Intersectional (Feminist) Activisms

This book includes essays that directly uncover how power asymmetries and related forms of marginalization and oppression function in the political and policy arenas with a special emphasis on the intersection of several systems of subordination.

This edited volume tackles two main questions: first, what are the main claims, struggles, and possibilities of contemporary intersectional feminisms; second, how shall we, as scholars, address intersectional (feminist) activisms in our research – theoretically, methodologically, and empirically. These issues are debated from several intersectional (feminist) perspectives, locations, and positionalities. The globally oriented and empirically grounded scope of this volume is undeniable. This book goes beyond the Western hegemony in intersectionality-related research and knowledge production, bringing in practices, experiences, and critical perspectives of intersectional (feminist) scholars and activists who are not necessarily located in the most privileged social, political, and financial milieus.

This book will be of interest to students and scholars from across the social sciences and humanities with an interest in intersectionality, gender, feminism, racism, LGBT+ and queer studies, activism and social movement studies. The chapters in this book were originally published as a special issue of *Journal of Women, Politics & Policy*.

Serena D'Agostino is Senior Researcher in Political Science at Vrije Universiteit Brussel and Universiteit Antwerpen, Belgium. Her work has been published in the *European Journal of Politics and Gender, International Feminist Journal of Politics, Journal of Diversity and Gender Studies, Journal of Women, Politics & Policy*, and *Politics, Groups, and Identities*, among others.

Nadia E. Brown is Professor of Government and Director of the Women's and Gender Studies Program at Georgetown University, Washington, DC, USA. She is the co-author of *Sister Style: The Politics of Appearance for Black Women Political Elites* (2021).

Intersectional (Feminist) Activisms
Global Practices and Experiences

Edited by
Serena D'Agostino & Nadia E. Brown

LONDON AND NEW YORK

First published 2025
by Routledge
2 Park Square, Milton Park, Abingdon, Oxon, OX14 4RN

and by Routledge
52 Vanderbilt Avenue, New York, NY 10017

Routledge is an imprint of the Taylor & Francis Group, an informa business

Introduction, Chapters 1-4, 8-10© 2025 Taylor & Francis
Chapter 5 © 2023 Rachel Simon-Kumar. Originally published as Open Access.
Chapter 6 © 2023 Fernando Tormos-Aponte, Shariana Ferrer-Núñez, and Carolina
Hernandez. Originally published as Open Access.
Chapter 7 © 2023 Fatima El Sayed. Originally published as Open Access.
With the exception of Chapters 5, 6 and 7, no part of this book may be reprinted or
reproduced or utilised in any form or by any electronic, mechanical, or other means, now
known or hereafter invented, including photocopying and recording, or in any information
storage or retrieval system, without permission in writing from the publishers. For details
on the rights for Chapters 5, 6 and 7, please see the chapters' Open Access footnotes.

Trademark notice: Product or corporate names may be trademarks or registered
trademarks, and are used only for identification and explanation without intent to infringe.

British Library Cataloguing-in-Publication Data
A catalogue record for this book is available from the British Library

ISBN13: 978-1-032-74924-2
ISBN13: 978-1-032-74925-9
ISBN13: 978-1-003-47154-7

DOI: 10.4324/9781003471547

Typeset in Minion Pro
by codeMantra

Publisher's Note
The publisher accepts responsibility for any inconsistencies that may have arisen during
the conversion of this book from journal articles to book chapters, namely the inclusion of
journal terminology.

Disclaimer
Every effort has been made to contact copyright holders for their permission to reprint
material in this book. The publishers would be grateful to hear from any copyright holder
who is not here acknowledged and will undertake to rectify any errors or omissions in
future editions of this book.

Contents

	Citation Information	vii
	Notes on Contributors	ix
	Introduction – Bringing Activism Back In	1
	Serena D'Agostino and Nadia E. Brown	
1	Studying Latina Mobilization Intersectionally, Studying Latinas Mobilizing Intersectionality	5
	Celeste Montoya	
2	Intersectional Feminist Activism and Practices of Transformation: Perspectives from Indian Feminisms	22
	Rukmini Sen	
3	At the Intersections of Gender Inequality and State Fragility in Africa	32
	Adryan Wallace	
4	De-Whitening Romani Women's Intersectional Experience	44
	Sebijan Fejzula	
5	Affirming Fissures: Conceptualizing Intersectional 'Ethnic' Feminism in Aotearoa New Zealand	54
	Rachel Simon-Kumar	
6	Intersectional Politics of the International Women's Strike	70
	Fernando Tormos-Aponte, Shariana Ferrer-Núñez and Carolina Hernandez	
7	Confronting Anti-Muslim Racism and Islamism: An Intersectional Perspective on Muslim Women's Activism in Germany	86
	Fatima El Sayed	
8	Solidarity Through Difference? How Italian and Spanish LGBTQIA* Organizations Frame Solidarity Through an Intersectional Lens	108
	Aurora Perego	

vi CONTENTS

9 Strategies of Resistance in the Everyday: The Political Approaches of Black
Women Living in a Public Housing Development in Chicago 125
Alex J. Moffett-Bateau

10 Feminists, Nationalist, Combatants, Activists. A Conversation with Vjosa
Musliu on the Multi-Faceted Role of Women in Kosovo 148
Vjosa Musliu and Enduena Klajiqi

Index 155

Citation Information

The chapters in this book were originally published in the *Journal of Women, Politics & Policy*, volume 44, issue 4 (2023). When citing this material, please use the original page numbering for each article, as follows:

Introduction
Introduction – Bringing Activism Back In
Serena D'Agostino and Nadia E. Brown
Journal of Women, Politics & Policy, volume 44, issue 4 (2023), pp. 401–404

Chapter 1
Studying Latina Mobilization Intersectionally, Studying Latinas Mobilizing Intersectionality
Celeste Montoya
Journal of Women, Politics & Policy, volume 44, issue 4 (2023), pp. 405–421

Chapter 2
Intersectional Feminist Activism and Practices of Transformation: Perspectives from Indian Feminisms
Rukmini Sen
Journal of Women, Politics & Policy, volume 44, issue 4 (2023), pp. 422–431

Chapter 3
At the Intersections of Gender Inequality and State Fragility in Africa
Adryan Wallace
Journal of Women, Politics & Policy, volume 44, issue 4 (2023), pp. 432–443

Chapter 4
De-Whitening Romani Women's Intersectional Experience
Sebijan Fejzula
Journal of Women, Politics & Policy, volume 44, issue 4 (2023), pp. 444–453

Chapter 5
Affirming Fissures: Conceptualizing Intersectional 'Ethnic' Feminism in Aotearoa New Zealand
Rachel Simon-Kumar
Journal of Women, Politics and Policy, volume 44, issue 4 (2023), pp. 454–469

Chapter 6

Intersectional Politics of the International Women's Strike
Fernando Tormos-Aponte, Shariana Ferrer-Núñez and Carolina Hernandez
Journal of Women, Politics & Policy, volume 44, issue 4 (2023), pp. 470–485

Chapter 7

Confronting Anti-Muslim Racism and Islamism: An Intersectional Perspective on Muslim Women's Activism in Germany
Fatima El Sayed
Journal of Women, Politics & Policy, volume 44, issue 4 (2023), pp. 486–507

Chapter 8

Solidarity Through Difference? How Italian and Spanish LGBTQIA* Organizations Frame Solidarity Through an Intersectional Lens
Aurora Perego
Journal of Women, Politics & Policy, volume 44, issue 4 (2023), pp. 508–524

Chapter 9

Strategies of Resistance in the Everyday: The Political Approaches of Black Women Living in a Public Housing Development in Chicago
Alex J. Moffett-Bateau
Journal of Women, Politics & Policy, volume 44, issue 4 (2023), pp. 525–547

Chapter 10

Feminists, Nationalist, Combatants, Activists. A Conversation with Vjosa Musliu on the Multi-Faceted Role of Women in Kosovo
Vjosa Musliu and Enduena Klajiqi
Journal of Women, Politics & Policy, volume 44, issue 4 (2023), pp. 548–554

For any permission-related enquiries please visit:
http://www.tandfonline.com/page/help/permissions

Notes on Contributors

Nadia E. Brown, Government and Women's & Gender Studies, Georgetown University, Washington, DC, USA.

Serena D'Agostino, Department of Political Science, Vrije Universiteit Brussel and Universiteit Antwerpen, Belgium.

Fatima El Sayed, Berlin Institute for Integration and Migration Research, Humboldt-Universität zu Berlin, Germany.

Sebijan Fejzula, Center for Social Studies, University of Coimbra, Portugal.

Shariana Ferrer-Núñez, Colectiva Feminista en Construcción, San Juan, Puerto Rico.

Carolina Hernandez, Department of Sociology, University of Pittsburgh, USA.

Enduena Klajiqi, Department of Political Science, Vrije Universiteit Brussel, Belgium.

Alex J. Moffett-Bateau, Department of Political Science, John Jay College of Criminal Justice – CUNY, USA.

Celeste Montoya, Women's and Gender Studies, University of Colorado Boulder, USA.

Vjosa Musliu, Department of Political Science, Vrije Universiteit Brussel, Belgium.

Aurora Perego, Sociology and Social Research, Università di Trento, Italy.

Rukmini Sen, School of Liberal Studies, Dr. B.R. Ambedkar University Delhi, India.

Rachel Simon-Kumar, School of Population Health, Waipapa Taumata Rau/The University of Auckland, New Zealand.

Fernando Tormos-Aponte, Department of Sociology, University of Pittsburgh, USA.

Adryan Wallace, Africana Studies, Stony Brook University, USA.

Introduction: Bringing Activism Back In

Serena D'Agostino and Nadia E. Brown

ABSTRACT

Two main questions animate our desire to produce this special issue: first, what are the main claims, struggles and possibilities of contemporary intersectional feminisms; and second, how shall we, as scholars, address intersectional feminist activisms in our research – theoretically, methodologically and empirically. In this special issue, these topics are debated from several intersectional feminist perspectives, locations and positionalities.

In July 2022, after the forced pause due to the COVID-19 pandemic, the *European Conference on Politics and Gender* (ECPG) finally took place at the University of Ljubljana (Slovenia). For most of us, this occasion was an opportunity to continue previous debates and share new thoughts about (the politics of) power, (in)equity, and difference. The idea for this special issue materialized at this conference. In particular, it developed around common concerns about the urgency to re-politicize intersectionality as a tool for attaining social justice. We felt it imperative to critically reflect on how to subvert the consolidated (European) praxis to "confin[e] intersectionality to an academic exercise of metatheoretical contemplation" (Bilge 2013, 405) and to recenter intersectional activisms in intersectionality studies (Broad-Wright 2017, 41).

These concerns were addressed at the conference roundtable discussion on contemporary intersectional feminist activisms in Europe and beyond.[1] Two main questions drove our conversation: first, *what are the main claims, struggles, and possibilities of contemporary intersectional feminisms*; and second, *how shall we, as scholars, address intersectional feminist activisms in our research – theoretically, methodologically, and empirically*. These issues were debated from several intersectional feminist perspectives, locations, and positionalities: from Black and Latina women's political activism in the US to emerging and old expressions of Islamic feminism in Europe, to the struggles and academic potential of Romani feminist activist-scholars, to the social and political challenges experienced by South-Asian and Indian feminists.

These two leading questions gave us much food for thought regarding intersectionality research in contemporary academia. They fostered reflection on the ongoing mainstreaming and (over)theorization of intersectionality, and the perils they might imply. In particular, the risk of neutralizing the critical potential of intersectionality by detaching it from its activist roots and "mov[ing] [it] away from the black feminist standpoint tradition of highlighting experiences" (Beaman and Brown 2019, 231). This special issue builds on the belief that for intersectionality not to become an empty signifier (Christoffersen 2021), intersectionality research needs to be empirically grounded. This means relocating intersectional (feminist) activists' experiences and practices of mobilization at the very heart of our inquiries. Methodologically, this signifies valuing and employing analytical tools that center situated and experiential knowledge (Dhamoon 2011) – such as narratives, storytelling, biography, and personal testimony.

When studying intersectionality as a mode of action, more empirical grounding is needed as the main claims, struggles, and possibilities of contemporary intersectional (feminist) activisms are context-specific. As shown elsewhere (see, for instance, D'Agostino 2021, 2023), intersectional mobilizations are indeed highly heterogeneous, which means that their specific characteristics depend on the historical legacies and the socio-political contexts where they emerge, develop and operate, their mission, strategies and repertoires, as well as activists' lived experiences and social locations. Keeping in mind the key role of "context" in intersectionality research, this special issue offers perspectives from a variety of settings and geographic locations worldwide. Doing so, we aim to bring the heterogeneity and fluidity of contemporary intersectional (feminist) activisms upfront. We want to create a space for reflection where we collectively engage with "ask[ing] the other question" (Matsuda 1991). It is with this spirit that we have decided to put the word "feminist" into brackets, and the term "activism" in plural. The research included in this special issue shows that women and other minoritized groups understand and experience "feminism" and "activism" in very different ways. Shedding light on this multitude of meanings and experiences is the main purpose of our joint endeavor.

The globally-oriented and empirically-grounded scope of this special issue is of undeniable value. On the one hand, it allows us to go beyond the Western hegemony in intersectionality-related research and knowledge production, bringing in practices, experiences, and critical perspectives of intersectional (feminist) scholars and activists who are not necessarily located in the most privileged social, political, and financial milieus. On the other hand, it creates the opportunity to start an open conversation about intersectional (feminist) activisms and the power and privilege dynamics that exist among different kinds of feminism, based on diverse (lived) experiences and situated knowledges. Intersectionality, a byproduct Black feminism or a Black feminist hometruth, is a historically contingent process of understanding that is rooted in social justice (Nash 2008). Therefore, our concentration on intersectional activism as a framework is used to address structures of reinforcing domination. This work is critical for understanding how politically salient identities – such as class, ethnicity, gender, nativity, race, sexuality – are marginalized and consequently lead to structural and institutional outcomes.

Our focus on intersectional (feminist) activisms includes politics, policy, and lived experiences. Not only do the essays in this special issue center on political processes, actors, and institutions, we also have manuscripts that address public policies that impact women's lives, as well as reflective papers that tackle broader epistemological concerns. Our issue includes essays that directly uncover how power asymmetries and related forms of marginalization and oppression function in the political and policy arenas with a special emphasis on the intersection of several systems of subordination – like racism, (hetero)sexism, classism, and so on – and their impact on the experiences of women and other minoritized groups. The devotion of the *Journal of Women, Politics, and Policy (JWPP)* to advancing knowledge through rigorous empirical research and the development of theory is why we selected the journal for this special issue.

JWPP is the ideal home for this work for two important reasons. First, we aim to reach a broader community of scholars who are part of the ECPG community but are keenly interested in global scholarship that centers intersectionality. Given its prestige and unique capability to offer special issues that examine women's experiences in a novel way, the *JWPP* was an appealing venue for this scholarship. The *JWPP* readership draws scholars from across the world but has a vibrant US readership. Although the origins of this special issue had its beginnings at the ECPG, we are excited about the possibility of US-based scholars and scholars of American politics engaging with this special issue. We were also thrilled about the opportunity to work with Becki Scola, one of the editors of the *JWPP*. She has been incredibly supportive and enthusiastic of this project. Taken together, these reasons make the *JWPP* a perfect fit for our special issue.

It is our sincere hope that the essays in this special issue solicit conversations about the importance of intersectional (feminist) activisms – both in scholarship and in practice. Engagement with these articles should elucidate a renewed interest of the politics of difference, inequity, and power with a focus on intersectional inquiry. As aforementioned, this special issue was intentionally developed to include a myriad of perspectives and vantage points. Of course, there are others that could be included. As a continued conversation, discussions should be ongoing on intersectional feminisms and its applicability in a variety of cases. To conclude, this special issue is conceived as a space for critical thinking where we can *become fluent in each other's histories* (Alexander 2005) and are pushed outside our comfort zone to contribute to a common goal: social justice. In sum, as a space where intersectionality is re-politicized.

Note

1. Endorsed by the ECPR Standing Group on Gender and Politics and sponsored by Bristol University Press and the *European Journal of Politics and Gender* (EJPG), this roundtable was organized and chaired by Serena D'Agostino (Vrije Universiteit Brussel). Speakers: Jean Beaman (University of California), Nadia Brown (Georgetown University), Iman Lechkar (Vrije Universiteit Brussel), Celeste Montoya (University of Colorado), Angéla Kóczé (Central European University), and Rukmini Sen (Ambedkar University Delhi). A heartfelt thanks goes to Rossella Ciccia (University of Oxford), Steering Committee Chair of the ECPR Standing Group on Gender and Politics, for her support and encouragement during the organization of this roundtable.

Disclosure statement

No potential conflict of interest was reported by the author(s).

ORCID

Nadia E. Brown ⓘ http://orcid.org/0000-0002-5145-2811

References

Alexander, M. Jacqui. 2005. *Pedagogies of Crossing: Meditations on Feminism, Sexual Politics, Memory, and the Sacred.* Durham, NC: Duke University Press.

Beaman, Jean, and Nadia E. Brown. 2019. "Sistas Doing It for Themselves: Black Women's Activism and #blacklivesmatter in the United States and France." In *Gendered Mobilization, Intersectional Challenges: Contemporary Social Movements in North America and Europe*, eds. Jill Irvine, Sabine Lang, and Celeste Montoya. London: ECPR Press, Rowman & Littlefield Intl, 226–43.

Bilge, Sirma. 2013. "Intersectionality Undone: Saving Intersectionality from Feminist Intersectionality Studies." *Du Bois Review* 10 (2):405–24. doi:10.1017/S1742058X13000283.

Broad-Wright, Kendal. 2017. "Social Movement Intersectionality and Re-Centering Intersectional Activism." *Atlantis: Critical Studies in Gender, Culture & Social Justice* 38 (1): 41–53.

Christoffersen, Ashlee. 2021. "The Politics of Intersectional Practice: Competing Concepts of Intersectionality." *Policy & Politics* 49 (3):1–18. doi:10.1332/030557321X16194316141034.

D'Agostino, Serena. 2021. "(In)visible Mobilizations: Romani Women's Intersectional Activisms in Romania and Bulgaria." *Politics, Groups, and Identities* 9 (1):170–89. doi:10.1080/21565503.2019.1629307.

D'Agostino, Serena. 2023. "Intersectional Feminist Activisms in Europe: Invisibility, Inclusivity and Affirmation." In *Handbook of Feminist Governance*, eds. Marian Sawer, Lee Ann Banaszak, Jacqui True, and Johanna Kantola. Cheltenham: Edward Elgar Publishing, 347–58. doi:10.4337/9781800374812.00037.

Dhamoon, Rita Kaur. 2011. "Considerations on Mainstreaming Intersectionality." *Political Research Quarterly* 64 (1):230–43. doi:10.1177/1065912910379227.

Matsuda, Mari J. 1991. "Beside My Sister, Facing the Enemy: Legal Theory Out of Coalition." *Stanford Law Review* 43 (6):1183–92. doi:10.2307/1229035.

Nash, Jennifer C. 2008. "Re-Thinking Intersectionality." *Feminist Review* 89 (1):1–15. doi:10.1057/fr.2008.4.

Studying Latina Mobilization Intersectionally, Studying Latinas Mobilizing Intersectionality

Celeste Montoya

ABSTRACT

Located at the intersection of multiple marginalities, US Latinas have often mobilized in ways that reflect this intersectional positioning. Their mobilization across and between various social movements is an important feature of their activism, which has been frequently overlooked, and studies that focus on this social movement intersectionality are an important means of locating it. But there are also important differences among Latinas, who may not all share the same intersectional locations or commitments. In this article, I argue the need for an open and expansive intersectional approach to studying US Latina activism, one that aims to identify and understand the intragroup differences in where, why, and how Latinas mobilize.

Latinas are rarely fully represented within US social movements or within scholarly explorations of movement histories. Like other women of color or groups at the intersection of multiple marginalities, the needs and experiences of Latinas can be overlooked or dismissed by movements organized along a single axis of identity or oppression (race-only, gender-only, class-only). Because of this, Latinas have often engaged in a broad array of mobilizing efforts, sometimes moving or shifting across multiple movements, or creating their own spaces within or between movements, so as to better address the multi-faceted nature of their lived experiences with discrimination and oppression (Blackwell 2011; Montoya and Galvez Seminario 2022; Roth 2004). Identifying what intersectional mobilization looks like and where to find it has been an important means of locating Latina activism. However, Latinas may vary in the way or extent to which they mobilize intersectionally. Some Latinas have remained rooted within single-axis movements where they might mobilize in more or less intersectional ways, with some, perhaps, never mobilizing intersectionally. There is a wide range of Latina activism, and recognizing that heterogeneity is vital.

In this article, I explore the ways in which a more nuanced and contextualized intersectional analysis can be used to better identify and explore the diversity of Latina activism. In the first section, I discuss the use of intersectionality as both an open analytical framework and as an object of study. I argue that there are important distinctions in studying Latina activism intersectionally and in studying Latina social movement intersectionality. Latina intersectional activism should be understood as a subset of Latina activism and not treated as a given. Even within the subset of Latina intersectional activism, there are important variations. Intersectionality is a tool for understanding the where, when, why, and how of Latina intersectional activism, including its absence. In the second section, I discuss developing a framework for Latina activism, using and adapting existing models of gender mobilization. Developing an open intersectional framework helps recognize not only the different types of mobilizing that Latinas engage in but also helps to interrogate the varied role that intersectionality may (or may not) play. I discuss three components of this framework: 1) recognizing the distinct but overlapping categories of Latinas in movement, Latina movements, and Latina intersectionality; 2) recognizing the multiple *dimensions* of identity and/or oppression around which Latinas might organize in single-axis ways or along various intersections; 3) recognizing the multiple *directions* that Latinas might organize based on diverging political consciousness (challenging or upholding the various dimensions of inequality).

Examining Latina activism intersectionally is a crucial means of locating Latina activism, whatever form it might take. It can also provide us with a deeper understanding of when, why, and how they organize. An open and expansive intersectional inquiry, one that aims to capture the gamut of Latina mobilization, can help us gain not only a deeper understanding of the dynamics of their mobilization, but also a stronger recognition of the significant contributions they have made throughout history.

Studying Latina activism intersectionally, studying Latina intersectional activism

Intersectionality refers to the understanding that systems of inequality (e.g., race, gender, class, sexuality, ability) are not mutually exclusive but interact with one another. It is an insight born out of the experiences of women of color and others residing at the intersection or multiple marginalities. It is an essential component of identifying and understanding diverging forms of Latina activism; however, it is important to acknowledge the difference between studying Latina activism intersectionally and studying Latina intersectional activism. In the former, *intersectionality* is understood as an analytical framework or heuristic. In the latter, it is understood as a political orientation and/or a way of doing politics. They are related, but distinct, and there is a lot of slippage in how the term is used. A comparative analogy might be found in how scholars have come to understand gender analysis and feminism. Intersectionality (as an orientation) is to intersectional analysis (a framework or heuristic) as feminism (an orientation) is to gender analysis (a framework or heuristic).

One of the crucial components of academic feminism has been to demonstrate the salience of gender and the need to incorporate it into a range of analyses. Early interventions focused on highlighting women and their experiences. Gender analyses have evolved into more expansive approaches that seek to demonstrate how gender functions within society. Similarly, the academic project of intersectionality (a product of women of color feminists) has been to highlight women of color and their experiences, demonstrating the salience of multiple and interconnected forms of oppression and the need to incorporate that analytical insight into a range of analyses. Collins (2012, 451) argues that the coinage of the term by Crenshaw (1989, 1991) marked "a juncture when the ideas of social movement politics were named and subsequently incorporated into the academy." In both cases, feminists created new forms of analysis that can be (and have been) applied to the study of social movements in different ways (see Figure 1). In the case of feminists forming a gender analysis,

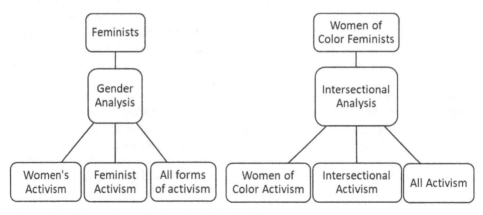

Figure 1. Structural Analysis as a Form of Activism for Studying Activism.

that analysis can be used to highlight women's activism and feminist activism (a distinct but over-lapping subset—something discussed later in the article), as well as to understand gendered dimensions of all activism or movements. In the case of intersectionality, it can be used to highlight women of color activism and/or intersectional activism (also a distinct but overlapping subset), as well as to understand the intersectional dimensions of all activists, activism, or movements.

Structural analysis, such as that provided by gender and intersectionality, is an important means of studying inequality and marginalization. Young (2002, 20) describes structure as denoting "the confluence of institutional rules and interactive routines, mobilization of resources, and physical structures, which constitute the historical givens in relation to which individuals act." She argues that they "connote the wider social outcomes that result from the confluence of individual actions within institutions relations." Gender, race, and class are examples of structures that are often studied separately. Intersectional analysis approaches them as interconnected. When we construct the categories of women, women of color, or even Latina activists, we are constructing categories based on their structural locations. This places groups and individuals within the context of historical patterns of inequality, something that may shape their activism (behavior); however, it does not dictate it. Connell (1987, 93) conceptualizes structures as practices that have been institutionalized over time, which create patterns of constraint on individual choices. While structure is deeply embedded within social relations, and serves to constrain, individuals still have agency. They can choose how they perform their gender, race, class, and sexuality in ways that are in accordance with or contrary to convention (Montoya 2016; Risman 2004).

While Latinas are often assumed (by definition) to share a race-gendered intersectional position, they might differ along other structural dimensions, such as class or sexuality. Even when they do hold the same position, their individual experiences and the ways in which they make sense of their position and experiences may shape their political consciousness in ways that lead to different social movement engagements or forms of mobilization. While social movements are often used to disrupt the historical patterns that make up structure, there are also movements that seek to uphold them. A single-axis mobilization often does both, even if the upholding is not conscious or intentional, but rather one of neglect. Latinas might mobilize in ways that challenge multiple interlocking forms of oppression, or in single-axis ways that combat oppression along one dimension, and ignore or even intentionally uphold structural inequalities along another. The action taken, and its direction, depends on the development of individual and/or collective group consciousness.

Scholars have long addressed the importance of political consciousness in motivating action aimed at challenging oppressive institutions and the larger structures they are embedded within, often in single-axis ways. Marxism focuses on the proletariat developing a class consciousness that is critical of the hierarchies created by capitalism (a consciousness that is not inherent) as necessary (but not always sufficient) for organizing a revolution. Similar distinctions between structural location and political consciousness are necessary for understanding mobilization along the lines of race and gender as singular dimensions but also in the particular understanding of multiple forms of interlocking oppression. The political consciousness of Latinas may vary because of their structural locations but also because of variations in how they understand those locations. Developing an intersectional consciousness requires "the recognition of oppression as constituted by multiple and interacting social structures" (Tormos 2017, 712). This may not be true for all Latinas, and they might vary in terms of which dimensions of oppression they recognize and/or see as most salient.

Studying Latina activism requires applying an open intersectional analysis that starts with a focus on structural positioning, yet interrogates the differences within that positioning as well as the differences that may occur in how Latinas experience their positionality, the sense they make of it (their consciousness), and how they mobilize those understandings (see Figure 2). While an intersectional positioning may lead to intersectional activism, there are also multiple points of divergence. Even if Latinas want to mobilize along multiple dimensions, they may be constrained or make strategic choices within different and/or shifting political environments. Latina engagement with movements

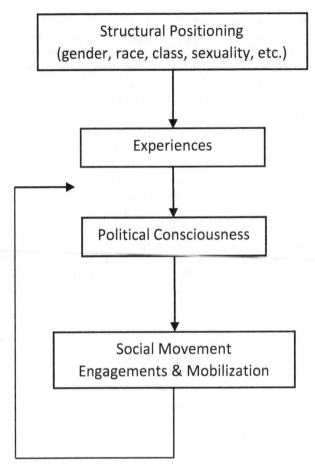

Figure 2. Intersectional Positioning, Consciousness, and Behavior.

can lead to new experiences that may shift their consciousness and the ways in which they mobilize. This is a dynamic process.

An open intersectional analysis will interrogate each part of this process, looking and allowing for variations at each stage. Where are Latinas structurally located? Even though they may share a race-gendered location, where are they in relation to class, sexuality, ability, and other potentially salient dimensions of inequality? How do they experience that location? How are those experiences raced, gendered, classed, etc.? Even Latinas who share intersectional locations may have different experiences that arise from personal circumstances (an individualistic consideration) or from variations in the temporal and geographic political environment (a contextual consideration). How are those political environments raced, gendered, classed, etc.? How do they make sense of these experiences? If they experience discrimination and oppression, do they understand it as such? Do they see their experiences as raced, gendered, classed? Do they see an alternative, the possibility of a different reality? Are they willing or able to act on it? Are their actions oriented in a particular direction that are raced, gendered, classed, etc.? Are they constrained from acting in particular ways that are raced, gendered, classed, etc.?

An open intersectional approach can help us understand why and how Latinas act in more or less intersectional ways. In the next section, I further expand on this framework to explore the different patterns of Latina mobilization.

Patterns of Latina mobilization

Latina activism can be found in a wide array of social movements. This includes movements and mobilizations that explicitly reflect their identity as Latinas as well as ones that do not. There is substantial variation in the role that identity does (or does not) play in their organizing. Scholars who study women's movements comparatively have argued the need to recognize important differences in how women organize and the role that gender might play. Beckwith (2000) makes the distinction between women in movement, women's movements, and feminist movements, and cautions against conflating these different patterns of mobilization. Women in movement is a broad category that can include the overlapping subsets of women's movements and feminist movements, but it can also include women in other types of movements, such as labor, racial justice, LGBT, peace, etc. (see Figure 3). Women's movements are defined as movements where women are the "primary core actors" and "where women make gendered identity claims as the basis for the movement, where they explicitly organize as women, or mothers, or as daughters, asserting a female gendered identity" (Beckwith 2007, 313). Feminist movements are then discussed as a type of women's movement (although they can include actors of other genders) that have a particular gendered consciousness, one that challenges patriarchy and its gendered hierarchy. In this framework, feminist movements might be considered a subset of women's movements, and women's movements a subset of women in movement.

Another way of conceptualizing this typology might be to recognize women's movements and feminist mobilization as two overlapping forms of gendered mobilization: one in which women are mobilizing their gender as an identity and then other in which they are mobilizing a particular form of gender consciousness (as feminists) (see Figure 4). Conceptualized in this way, feminist mobilization can happen within the context of women's movements, feminist movements, or in other movements. It allows space for recognizing feminist interventions that may occur in a more limited manner but in a wide array of contexts.

While these typologies help us to identify and use gender in different ways, it is important to recognize that the boundaries between movements are messy and fluid, and activists might shift their mobilization over time. In Beckwith's (2000, 433–434) article, she discusses the need to problematize

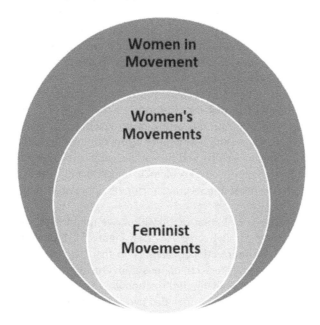

Figure 3. Women's Mobilization (Model 1).

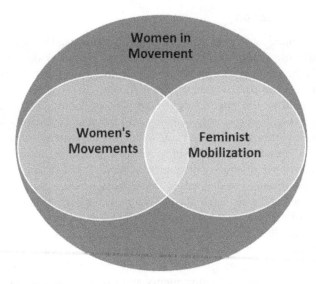

Figure 4. Women's Mobilization Model 2.

gender, such that it is understood as a dynamic engagement with women's "specific locations and history of struggle" (Youngs, Jones, and Pettman 1999, as quoted in Beckwith 2000). Women might start in a movement that is not mobilized around gender, but within the context of the movement, gender becomes more salient to them. They might then begin to organize around gender, within or outside that original movement. Separate identity-based organizing within movements has been a means for groups to articulate and act on concerns of exclusion, making interventions that create a more inclusive and enduring movement (Montoya 2019; Weldon 2012). Experiences of sexism in other movements often has been a motivation for women to organize on their own and can be accompanied by the development of a feminist consciousness that can be mobilized within or outside of that movement. However, women might also organize around gender in ways that do not challenge gender hierarchies or necessitate a feminist consciousness, such as in the creation of auxiliary groups or mothers' movements. Here, gender is salient, such that women are organizing as woman and perhaps (but not always) making gendered claims, but their mobilization is not necessarily feminist (aimed at combating gender oppression). When women are in movement and/or in women's affinity groups within those movements, and they do start to develop a feminist consciousness (or that consciousness becomes more salient), they may continue to mobilize within that movement (or affinity group), perhaps making feminist interventions, or they may shift the mobilization so as to join or create a separate and autonomous feminist movement. An open and dynamic gender analysis—where we ask when, where, and how gender is functioning—helps us to distinguish between different uses or understandings of gender and how it is used in mobilization as well as to recognize the different gendered shifts that may occur. Problematizing gender also allows us to explore when and how race, class, sexuality, and other intersecting forms of oppression may become a part of that mobilization.

In exploring different patterns of Latina mobilization, we might start with the second model of women's mobilization, creating parallel categories (see Figure 5). Latinas in movement is the all-encompassing category. It is an intersectional category in that the actors being identified (Latinas) occupy a particular (race-gendered) intersectional position. One way of studying this group would be to ask whether and how they are mobilizing intersectionally. As with the second model of women's mobilization, this model of Latina activism includes two overlapping categories within the larger: 1) Latina movements—where Latinas are mobilizing their race-gendered identity as Latinas and 2) Latina intersectionality—where Latinas are mobilizing to combat multiple forms of oppression.

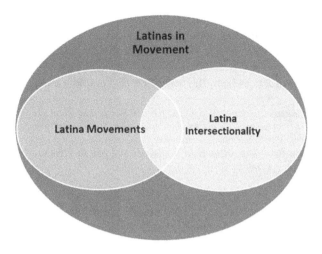

Figure 5. Latina Activism.

This conceptualization allows us to make the distinction between two different types of social movement intersectionality. When Latinas mobilize as Latinas, they are mobilizing an intersectional (race-gendered) position. When they mobilize intersectionality, they are mobilizing an intersectional consciousness, one aimed at combating multiple forms of oppression. These two forms of mobilization might overlap, but they do not always. An example of this distinction can be focusing on some of the race-gendered mobilization of Latinas in racial justice movements, a dimension of oppression that has often been one of the most salient in their activism. In *500 Years of Chicana Women's History*, Martínez (2008) traces Chicana activism back through the complicated shifts of different eras, including the role they played in independence and anti-colonial movements as the borders of the Southwest were redrawn, often via violence. She focuses on their work in the region during the early 1900s, when Mexican-Americans were subjected to many of the same forms of oppression experienced by African Americans in the Jim Crow South (e.g., lynchings, racial segregation, voter suppression) and later in the Chicano movement of the 1960s where they continued those battles both locally and nationally. Latinas mobilized against racial injustice in single-axis ways in which their gender may have had little to no salience. They also mobilized as Latinas (mobilizing their intersectional race-gendered identity) in ways that still focused predominantly on race and without explicitly challenging gender hierarchies. For example, in the early 1900s, they mobilized within mutual aid societies, often doing charity and fundraising work in women's auxiliaries. They also helped form and teach in *esqualitas* (little schools) when their children were excluded from public schools, mobilizing their gendered roles as caregivers. Later, the League of United Latina American Citizens formed the "Ladies LULAC Councils" that worked with the larger organization to address school segregation and voting rights. There was also a women's auxiliary to the American GI Forum, a civil rights organization chartered by Mexican-American Veterans after WWII, when soldiers were met with the same racist treatment that they had experienced before leaving.

Mobilizing intersectionality (a particular political orientation) can, and often has, overlapped with mobilizing intersectionally. In fact, as discussed earlier, intersectionality came out of women of color movements. Social scholars discuss the mobilization of intersectionality as *intersectional praxis*: the ways in which activists might put their commitments (to combating multiple and intersectional forms of oppression) into practice (Lépinard 2014; Montoya and Galvez Seminario 2022; Montoya and Guerrero 2023; Tormos 2017; Townsend-Bell 2011). In discussing Chicana intersectionality, Cotera, Blackwell, and Espinoza (2018) work with the concept of *movidas* (moves), the praxis of resistance forged by Chicanas as they moved within and between sites of struggle, developing innovative new concepts and tactics at the intersection of race, class, gender, and sexuality. They build on the conceptualizations made by Chicana feminists Gloria Anzaldúa and Chela Sandoval. Anzaldúa differentiated the praxis (theory/practice) of women of color activism from the grand narratives of social movements, placing more of an emphasis on the small acts of rebellion that can reshape movement discourses and practices from the inside out (Cotera, Blackwell, and Espinoza 2018, 2):

> We have not one movement but many. [...] Ours are individual and small group movidas, unpublicized movimientos—movements not of media stars or popular authors but of small groups or single mujeres. [...] Though unnoticed, right now in small towns women are organizing, attending meetings, setting up retreats or demonstrations. [...] Now here, now there, aquí y alla, we and our movimientos are firmly committed to transforming all our cultures. (Anzaldúa 1990, xxvii)

Sandoval (2000, 182) builds on Anzaldúa's conceptualization in her identification of *movidas* as a repertoire of "revolutionary maneuvers," a political site for the third meaning that shines through binary opposition. Cotera, Blackwell, and Espinoza (2018, 2) argue that this concept of *movidas* offers a "fruitful critical frame for scholars who wish to uncover the central yet still largely unexplored terrain of Chicana feminist movidas during the movement years." I argue that the concept of *movidas* might go further than that and help to elucidate the myriad of ways that Latinas have engaged in *intersectional praxis* in a wide array of movement settings, including those that are not explicitly Latina.

Latinas intersectional *movidas*, like intersectional social movement praxis more broadly, can take multiple forms. They might include: 1) intersectional interventions within the large mainstream single-axis movements, either by addressing oppression within the movement or attempting to expand the movement agenda to address intersectional issues; 2) working across movements—transversally, where they might make similar intersectional interventions to single-axis movements (addressing exclusions and/or expanding agendas) or through their "bridging" or coalitional work (Collins 2017; Irvine, Lang, and; Montoya 2019, 2021; Yuval-Davis 2006); and/or 3) organizing between movements—interstitially, creating their own organizations where they might chose when, where, or even whether to engage with mainstream movements (Irvine, Lang, and Montoya 2019; Montoya 2021; Roth 2004; Springer 2001, 2005).

Focusing on *movidas*, we can find numerous examples of the varied and overlapping forms of Latina intersectional praxis throughout history. In the early 1900s, activists like Jovita Idár mobilized across movements, working to combat the lynching of *Tejanos* by the Texas Rangers and the numerous racial segregation laws, in particular the discriminatory education policies and practices, but also by fighting for women's suffrage and education. She also helped to create Latina specific spaces, such as the *Liga Femenil Mexicanista* [Mexican Women's League], an organization that also fought for economic and political rights for Latinas. Within the Chicano movement, Chicana feminists started to challenge sexism within and outside of the movement and then in autonomous organizations. Vasquez (2016) wrote about women speaking at the United Farm Workers Organizing Committee conference in Castroville, Texas, warning men that sexist attitudes and disputes around women's rights would divide the farm worker's struggle. At the 1969 National Chicano Youth Liberation Conference in Denver, a group of Chicanas organized a Chicana Caucus and workshop to discuss (and debate) equality for women and the role of women in the movement. Latinas formed the Raza Unidas Party Mujeres Caucus and held their own conference to fight for better representation within the party. Latinas also formed their own autonomous organizations with more intersectionally explicit orientations, such as the *Comisión Femenil Mexicana*—an organization focused on increasing Chicana leadership within the movement and also advocating on their behalf (Nieto-Gómez 2018).

As with gender mobilization, how Latinas mobilize, intersectionally or not, or what form of intersectional praxis they engage can be, and often is, dynamic. The recognition of interlocking dimensions does not necessarily mean that all dimensions will hold equal or consistent meaning and importance (Bedolla 2007; Hancock 2007; Townsend-Bell 2011; Weldon 2006; Yuval-Davis 2006). Latina activism may shift to different locations as the meaning and salience of particular dimensions shift for particular Latinas based on new experiences and/or changes in their political environments.

Latinas might start in a particular location but not stay there, shifting as the environment does, or as they develop different forms of political consciousness. Many Latinas started their activist journey in single-axis movements. It was the exclusions within single-axis movements that led many (but not all) women of color to start exploring, articulating, and enacting new intersectional forms of politics, both within and outside of those movements.

At the same time, not all Latinas (or women of color) followed this pathway. Some stayed within those single-axis movements, sometimes forming their own organization within those mobilizations, sometimes not. When faced with exclusion or more blatant forms of mistreatment within social movements, groups can choose how they respond. As with other groups and in other contexts, Latinas can choose exit, voice, or loyalty. In the next two subsections, I address the need to attend to the multiple *dimensions* around which Latinas might mobilize and the different *directions* their activism might take around those dimensions.

The multiple dimensions of Latina mobilization

While Latinas in movement, Latina movements, and Latina intersectionality captures a wide array of Latina activism, not all forms of intersectional mobilization are equally visible. The race-gendered intersection is most prominent, potentially overlooking other salient dimensions of mobilization that might be explored in a more open intersectional analysis. While race and gender may be likely dimensions of Latina activism, there might be other dimensions or intersections that take a more prominent role in their organizing. For example, class has been a highly salient dimension of Latina activism. Like with racial justice, some of this mobilization has been in more single-axis ways, with class most prominent. However, the most common type of class-based mobilization has been in the form of labor movements. Because workplaces are often segregated in race, gendered, or race-gendered ways, so too are mobilizations aimed at combating workplace injustices.

Latinas, like other women of color, have been active in fighting for workers' rights in an array of settings, from fields and mines to factories, hospitals, and hotels, as well as in domestic work. Martínez (2008) writes about Latinas active in the labor movements of the 1930s, where they organized and participated in strikes as cotton workers, garment workers, pecan shellers, laundry workers, on the cannery line, and more. They were also a part of the farmworkers movements in the 1960s and 1970s that overlapped with racial justice movements. Latina labor activism continued into the subsequent decades and can be see most recently in activism to raise the minimum wage and to address the exploitative practices arising in in the wake of the coronavirus pandemic—where workers (particularly those who were undocumented) faced wage theft, overwork, and an absence of health protections (Chitnis 2021; Montoya and Guerrero 2023). In each of these settings, you can find examples of Latinas mobilizing their intersectional identities and/or intersectionality, but perhaps with emphasis on different dimensions or intersections of their structural positions.

Similar patterns are found in organizing around other classed issues, such as housing. Many housing justice movements have more prominent race-class dimensions to the mobilization, however, sometime gender (and even sexuality) can play a role. For example, Montoya and Galvez Seminario (2022) discuss a housing justice organization that forged a Brown-Black coalition to fight gentrification under the initial leadership of a Latina feminist. While the race-classed dimensions of the activism are most prominent, there were numerous examples indicative of an intersectional praxis (or *movidas*) that included gender and sexuality, such as in their leadership, their messaging, and their coalitional patterns.

Thus, expanding our studies of Latina activism and Latina social movement intersectionality should more fully consider the different dimensions of their structural location around which they might mobilize, as well as the various combinations thereof. In considering the three most frequently salient dimensions (race, class, and gender), you might see mobilization around: gender, race, class,

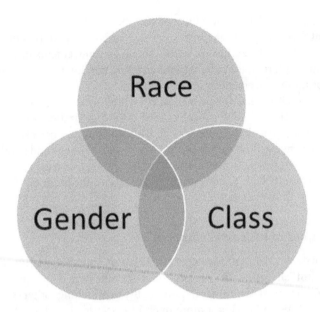

Figure 6. Different Dimensions of Latina Activism.

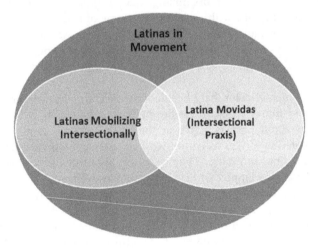

Figure 7. Latina Activism Model 2.

race-gender, race-class, class-gender, race-class, and race-gender-class (see Figure 6). There are also additional dimensions that could and should be considered, making an open intersectional inquiry all the more necessary. In order to better consider the possibility of other salient intersections, we might make a slight adjustment to categorizing patterns of mobilization to include: Latinas in movement, Latinas mobilizing intersectionally—of which Latina movements are a subcategory—and Latinas mobilizing intersectionality—in which we consider a wide array of intersectional praxis or *movidas* (see Figure 7).

The multiple directions of Latinas mobilization

A final consideration for a framework of Latina mobilization requires opening up the various categories of identity so as to better interrogate the meaning they hold for Latinas and Latina mobilization. While race, gender, and even class, can be understood as structures capable of shaping material reality, they are also constructed and contested categories that hold different meanings across time and place, as well as for individuals. Recognizing them as such can help us to better understand why Latinas in ostensibly similar social locations, might mobilize in diverging directions.

In the previous section, I discussed some of the different ways that Latinas might mobilize, intersectionally or not, noting that it should not be assumed that all Latinas will always (or ever) act in intersectional ways. In this section, I want to discuss the whether and when of intersectional mobilization, by exploring some of the dynamics of identity and different formations of group consciousness. Not only do we need to consider the variation between Latinas that might exist outside their "shared" racial and gender identities (such as class and sexuality), but we must also interrogate the categories of race and gender themselves.

Crenshaw (1991) argues that all identities, even those grounded in structural inequalities, are coalitions, something that allows us to trouble the idea of "natural" affinity groups that can be mobilized (Carastathis 2013; Cole 2008; Montoya 2021). Instead, we must treat identity as fluid, relative, and contested, taking an approach that destabilizes these categories without dismissing them or their potential relevance (Bedolla 2007; Cohen 1997). For Latinas, an important part of understanding variations in intersectional consciousness, means deconstructing the different dimensions of identity, starting with race and gender, the two intersecting dimensions most often associated with Latinas. Along these two dimensions, we might see variance in the level of salience, differences in the orientation (upholding or challenging traditional hierarchies), and different constructions altogether.

The complexities of Latina ethno-racial mobilization

Historically, race has been one of the most salient dimensions of Latina activism. However, it is also one of the most complicated ones. First, not all Latinas (or Latinos) may assert a politicized racial group consciousness. A key finding in the study of racial group consciousness is the pivotal role played by linked fate—the belief that what happens to the group will impact the individual (Dawson 1994; Tate 2004). Linked fate has been an important means of mobilizing African Americans. While linked fate has been found among other minoritized groups, such as Latinos and Asian Americans, it is less prevalent and more variable (Sanchez and Masuoka 2010; Vargas, Sanchez, and Valdez 2017). While shared experiences with discrimination can (and have) facilitate a collective sense of identity among Latinos (pan-ethnically and cross-racially), the heterogeneity of the group means that there can be substantial variations in which racialized groups(s) they identify and mobilize with.

It is important to note that "Latino" is a newer and pan-ethnic identity that groups together diverse communities with distinct histories. Scholars have noted that the concept or construction of *Latinidad* is one rife with complexities and contradictions involving issues of immigration, colonialism, conquest, race, color, and language, along with intersecting elements of gender, class, and sexuality (Beltrán 2010; Rodríguez 2003). Patterns of racialization vary among Latinos, or in this case, Latinas, in a way that have important implications for group consciousness and mobilization (Bedolla 2005). Until more recently, Latino struggles for civil rights and racial justice were organized around identities emphasizing national origins and related to their distinctive colonial, geo-political histories.

While pan-ethnic identity and organizing did exist during and prior to the civil rights movement, it was less prevalent and often involved another intersecting dimension that helped to forge the coalition, such as class in the labor movement, or even gender in the feminist movement (discussed more in the next section). Pan-ethic Latino identity became more prevalent as the set of Spanish speaking and origin populations grew in size, became closer in residential proximity, and had shared interests (García 2003; Monfortí 2014). Discrimination and social movements have also played a key role in the development of a Latino pan-ethnic identity. Drawing on Omi and Winant's (1994) theory of "racial formation"—which contends the development of racial identities in the US is significantly influenced by state policies, various forms of discrimination perpetrated by members of the majority, and the political activism of minoritized groups—Zepeda-Millán and Wallace (2013) discuss how anti-immigrant policies and the resulting immigrant rights movement in 2006, contributed to Latino identification as a distinct racial group. In the post-civil rights era, pan-ethnic and cross-racial organizing became more prevalent, and Latinas have played a vital role in an array of these movements (Montoya and Galvez Seminario 2022; Montoya and Guerrero 2023).

The often hybrid or *mestizo* nature of Latino racial identity is one that could be conducive to bridge-building between ethno-racial groups (Anzaldúa 1987; Barvosa 2008). For example, Latinas might develop a racial consciousness that includes a sense of minority-linked fate (Bejarano et al. 2021; Gershon et al. 2019), which might be mobilized in women of color or people of color coalitions and movements. It might, however, go in a different direction. When members of a racial minority feel socially rejected, they may be more inclined to see other groups (including racial minorities) as threats (Bobo and Hutchings 1996; Hutchings et al. 2011; Pérez, Robertson, and Vicuña 2023). Colorism, internal and external, to Latino communities (or even individuals) can become a component of political consciousness and behavior, as can the often related patterns of assimilation. Scholars of Latino politics discuss an ideological whitening in some Latinos (that can be, but is not necessarily related to their skin color) who may adopt a color-blind approach that rejects the recognition of interpersonal or structural racism and/or solutions to address racism as a means of positioning themselves with the hegemonic in-group (Vargas 2018). This can lead to a different, potentially more conservative racial consciousness. Zambrano (2018) analyzes the activism of "Latinas for Trump" through these alternative processes of identity by which activists construct their own self-representation by emphasizing commonalities with those in more privileged positions, even as Trump was constructing them by both race and gender.

The complexities of Latina gender mobilization

Earlier in the essay, I discussed a typology of women's mobilization in different types of movements, all in which gender was salient, albeit in different ways. Such has been true for Latinas. The degree to which gender is salient may vary, as may the type of gender consciousness and orientation that develops. Latinas have mobilized as feminists, seeking to overturn traditional gender hierarchies that subordinate women. They have, too, mobilized in more conservative directions, seeking to uphold traditional gender values, even when they are working for racial liberation.

They have also mobilized in gendered ways that are more complicated than these two alternatives might suggest, and intersectional considerations are an important part of engaging the various tensions and complexities. Scholars have critiqued feminist tendencies to prioritize gender liberation over the other concerns that might be held by women who are simultaneously experiencing class and racial oppression (hooks 1984; Marchand 1995). They have also cautioned against conflating adherence to "tradition" as conservatism or submission to patriarchy. Pardo (1990) argues that Mexican-American women, such as the "Mothers of East Los Angeles," transformed "traditional" networks and resources based on family and culture into political assets, and often speak of their communities and their activism as extensions of their family and household responsibilities.

Within the US labor movement, Latinas have participated in an array of mobilizations based on their class positions, both as active workers within exploitative industries and as leading organizers engaged in direct action to support men's labor struggles (Gutierrez de Soldatenko 2002; Montoya and Guerrero 2023; Soldatenko 2000). Within this context, they have mobilized as women implicitly, due to gender segregation and/or the feminization of work places. Latinas have also mobilized as women more explicitly, to address issues such as sexual harassment. In both scenarios, they blur the line of a feminist-feminine dichotomy. Sometimes they have taken more explicitly "feminist" positions, such as when they challenge the sexism with the labor movement and/or make demands to include issues of gender equality on the agenda.

Within the context of racial justice and civil rights, the issue of gender inequality has been a contentious one at times, even among Latinas, who articulated different types of gender consciousness. In the Chicano movement, debates developed between Chicana traditionalists who held that women's role was to support the men and the feminists who insisted that their struggle was to achieve equality and self-determination for both Chicanos and Chicanas (Nieto-Gómez 2018, 45–46). Even between those who supported liberation, there might be differences. Akin to Black womanism is mujerismo, a Latina womanism (Bryant-Davis and Comas-Díaz 2016; Comas-Díaz 2008; Isasi-Diaz et al. 1992). Like womanism, mujerismo emerged as an alternative to White-dominant feminisms that failed to address women of color's lived experience. While there are different iterations of mujerismo, it often focuses on the centrality of community and collective liberation, where the needs of the whole group (a category constructed along race) are prioritized, and in which antiracism and decolonization is essential.[1] One of the primary divergences between mujeristas and Latina feminists is their understanding of and approach to community. Whereas mujeristas often stress cooperation and interdependence between women and men, some Latina feminists have been more openly critical in articulating the sexism within community and liberation movements, sometimes engaging in more separatist approaches to mobilization.

Chicana feminists frustrated with the mainstream movements (both the Chicano and women's liberation movement) created their own women's organizations. They organized as Chicanas, but sometimes with another race-gendered consciousness, as women of color or third world women (Montoya and Guerrero 2023; Montoya and Killen 2023). Here is where some of the ideas and practices of intersectionality emerged. *The Kitchen Table: Women of Color Press* is an example of these cross-racial communities of women. It was co-founded in 1980 by Black feminists active in the well-known Combahee River Collective, who helped initiate it, but also by Latinas such as Cherríe Morraga, Ana Oliveira, Rosío Alvarez, and Alma Gomez. The intersectional approach of women of color and third world feminism often included an integrated analysis of gender, race, and class, but also of sexuality. It is perhaps no coincidence that many of the scholars and activists articulating and/or practicing intersectional politics were also queer. The intersecting dimension of sexuality is an important one that has yet to be fully explored, and may, in fact, play an important role in understanding some of the divergences that occurred in gender consciousness. Whereas traditional gender roles were embraced by some Latinas, and seen as compatible with—if not vital to—(racial) liberation, for queer Latinas, these gender ideologies contributed to their exclusion within the community, and were thus not a path to liberation.

Contemporary discussion of Latina (or Latinx) activism might, and perhaps should, further problematize the category of gender, including that of woman, to be trans-inclusive. The term Latinx, with roots in feminist and queer intersectional organizing, challenges gender binaries and hierarchies, both in the Spanish language and in society (Guidotti-Hernández 2017; Juárez 2018; Montoya and Galvez Seminario 2022; Vidal-Ortiz and Martinez 2018). Latinas, as well as those with trans and non-binary identities, are identifying and organizing in transformative ways in a range of progressive movements (immigration, voting rights, housing, reproductive justice).

At the same time, there are still Latinas engaged in activism that upholds traditional gender binaries and hierarchies. They may follow patterns of conservatism found among women more broadly, such as those rooted in a religious social conservatism or a more *laissez-faire* rejection of gender inequality or solutions to address it (Schreiber 2008). More recently, there has been increased media attention given to Latinas of the far-right, yet there is still relatively little (if any) research exploring the intersectional dynamics of Latina conservative activism.

Conclusion

In her study of Chicana feminism, Blackwell (2011, 26–27) argues that women of color, lesbians, and working-class women are not clearly registered in dominant frames because they often engage in multi-issue organizing or work on multiple fronts. Their *movidas* take many different forms. Studies of social movement intersectionality help highlight different modes of mobilizing that have traditionally been overlooked or underexplored in the broader study of social movements. At the same time, not all Latinas have mobilized intersectionally. There is a risk that portrayals of Latina intersectional activism oversimplify the complicated realities of what Latina activism looks like. Often, highlighting groups that are previously obscured focuses on what might make them different from other groups (inter-group differences), and less on the heterogeneity within the group itself (intra-group differences). This is not because existing studies are necessarily flawed, but that there are still comparatively few of them. Increasing the number and broadening the scope of studies, so as to better include different mobilizations or forms of mobilizing, can help prevent overgeneralizations.

Latina activism is often overlooked within movements, both as a function of their marginalization within them, but also because scholars might miss their contributions. When scholars take a single-axis approach to the study of social movements, they not only reflect but can also reify exclusionary boundaries. Social movement scholars often construct ideal-type movements that can be helpful in achieving social science goals of parsimony and generalizability, but that often minimize the complex nature of mobilization (Ferree and Roth 1998; Irvine, Lang, and Montoya 2019; Montoya 2021). Mayo-Adams (2020, 1) describes social movements as "dynamic and volatile entities that are never formed, but always forming." Thus, movement boundaries are often porous and temporal, with overlaps and shifts across and within cycles of protests. Latinas can—and often do—reside within this messiness, mobilizing between and across movements, responding to and even instigating some of the changes in movement constructions.

How Latinas mobilize, intersectionally or not, or what form of intersectional praxis they engage, can be, and often is, dynamic. The recognition of interlocking dimensions does not necessarily mean that all dimensions will hold equal or consistent meaning and importance (Bedolla 2007; Hancock 2007; Townsend-Bell 2011; Weldon 2006; Yuval-Davis 2006). Latina activism may shift to different locations as the meaning and salience of particular dimensions shift for particular Latinas in changing political environments. It might also shift due to perceptions of the opportunities and constraints of the environment. Latinas might start in a particular location but not stay there, shifting as the environment does or as they develop different forms of political consciousness.

In this article, I have discussed the ways in which an open and dynamic intersectional analysis might help us to better recognize and understand the varied forms of Latinas mobilization. I have argued the need to distinguish between studying Latina mobilization intersectionally (an approach to understanding all facets and types of Latina mobilization) and studying Latina intersectionality (as an object of study – and a subset of Latina mobilization). I discuss different considerations for studying these patterns, starting with a broad framework of questions that looks to interrogate the dynamic intersectional variations in and connections between Latina structural locations, experiences, orientations, and political behaviors. I provide models for categorizing different patterns of Latina mobilization aimed at recognizing their activism in single-axis movements as well as their mobilization of intersectional identities and/or orientations. I also discuss the need to open up intersectional analysis so as to not only recognize the different possible dimensions of mobilization, but to interrogate the constructions and understandings of those dimensions to better understand the how, where, and why Latinas might develop more or less intersectional politics and practices.

Ultimately, my aim in writing this article is one similar to that of other women of color who brought intersectionality into the academy—to highlight Latinas and their social movement activism in all its forms. An open and expansive intersectional inquiry often means delving into the messiness of lived experience, one that can be at odds with traditional social science goals and methods. The considerations I have laid out are not meant to serve as a checklist for how to study Latina activism, but rather a way to visualize or imagine a larger terrain of exploration so that we can continue pushing and working toward a wider and deeper understanding of the dynamic and varied nature of Latina mobilization. In doing so, we can gain a stronger recognition of the significant contributions that Latinas have made and will continue to make in social movements.

Note

1. Another defining characteristic is the spiritual side to this gendered activism. Isasi-Diaz et al. (1992) discusses mujerismo as being rooted both in Catholic liberation theology, where the goal of liberation is informed by spiritual obligations to the most marginalized populations. Here, activism is a sacred calling and structural oppressions such as racism, classism, colonialism, and sexism are understood within a Christian framework (Montoya and Guerrero 2023).

Disclosure statement

No potential conflict of interest was reported by the author(s).

References

Anzaldúa, Gloria. 1987. *Borderlands/La Frontera: The New Mestiza*. San Francisco: Aunt Lute Books.

Anzaldúa, Gloria. 1990. "Haciendo caras, una entrada." In *Making Face, Making Soul: Haciendo Caras*, ed. Gloria Anzaldúa. San Francisco: Aunt Lute Books, xv–xxvii.

Barvosa, Edwina. 2008. *Wealth of Selves: Multiple Identities, Mestiza Consciousness and the Subject of Politics*. College Station, TX: Texas A&M Press.

Beckwith, Karen. 2000. "Beyond Compare? Women's Movements in Comparative Perspective." *European Journal of Political Research* 37 (4):431–68. doi:10.1111/1475-6765.00521.

Beckwith, Karen. 2007. "Mapping Strategic Engagements: Women's Movements and the State." *International Feminist Journal of Politics* 9 (3):312–38. doi:10.1080/14616740701438218.

Bedolla, Lisa García. 2005. *Fluid Borders: Latino Power, Identity, and Politics in Los Angeles*. Berkeley: University of California Press.

Bedolla, Lisa García. 2007. "Intersections of Inequality: Understanding Marginalization and Privilege in the Post-Civil Rights Era." *Politics & Gender* 3 (2):232–48. doi:10.1017/S1743923X07000050.

Bejarano, Christina, Nadia Brown, Sarah Allen Gershon, and Celeste Montoya. 2021. "Shared Identities: Intersectionality, Linked Fate, and Perception of Political Candidates." *Political Research Quarterly* 74 (4):970–85. doi:10.1177/1065912920951640.

Beltrán, Cristina. 2010. *The Trouble with Unity: Latino Politics and the Creation of Identity*. New York: Oxford University Press.

Blackwell, Maylei. 2011. *Chicana Power! Contested Histories of Feminism in the Chicano Movements*. Austin: University of Texas Press. doi:10.7560/725881.

Bobo, Lawrence, and Vincent L. Hutching. 1996. "Perceptions of Racial Group Competition: Extending Blumer's Theory of Group Position to a Multiracial Social Context." *American sociological review* 61 (6): 951–72.

Bryant-Davis, Thema, and Lillian Comas-Díaz eds. 2016. "Introduction: Womanist and Mujerista Psychologies." In *Womanist and Mujerista Psychologies: Voices of Fire, Acts of Courage*, The American Psychological Association. doi:10.1037/14937-000.

Carastathis, Anna. 2013. "Identity Categories as Potential Coalitions." *Signs: Journal of Women in Culture & Society* 38 (4):941–65. doi:10.1086/669573.

Chitnis, Rucha. 2021. "Garment Workers Organize to End Wage Theft." *YES! Magazine*, December 28. https://www.yesmagazine.org/social-justice/2021/12/28/garment-workers-fashion-industry-wage-theft

Cohen, Cathy J. 1997. "Punks, Bulldaggers, and Welfare Queens: The Radical Potential of Queer Politics." *GLQ: A Journal of Lesbian & Gay Studies* 3 (4):437–65. doi:10.1215/10642684-3-4-437.

Cole, Elizabeth R. 2008. "Coalitions as a Model for Intersectionality: From Practice to Theory." *Sex Roles* 59 (5–6):443–53. doi:10.1007/s11199-008-9419-1.

Collins, Patricia Hill. 2012. "Intersectionality's Definitional Dilemmas." *Annual Review of Sociology* 41 (1):1–20. doi:10.1146/annurev-soc-073014-112142.

Collins, Patricia Hill. 2017. "On Violence, Intersectionality, and Transversal Politics." *Ethnic and Racial Studies* 40 (9):1460–73. doi:10.1080/01419870.2017.1317827.

Comas-Díaz, Lilian. 2008. "2007 Carolyn Sherif Award Address: Spirita Reclaiming Womanist Sacredness into Feminism." *Psychology of Women Quarterly* 32 (1):13–21. doi:10.1111/j.1471-6402.2007.00403.x.

Connell, R. W. 1987. *Gender and Power: Society, the Person, and Sexual Politics*. Redwood City, CA: Stanford University Press.

Cotera, María, Maylei Blackwell, and Dionne Espinoza. 2018. "Introduction: Movements, Movimientos, and Movidas." In *Chicana Movidas: New Narratives of Activism and Feminism in the Movement Era*, eds. Dionne Espinoza, Maria Eugenia Cotera, and Maylei Blackwell, 1–30. Austin: University of Texas Press. doi: 10.7560/315583-002.

Crenshaw, Kimberlé. 1989. "Demarginalizing the Intersection of Race and Sex: A Black Feminist Critique of Antidiscrimination Doctrine, Feminist Theory, and Antiracist Politics." *The University of Chicago Legal Forum* 140: 139–67.

Crenshaw, Kimberlé. 1991. "Mapping the Margins: Intersectionality, Identity Politics, and Violence Against Women of Color." *Stanford Law Review* 43 (6):1241–99. doi:10.2307/1229039.

Dawson, Michael. 1994. *Behind the Mule: Race and Class in African-American Politics*. Princeton: Princeton University Press. doi:10.1515/9780691212982.

de Soldatenko, Gutierrez, and Maria A. de. 2002. "ILGWU Organizers: Chicana and Latina Leadership in the Los Angeles Garment Industry." *Frontiers: A Journal of Women Studies* 23 (1):46–66. doi:10.1353/fro.2002.0013.

Ferree, Myra Marx, and Silke Roth. 1998. "Gender, Class, and the Intersection Between Social Movements: A Strike of West Berlin Care Workers." *Gender & Society* 12 (6):626–48. doi:10.1177/089124398012006003.

García, John A. 2003. *Latino Politics: Community, Culture, and Interests*. Lanham, MD: Rowman and Littlefield.

Gershon, Sarah Allen, Celeste Montoya, Christina Bejarano, and Nadia Brown. 2019. "Intersectional Linked Fate and Political Representation." *Politics, Groups & Identities* 7 (3):642–53. doi:10.1080/21565503.2019.1639520.

Gillian, Youngs, Kathleen B. Jones, and Jan Jindy Pettman. 1999. ""New Spaces, New Politics." *International Feminist Journal of Politics* 1 (1): 1–13.

Guidotti-Hernández, Nicole M. 2017. "Affective Communities and Millennial Desires: Latinx or Why My Computer Won't Recognize Latino/A." *Cultural Dynamics* 29 (3):141–59. doi:10.1177/0921374017727853.

Hancock, Ange Marie. 2007. "When Multiplication Doesn't Equal Quick Addition. Examining Intersectionality as a Research Paradigm." *Perspectives on Politics* 5 (1):63–79. doi:10.1017/S1537592707070065.

Hooks, bell. 1984. *Feminist Theory: From Margin to Center*. Boston: South End Press.

Hutching, Vincent L., Cara Wong, James Jackson, and Ronald E. Brown. 2011. "Explaining Perceptions of Competitive Threat in a Multiracial Context." In *Race, Reform, and Regulation of the Electoral Process: Recurring Puzzles in American Democracy*, eds. Charles Guy-Uriel E, Heather K. Gerken, and Michael S Kang, 52–74. New York: Cambridge University Press.

Irvine, Jill, Lang Sabine, and Montoya. Celeste. 2019. "Gendered Mobilizations and Intersectional Challenges." In *Gendered Mobilization and Intersectional Challenges: Contemporary Social Movements in North America and Europe*, eds. Jill Irvine, Sabine Lang, and Celeste Montoya, 1–22. London: ECPR Press.

Isasi-Diaz, Ada Maria, Elena Olazagasti-Segovia, Sandra Mangual-Rodriguez, Maria Antonietta Berriozábal, Daisy L. Machado, Lourdes Arguelles, and Raven-Anne Rivero. 1992. "Roundtable Discussion: Mujeristas Who We are and What We are About." *Journal of Feminist Studies in Religion* 8 (1): 105–25.

Juárez, Melina. 2018. "Queering Latinidad: Latinx Politics Beyond Nativity." Diss., University of New Mexico.

Lépinard, Eléonore. 2014. "Doing Intersectionality: Repertoires of Feminist Practices in France and Canada." *Gender & Society* 28 (6):877–903. doi:10.1177/0891243214542430.

Marchand, Marianne H. 1995. "Latin American Women Speak on Development: Are We Listening Yet?" In *Feminism/postmodernism/development*, eds. Marianne H. Marchand and Jane L. Parpart, 56–72. London: Routledge.

Martínez, Elizabeth, Betita. 2008. *500 Years of Chicana Women's History*. New Brunswick, NJ: Rutgers University Press.

Mayo-Adams. 2020. *Queer Alliances: How Power Shapes Political Movement Formation*. Palo Alto, CA: Stanford University Press. doi:10.1515/9781503612808.

Monfortí, Jessica Lavariega. 2014. "Identity Revisited: Latinos(as) and Panethnicity." In *Latino Politics En Ciencia Política: The Search for Latino Identity and Racial Consciousness*, eds. Tony Affigne, Evelyn Hu_Dehart, and Marion Orr, 51–73. New York: New York University Press.

Montoya, Celeste. 2016. "Institutions." In *The Oxford Handbook of Feminist Theory*, eds. Lisa Disch and Mary Hawkesworth, 367–84. New York: Oxford University Press. doi:10.1093/oxfordhb/9780199328581.013.19.

Montoya, Celeste. 2019. "From Identity Politics to Intersectionality? Identity-Based Organizing in the Occupy Movement." In *Gendered Mobilization and Intersectional Challenges: Contemporary Social Movements in Europe and North America*, eds. Jill Irvine, Sabine Lang, and Celeste Montoya, 135–53. London: ECPR Press.

Montoya, Celeste. 2021. "Intersectionality and Social Movements: Intersectional Challenges and Imperatives in the Study of Social Movements." *Sociology Compass* 15 (8):1–12. doi:10.1111/soc4.12905.

Montoya, Celeste, and Mar Galvez Seminario. 2022. ""*Guerreras Y Puentes*: The Theory and Praxis of Latina(x) Activism." *Politics, Groups & Identities* 10 (2):171–88. doi:10.1080/21565503.2020.1821233.

Montoya, Celeste, and Kimberly Killen. 2023. "Genealogies of Intersectionality in International Relations." *Oxford Research Encyclopedia of International Studies*. International Studies Association and Oxford University Press. doi:10.1093/acrefore/9780190846626.013.730.

Montoya, Celeste, and Raquel Hernandez Guerrero. 2023. "Latina Activism in the United States: Intersectional Positions and Praxis." In *Routledge Handbook of Intersectionality Studies*, eds. Kathy Davis and Helma Lutz, 304–16. London: Routledge University Press. doi:10.4324/9781003089520-28.

Nieto-Gómez, Anna. 2018. "Francisca Flores, The League of Mexican American Women, and The Comisión Feminil Mexicana Nacional, 1958-1975." In *Chicana Movidas: New Narratives of Activism and Feminism in the Movement Era*, eds. Dionne Espinoza, María Cotera, and Maylei Blackwell, 33-50. Austin: University of Texas Press. doi:10.7560/315583-003.

Omi, Michael, and Howard Winant. 1994. *Racial Formation in the United States*. 2nd ed. New York: Routledge.

Pardo, Mary. 1990. "Mexican American Women Grassroots Community Activists: Mothers of East Los Angeles." *Frontiers: A Journal of Women Studies* 11 (1):1–7. doi:10.2307/3346696.

Pérez, Efrén, Crystal Robertson, and Bianca Vicuña. 2023. "Prejudice When Climbing Up or Falling Down? Why Some People of Color Express Anti-Black Racism." *American Political Science Review* 117 (1):168–83. doi:10.1017/S0003055422000545.

Risman, Barbara J. 2004. "Gender as a Social Structure." *Gender & Society* 18 (4):429–50. doi:10.1177/0891243204265349.

Rodríguez, Juana María. 2003. *Queer Latinidad: Identity Practices, Discursive Spaces*. New York: New York University Press.

Roth, Benita. 2004. *Separate Roads to Feminism: Black, Chicana, and White Feminist Movements in America's Second Wave*. Oxford: Oxford University Press. doi:10.1017/CBO9780511815201.

Sanchez, Gabriel R., and Natalie Masuoka. 2010. "Brown Utility Heuristic? The Presence and Contributing Factors of Latino Linked Fate." *Hispanic Journal of Behavioral Sciences* 32 (4):519–31. doi:10.1177/0739986310383129.

Sandoval, Chela. 2000. *Methodology of the Oppressed. Minneapolis*. University of Minnesota Press.

Schreiber, Ronnee. 2008. *Righting Feminism: Conservative Women and American Politics*. New York: Oxford University Press.

Soldatenko, Maria Angelina. 2000. "Organizing Latina Garment Workers in Los Angeles." In *Las Obreras: Chicana Politics of Work and Family*, ed. Vicki Ruiz *Aztlan Anthology Series* Vol. 1, Los Angeles: UCLA Chicano Studies Research Center Publications, 137–157.

Springer, Kimberly. 2001. "The Interstitial Politics of Black Feminist Organizations." *Meridian* 1 (2):155–91. doi:10.1215/15366936-1.2.155.

Springer, Kimberly. 2005. *Living for the Revolution*. Duke University Press.

Tate, Katherine. 1994. *From Protest to Politics: The New Black Voters in American elections*. Cambridge: Harvard University Press.

Tormos, Fernando. 2017. "Intersectional Solidarity." *Politics, Groups & Identities* 5 (4):707–20. doi:10.1080/21565503.2017.1385494.

Townsend-Bell, Erica. 2011. "What is Relevance? Defining Intersectional Praxis in Uruguay." *Political Research Quarterly* 64(1):187–99. doi:10.1177/1065912910382301.

Vargas, N. 2018. "Ideological Whitening: Does Skintone Shape Colour-Blind Ideology Adherence for Latina/os?" *Ethnic and racial studies* 41 (14): 2407–25.

Vargas, Edward, Gabriel R. Sanchez, and Juan A. Valdez. 2017. "Immigration Policies and Group Identity: How Immigrant Laws Affect Linked Fate among U.S. Latino Populations." *Journal of Race, Ethnicity, & Politics* 2(1): 35–62. doi:10.1017/rep.2016.24.

Vasquez, Enriqueta L. 2016. *The Women of La Raza: An Epic History of Chicana/Mexican-American Peoples*. El Grito del Norte Publication.

Vidal-Ortiz, Salvador, and Juliana Martinez. 2018. "Latinx Thoughts: Latinidad with an X." *Latino Studies* 16 (3):384–95. doi:10.1057/s41276-018-0137-8.

Weldon, S. Laurel. 2006. "The Structure of Intersectionality: A Comparative Politics of Gender." *Politics & Gender* 2 (2):235–48. doi:10.1017/S1743923X06231040.

Weldon, S. Laurel. 2012. When Protest Makes Policy: How Social Movements Represent Disadvantaged Groups. Ann Arbor: University of Michigan Press.

Young, Iris Marion. 2002. *Inclusion and Democracy*. New York: Oxford University Press.

Yuval-Davis, Nira. 2006. "Intersectionality and Feminist Politics." *European Journal of Women's Studies* 13:193–209. doi:10.1177/1350506806065752.

Zambrano, Mayela. 2018. "Latinas for Trump Analysis of Processes of Identification and the Use of Narratives to Construct Subject-Positions." *Pragmática Sociocultural/Sociocultural Pragmatics* 6 (2):197–214. doi:10.1515/soprag-2018-0004.

Zepeda-Millán, Chris, and Sophia J. Wallace. 2013. "Racialization in Times of Contention: How Social Movements Influence Latino Racial Identity." *Politics, Groups & Identities* 1 (4):510–27. doi:10.1080/21565503.2013.842492.

Intersectional Feminist Activism and Practices of Transformation: Perspectives from Indian Feminisms

Rukmini Sen

ABSTRACT

While it is true that there have been and continues to be multiple ways in which intersectional feminist agendas are invisibilized, it is equally important to foreground ways in which intersectional feminists affirm themselves as transformatory agents and create new directions in practice and pedagogy. This article will engage with three legal moments of intersectional feminist transformation: legislation on transgender persons (2019), an intersectional political mobilization against (contested) legislation on citizenship (2019–2020), and responses to a gang-rape on women from *dalit* community (2020). This article analyzes legislation, interprets posters and interviews given by participants in the anti-Citizenship Amendment Act mobilizations, and uses newspaper archives to understand a narrative of invisibility. In conclusion, the article proposes ways that feminist assessments of intersectional political moments can provide a more holistic pedagogical practice in the teaching of intersectional feminisms.

Intersectional feminism: politics and pedagogy

In this article, three contemporary moments of feminist activism will be discussed in order to understand the transformatory potential of intersectional feminist alliances. The first is a law-making moment in 2019, albeit as a result of years of activism as well as a "promising" 2014 Supreme Court judgment. The second is a moment of mass-scale mobilization against proposed legislation for four months between December 2019 and March 2020. The third is an incident of gang-rape in September 2020, which led to questions of (in)access to justice. The first moment was particularly important for the transgender community, the second saw Muslim women leading the protests against citizenship legislation, and the third witnessed the travesty of justice in relation to the gang-rape of a 19-year-old *dalit* woman. Although these three moments may have been about three distinct identities, in all of them there were intersectional alliances.

This article engages with these complex and contested intersectional feminist claims and contemporary struggles in order to think about the possibilities of citizenship that each of these moments, in specific ways, opens up. While intersectionality was not the lens through which these three moments played out, by bringing these three moments together I affirm the potential of intersectional feminist politics, from the global south context, toward a possible repertoire of alliances. The article both highlights contemporary intersectional feminist moments in India and foregrounds the importance of an intersectional feminist pedagogy.

What I attempt to bring together through these three moments are the following: legislation that was critiqued by the community for whom it was meant, a site of protest in which an intersectional collective raised questions about legislation proposed by the Union government, and the travesty of justice through government institutions after the gang-rape of a *dalit* woman.

For each of the moments, I consider the legislation, newspaper archives reporting about the incident, or interviews conducted by other researchers bringing out the intersectional feminist voice.

There are several intersectional themes that connect the three moments:

(a) Use of/need for mobilization at local/community/national level;
(b) Engagement with the legal sphere – either the legislation is the start of mobilization or the attempt to receive justice through the court;
(c) Violence, as the founding basis through a direct act of violence (gang-rape) or causing symbolic violence (Citizenship Amendment Act or Transgender Persons Act);
(d) Claiming justice is an integral aspect of all the three moments. Justice may be the means to an end or the end in itself; but all three moments essentially are connected to processes of justice. Access or the in-access to justice or efforts to accessing justice have been the fulcrum in all the three moments;
(e) Establishing citizenship, pushing the contours of citizenry and promoting a more inclusive citizenship is a fundamental feature across all the three moments.

Intersectionality was conceived as a mechanism for understanding that gender does not exist in isolation from race, caste, class, religion, and ability, among others – that these identities are multiple and intersecting, and therefore the resultant power and privilege, inequalities, and exclusion cannot be understood and addressed through single-axis frameworks (Crenshaw 1989). In the Indian feminist context, intersectionality has been articulated from the late 1990s either through feminist academic writings (Rege 1998) or through memoirs written by *dalit* women (Bama 1992) or expressions made by *dalit* feminist activists like Ruth Manorama (2008). Another academic debate on intersectionality happened in feminist discourses and through the pages of a premier social science journal in India in 2015, with Indian feminists taking positions for or against a universal framework of intersectionality. Menon (2015) taking a position on the limitedness of the universal concept of intersectionality (which has been valuable for states and international funding agencies) proposed that caste, religious identity and sexuality reconfigure women and at the same time are unstable identities themselves. While not providing an alternative concept to intersectionality, what Menon did was to articulate her imagination of feminist politics, which has the potential to motivate people affirming themselves as feminists in different contexts. She points to the internal question of intersectionality regarding whether it should be understood as a theory of marginalized subjectivity or a generalized theory of identity (Nash 2015).

John (2015) critiques Menon to suggest that being trapped in "false particularisms" could be as troubling as understanding that there are false universalisms. She puts forth the question as to whether there has been a radical decentering of the upper caste subject of feminist politics, although *dalit* feminists may have been inspired by Black women, where, according to John, the concept of intersectionality may prove useful. Gopal (2015) in her critique of Menon primarily speaks of the absence of class in most of Menon's articulations or examples and critiques the binary opposition that Menon suggests between caste politics and feminist politics, since the overlaps are evident from different mobilizations. Banerjee and Ghosh (2018) argue for using intersectionality as primarily an organizing principle – a principle which asks for reflexivity in the study of social characteristics, such that one marginality is not substituted by another and lived experiences are not treated as generic and undifferentiated. The value of intersectionality does not lie only in locating hierarchies of social characteristics but also in examining ways in which they become currencies of power. Taking the lens of intersectionality in feminist teaching, Govinda (2022) argues that in order for her students to truly understand that the classroom is not (and cannot) be constructed as a community of equals and yet engage with the intersectionality of identity and structures and how these produce marginality and oppression, then there is a need to reflect on intersectional privilege. Building conversations with some of these perspectives, this

24 INTERSECTIONAL (FEMINIST) ACTIVISMS

article, in engaging with the three moments, will understand the emergence of intersectional feminist politics and pedagogy and end with proposing the methodological promise of intersectionality: what are the intersectional lessons to be learnt from these moments?

Transgender discourse – from self-identification to expert certification

In India, the sexuality rights discourse began with decriminalizing a penal provision on same-sex relationships, which was finally made possible through a Supreme Court judgment in 2018 (after nearly 20 years of struggle by the queer community). The other parallel legal journey has been from the transgender community. According to The Transgender Persons (Protection of Rights) Act, 2019, "transgender person" means a person whose gender does not match with the gender assigned to that person at birth and includes trans-man or trans-woman (whether or not such person has undergone Sex Reassignment Surgery or hormone therapy or laser therapy or such other therapy), person with intersex variations, genderqueer and person having such socio-cultural identities as *kinner, hijra, aravani* and *jogta*. The 2019 Act gives the district magistrate (DM) the power to recognize a person as trans, while the Supreme Court National Legal Services Authorities (NALSA) judgment of 2014, the precursor to the 2019 Act, allowed self-identification of gender. The NALSA judgment had further said that any insistence on sex reconstruction surgery (SRS) was immoral and illegal. It stressed that self-determination of gender is integral to one's personality and dignity.

However, the 2019 Act specifies that to identify as male or as female, one must supply proof of surgery to the magistrate. The Act makes it mandatory for the individual to apply for a "Transgender Certificate," which will label their gender as transgender (Jain 2020). The new rules, however, require the individual to submit a psychologist's report for the "Certificate of Identity." Moreover, if the individual undergoes surgery to change their gender to male or female, they require a "revised certificate" issued by the District Magistrate. The District Magistrate (DM) has the power to judge the "correctness" of the application, albeit if they are able to submit proof of their gender confirmation surgery.

The draft rules make the process of gender identification and reassignment cumbersome and intrusive. Transactivists say this gives immense power to the DM, leading to the possibility of arbitrariness and misuse (Ram Mohan 2020). There is strong resistance from the members of the trans community toward the legislation, suggesting how it is limited to assess intersectional subjectivity, thereby causing symbolic (and also real) violence on the community itself:

> We will continue to oppose this. Our throats cracked ages ago, hands bled and bodies tired. None of it has put a halt to our demand for what is rightfully ours. Through the fight we spent moments mourning our losses, these weren't losses in courts or in legislation; these were losses of our kith and kin. These were losses when our partners in the fight were stripped naked and paraded, their bodies examined, their bodies raped, bodies stared at till they were bloodied in shame, minds torn apart and pushed to them taking their own lives (Mudraboyina, Jagirdar, and Philip 2019).

The 2019 Act which was purportedly enacted to eliminate discrimination against transgender persons by other persons or establishments does not even prescribe a punishment for discrimination. The 2020 Transgender Rules say that even for self-identification as a transgender person, you need a psychologist's certificate. The NALSA judgment had stressed that self-identification is enough and rights should flow from it. The judgment created the category of Third Gender and suggested, "A person's sex is usually assigned at birth, but a relatively small group of persons may be born with bodies which incorporate both or certain aspects of both male and female physiology." According to the judgment, the discrimination on the basis of "sex" under Articles 15 and 16, would include discrimination on the basis of gender identity. The expression "sex" used in Articles 15 and 16 is not just limited to biological sex of male or female, but intended to include people who consider themselves to be neither male nor female. Gender identity is integral to the dignity of an individual and is at the core of "personal autonomy" and "self-determination." Hijras/Eunuchs, therefore, have to be considered as Third Gender, as per the judgment, over and above binary genders under our Constitution and the laws.

The intense contestations around the category of "transgender" proves how even as the state tries to order gender, it fails to do so in the face of proliferating oppositional accounts of self-making. These oppositional narratives are rooted in complex lived realities that exceed the mandate of law (Bhattacharya 2019). Moreover, the operative part of the judgment states that the third gender should be treated as socially and educationally backward classes of citizens and extends all kinds of reservation in cases of admission in educational institutions and for public appointments. Ironically, none of these intersectional social justice affirmations finds a place in the 2019 legislation. The 2019 Act says if anyone harms or injures or endangers the life, safety, health, or well-being, whether mental or physical, of a transgender person or tends to do acts including causing physical abuse, sexual abuse, verbal and emotional abuse, and economic abuse, shall be punishable with imprisonment for a term which shall not be less than six months but which may extend to two years and with fine. This section has been critiqued by various transactivists suggesting that the harm caused to a transgender body is clearly lower in the eyes of the law, than when it is caused on a cisgender body. What is equally important to point out, however, is that while the 2014 judgment made references to the question of livelihood, the legislation completely erases the class, caste, or other specificities connected with the transgender.

Another important point of critique of the Act that has come from transgender activists is the way the "family" is understood – that is, through a banal definition, even after multiple clarifications made by members of the community with regard to the need to expand the meaning of "family." Most transpersons do not live with their biological family because of the discrimination and violence they face from their biological family and their immediate community. Therefore, a need to include chosen family within the ambit and definition of "family" was essential (Mudraboyina, Jagirdar, and Philip 2019). Since it is through the chosen family that most transpersons get support and are able to find their kith and kin. Thus, although the state is recognizing an intersectional identity through this legislation, that identity lacks intersections with labor and intimacies. Providing the transgender community equal constitutional rights with a comprehensive recognition of the challenges to the heteronormative structures that the community does is essential to reduce social stigmas, improve their socio-economic position and support their quest for intersectional justice.

Sisterhood of democracy: Shaheen Bagh and (Muslim) women question

At the core of the movement were Muslim women, who are often painted as deeply marginalized. The image that Shaheen Bagh (a site which is a geographical location in South West Delhi[1]) evoked was a pulsating space of/for democracy. A democracy which is imagined by women of all ages – a space that is a conglomeration of people of different communities, there is a multiplicity of colors – green, saffron, blue and red. There is also a co-existence of Gandhi, Ambedkar, Nehru, Azad, Savitribai Phule – different national leaders from different political ideologies and yet all united in their anti-colonial politics. Shaheen Bagh became more than a site; it evoked the emotions of protest and peace at the same time. A name which became a symbol in other parts of the country, like Shaheen Bagh in Hyderabad (a city in Southern part of the country) or Kolkata (a city in the eastern part of the country), where women were sitting in a peaceful manner, to protest against legislation proposing an enumeration system meant to exclude rather than include the already present – the Citizenship Amendment Act (CAA), 2019. The Act made citizenship conditional upon religion, for the first time in India. The 2019 CAA entrenches a majoritarian and exclusionary idea of citizenship by giving citizenship to "persecuted minorities," viz., Hindus, Sikhs, Christians, Buddhists, Jains, and Zoroastrians, from Afghanistan, Bangladesh, and Pakistan – the three Muslim majority countries. With this reconfigured citizenship, India has moved toward "an idea of racial citizenship," something that members of the Constituent Assembly had avoided (Jayal 2019, 34). Kinship lineage and religion became connected with the acquiring of citizenship and that clearly led to feminist anxieties around it.

Some of these feminist engagements were captured in the following posters that have been written in the wake of the protests against this amendment to citizenship act:

(a) I had to run away from my natal family to get married, how do I get documents to prove my citizenship?
(b) How many women have property on their names, how can we show tenancy documents?
(c) My documents were burnt during the Gujarat riots (2002 Hindu-Muslim religious riots in the state of Gujarat) how do I prove my citizenship?
(d) We people from Denotified communities (erstwhile Criminal Tribes) do not have property documents. What policies have been made for us?
(e) First protect minorities in your own country, before giving citizenship to persecuted minorities from other countries.

There was a continuous articulation of intersectional politics in the movement – it was about various kinds of crosscutting marginalities mentioned above, together with belonging to a certain religion. At Shaheen Bagh women, men, and children came in ones, twos, threes, as well as in groups of numerous sizes to join the protest against the discriminatory citizenship law. The women who came to the protest were of all ages – from grandmothers (*dadis*) to women with young and old children, and young girls (Chopra 2021). They held the Indian flag caps and mufflers on their head and had anti-CAA bands wrapped around their foreheads; "No to CAA" emblazoned on their cheeks or bare chest; anti-NPR-NRC-CAA badges stuck on their chests (Hashmi 2022). Shaheen Bagh remained a site of resistance for 101 days. It also led to the reclaiming of public spaces where many people of diverse origins conglomerated, and destabilized the meaning of protest through marches by, instead, sitting-in through the night, occupying a public road yet letting school buses, ambulances etc. pass by so that these services were not hampered. The *Bharatiya Muslim Mahila Andolan* (BMMA), *Pinjra Tod*, and the National Women's Association were among organizations that joined and collaborated with the Shaheen Bagh women, explicitly mobilizing respective members to come and protest. Farmers from Punjab were most notable in setting up a langar just outside the tent and supplying women protestors with free food (Chopra 2021).

Shaheen Bagh could be summed up as a metaphor of public performance having a multiplicity of actors and teachers (Hashmi 2022). Songs like *Hum Dekhenge*, or slogans like *Sambidhan Zindabad*, dominated the protests. One of the reverberating songs has been *Hum Dekhenge—We will see, It is inevitable that we (too) shall see, The day that has been promised, That has been written in the book of destiny, We too shall see*. This *nazm*/song, originally written by Faiz Ahmed Faiz[2] in the context of an oppressive regime in Pakistan in the 1970s, was being sung and reclaimed by peace protestors in Shaheen Bagh. The overwhelming presence of this song definitely indicated shared histories of cultural activists across South Asia, using their poems, songs, music in different post-colonial moments in South Asia, more so with sisterhood dominating the democratic struggle.

The other sound that Shaheen Bagh generated was "*Samvidhan Zindabad*" – Long Live the Constitution. This was a very interesting spinoff of the otherwise common *Inquilaab Zindabaad*, Long Live the Revolution, that most protest marches would chant. Reclaiming the Constitution, collective reading of the Preamble to the Indian Constitution, in multiple Indian languages – which has the principles of Liberty, Equality, Fraternity, Justice, Dignity enshrined brought the Constitution to the streets of India, and made it a living document, with potential to be revolutionary and in contravention to the proposed legislation. Its principles were being claimed, understood, chanted, demanded by the sisters of/from Shaheen Bagh. "We the people of India" – the first few words with which the Constitution begins was always significant, but in the current juncture, when women of all ages and communities read it together, it becomes another reverberation – the melody of our intersectional democratic citizenry. On India's Republic Day, January 26, 2020, the mothers of Rohith Vemula (a *dalit* university student who had died by suicide) and the "*dadis* (grandmothers) of Shaheen Bagh," Asma Khatoon (90 years old), Bilkis Bano (82) and Sarwari (75) hoisted the national flag amid chanted "*samvidhan ki raksha, desh ki raksha*" (defense of the constitution is defense of the country). Indeed, expropriating the national flag and the constitution as symbolic of their struggle was a powerful move to undermine the mobilization of majoritarian nationalism by the BJP government (Rai 2020).

Shaheen Bagh brought citizenship as a daily practice, strengthened social bonding and focused on civility and solidarity. Through all of this it brought women of intersectional organizations and communities together, making the (excluded) citizenship question as an intersectional feminist pedagogic question.

Dalit woman gang-rape: tracing invisibility and in-accessible justice

"We will frame a large photo once justice is delivered," said the mother of the 19-year-old *dalit* woman (of the Valmiki community) of Hathras (Uttar Pradesh in north India) gang-raped by four upper caste men (Taskin 2021). "Until then, I will continue to take care of her (*tulsi*) plant; it reminds us of her, and it's growing beautifully." One year after the incident of gang-rape, this was the resilience with which the mother spoke. The incident had happened on one September morning in 2019 when the mother and the daughter had gone to the fields to collect fodder for the cattle. The daughter had succumbed to sexual violence about 15 days later in a public hospital in Delhi, the most troubling situation arose subsequent to her death when she was cremated forcibly by Uttar Pradesh government officials on the early morning hours, without consent from the family. "We will never leave this village, this is our home, we have her memories in every corner," the father said (Taskin 2021).

All three *dalit* families of that village have been isolated and the caste divide has sharpened. The lawyer of the *dalit* family has experienced threats and harassments in the special Scheduled Caste/Scheduled Tribe court of Hathras where the trail takes place.[3] The upper caste narrative is the invisibilization of gang-rape and propagating "honor killing," indicating that the woman had a romantic relationship with one of the Thakur men (alleged accused) and was killed by her own brother as a result of that. While the case was taken over by the Central Bureau of Investigation, after widespread protests, four men were charged with gang-rape.

The Allahabad High Court in July, 2022, directed the Uttar Pradesh government to consider giving employment to a family member of Hathras gang-rape victim within three months. The Lucknow bench of High Court (PTI 2022), while looking at the relief and rehabilitation aspect of the case, also directed the state authorities to consider relocation of the victim's family outside Hathras but within Uttar Pradesh, keeping in mind the family's social and economic rehabilitation and also the educational needs of the children of the family, within six months. As per the judgment, one of the submissions made by the family's lawyer was, "[t]he family feels highly insecure, socially, economically, mentally and psychologically. Children are unable to go to school as the mother is afraid to send them for studies in the vicinity of the village or even nearby." In March 2023, the final court judgment acquitted three people and convicted one with culpable homicide while not invoking the rape clause even for the conviction.

While the protests at Shaheen Bagh were one of the last public protests before the pandemic-induced strict lockdown, a protest after the forced cremation of the Hathras gang-raped woman, at the popular protest site in Delhi's Jantar Mantar, was one of the first public outrage post pandemic when citizens felt the need to come out of their homes. One of the protestors articulated that "[t]his entire pandemic period has been very much as an opportunity and as fortune by the government to quell dissenting voices and to curb protests in any form." The space for dissent for women from marginalized communities had shrunk further (Lalwani 2020), and her community was given a clear message that they do not have the right to dissent by the bureaucracy, by the administration, and by the UP police.

There were leaders of opposition political parties voicing their anger and protest against both the Uttar Pradesh government as well as the Central government since both are controlled by the Bhartiya Janta Party (BJP) just after the incident of forcible cremation. However, a year and a half after the gang-rape no opposition political party leader would visit the aggrieved family at the village in Hathras. A group of women's organizations had called for a nationwide protest on October 29, 2020, one month after the death, and demanded the resignation of the Uttar Pradesh Chief Minister. A joint statement signed by the All India Democratic Women's Association, National Federation of Indian Women, All India Progressive Women's Association, Pragatisheel Mahila Sangathan, and others said that that the organizations and activists working to preserve the right to life, livelihood, democratic rights, and a violence-free life are extremely concerned at the way the inquiry in the Hathras case is being compromised (PTI 2020).

A few questions must be raised in the context of this incident. First, while this was gang-rape of a *dalit* woman, in the discourse around the protests the political anger against the government and institution came to be emphasized much more than the intersectional nature of the violence itself. The question of rape cannot be grasped merely in terms of class, criminality, or as a psychological aberration, or an illustration of male violence. The caste factor (its erasure) also has to be taken into account which makes sexual violence against *dalit*/lower caste women much more severe in terms of intensity and magnitude. It is as much important to remember what Rege (1998) had to say in her dialogue with Guru: the "difference" of *dalit* women does not only exist in some separable non-woman (caste) part of them, there is an inseparability (and if I may add not just intersectionality) of caste and gender. Rege (1998) confirmed that in Ambedkar's formulation intra-group organization of reproduction, violent control of surplus women's sexuality and legitimizing control practices through ideology explained the origin and development of caste. Thus the interconnectedness of caste with patriarchal violence is in its origin, existence and survival; there is nothing exceptional about it.

It is also pertinent to ask why the 2012 Delhi gang-rape of Jyoti Singh Pandey led to nationwide protests, changes in the criminal law, capital punishment pronounced by the judiciary against the migrant men who were rapists, and yet the Hathras gang-rape less than 10 years later did not generate anything close to the feminist outrage seen post 2012. After the suicide of Rohith Vemula (in Hyderabad), his mother, Radhika Vemula, had raised a question: "Why was Nirbhaya's (meaning Fearless and referring to Jyoti) caste never asked, while her son's caste identity is repeatedly discussed?." The nature of the question or critique is similar to the one that can be asked after the lack of outrage post the Hathras gang-rape and now court judgment. Ironically and insensitively, the Hathras gang-raped woman was referred to as the Nirbhaya of Hathras by the Congress President (HT Correspondent 2020).

Why will Jyoti's gang-rape go down in the women's movement/studies discourses as a critical event, a moment of transformation, while the Hathras gang-rape, like those previously – Bhanwari Devi gang-rape (1992, Rajasthan), Khairlanji gang-rape and murder (2006, Maharashtra), or the Bhagana gang-rape (2014, Chandigarh), all gang-rapes of *dalit* women – have rarely become intersectional feminist moments of activism or learning. According to Paik (2009), it is important not to subsume *dalit* feminism into the overarching rubric of Indian feminism, for one must comprehend the specific context of the femininity and oppressed sexuality of *dalit* women. The violent, discriminatory experiences of *dalit* castes, the specific *dalit* histories, culture and religion, class, personal lives, and self-hood need to be analyzed in their own contexts.

Dalit women have minimal access to resources and power, unlike upper caste women, and they cannot risk struggling against both sexism and casteist tendencies. It is possible for the outsider to develop sympathy and empathy toward the suffering and oppression that being a *dalit* entails. Paik (2009) argues for a porous struggle, thus building many bridges across feminist movements, and *dalit* movements, and the borders or boundaries here may not be defined and fixed. Such an agenda is to forge informed and engaged solidarities among ourselves, in order to contest all sorts of and forms of Brahmanism. While access to the juridical remains necessary and yet characterized with delay, denial, resistance, clearly indicating the complicity with *brahmanical* patriarchy; but equally important is to raise the question of recognition and nonrecognition of caste intersecting gender and patriarchal violence in the feminist agenda on resistance.

Intersectional methodology: promise and perspective

None of the three contemporary moments discussed in this article are situations that have happened for the first time in India, however there are three intersectional feminist methodological lessons learnt from them. Firstl, waiting for justice, hope and dialogue despite institutional hierarchies. The Shaheen Bagh moment represented this importance of dialogue in a very significant way. The creation of the temporary Fatima Sheikh-Savitribai Phule Library on a bus stand close to the protest site was an imaginative space created with the spirit of conversation (Bhura 2020). Second, creation of new forms and communities of citizenship. The process of legislation formulation, while it may seem to happen in the parliament and the court, is always as a result of what has already occurred in the streets or at the level of collectivization. The formation of transgender collectives, the creation of (medicalized) transgender identity through state legislation and the critique of the legislation through community voices all indicate the different forms of articulating citizenship – their civil, political and economic rights. Third, the co-existence and belief in resistance and resilience. The resistance of the Hathras family lies in taking recourse to the justice delivery system, reaffirming their hope in the judiciary in an otherwise caste and patriarchy ridden social hierarchy. This co-existence of resistance and resilience is seen in all the three intersectional feminist moments, building alliances across differences, resisting the law as well as taking recourse to the legal.

As someone who does not belong to the transgender, Muslim, or *dalit* community, these intersectional feminist pedagogic lessons learnt to connect with the five conceptual themes laid down in the introduction and discussed in three incidents through which the arguments have traveled. It is this feminist intersectionality which will take the project much beyond the identity question, but a pedagogic/methodological question with intersectional feminist politics and perspective underlying it.

I end with a reflection from one of the Shaheen Bagh (Hindu woman) protestor:

> I used to travel back and forth every day but not anymore. Now I go back home once a week. I spend the day at the protest site and at night I sleep at the house of any of my Muslim friends. I did not know any of them when I came here and now they are like family. They take care of me, they invite me to have meals with them and have opened their doors for me—quite literally. I go and sleep in their homes like it is my home. I've received so much love and affection here. It feels like we were never strangers. At any other crowded place like a carnival or a market, it is impossible for a woman to move around without getting jostled. Even I'm not spared despite my age. This safety and respect that I found in Shaheen Bagh has changed my life. Where else can you find this sense of security? I'm a Hindu in a Muslim neighborhood and I feel completely safe. There's no sense of fear. (Prakash Devi, a regular at the Shaheen Bagh protest site, quoted in Mustafa 2021)

The hope in resistance and the ethics of resilience are what intersectional feminist pedagogy exemplifies from the global south, Indian context. The poem signifies this intersectionality:

> *Apna haq chheen-ne ko nikal aaye hum*
> *apne aanchal ko parcham bana hi liya.*
> *Koi tabdeel karne chala tha jise*
> *Us tirange ko humne bacha hi liya.*
> *Dekhiye aap himmat toh shaheen ki*
> *Aasmanon pe kabza jama hi liya.*
>
> (We have emerged to take our rights back
> We have made banners of our scarves.
> They thought that they could change it;
> Behold the courage of the falcon!
> It has made the entire sky its dominion.)

–Poem by Waseem Rashid, a resident of Shaheen Bagh, Quoted in Mustafa, 2021

Notes

1. It is on the UP border and southernmost colony of the Okhla (Jamia Nagar) area, situated along the banks of the Yamuna.
2. Faiz was a Pakistani poet, and author of Urdu and Punjabi literature. He was one of the most celebrated Pakistani Urdu writers of his time. Outside literature, he has been described as "a man of wide experience," having been a teacher, an army officer, a journalist, a trade unionist and a broadcaster.
3. These are the courts that would deal with cases only of scheduled caste and scheduled tribe people and under the specific legislation Scheduled Caste/Scheduled Tribe (Prevention of Atrocities) Act.

Acknowledgments

Thanks to the organizers of the plenary (hybrid) roundtable on 'Contemporary Intersectional Feminist Activisms in Europe and Beyond' at the European Conference on Politics and Gender, University of Ljubljana, Slovenia 6–8 July. Some of the broader feminist ideas written in this article were first articulated at the roundtable.

Disclosure statement

No potential conflict of interest was reported by the author.

References

Bama. 1992. *Karukku Kalachuvadu Publications Pvt.* Ltd.

Banerjee, Supurna, and Nandini Ghosh. 2018. "Introduction. Debating Intersectionalities: Challenges for a Methodological Framework." *South Asia Multidisciplinary Academic Journal* 19. doi:10.4000/samaj.4745.

Bhattacharya, Sayan. 2019. "The Transgender Nation and Its Margins: The Many Lives of the Law." *South Asia Multidisciplinary Academic Journal* 20. doi:10.4000/samaj.4930.

Bhura, Sneha. 2020. "The Story Behind the Library at Shaheen Bagh." *The Week*, February 18. Accessed May 13, 2023. https://www.theweek.in/news/india/2020/02/17/the-story-behind-the-library-at-shaheen-bagh.html

Chopra, Deepta. 2021. "The Resistance Strikes Back: Women's Protest Strategies Against Backlash in India." *Gender & Development* 29 (2–3):467–91. doi:10.1080/13552074.2021.1981698.

Crenshaw, Kimberly. 1989."Demarginalizing the Intersection of Race and Sex: A Black Feminist Critique of Antidiscrimination Doctrine, Feminist Theory and Antiracist Politics." *University of Chicago Legal Forum* 1989 (1):8.

Gopal, Meena. 2015. "Struggles Around Gender: Some Clarifications." *Economic and Political Weekly* 50 (33): 76–77.

Govinda, Radhika. 2022. "Interrogating Intersectionality: Dalit Women, Western Classrooms, and the Politics of Feminist Knowledge Production." *Journal of International Women's Studies* 23 (2): 72–86.

Hashmi, Fahad. 2022. "Citizenship, Religion, and the Politics of Belonging: A Case Study of Shaheen Bagh." *South Asia Multidisciplinary Academic Journal* (28):28. doi: 10.4000/samaj.7690

HT Correspondent. 2020. "Nirbhaya of Hathras Killed by Insensitive Government: Sonia Gandhi." *Hindustan Times*, September 30. Accessed on May 12, 2023. https://www.hindustantimes.com/india-news/nirbhaya-of-hathras-killed-by-insensitive-government-sonia-gandhi/story-oYa6FgpsyeCTBMq4Bg9hMO.html

Jain, Shruti. 2020. "Pride Month 2020: Evaluating the Transgender Persons Act, 2019." Observer Researcher Foundation, July 20. Accessed May 10. https://www.orfonline.org/expert-speak/pride-month-2020-68965/

Jayal, Niraja Gopal. 2019. "Reconfiguring Citizenship in Contemporary India." *South Asia: Journal of South Asian Studies* 42 (1):33–50.

John, Mary. 2015. "Intersectionality: Rejection or Critical Dialogue?" *Economic and Political Weekly* 50 (33): 72–76.

Lalwani, Vijeta. 2020. "'UP Situation More Dangerous Than coronavirus': Protests Erupt in Delhi Over Hathras Gang Rape." *The Quint*, October 3. Accessed May 10, 2023. https://www.thequint.com/news/india/hathras-gang-rape-allahabad-high-court-hc-up-government-job-to-victims-family-member

Manorama, Ruth. 2008. "Dalit Women: The Downtrodden Among the Downtrodden." In *Women's Studies in India: A Reader*, ed. Mary E. John. New Delhi: Penguin.

Menon, Nivedita. 2015. "Is Feminism About 'Women'? A Critical View on Intersectionality from India." *Economic and Political Weekly* 50 (17): 37–44.

Mudraboyina, Rachana, Sammera Jagirdar, and Philip C. Philip. 2019. "A Critique of Transgender Persons (Protection of Rights) Bill, 2019." *Feminism in India*, August 5. Accessed May 13, 2023. https://feminisminindia.com/2019/08/05/critique-transgender-persons-protection-of-rights-bill-2019/

Mustafa, Seema, ed. 2021. Pasha, Seemi (2021) Voices from Shaheen Bagh February-March 2020 in Mustafa, Seema. *Shaheen Bagh and the Idea of India: Writings on a Movement for Justice, Liberty and Equality*. New Delhi: Speaking Tiger.

Nash, Jennifer C. 2015. "The Institutional Lives of Intersectionality." *Economic and Political Weekly* 50 (38): 74–76.

Paik. 2009. "Sailaja Amchya Jalmachi Chittarkatha (The Bioscope of Our Lives): Who Is My Ally?" *Economic & Political Weekly* 44 (40 Oct): 3–9.

PTI. 2020. "Women's Groups Call for Nationwide Protest Against Hathras Gang-Rape." *Business Standard*, October 22. Accessed May 12, 2023. https://www.business-standard.com/article/current-affairs/women-s-groups-call-for-nationwide-protest-against-hathras-gang-rape-120102200017_1.html

PTI. 2022. "'Consider Giving Job to the Victim's family': HC to UP Govt on Hathras Gang Rape." *Business Standard*, July 27. Accessed May 10, 2023. https://www.thequint.com/news/india/hathras-gang-rape-allahabad-high-court-hc-up-government-job-to-victims.family-member

Rai, Shirin. 2020. "Feminist Dissent: Shaheen Bagh, Citizens and Citizenship." *Feminist Dissent* 5 (5):265–74. doi:10.31273/fd.n5.2020.768.

Ram Mohan, G. 2020. Halt Implementation of the Trans Act 2019: Activists, The Wire. June 5, 2020. Accessed May 10, 2023. https://thewire.in/lgbtqia/trans-act-2019-rules-feedback-activists

Rege, Sharmila. 1998. "Dalit Women Talk Differently: A Critique of 'Difference' and Towards a Dalit Feminist Standpoint Position." *Economic and Political Weekly* 33 (44): WS39–WS46.

Taskin, Bisme. 2021. "1-Year Since Hathras 'Gang rape': Caste Divide is Deeper, Memories Don't Fade, Drama in Court." *The Print*, September 14. Accessed May 12, 2023. https://theprint.in/india/1-yr-since-hathras-gang-rape-caste-divide-is-deeper-memories-dont-fade-drama-in-court/732819/

At the Intersections of Gender Inequality and State Fragility in Africa

Adryan Wallace

ABSTRACT

Intersectionality has become a widely used theoretical lens through which scholars examine women's political and economic participation. Intersectional frameworks analyze the ways in which formal state structures produce gender inequalities. It is precisely this conceptual and empirical strength that make a theory originally rooted in the experiences of Black women in the United States, applicable to other groups of women in a range of national contexts. Extensive debates surround the generalizability of intersectional theory. Using my work on gender inequality as a predictor of state fragility in the African region, this piece addresses these questions both conceptually and methodologically. My larger project is a cross-national study; however, I will use original country case study datasets from women's local civil society organizations in Nigeria and Ghana to illustrate the relationships between institutionalized inequalities and the mobilization efforts of different groups of women. First, I begin by defining intersectionality. Next, I combine African feminists and African Muslim feminists' theoretical contributions which extend and expand intersectionality. This piece contributes to conversations about the ways in which intersectionality can be applied to other groups of Black women outside of the United States. Third, I demonstrate how intersectionality is used to capture the range of priorities and strategies activists used to define and promote gender equality within formal state structures.

Introduction

Intersectionality has become a theoretical framework used by feminist scholars to explore the political and economic activities of different groups of women around the world (Carbado et al. 2013; Crenshaw 2017; Meer, Talia, and Alex Müller 2017; Davis 2022). The utility of intersectionality has been recognized in multiple spheres. It serves as a theoretical framework, a site of activist organizing and a set of methodological tools for addressing gender equality and inclusivity (Nash 2008; Alexander-Floyd 2012; Blige 2013). The resonance with other feminist theories describing the ways in which structural inequalities impact the material realities of women in different ways is extensive (Crenshaw 2012). There is a long history of engagement of Black feminist theorists with other women of color inside the west and within global majority countries (Montoya 2021). Establishing networks of mutual support around activism and feminist theory building normalized blending frameworks from multiple national contexts (Bose 2012; Lozano and Paredes Grijalva 2022). The need to understand the experiences of different groups of women encountering institutional biases made generalizing intersectionality appealing to feminists in other regions.

I cultivated a conceptual framework to support my model which uses gender inequalities to predict state fragility. I argue that while there are commonalities, it is critical not to treat the experiences of women of African descent as a monolith. Intersectionality coupled with African feminist theories can be applied to Black women outside of the US to understand gender equality and state effectiveness through security. African feminist theories and methodological approaches can capture intersecting inequalities and sites of resistance (Wallace 2022). My model illustrates how the structural inequalities, which I term *constellations of inequalities*, produce gender inequalities and disparities. The constellations of inequalities serve to outline broader collective goals for structural changes. Here, the interests and experiences of women with less affluence reimagine conceptualizations of power and in turn, demonstrates a key component of intersectionality. The ability to center women of color by applying their experiences into intersectional analysis of legal structures (Crenshaw 1989) suggests that it can be applied to other state institutions tasked with making complicated policy prescriptions with specified desired outcomes. Gender inequality is a predictor of state fragility in Africa, which mandates an intersectional approach that is both a theoretical lens and methodological (Wallace 2022).

In this essay, I use country case study datasets from local women's groups in Nigeria and Ghana to focus on two critical components. First, I contribute to conversations exploring the application of intersectionality to Black women outside of the United States. This section examines the critical theoretical contributions developed by African feminist scholars and particularly Islamic feminisms to expand intersectional analysis to address social institutions. The extent to which local feminist frames are used to extend intersectional analysis is explored. I demonstrate the benefit of applying the framework to generate a synthesis of other feminist voices and experiences. Next, I explore how intersectionality contributes to knowledge production in security studies. Finally, I use intersectional methods to illustrate how gender activists and women working through civil society are mobilizing, which has implications for addressing institutional bias and gender inequality.

What is intersectionality?

Before outlining the role of intersectionality and African feminisms in security studies and related fields, I need to specify how I am defining intersectionality. Intersectionality was developed in the 1980s within critical legal studies to challenge the biases that prevented Black women from seeking legal recourse as a protected class from the state (Crenshaw 1989; King 1988). Although the initial piece focused on workplace and labor force discrimination, Crenshaw recognized that the ideological constructs that created institutional inequalities within legal systems perpetuated them in political, economic, and social institutions as well. Intersectional stigma and discrimination traced the ways in which legal and policy prescriptions created binary categories that flattened out the experiences of minoritized groups (Berger 2010). The utility of the framework extended beyond legal studies (Crenshaw 1990). The expansion conceptualized structural intersectionality, political intersectionality, and representational intersectionality (Crenshaw 1990). The institutional biases encountered by Black women were forged at the intersections of their racialized and gendered identities, requiring the development of a theoretical framework capable of recognizing interconnected structural disparities. Intersectionality creates space to examine the impacts of geopolitical dynamics on local and regional comparative perspectives (Walsh and Xydias 2014; Wilson 2015). The political project of formally responding to the concerns of underrepresented groups is a central feature of the praxis. Variations in the political claims made by women around the world can be captured.

The utilization of African feminist theories with intersectionality prevents us from superimposing the same social stratifications and politicization of identity categories in the US onto the domestic social landscape in other countries. Several African feminists have recognized the important role that intersectionality contributes to local feminist movements and scholarship (Imam, Sow, and Mama 1997; Gouws 2017; Mohammed 2022). More specifically intersectionality and African feminisms together help explain the relationship between gender equality and state fragility. Works examining how gender equality is produced by combinations of social, political, and economic institutions extend intersectional analysis and methods in three ways. First, it provides an analytical lens flexible enough to capture different types of institutional marginalization while recognizing that socially constructed identity categories are fluid (Mama 2004, 2011; Beoku-Betts and Ampofo 2021; Salem 2018). Second, the relationships among an individual and the larger demographic communities in which they have membership is explored (Lozano and Paredes Grijalva 2022). Third, the responses of activists and women's organization to inequalities are revealed (Bonnie and Grzanka 2017; Brown et al. 2017; Tormos 2017).

Yet, the intellectual connections between intersectionality as a US-based theory to African feminisms are clear. For example, Wunpini Mohammed (2022) describes the benefits of applying intersectionality with national feminist scholarship and movements in Africa. Mohammed argues that Black feminist theories contribute to the radical Ghanaian feminist agenda because they place the most marginal groups at the center of all theorizing. The use of the theory therefore can include and incorporate all marginalized identities and the role of gender includes some men in this framework as well. It captures the ways in which constellations of inequalities can be remedied with net positive impacts for many groups while being based on the needs and interests of the most vulnerable groups of women and other marginalized identities. Wunpini's work examines outcomes, and the matrix of domination analogy used by Amanda Gowus (2017) describes the institutional biases that generate them.

The work by Adamu (1999, 2005) provides a perfect example of the conceptual benefits of disaggregating the experiences of different groups of women. The impacts of individual and community connections through social institutions, which support political and economic structures, are explored in her work. She highlights the tensions African Muslim Feminists face in advancing their own definitions of gender equality while resisting both the western feminist critiques that cast Muslim women as passive victims and the conservative male counterparts that argue feminism is a western and not a local movement. Adamu explains how African Muslim Feminists reject both external constructions which seek to delegitimize their work as feminists and as Muslims. Her work assesses the role of social institutions and affluence on women's agency.

The larger communities in which African Muslim Feminists are connected, e.g., national identities, Muslim communities, and women, cannot be fully separated from their individual embodiment of each simultaneously. Intersectionality benefits from being paired with the work of Adamu and other African Muslim Feminists by interrogating the interactions among social institutions and the disparities in political and economic and legal outcomes across different groups of women (Mama 2001; Imam 1997). The ability of the state to provide the same resources to populations equally is a fundamental metric for state legitimacy. Prior to armed conflict political and economic institutions are often perceived as biased against or unresponsive to the needs of demographic groups. Being able to identify multiple combinations of limited state capacity to deliver goods and services can reveal thresholds that are attained before a state is considered ineffective, leading to destabilization and potentially armed conflict. Understanding these differences domestically can provide insight into the endogenous factors that contribute to state fragility.

Intersectionality and post-colonial critiques are used to contextualize the #FeesMustFall, #RhodesMustFall, and #OpenStellenbosch movements in South Africa. Student protests are described in the piece as sites of "radical, intersectional African feminists" (Gouws 2017, 19). The intersectional oppressions described in her work parallel the epistemological conceptualizations of intersectionality by Crenshaw. The educational movements pushed for decolonization of education and criticized the absence of linguistic diversity and heritage in the methods of instruction. Activists used intersectional methods to promote the priorities of multiple groups of students around issues such as gender-based violence (GBV) (Gouws 2017).

The matrix of oppression concept that Gouws (2017) introduces is significant because it provides another lens through which intersecting oppressions can be analyzed across time and geographic locations. There are some key distinctions between the matrix of domination and my *constellation of inequalities* concept. First, my constellations examine the impact on the individual and the institutions. Next, my constellations are examined in relationship to each other to determine when the efficacy of the state is undermined. Additionally, the ways in which different constellations of inequality produce varied impacts on the state is captured. In other words, the same level of economic and political marginalization in one country may not generate the same outcomes in another country. The impacts of different levels of privilege on feminist activism is underscored in my study.

In this essay, I center the experiences of blending intersectionality with feminist scholarship of Black women outside of the United States specifically African feminist research. Examining the impact of compounded gender inequalities on the ability of the state to function (i.e., treat populations equally) and remain stable through an intersectional lens provides critical insights into the effects of institutional bias. In what follows, I illustrate the application to state fragility and security studies.

Intersectionality and state fragility

States attain security for their populations through a combination of political stability and addressing economic needs and inequalities. Ideally, states represent the interests of their populations and are held accountable if those populations' interests are excluded. States become fragile when groups experience marginalization and exploitation, and national identities become fragmented – all of which can be precursors to inter- and intra-state conflict (Caprioli 2005). The relationship between inequality and political instability has been well-established (Baker 2017; Buvinic et al. 2013; Forsberg and Olsson 2016; Hudson, Bowen, and Nielsen 2016; Pyle and Ward 2003; Cramer 2005; Ostby, Nordas, and Rod 2009), with gender inequality yielding similar predictive results. Inequality is defined as variations in access to resources and opportunities because of membership in particular demographic categories (i.e., gender, race, nationality, religion, gender identity, sexual orientation). These inequalities can extend across political, economic, social, and legal systems and include instances of discrimination and bias. In response to concerns around gender disparities, states and regional economic cooperative groups have adopted quotas and policies to promote gender equality.

There are multiple components attributed to state failures, including quality of life, functioning democratic structures, and participation in global trade (Esty et al. 1998). Security studies scholars have established an empirical link between high levels of inequality (Robinson 2003; Cramer 2005), specifically gender inequality, and high levels of inter and intrastate conflict (Caprioli 2005; Forsberg and Olsson 2016). The majority of these studies theorize gender along three dimensions: a) norms, b) social capacity, and c) socioeconomic status (SES). Socioeconomic status, the most recently added component (Forsberg and Olsson 2016), is defined as a combination of income, occupation, and formal education. While critical, this conceptualization of SES does not reveal how *privilege* functions, allowing some women more autonomy to define work on their own terms and cope with institutional barriers. There is a need to develop models that can unpack such complexities of inequalities. If we can understand how privileges and inequalities intersect, states can more effectively address the fiscal needs of their citizens. Understanding the complexities surrounding how identities impact the ways in which individuals perceive their autonomy and power within the state includes understanding individuals' willingness to negotiate and cooperate to avoid conflict (Suedfeld 2010, 2011; Conway et al. 2018).

The potential capacity of intersectionality to address structural disparities through feminist policy and programmatic interventions has been explored by feminist scholars as an important component of state effectiveness vis-à-vis policy formation, institutional norms, and governmental structures (Hankivsky et al. 2014; Olena and Jordan-Zachery 2019; Smooth 2013). Hancock (2007, 2019) attempts to demonstrate the utility of applying intersectionality to public policy. There are clear parallels between the reliance of legal and policy systems on binary oppositional categories and the tendency to homogenize the requirements and experiences of groups.

State fragility occurs when the state has lost legitimacy and/or the ability to be effective (Marshall and Cole 2008). The goal of my larger project is to develop and test a theoretical framework using gender inequality to predict state fragility and dysfunction. I am operationalizing effectiveness as the capacity to provide security, good governance, economic opportunities, and social development (Marshall and Cole 2008). Women cannot be treated as a monolith; disparities in access to resources intersect with other demographic categories and factors. To capture the variations in women's individual economic experiences, I have developed an *Index of Agency (IOA)*. I conceptualize agency as having the autonomy to determine one's own economic activities and to successfully address institutional obstacles that are encountered. Agency measures the ability to access resources from the state. My *Gender Inequality as a predictor of State Fragility (GISF)* predictive model uses the *IOA* to reveal how combinations of inequalities produced by political, economic, and social institutions combine to impact women's economic security. I argue that gender inequalities ultimately make the state fragile. This model generates rich data that allow us to identify weaknesses in state structures that are producing inequalities and develop sustainable approaches to addressing inequalities. The *IOA* uses intersectionality to examine how different combinations of identity categories and privilege across women impact their ability to make choices and have their issues addressed by state institutions. The index identifies how privilege is constituted within and across countries. Any differences in the kinds of fiscal or social capital on structural discrimination is uncovered.

Examining activist approaches through an intersectional lens in Nigeria & Ghana

The theoretical benefits of synthesizing intersectional and African feminist approaches provide for a conceptualization of women's experiences with inequality that vary based on levels of privilege and which results in how they strategize to address these issues. The aggregate inequality outcomes for individuals and communities can also be discerned through an examination of the other demographic categories that intersect with gender. This section will focus on the methodological benefits of applying these hybrid feminist theories to illustrate the mobilization efforts on the ground around inequality.

Methodological approach

Women's economic experiences and how women define gender equality and their priorities for structural change are revealed using intersectional analysis, producing dynamic pictures of the relationships among underlying political, economic, and social factors. Through the incorporation of original datasets that I created from 2022 the study can identify contemporary issues contextualized with field work from 2012. The qualitative data collected through the first round includes 150 interviews and content analysis of local women's organizations and will provide detailed pictures of women's lived experiences that will be integrated into the *GISF* model. The women participating in this study are a representative sample of women across levels of privilege and engaged in a range of economic activities.

The *IOA* uses individual-level gender indicators (e.g., labor force participation, decision making authority) to identify relationships to components of state fragility, providing a method for coding gender indicators to test short-term and long-term effects on conflict forecasting models. Typologies of the combinations of weakened state and social institutions that can culminate in conflict are captured by this study and contextualized at the household and national levels. The *IOA* supports a series of insights into motivational factors used in conflict forecasting through capturing the perspectives of multiple groups on the ground. There are two sets of data: the first examines the relationships between the levels of privilege *(IOA)* and the types of mobilization through civil society organizations; the second summarizes the kinds of institutional barriers faced by women with the least amount of privilege across two country case studies.

Description of participants

The women participating in this study are a representative sample of women across levels of privilege and engaged in a range of economic activities. Participants come from multiple economic sectors, firms of all sizes, private and not-for profit organizations, and government agencies. The age ranges of women will extend into their 80s because labor does not end at 64 years of age – as common in

Western democracies – but continues throughout the lifecycle (Wallace 2018). Women were interviewed in urban and rural communities within Nigeria and Ghana to obtain internal domestic geographic differences. The data from Nigeria features women from the northern part of the country. Northern Nigeria has a predominantly Muslim population and has operated under Sharia Law (Islamic law) since 1999. The women represent the intersections of multiple ethnolinguistic groups (majority and minority status), income (individual and household), family lineages, formal education, Islamic education, marital status (married-polygamous/monogamous, unmarried, widowed, divorced). The selection of case study data from Nigeria and Ghana provides a contrast between a majority and minority Muslim populations.

The specific types of work included are: a) private sector small- and medium-sized enterprises (industries/sectors-agriculture, food stuffs, technology, banking, telecommunications, fashion/clothing, beauty, health, education, child/elder care); b) women in civil society organizations, NGOs, CBOs; c) national women political officials (ministers, legislators, executive); d) sub-regional women political officials (RECs, RIOs); e) work without monetary remuneration (care work). I selected labor sectors where women are over or underrepresented. The case study data summary shared below focuses on women's organizations. The CBO and NGO data were selected because these women represent a cross section of labor sectors and their constituents are some of the most vulnerable women.

Index of agency

The *IOA* highlights the micro-level economic experiences of women including: 1) their ability to make decisions about the types of work they undertake; 2) the specific institutional barriers they encounter; 3) the strategies they employ to address any obstacles; and 4) their success in removing structural impediments. The *IOA* includes a survey and semi-structured interviews. A total of 150 women in each country case study were interviewed in Nigeria and Ghana, respectively.

A qualitative content analysis of the semi-structured interviews was conducted to identify themes and sub-themes to compile a detailed description of the level of agency based on the four measures of gender equality described above. The demographic factors that are included in the index are age, lineage, level of formal education completed, level of religious education, income, sector of economic participation, ethnolinguistic group, religion, and language. While education and income are critical, the ability to leverage relationships with powerful individuals in formal systems must be included when quantifying privilege. Direct connections to decision-makers within formal institutions is measured through social network mapping. Understanding how privilege is constituted and perceived by individual actors is a complex process. Conducting a qualitative content analysis allowed me to drill down and reveal how demographic factors interacted with proximity to institutional power to increase or decrease the ability of participants to decide in which economic sector to work, determine the types of obstacles they encounter, influence how they address barriers and if they can successfully remove an impediment they face. The larger themes are derived from common issues that participants highlighted across levels of privilege and are used to create the constellations of inequalities. The sub-themes are then outlined under each larger institutional theme/barrier to gender equality. The sub-themes provide data about specific interventions or policy provisions required to address concerns. The relationships among individual privilege, organizational responses and inequalities are explored through examining how civil society organizations define gender equality priorities and provide accountability mechanisms to help ensure that the collective agenda is based on the interests of women in each echelon of society, not just women with greater levels of social capital.

Constellations of inequality

The preliminary country case study data has qualitatively highlighted particular institutions that impact gender equality and intersecting points of discrimination. The qualitative data is reflective of two country case studies and includes interviews from women engaged in local NGOs, political officials, and women engaged in small scale and micro enterprises. The data used to develop the constellations of inequalities are from the West African dataset (Nigeria and Ghana) from the first preliminary pilot round of data. There are six kinds of institutions that will be incorporated into my *GSIF* model: a) economic institutions, b) political institutions, c) social institutions (cultural and religious), d) educational institutions, e) information communication technology (ICT) infrastructure, and f) public health institutions. The specific sets of metrics for each of these six institutional factors are detailed below. These were the recurring themes about institutions in the interviews.

Description of data and analysis

Table 1 summarizes the mobilization data from women's organizations (NGOs and CBOs) to address gender equality, including efforts to define the larger feminist agenda and to hold grassroots organizations accountable to their constituents. The levels of privilege are captured by the *IOA* and mapped onto the organizational structures. The results of the interviews are used to distill the specific kinds of structural barriers that result in inequalities experienced by women. The results of the qualitative content analysis were disaggregated by the results of the *IOA* survey to determine points of congruence and divergence, and to determine any additional probing questions that need to be added to the survey prior to distribution. The *IOA* is broken down into three tiers (A, B, C) with a range of 1–3 within each. The experiences of women in the lowest sphere, with the least amount of agency, are included in this study because they represent the most vulnerable groups. Successfully addressing the issues faced by women that are the most institutionally marginalized across multiple sectors can help improve the conditions for other cross-sections of society and strengthen formal economic, political, and social structures and mechanisms of the state, regional, and sub-regional governing organizations. The thematic results of the semi-structured interviews help ensure that the reported economic experiences of women can be further contextualized through their own stories. Women involved in NGOs work to have more privilege than women involved in community-based organizations (Wallace 2018).

Table 1 summarizes the ways in which different local women's groups in Nigeria and Ghana define their gender equality priorities to promote economic engagement and the presence of structures to help ensure that women that are represented by the organizations provide feedback and hold the groups accountable for representing their different interests. The concrete institutional barriers that they encounter and need to have removed are depicted. The greater specificity of the local women's organizations moves beyond broader themes and outlines ways to concretize them and generate structural changes that perpetuate the disparities.

In Nigeria, the NGOs that served as the focal point of this study included umbrella groups, single-issue organizations (e.g., education, health), and faith-based organizations. The women that had the highest scores on the *IOA* were running these groups and comprised their constituents, A {1–3} and B {1–3}. The NGOs made addressing development, democracy (good governance-anti-corruption), health, and vulnerable populations their key areas of work. The definitions of gender equality centered on addressing institutional barriers and capacity building for women in their respective economic sectors. It is important to note that women with a C {1} *IOA* score were also involved in NGO activity. They comprised the smallest percentage of women involved in NGO work. Many of these women were present through umbrella Muslim women's organizations. The consensus model of decision making is largely responsible for their participation in NGOs. During meetings, issues and decisions are discussed and debated until everyone agrees with the outcome instead of relying on majoritarian votes. It does require more time to reach agreements however the concerns of everyone involved are addressed before the group can act or move forward. The presence of women with less privilege in the umbrella organizations increases the extent to which they are able to place their issues on the larger agenda of the NGO through their connections to more institutionally powerful women. NGOs often partner with the federal and state governments on programs and interventions around gender. In Ghana, the NGOs had similar agenda items. The women involved in the NGO work are predominantly women with the highest scores on the *IOA*. The more direct partnerships with the state are less robust than in the Nigerian context.

INTERSECTIONAL (FEMINIST) ACTIVISMS

Table 1. Impact of Privilege on Local Women's Groups Gender Equality Activism Nigeria & Ghana.

Type of CSO	IOA Score A {1–3} B {1–3} C {1–3}	Conceptualizations of Gender Eequality (Local Women's CSO)	Mechanisms of Organizational Accountability (Local Women's CSOs)
NIGERIA Non-Governmental Organizations (NGOs) *umbrella organizations *individual NGOs *faith-based groups *issues: health, education, democracy, vulnerable populations	A {1–3} B {1–3} C {1}	*increase access to fiscal capital *removing collateral requirement *business development *basic fiscal literacy *trainings for health care work *increase access to contract set asides *better telecommunications network stability and access *inclusion in designing gender equality policies	*direct connectivity NGO umbrella and CBOs *decision making via consensus vs majoritarian votes *autonomy to form coalitions
Community-Based Groups (CBOs) *issues: development committees, trading cooperatives, traditional birth attendants, small scale food stuffs	C {2–3}	*increase access to healthcare facilities *increase access to fiscal capital *removing collateral requirement *trainings for health care work, traditional birth attendants *better telecommunications network access	
GHANA Non-Governmental Organizations (NGOs) *issues: political engagement, LGBTQ+ groups, faith-based groups, health, education	A {1–3} B {1–3}	*increased access to capital *increased access to equipment and facilities *increases in local government institutional support *inclusion in designing gender equality policies *increase access to health care services and medications	*direct NGO-CBO missing link among some demographically minority groups
Community-Based Groups (CBOs) *issues: development committees, trading cooperatives, textile/clothing production, sub-regional groups, small scale food stuffs	C {1–3}	*increases in local government *increases in resources to zongo *increased access to capital through government programs	

The CBOs in Nigeria tend to focus on issues that can be addressed if the individual has more fiscal resources. The emphasis on increasing access to the internet, healthcare facilities, and trainings for traditional birth attendants are necessary when people cannot cover the costs of purchasing services from private sector vendors or the associated hidden costs. In contrast, CBOs in Ghana, particularly those run by women that are members of ethnolinguistic and religious minority groups, mobilized around attaining more resources for local governments at the community levels (zongos). The multiple minority statuses of women in these organizations culminated in a closer institutional relationship to local political officials as a mechanism to obtain support to address gender equality over the sub-national or national government. The experiences of Muslim women that are members of non-majority ethnolinguistic groups, and women in the northern region of the country compared to the areas around the capital and the southern part of the country, articulate this clearly.

In addition to testing the connections between privilege and organizational responses, the index outlines the themes and sub-thematic issues that are more prevalent among women based on their *IOA* scores. The institutions that participants perceived responsible for gender disparities are listed in Table 2. The barriers specified in each theme (sub-themes) are outlined as well.

The six themes of institutional bias that were reported most often by participants include: economic institutions, political institutions, social (religious and cultural) institutions, educational institutions, ICT infrastructure, and public health institutions. The data in Table 2 combines the results of the interviews with women that scored in the lowest category on the *IOA*, tier C {1–3} with each type of formal institution they encounter. The factors that resulted in their scores being in tier C include lack of formal education, income, social capital, and limited autonomy to determine if they would participate in the external labor force market and if they decided to participate, they were not able to select their preferred types of economic activities. They are also the participants that were the farthest removed from decision makers within formal structures. Each participant was interviewed twice which provided me with the opportunity to ask follow-up questions based on information gathered in the initial interview. The participants that generated the data in Table 2 represent a cross-section of women of varying ages that were involved in the following economic sectors: micro-enterprises (food stuffs, incense burners, trading cooperatives), domestic care work (childcare, elder-care), community-based organizations, and textiles-clothing. The sub-issues that people wanted to resolve are included under each larger theme.

Women that scored in this last tier had little flexibility to determine the conditions under which their labor occurred. The social network maps of these women were often characterized by differing degrees of separation among decision makers in formal economic and political institutions and social, cultural, and religious ones. The other factors that were important include their domestic sub-regional location and the majority and minority statuses of demographic categories such as religion. Finally, many of the women interviewed in both country case studies while engaging in informal economic activity that includes renumeration, they are also providing labor in both the formal and informal sectors that is not compensated monetarily.

Table 2. Continuity in Gender Equality Institutional Barriers in Nigeria and Ghana Among Women with Lowest IOA Scores.

Economic Institutions	Political Institutions	Social (Religious and Cultural) Institutions	Educational Institutions	ICT Infrastructure	Public Health Institutions
Ability to access capital (firm registration)	Existence of gender equality policies and quotas	Authority to change cultural gender norms	Adult literacy rates	Inclusive ICT policy	Healthcare access
Need human capital investments	Date of adoption of policies and quotas at all levels of government	Authority to change religious gender norms	Literacy rates for girls and boys	Internet Access (Broadband subscription)	Mental Healthcare access
Wage gaps	Presence of enforcement mechanisms	Leadership positions in cultural institutions	Primary School Completion	Technology innovation and access	Insurance coverage
Access to formal financial institutions	Increase women in legislatures and executive office	Leadership positions in religious institutions	Secondary School Completion	Improved Roads in all areas	Treatment access
Labor force participation with renumeration	Legal protections (criminal-workplace)	Public changes in women's roles within cultural institutions	Tertiary education completion	Access to Water	Medication provisions
Investment in women-led economic sectors	Invoking gender based legal precedents	Public changes in women's roles within religious institutions	Post-graduate education completion	Sanitation	Accessibility to personnel

Institutional barriers faced by women with the least amount of privilege document similar encounters in both Nigeria and Ghana. The continuity between these sets of challenges shows that the *IOA* score can be used to predict gender inequalities and corresponding institutional weaknesses in multiple national contexts. The similarities in the issues that participants in Nigeria and Ghana reported facing are depicted with their corresponding institutions in Table 2. Under each structural barrier a list of the top six potential interventions have been outlined. The points of congruence across the two country case studies are highlighted in order to outline specific structural changes that can address these gender inequalities and fortify the connected state institutions from the perspectives of the most vulnerable.

There are differences between the economic experiences of women in Nigeria and Ghana, however I emphasize understanding the issues that both cases had in common. Implementing gender equality policy prescriptions based on the cross-cutting issues identified in both country case studies can also provide further insight into how intersectional methods can be used to illustrate the experiences of intersectional identities to strengthen state structures, allowing them to provide all segments of their populations with resources and opportunities. Given the key role that RECs play in addressing gender equality for all their member states, it is important that the variations in women's interests and needs are understood across levels of affluence. The policy recommendations that can result from using the *IOA* and *GSIF* are concrete, specific, and measurable.

Concluding thoughts on comparative intersectionality in global context

Originally rooted in the experiences of Black women in the United States, intersectionality as a conceptual framework has been applied to other groups of women in a range of national contexts. The incorporation of intersectional frames underscores the importance of local feminist praxis and concepts. The context in which intersectionality was developed is precisely what makes it so valuable. Adding identity categories together or treating them as static in various categories is a critical misstep that violates the ethical tenets of this theory. The impacts on national domestic feminist movements provide greater insights into the other ways that identity categories are made and unmade and the particular outcomes of their combinations that yield resources from the state. Comparative perspectives can shed light on the ways in which we identify and strategize to generate feminist theories and address discrimination and inequalities.

Placing intersectionality in conversation with scholarship and activism by Black women outside of the US provides for an examination of how other forms of institutional biases as measured through gender inequalities can be addressed. Conceptualizing security through an African feminist-focused model of intersectionality elucidates methodological approaches that are capable of capturing the varying experiences, interests, and priorities of different groups of women while simultaneously examining how marginalized groups engage with these institutions and structures.

Examining gender equality as a predictor of state fragility allows me to share an example of the benefits of intersectionality in conjunction with African feminisms in practice by illustrating what it looks like theoretically and as a method that yields empirical results. I began by describing the ways in which African feminisms extend intersectional analysis in three ways. First through the identification of different types of institutional bias and marginalization. Second, the impacts of the individual to other communities are enhanced. Third, the impact of privilege on women's experiences was explored. Finally, the utility of intersectional methods was demonstrated using the *IOA* to explain variations in women's organizing around gender equality and to outline the types of institutional barriers the most vulnerable women face. In sum, combining intersectionality with African feminism can help fortify state institutions before the next set of exogenous stressors place more pressure on existing systems.

Disclosure statement

No potential conflict of interest was reported by the author.

References

Adamu, Fatima L. 1999. "A double-edged sword: Challenging women's oppression within Muslim society in Northern Nigeria." *Gender & Development* 7 (1):56–61.

Alexander-Floyd, Nikol G. 2012. "Disappearing acts: Reclaiming intersectionality in the social sciences in a post—Black feminist era." *Feminist Formations* 1–25.

Baker, Pauline H. 2017. *Exploring the Correlates of Economic Growth and Inequality in Conflict Affected Environments Fault Lines and Routes of Recovery.* Washington, DC: Creative Associates International.

Berger, Michele Tracy. 2010. *"Workable sisterhood: The political journey of stigmatized women with HIV/AIDS."* Princeton University Press.

Bilge, Sirma. 2013. "Intersectionality undone: Saving intersectionality from feminist intersectionality studies 1. Du Bois review." *Social science research on race* 10 (2):405–24.

Bose, Christine E. 2012. "Intersectionality and Global Gender Inequality." *Gender & Society* 26 (1):67–72. doi:10.1177/0891243211426722.

Brown, Melissa, Rashawn Ray, Ed Summers, and Neil Fraistat. 2017. "#sayhername: A Case Study of Intersectional Social Media Activism." *Ethnic and Racial Studies* 40 (11):1831–46. doi:10.1080/01419870.2017.1334934.

Buvinic, Mayra, Monica Das Gupta, Ursula Casabonne, and Phillip Verwimp. 2013. "Violent Conflict and Gender Inequality: An Overview." *The World Bank Research Observer* 28 (1):110–38. doi:10.1093/wbro/lks011.

Caprioli, Mary. 2005. "Primed for Violence: The Role of Gender Inequality in Predicting Internal Conflict." *International Studies Quarterly* 49 (2):161–78. doi:10.1111/j.0020-8833.2005.00340.x.

Carbado, Devon W., Kimberl Williams. Crenshaw, Vickie M. Mays, and Barbara. Tomlinson. 2013. "INTERSECTIONALITY: Mapping the Movements of a Theory1." *Du Bois Review: Social Science Research on Race* 10 (2):303–12.

Conway III, Lucian., Lucian, Gideon, Suedfeld Peter, Tetlock, and Phillip. E. 2018. *"Integrative complexity in politics."* The Oxford Handbook of Behavioral Political Science.

Cramer, Chrisopher. 2005. "Inequality and conflict: A review of an age-old concern." Geneva: United Nations Research Institute for Social Development.

Crenshaw, Kimberle. 2012. *"On intersectionality: The seminal essays."*

Crenshaw, Kimberl W. 2017. *"On intersectionality: Essential writings."* The New Press.

Davis, Martha F. 2022. "(G) local Intersectionality." *Washington and Lee Law Review* 79:1021.

Esty, Daniel C., Jack A. Goldstone, Ted Robert. Gurr, Barbara. Harff, Marc. Levy, Geoffrey. Dabelko, and Alan N. Unger. 1998. *State Failure Task Force Report: Phase II Findings.* McLean, VA: Science Applications International Corporation.

Forsberg, Erika, and Louise Olsson. 2016. "Gender Inequality and Internal Conflict." *Oxford Research Encyclopedia of Politics.* doi:10.1093/acrefore/9780190228637.013.34.

Gouws, Amanda. 2017. "Feminist intersectionality and the matrix of domination in South Africa." *Agenda* 31 (1):19–27.

Gouws, Amanda. 2017. "Feminist Intersectionality and the Matrix of Domination in South Africa." *Agenda* 31 (1):19–27. doi:10.1080/10130950.2017.1338871.

Hancock, Ange-Marie. 2007. "Intersectionality as a normative and empirical paradigm." *Politics & Gender* 3 (2):248–54.

Hankivsky, Olena, Daniel Grace, Gemma Hunting, Melissa Giesbrecht, Alycia Fridkin, Sarah Rudrum, Olivier Ferlatte, and Natalie Clark. 2014. "An Intersectionality-Based Policy Analysis Framework: Critical Reflections on a Methodology for Advancing Equity." *International Journal for Equity in Health* 13 (1):1–16. doi:10.1186/s12939-014-0119-x.

Hudson, Valerie M., Donna Lee Bowen, and Perpetuya Lynne Nielsen. 2016. "We are Not Helpless: Addressing Structural Gender Inequality in Post-Conflict Societies." *Prism* 6 (1): 122–39.

Imam, A. 1997. *The Dynamics of WINning. Feminist Genealogies, Colonial Legacies, Democratic Futures*, M. Jacqui Alexander, eds., Chandra Mohanty and Chandra Mohanty, 230–307

Imam, Ayesha MT., Amina A. Mama, and Fatou. Sow. 1997. "Engendering African social sciences."

Josephine, Beoku-Betts, and Adomako Ampofo. Akosua. 2021. "Positioning Feminist Voices in the Global South." In *Producing Inclusive Feminist Knowledge: Positionalities and Discourses in the Global South*, eds. Akosua Adomako Ampofo and Josephine Beoku-Betts. Bingley, UK: Emerald Publishing Limited, 1–19. doi:10.1108/S1529-212620210000031001.

King, Deborah K. 1988. "Multiple jeopardy, multiple consciousness: The context of a Black feminist ideology." *Signs: Journal of Women in Culture & Society* 14 (1):42–72.

Lozano, Betty Ruth, and Daniela Paredes Grijalva. 2022. "Feminism Cannot Be Single Because Women are Diverse: Contributions to a Decolonial Black Feminism Stemming from the Experience of Black Women of the Colombian Pacific." *Hypatia* 37 (3):523–43. doi:10.1017/hyp.2022.35.

Mama, Amina. 2001. "Challenging Subjects: Gender and Power in African Contexts." *African Sociological Review/Revue Africaine de Sociologie* 5 (2):63–73. doi:10.4314/asr.v5i2.23191.

Mama, Amina. 2004. "Demythologising Gender in Development: Feminist Studies in African Contexts." *IDS Bulletin* 35 (4):121–24. doi:10.1111/j.1759-5436.2004.tb00165.x.

Mama, Amina. 2011. "What Does It Mean to Do Feminist Research in African Contexts?" *Feminist Review* 98 (1_suppl): e4–e20. doi:10.1057/fr.2011.22.

Marshall, Monty G., and Benjamin R. Cole. 2008. "Global Report on Conflict, Governance and State Fragility 2008." *Foreign Policy Bulletin* 18 (1):3–21. doi:10.1017/S1052703608000014.

Meer, Talia., and Alex. Müller. 2017. "Considering intersectionality in Africa." *Agenda* 31 (1):3–4.

Mohammed, Wunpini Fatimata. 2022. "Why we need intersectionality in Ghanaian feminist politics and discourses." *Feminist Media Studies* 1–17.

Montoya, Celeste. 2021. Intersectionality and social movements: Intersectional challenges and imperatives in the study of social movements. *Sociology Compass*. 15 (8):e12905.

Moradi, Bonnie, and Patrick R. Grzanka. 2017. "Using Intersectionality Responsibly: Toward Critical Epistemology, Structural Analysis, and Social Justice Activism." *Journal of Counseling Psychology* 64 (5):500–13. doi:10.1037/cou0000203.

Nash, Jennifer C. 2008. "Re-thinking intersectionality." *Feminist review* 89 (1):1–15.

Hankivsky, Olena, and Julia S., Jordan-Zachery, eds. 2019. *The Palgrave Handbook of Intersectionality in Public Policy.* Basingstoke: Palgrave Macmillan. doi:10.1007/978-3-319-98473-5.

Østby, Gudrun., Ragnhild. Nordås, and Jan Ketil. Rød. 2009. "Regional inequalities and civil conflict in Sub-Saharan Africa." *International Studies Quarterly* 53 (2):301–24.

Pyle, Jean L., and Kathryn B Ward. 2003. "Recasting Our Understanding of Gender and Work During Global Restructuring." *International Sociology* 18 (3):461–89. doi:10.1177/02685809030183002.

Robinson, James A. 2003. "Social identity, inequality and conflict." In *Conflict and Governance*. Berlin, Heidelberg: Springer, 7–21.

Salem, Sara. 2018. "Intersectionality and Its Discontents: Intersectionality as Traveling Theory." *European Journal of Women's Studies* 25 (4):403–18. doi:10.1177/1350506816643999.

Smooth, Wendy G. 2013. "Intersectionality from Theoretical Framework to Policy Intervention." In *Situating Intersectionality: Politics, Policy, and Power*, ed. Angelia R. Wilson. New York: Palgrave Macmillan, 11–41. doi:10.1057/9781137025135_2.

Suedfeld, Peter. 2010. *The Scoring of Integrative Complexity as a Tool in Forecasting Adversary Intentions: Three Case Studies.* https://apps.dtic.mil/sti/pdfs/ADA526439.pdf

Tormos, Fernando. 2017. "Intersectional Solidarity." *Politics, Groups & Identities* 5 (4):707–20. doi:10.1080/21565503.2017.1385494.

Wallace, Adryan. 2018. "Agency and Development, Hausa Women's CSOs in Kano Nigeria." In *Gender and Economics in Muslim Communities: A Critical Feminist and Postcolonial Analyses*, eds. Ebru Kongar, Jennifer C. Olmsted, and Elora Shehabuddin. New York: Routledge, 281–305. doi:10.4324/9781315228617-12.

Wallace, Adryan. 2022."The Intersections of Gender Inequality, Regional Economic Integration, and State Fragility." Compendium of Papers Presented at the Academic Conference: Africa's Fiscal Space, Fragility and Conflict, United Nations Office of the Special Adviser on Africa (OSAA) & the African Capacity Building Foundation, 22–24 February. United Nations, New York, NY, 26–51.

Walsh, Shannon D., and Christina Xydias. 2014. "Women's Organizing and Intersectional Policy-Making in Comparative Perspective: Evidence from Guatemala and Germany." *Politics, Groups & Identities* 2 (4):549–72. doi:10.1080/21565503.2014.969743.

Wilson, Kalpana. 2015. "Towards a Radical Re-Appropriation: Gender, Development and Neoliberal Feminism." *Development and Change* 46 (4):803–32. doi:10.1111/dech.12176.

De-Whitening Romani Women's Intersectional Experience

Sebijan Fejzula

ABSTRACT

This article critically examines the whitening of Romani women's intersectional experience by white feminist movements and its implications for the perpetuation of anti-Roma racism. It argues that the dismissal of race is not a mere oversight, but rather a deliberate political strategy aimed at maintaining existing power dynamics. The centralization of race as a political lens is explored as a means to understand and address the challenges faced by Romani women in their struggle for emancipation and political agency.

Introduction

I Ain't Your Sister!
While you claimed your "sisterhood"
My prima was forcedly sterilised
To which you "sisters" were color-blinded!
While you screamed "women rights"
My mother was running from the police raid,
To which you "sisters" remained silenced!
While you claimed your "universal feminism"
There were bullets running over my head,
To which you sisters did nothing!
While you "sisters" called my husband "the oppressor,"
The State took my daughter from me,
The school segregated my son,
The system killed my father,
And to which you "sisters" once again remained ignorant!
Now ... the Roma sister asks you "sisters"
Who the oppressor is?

Over the past few years, I have experienced one of the most challenging tasks as a Romani woman, both as an activist and academic: discussing and theorizing about the struggle of Romani women in Europe. This epistemic struggle occurs due to the political unthinking of race and racism as a structural condition in Europe that shapes the lives of racialized people. The relevance of race is structurally denied in Europe. As Lentin (2008, 487) describes, "the silence about race in Europe allows European states to declare themselves non-racist, or even anti-racist, while at the same time continuing to imply an inherent European superiority (...) with those seen as 'in but not of Europe' within its domestic spheres." This denial is an integral part of the dominant narratives and political project of a raceless Europe (Goldberg 2006), primarily sustained by the idea that racism is a thing of the past, mainly connecting it to the Holocaust, thus leading toward the personalization and individualization of racism, which reduces its structural component. Academia as an institution that shapes power-relations is one of the pillars that placed the discussion on race and racism within the unspoken subtext (Goldberg 2006). While academia has been actively producing knowledge about racialized people, it has been dominated by paternalist approaches that have excluded the historical and current structural conditions of the struggle. Academic institutions have also discredited, excluded, and/or silenced knowledge on race, racism, and whiteness produced by racialized people with the excuse that these types of knowledge are not scientific and/or objective enough. As pointed out by various racialized scholars and activists, this is a colonial practice driven by the idea that the racialized/subalterns have no knowledge of themselves and that they can only be explained by the power/white (Fejzula and Fernández 2022; Kilomba 2016; Tuhiwai Smith 2012).

Romani women are not immune to this European political framework of depoliticized culture that has institutionally converted them into permanent objects of intervention (Fejzula and Fernández 2022). Historical narratives that expose racial antagonism as embedded in the formation of modern societies are excluded. Consequently, the dominant policy and/or academic approach toward Romani women's intersectional experience is mainly from a gender perspective and has a civilizational orientation. In this reflection essay, I argue that this approach leads to the whitening of the intersectional experience of Romani women, becoming a new fashionable instrument to keep silencing race issues in Europe, to keep ignoring the racial experiences of Romani women, which are also addressed in the above-mentioned poem "I Ain't Your Sister!". As Bilge (2014, 1) explains, "in European academic feminist circles, intersectionality is seen as the brainchild of feminism and gender studies. This narrative puts gender at the core of the intersectional project and leaves out the constitutive role of race." It is within such hesitations that I am also writing this article. Despite the current academic feminists' demand to produce knowledge based on situated experiences, when the racial struggle is placed at the center of the analysis, evidence has shown that academia is not yet ready to question its own colonial production. Hence, decolonizing academia should not be a cosmetic operation but a political will to break up with its forms of domination, assuming that the political dialogue does not have to be based on academic standards. In fact, Sirma Bilge reminds us that hierarchies are also shaped based on:

> whose texts are deemed foundational and included in the translated "canon"; who gets invited to major scientific events where the new knowledge product is launched and confronted by local expertise; who gets the credit for introducing it; whose career benefits from it; who are included to be a part of local expertise, who is side-lined; who is empowered by this introduction, and who is not. Thus, debates about intersectionality also reflect power struggles, opportunity structures, and turf wars internal to specific disciplines and fields. (Bilge 2013, 410)

This article argues that the depoliticizing of Romani women's intersectional experience is not a white mistake but a matter of power-relations. Taking the white feminist agendas as my object of study, I will point out that their mainstream approaches toward our intersectional experience reproduce anti-Roma racism by ignoring/silencing/diminishing our racial antagonism while notably arguing for the need for Romani women's salvation. The whitening of Romani women's intersectional experience by white feminist agendas is part of the broader anti-Roma framework in Europe which is that of integration/civilization. Therefore, I draw on the definition of white feminism by the decolonial thinker Vergès (2021, 4–5) as "civilizational" "because, in the name of an ideology of women's rights, it has undertaken the mission of imposing a unique perspective that contributes to the perpetuation of domination based on class, gender, and race." In this regard, dismissing race is not a naïve mistake but a political condition aiming to maintain power relations. My main argument lies on the foundation that Romani women's intersectional experience can only be understood if race is placed at the center of the analysis "as an essential axis of domination and oppression, shaped by political and institutional elements that operate in a relational way" (Fejzula and Fernández 2022, 392). This article aims to contribute to the theoretical and political discussions on (de)whitening the intersectional experiences of Romani women from a decolonial (feminist) perspective, as politics that "(. . .) assert[s] its right to existence" (Vergès 2021, 10) as racialized women. More concretely, the decolonial perspective allows the reading of white feminist agendas within the racial logics of Modernity, and it enables knowledge production from the standpoint of "otherness," "[…) providing a space for the voices and experiences of silenced 'othered' women […]" (Manning 2021, 1204).

In the following section, I discuss the political framework prevailing in Europe in regard to anti-Roma racism. Next, I discuss the whitening of the Romani women experience by the white feminist agendas as part of that same anti-Roma framework. Finally, I conclude on the necessity to reclaim the centralization of race to challenge the erasure and silencing of Romani women's experiences, demanding a more comprehensive understanding of their intersecting identities and the specific forms of oppression they face.

Anti-Roma racism in Europe

As a Romani woman, I have found it challenging to place myself within notions of women's liberation, women's rights, feminism, democracy, and human rights. These labels have been emphasized in the exercise of white domination over Romani people for the sake of integration. This creates a dichotomy between Modernity and being a Romani woman because European modernity is built on the dehumanization of Roma, which stems from anti-Roma racism, defined in this article as a:

> race-based system of domination that has historical roots in modernity and that obeys the construction of the European white man as the model of humanity, thus dehumanizing all others. As Roma, we are considered as not human enough, therefore, we are denied this political capacity of self-determination and, at the same time, to close the circle, this serves as a justification for the implementation of an "ideology of integration" that seeks to "civilise" us within what they consider to be civilisation. That is why, the battle against anti-Gypsyism cannot be limited to trying to change prejudices or certain misconceptions in the minds of the gadje, but to understand that this system of domination is rooted in the State itself and its institutions. (Fernández 2020)

To comprehend this dichotomy, it is necessary to pay attention to the historical construction of white narratives about Roma people depicted through white fictional representations. The Romani thinker Cayetano Fernández argues that the conception of "Roma history" is a white creation about us and our ancestors, a Gadji[1] view of us that amounts to nothing more than an ontological search for white identity and legitimation" (Fernández 2021, 205). Similarly, Matache (2017, 3) points out that "scholarly research has advanced the image of the uncivilized and uneducated Gypsies." These historical colonial and civilizing approaches date back to the nineteenth century when George Borrow, one of the fathers of "gypsyology" (Fernández 2016), claimed "[t]he Romas have no history" (Borrow 1841, 159). He, among many other white scholars, policymakers, reporters, etc., have institutionally converted the Roma body into the permanent object of intervention: "as the intervened, the ones who are in constant need of interventions. This is because of the dominant understanding that we, as Roma people, are incapable of organizing ourselves politically, hence unable to govern ourselves" (Fejzula and Fernández 2022, 389). This racial exclusion has placed us to be in a permanent need of white salvation, and has also robbed our self-agency and autonomy. The historical racial construction of Roma people as non-European and non-human became one of the foundations of the imaginary European project of civilization. Narratives of dishonest and criminal Gypsies surrounded Roma in chronicles, and even humanists such as Jacobus Thomasius concluded that "these black-looking heathen foreigners, speaking a strange tongue, were not fully human" (cited in Lewy 2000, 2). Since then, the principal aim of states has been to control Roma lives, with various measures ranging from forced sterilizations of Romani women (see European Roma Rights Center, ERRC 2016), to cases of police brutality and placement in ghettos. The "Roma ghettos" in Europe serve as twentieth-century prisons without walls in which Roma lives are controlled by different state institutions such as police, social services, and education centers, all serving the same purpose: to control the uncivilized Roma people. This systematic control is driven by racial fear and historical criminalization of Roma bodies.

This racial context is particularly relevant to understanding how anti-Roma racism in Europe is dealt with, given that the political approach of "Roma integration" has become the ultimate goal of the Roma's emancipation. In her analysis on the racist beliefs in the formulation and the implementation of the former EU Framework for National Roma Integration Strategies up to 2020, the Romani scholar

Margareta Matache (2017, 3) argues, for instance, that "gadjo stakeholders have designed legislation and policies for Romani children relying on a popular idea that Romani cultural patterns reject education, an assumption that neglects and simplifies the multiplicity of Romani identity." According to Matache (2017), Roma integration policymakers have failed to tackle the continual racism, white privileges and power and their influence on Roma children. Although Matache's analysis focuses on the policies for Romani children in education, her well established critique could be expanded to the entire former EU policy framework on Roma integration. The structural racism component of the Roma struggle and the role of whiteness in the oppression of Roma people have not been fully addressed in European policies. The exclusion of a clear and overt debate about anti-Roma racism has prevented the conditions for Roma's self-agency, political definition, and participation. These civilizatory-oriented projects and initiatives have served the purpose of avoiding any political discussion of whiteness, its privileges, consequences, and possible reparatory measures, while "granting more symbolic and material value and powers to gadjo-ness" (Matache 2017, 10).

More recently, European Roma policies have shifted from a prevailing logic of integration toward a new approach based on political participation and the fight against anti-Roma racism, also known as antigypsyism. The current EU Roma Strategic Framework for Equality, Inclusion, and Participation for 2020–2030 has indeed received institutional acclaim due to its explicit inclusion of and reference to antigypsyism. However, altering the language and formulation of certain policies does not necessarily diminish their underlying civilizational and neocolonial nature, as exemplified below:

> Europe has a duty to protect its minorities from racism and discrimination. We must replace antigypsyism with openness and acceptance, hate speech and hate crime with tolerance and respect for human dignity, and bullying with education about the Holocaust. Above all, we must promote diversity as a wonderful gift that makes Europe strong and resilient. This is why the Commission calls on all Member States to join the pledge to end racism and discrimination, which blatantly affects our large ethnic Roma minorities. We urge Member States to commit to a new EU Roma strategic framework for equality, inclusion and participation to bring social fairness and more equality in all senses of the word. (European Commission 2020)

What we observe is a superficial and diluted incorporation of antigypsyism: vague formulation and moralizing narratives contribute to fostering a depoliticizing approach that fails to address the fundamental structural dimensions of anti-Roma racism. Consequently, this framework risks hampering the development of meaningful anti-racist initiatives that could foster Roma self-agency, political definition, and inclusive participation in emancipatory projects aimed at improving Roma lives. It is not my specific intention to analyze the EU Roma Framework itself, but rather to discuss the whitening of Romani women's intersectional experience by white feminist agendas as part of the broader anti-Roma framework in Europe, as expounded in the following section.

Whitening the intersectional experience of Romani women

The issue of Romani women in Europe has gained increasing attention in recent years, with a growing focus on intersectionality. Romani women activists and feminists have emphasized that their struggle is multilayered, with ethnicity,[2] gender, and class intersecting continually in their lives (see Kóczé and Maria Popa 2009). However, these intersections are often not recognized by white feminist agendas, leading to a need for new knowledge and practices that consider the experiences of Romani women:

> Intersectional discrimination on Romani women within activist circles seem to affect some Romani women to move "back" to understanding of identity dimensions (such as "being Roma" and "being woman") and inequalities based on "ethnicity" and "gender" as competing and not as intersecting. Intersectional discrimination Romani women activists face may also be the reason why recently some young Romani feminists expressed resistance to "gadze feminism" and a need to produce knowledge as "Romnja feminists." (Jovanovic, Kóczé, and Balogh 2015, 12)

Despite their urgent call for systematic integration of this intersectional dimension into studies and policies aiming to improve the position of Romani women, anti-Roma racism and its effect on Romani women are hardly addressed. This leaves historical and current issues such as Roma women's racialization, criminalization, and persecution to be an ongoing normalized practice. As mentioned previously, the notion of "Gypsy criminality" has been systematically employed as a means to target Roma individuals, reflecting the state's desire for control and order in contemporary Europe (Fejzula 2021). The association of crime with the Roma community has led to heightened control and policing of Roma "ghettos," often associated with drug-related issues (Fejzula 2021). An investigation conducted by the Baraññí research project in 1999 revealed a stark overrepresentation of Romani women in Spanish prisons, with their numbers being 20 times higher compared to non-Romani women (Palomo 2002). The project aimed to analyze the history of criminalization and imprisonment of Romani women to avoid repeating past mistakes and identify areas for improvement or change within the Spanish context. While the Roma population in Spain represents approximately 1.4% of the total population, Romani women account for 25% of all female prisoners (Palomo 2002, 149). This overrepresentation far exceeds that of other traditionally marginalized ethnic groups. The author draws a comparison between the high percentage of Romani women in prisons and the Black population in the United States of America or indigenous peoples in Australia, highlighting the historical exclusion of the Roma from "normalized" sociocultural and economic relationships in Spanish society (Palomo 2002, 152). Despite the alarming overrepresentation of Roma individuals in Spanish prisons, the discussion of anti-Roma racism and its connection to security policies remains marginalized within Spanish society. Moreover, the structural component of this issue is often overlooked, leading to the reduction of police brutality incidents as mere "misbehaved individual actions" (Fejzula 2021, 296). According to a survey conducted by the University of Valencia (García Añón 2013), only six percent of white individuals reported experiencing a police checkpoint in the previous two years, compared to 22% of Latin Americans, 39% of Black people, 45% of Arabs, and 65% of Roma individuals.

Similar findings were observed in a 2008 study conducted by the European Union Fundamental Rights Agency (FRA). In 2016, the Pro Human Rights Association of Andalusia (APDHA) conducted a direct observation study of police checks at the main bus station in Granada, revealing a ratio of 12:1 for Roma individuals (Povic and Jiménez Bautista 2016). In their discussion and analyzes of relevant research and policy efforts in regard to the situation of Romani women, Angela Kóczé and Raluca Maria Popa concluded that:

> While policy studies and recommendations that include a focus on Romani women suggest certain advances on the anti-discrimination, gender equality, and human development agendas, they still fail to achieve an integrated and coordinated policy response to the exclusion, inequality, and discrimination experienced by Romani women. (Kóczé and Popa 2009, 22)

Based on the latest report published in 2022 by the European Union Agency for Fundamental Rights,[3] there has been little change in the lives of Romani women over the past few decades. This report corroborates the findings of Kóczé and Maria Popa (2009). The report reveals that exclusion, deprivation, discrimination, and racism continue to be prevalent in the daily lives of many Roma individuals. In particular, Roma women face significant challenges. The data collected in 2021 indicates that Roma women have a life expectancy that is, on average, 11 years shorter than that of women in the majority population. Additionally, only 28% of Roma women aged 20 to 64 are employed (FRA 2022; 17–18). The data highlighting the ongoing racial antagonism experienced by Roma individuals in Europe is deeply concerning. However, it remains largely unnoticed in academic and policy discussions concerning the Roma community.

White feminism and its (re)production of anti-Roma racism

The exclusion of race in discussions and actions perpetuates the whitening of Romani women's struggles and overlooks the historical and ongoing effects of racism. It is imperative to dismantle the structures of power that perpetuate racial inequalities and recognize the intersecting forms of oppression they face. Even within white feminist agendas, which have traditionally focused on gender-related inequalities, this issue goes unrecognized. White feminist agendas are complicit in upholding existing power structures (Espinosa-Miñoso 2014). According to the decolonial feminist Yuderkys Espinosa-Miñoso (2014), by focusing solely on gender equality within the current system, white feminism fails to challenge the broader structures of white supremacy, capitalism, and colonialism that perpetuate inequality and marginalization. This critique emphasizes the need for a more comprehensive and intersectional analysis of power dynamics. It is within such context of silencing race relations that I argue that processes of whitening Romani women's intersectional experiences form part of the contemporary approach to racism in politics.

The political slogan "we are all equal," has indeed created a "silent protocol on race" aimed to contain the "reaction" to racism, rather than combat this historical and political phenomenon (Araújo and Maeso 2021, 187). Within the same racial silencing context, the claim that "we are all women" stems from the same ideology that aims to dismiss processes of racialization that allow white women to exist. Spillers (as cited in Broeck 2018, 26) argues that there exists no relation of differentiation between white women ("the empowered") and Black women, but an antagonistic opposition ("nemesis") between being and "nonbeing." In contrast to white women historically marked as being inferior, a Black woman is marked by the "paradox of nonbeing" which aligns Black male and female existence as absolutely equal. Based on this antagonist opposition, the omission of racial considerations in European policymaking regarding the Roma community is not a mere oversight. Rather, it is a product of the broader political framework that perpetuates anti-Roma racism and seeks to integrate Roma individuals into society based on a civilizational paradigm. These approaches effectively silence the racial antagonism faced by the Roma community by solely focusing on ethnicity and culture.

In this regard, I suggest a decolonial feminist reading of the Romani women's struggle because it permits us to establish a basis for gender-focused approaches within a larger political context that often disregards the issues of race and racism, despite the ongoing oppression deeply rooted in racial relations. In fact, decolonial feminism, emerging as a response to the colonial governance of racialized populations, provides the analytical tools to critically analyze the racial logics of Western civilization and progress. It also enables us to develop strategies for liberation based on our situated knowledge and experiences with whiteness. As Vergès (2021, 12) asserts, "a feminism that advocates solely for gender equality while ignoring how integration exposes racialized women to brutality, violence, rape, and murder, ultimately becomes complicit in it." Sara Ahmed (2021, 157) emphasizes that "whiteness remains invisible to those who inhabit it or become accustomed to its presence, even when they are not themselves white."

Throughout history and in the present political landscape, white feminist agendas have actively participated in constructing and upholding a white order that equates civilization and progress with whiteness. Rather than being naive, these agendas have silenced racial antagonism and generated feminist knowledge solely based on the experiences of middle-class white women. This approach has led to the normalization of white feminism as the only acceptable form of feminism (Zakaria 2021). Through their whitening approaches, white feminist agendas depoliticize the experiences and knowledge of Romani women in academia and social movements, effectively serving the interests of whiteness and contributing to the (re)production of anti-Roma racism. Françoise Vergès (2021) further characterizes white feminists and their role in perpetuating the white order as follows:

> As active accomplices of the racial capitalist order, civilizational feminists do not hesitate to support imperialist intervention policies, as well as policies rooted in Islamophobia and even "Negrophobia." (Vergès 2021, 12)

Many racialized women, mostly decolonial scholars and activists, have criticized white feminism for its colonial, and thus racist, ideology (cf. Bouteldja and Contreras Castro 2017; Vergès 2021, among others), precisely because of its role in normalizing dehumanized relations between white and racialized women. As a Romani woman from North-Macedonia, I have witnessed the extreme exploitation faced by Romani women, including my mother, who work in precarious conditions cleaning the houses of white women. These Romani women receive low wages, lack employment contracts, and have no access to social insurance. This racial exploitation directly contributes to the significantly shorter average lifespan of Romani women compared to women in the majority population.

> The comfortable life of bourgeois women around the world is possible because millions of exploited and racialized women maintain this comfort by making their clothes, cleaning their homes and the offices where they work, taking care of their children, and by taking care of the sexual needs of their husbands, brothers, and partners. (Vergès 2021, 2–3)

Very rarely, if ever, do we see white women, white academics, as well as white policies and strategies, challenging these hierarchical positions that are based on race. On the contrary, due to their structural ignorance, they have become normalized. On a similar note, Romani activist and scholar Alexandra Oprea asks, "[h]ow can one stand for women's equality without examining racism within one's own ranks and looking at disparities among white women and Romani women (e.g., in terms of earning potential, educational level, access to the justice system, treatment by law enforcement officials, etc.)?" (as cited in Kóczé and Maria Popa 2009, 22). Instead, during the last years, various international reports on gender-based violence against Romani women were published. For instance, according to a 2018 report, "poverty in Roma communities is both a consequence and a determinant of a lack of access to education" (Milenković 2018, 4).[4] The report highlights that gender roles come along with strict rules and expected behaviors, noting that Roma girls are brought up being told that their role is to become wives, mothers and housewives (Milenković 2018, 9), and that Roma girls who live in Roma settlements are not expected to complete their education or find jobs (Milenković 2018, 9). I argue that the production of any report on Roma communities, particularly one focused solely on gender perspectives without conducting a comprehensive analysis of the intersectional experiences of Romani women with the anti-Roma system (e.g., the educational system's violence toward Roma women), perpetuates the idea of Roma as uncivilized people culturally unsuited to living in Europe. These imaginary ideas lead to the justified systemic persecution of Roma people and reinforce the perception that they are permanently in need of intervention. Additionally, the isolation of the discussion of an alleged "Roma patriarchy" from the construct of white patriarchy contributes to a misallocation of the origin of the problem. It deflects attention from the systemic nature of anti-Roma racism and the white perspective that underlies such approaches, instead promoting an essentialist understanding of Roma culture. Consequently, all these elements contribute to whitening Romani women's experience and maintaining the status quo based on colonial ideology.

Therefore, it becomes crucial to situate white feminist agendas as an institutional political framework that contributes to maintaining whiteness and, consequently, Romani women's racialization by reproducing the: (I) denial of Romani women's self-agency; (II) invisibilization of race; and (III) whitening of their struggle. White feminists' production about Romani women cannot be understood as isolated logics and politics. Instead, it builds upon and fuels a set of anti-Roma beliefs, practices, and politics embedded in racial formation and with a civilizing mission. In the next section, I conclude on the importance of centering race in the urgent call for decolonization within the struggle of Romani women. Centering race in the decolonization of Romani women's struggle allows us to confront the historical and political forces that have shaped our experiences. By doing so, we can work toward dismantling the systemic barriers and biases that hinder Romani women's empowerment and full participation in society.

Discussion and conclusion: race as a central intersection

In Europe, intersectionality in practice is whitened in feminist studies and movements, as a result, so are the experiences of Romani women. In light of the decolonial (feminist) framework discussed above and the daily racial experiences of Romani women, I composed the poem "Ain't Your Sister." This poem serves as an effort to expose our realities as Romani women within what I perceive to be Anti-Roma Europe. It highlights the history of European racial silence, the interrelatedness of racially constructed institutions, and the universalism of white feminism. The poem represents the anger of a Romani woman, an anger that Sara Ahmed characterizes as a judgment that something is wrong: "we are angry about racism, about forms of violence and power that are hidden under the signs of civility and love. [...] Your anger is judgment that something is wrong" (Ahmed 2009, 49–50). This anger is distinct from the stereotype of anger that has long been attributed to racialized women by the white imaginary vision. Instead, it is the anger that Audre Lorde describes in her discussion of racism against Black women:

> My response to racism is anger. I have lived with that anger, ignoring it, feeding it, learning to use it, before it laid my visions to waste for most of my life. Once I did it in silence, afraid of the weight. My fear of anger taught me nothing ... Anger expressed and translated into action in the service of our vision and our future is a liberating and strengthening act of clarification ... Anger is loaded with information and energy. (Lorde 1984, 127, quoted in Ahmed 2009, 51)

This anger of a Romani woman underscores the manipulations of intersectionality as a theory and practice in relation to our experiences, due to its "silent protocol on race" - a consequence of whitening the theory of intersectionality, in order to "rearticulate it around Eurocentric epistemologies" (Bilge 2014, 16). As Romani scholar Angéla Kóczé (2011) has correctly analyzed, intersectionality offers us with instruments for further developing our knowledges about the political and social activism as interconnected practice aiming at questioning the structural reproduction of inequality. However, when intersectionality is solely focused on gender (e.g., in cultural practices), it can (re)produce and/or (re)enforce the notion of "uncivilized Roma bodies." In this article, I conclude that this depoliticization of the Romani women's struggle leads to "neutralizing the critical potential of intersectionality for social justice-oriented change" (Bilge 2013, 405). Moreover, as Kimberlé Crenshaw (1993) has pointed out, "political actions that tackle only some subordinating ideas and actions while not questioning the upholding hierarchies, the consequence is in oppositionalizing race and gender discourses" (pp. 112–113). In this piece, I discussed the pressing need to centralize race in order to decolonize Romani women's struggle; namely, the need for de-whitening Roma women's intersectional experience. Doing so would provide the theoretical and political tools necessary for interpreting the power relations maintained over Romani women, and it would allow them to speak from a position of authority and have the right to define their own realities and identities (hooks 1989).

When addressing the Romani women's intersectional experience from a decolonial perspective, centralizing race allows for the following interpretation. First, it places Romani women's experiences as crucial in the process of dismantling anti-Roma racism by centering racially marked experiences as political processes of racialization.

Second, it rearticulates, reinterprets, and places the category of "woman" within the context of whiteness. Following Lugones (2007) proposal, the relationship between the colonizer and the colonized should be interpreted in terms of gender, race, and sexuality. For Lugones (2007), this requires a re-reading of modern capitalist colonial modernity itself. The author argues that this is vital due to the colonial imposition of gender, which manifests in different forms, to see what is blurred in our understanding of both race and gender.

Third, it undoes categories such as "diversity," "interculturality," and "multiculturality," which serve only as politics of representation rather than leading to structural changes regarding the experiences of Romani women. These categories are once again used to dismiss any discussions on racism, thereby excluding any reparatory measures and anti-racism projects of liberation. Hence, it is necessary to recognize the limitations of not understanding the historical perspective of anti-Roma racism as a matter of structuring order.

Fourth, it creates an anti-racist Romani women's struggle with a political agenda. The anti-racist struggle entails the opportunity to critically interpret the universal order in which we live, allocate key counter-hegemonic narratives that prove the continuum of anti-Roma racism, while simultaneously rejecting the project of modernity. As a result, this would also mean an epistemic potentiality to disturb any type of integratory approaches to anti-Roma racism that Romani women face. Understanding the anti-racist struggle as a project of liberation requires challenging the idea of universal feminism and the neoliberal thinking of liberation to move beyond notions of inclusion or integration. In short, it requires the ability to trace the connections between feminism as a progressive movement and the racial logics inherited by European White Modernity. Centering

Notes

1. *"Gadje"* in the plural, and *"gadjo"* and *"gadji"* as the masculine and feminine forms, are Romani words which refer to non-Roma or white people (Fernández 2021).
2. Please note that the inclusion of the term "ethnicity" in the mentioned sentence is solely due to its usage by certain Romani feminists and activists. This usage is the product of wider historical and political categorization of Roma as an ethnic group, emphasizing their cultural identity. Analyzing Roma related issues from an ethnic point of view limits our ability to recognize and address the underlying structural condition of anti-Roma racism, specifically rooted in whiteness. By recentering the concept of race, I aim to also move away from the very problematic "ethnicization" of the Roma, which has dominated Romani studies.
3. "This report presents findings from FRA's 2021 survey on Roma in Croatia, Czechia, Greece, Hungary, Italy, Portugal, Romania and Spain, as well as in North Macedonia and Serbia. The survey includes interviews with more than 8,400 Roma, collecting information on more than 20,000 individuals living in their households. By focusing on Roma, the survey provides unique data and information that are not available from European general population surveys, which do not disaggregate on grounds of ethnic origin. The findings present a bleak but familiar picture of exclusion, deprivation, discrimination and racism." (FRA 2022).
4. This report was produced by the UNDP Istanbul Regional Hub. For more detailed analyses visit: https://www.undp.org/eurasia/publications/nowhere-turn-gender-based-violence-against-roma-women

Disclosure statement

No potential conflict of interest was reported by the author.

References

Ahmed, Sara. 2009. "Embodying Diversity: Problems and Paradoxes for Black Feminists." *Race Ethnicity and Education* 12 (1):41–52. doi:10.1080/13613320802650931.

Ahmed, Sara. 2021. "A Phenomenology of Whiteness." In *Fanon, Phenomenology, and Psychology*, eds. Leswin Laubscher, Derek Hook, and Miraj U. Desai. New Ork: Routledge, 229–46. doi:10.4324/9781003037132-22.

Araújo, Marta, and Silvia Maeso. 2021. "The Power of Racism in Academia: Knowledge Production and Political Disputes." In *The Pluriverse of Human Rights: The Diversity of Struggles for Dignity*, eds. Boaventura de Sousa Santos, and Bruno Sena, Martins. New York: Routledge, 186–204. doi:10.4324/9781003177722-12.

Bilge, Sirma. 2013. "Intersectionality Undone: Saving Intersectionality from Feminist Intersectionality Studies." *Du Bois Review: Social Science Research on Race* 10 (2):405–24. doi:10.1017/S1742058X13000283.

Bilge, Sirma. 2014. "Whitening Intersectionality: Evanescence of Race in Intersectionality Scholarship." In *Racism and Sociology*, eds. Wulf D. Hund and Alana Lentin. Berlin: LIT Verlag Münster, 175–206.

Borrow, George Henry. 1841. *The Zincali: Or, an Account of the Gypsies of Spain*. London: J. Murray.

Bouteldja, Houria, and Anabelle Contreras Castro. 2017. *Los blancos, los judíos y nosotros: hacia una política del amor revolucionario*. Mexico City: Akal.

Broeck, Sabine. 2018. *Gender and the Abjection of Blackness.* Albany, NY: SUNY, State University of New York Press.

Crenshaw, Kimberlé Williams. 1993. "Beyond Racism and Misogyny: Black Feminism and 2 Live Crew." In *Words That Wound: Critical Race Theory, Assaultive Speech, and the First Amendment,* eds. Mari J. Matsuda, Charles R. Lawrence III, Richard Delgado, and Kimberlé Williams Crenshaw. Boulder, CO: Westview Press, 111–32. doi:10.4324/9780429502941-5.

Espinosa-Miñoso, Yuderkys. 2014. "Una crítica descolonial a la epistemología feminista crítica." *El Cotidiano-Universidad Autónoma Metropolotana Unidad Azcapotzalco México* 184: 7–12.

European Commission. 2020. "European Roma Holocaust Memorial Day: Statement by President von der Leyen, Vice-President Jourová and Commissioner Dalli." Accessed May 2, 2023. https://ec.europa.eu/commission/presscorner/detail/en/STATEMENT_20_1423

European Roma Rights Center (ERRC). 2016. "Coercive and Cruel: Sterilisation and Its Consequences for Romani Women in the Czech Republic (1966-2016)." http://www.errc.org/reports-and-submissions/coercive-and-cruel-sterilisation-and-its-consequences-for-romani-women-in-the-czech-republic-1966-2016

Fejzula, Sebijan. 2021. "A Europa "civilizada" e a sua violência contra o povo Roma." In *O Estado do Racismo em Portugal: Racismo Antinegro e Anticiganismo no Direito e nas Políticas Públicas,* ed. Silvia Rodríguez Maeso. Lisbon: Tinta da China, 289–98.

Fejzula, Sebijan, and Cayetano Fernández. 2022. "Anti-Roma Racism, Social Work and the White Civilisatory Mission." In *Handbook of Critical Social Work,* eds. Stephen A., Webb. 2nd ed. New York: Routledge, 389–402. doi:10.4324/9781003211969-32.

Fernández, Cayetano. 2016. "Who's Teaching Romani Studies? Increasingly, Roma Themselves." *Open Society Foundations* (blog), January 15. https://www.opensocietyfoundations.org/voices/two-milestones-put-romani-cultural-discourse-hands-roma-themselves

Fernández, Cayetano. 2020. "Anti-Roma Racism is a Historical Product of European Modernity." *Kale Amenge* (blog), January 13, 2020. https://www.kaleamenge.org/en/anti-gypsyism-is-a-historical-product-of-european-modernity/

Fernández, Cayetano. 2021. "The Roma Collective Memory and the Epistemological Limits of Western Historiography." In *The Pluriverse of the Human: Struggles for Dignity and Human Rights,* eds. Boaventura Sousa, Santos, and Bruno Sena, Martins. London, New York: Routledge, 205–17. doi:10.4324/9781003177722-13.

FRA - European Union Agency for Fundamental Rights. 2022. "Roma in 10 European Countries - Main Results." October 17. http://fra.europa.eu/en/publication/2022/roma-survey-findings

García Añón, José, ed. 2013. "*Identificación policial por perfil étnico en España: informe sobre experiencias y actitudes en relación con las actuaciones policiales.*" Derechos humanos 22. Valencia: Tirant lo Blanch. https://roderic.uv.es/handle/10550/56187.

Goldberg, David Theo. 2006. "Racial Europeanization." *Ethnic and Racial Studies* 29 (2):331–64. doi:10.1080/01419870500465611.

hooks, bell. 1989. *Talking Back: Thinking Feminist, Thinking Black.* Boston: South End Press.

Jovanovic, Jelena, Angela Kóczé, and Lídia Balogh. 2015. *Intersections of Gender, Ethnicity, and Class: History and Future of the Romani Women's Movement.* Budapest: Friedrich-Ebert-Stiftung Budapest -Central European University.

Kilomba, Grada. 2016. *Plantation Memories: Episodes of Everyday Racism.* 4th edition ed. Münster: Unrast.

Kóczé, Angela. 2011. *Gender, Ethnicity and Class: Romani Women's Political Activism and Social Struggles.* Budapest: Central European University Press.

Kóczé, Angela, and Raluca Maria Popa. 2009. *Missing Intersectionality: Race/Ethnicity, Gender, and Class in Current Research and Policies on Romani Women in Europe.* Budapest: Central European University Press.

Lentin, Alana. 2008. "Europe and the Silence About Race." *European Journal of Social Theory* 11 (4):487–503. doi:10.1177/1368431008097008.

Lewy, Guenter. 2000. *The Nazi Persecution of the Gypsies.* New York: Oxford University Press.

Lugones, María. 2007. "Heterosexualism and the Colonial/Modern Gender System." *Hypatia* 22 (1):186–219. doi:10.1111/j.1527-2001.2007.tb01156.x.

Matache, Margareta. 2017. "Biased Elites, Unfit Policies: Reflections on the Lacunae of Roma Integration Strategies." *European Review* 25 (4):588–607. doi:10.1017/S1062798717000254.

Milenković, Nataša. 2018. *Nowhere to Turn: Gender-Based Violence Against Roma Women.* UNDP: Roma Inclusion Series. https://www.undp.org/eurasia/publications/nowhere-turn-gender-based-violence-against-roma-women

Palomo, Martin Teresa. 2002. "Mujeres gitanas y el sistema penal." *Revista de Estudios de Género La Ventana* 2 (15):149–174.

Povic, Mirjana, and Francisco Jiménez Bautista. 2016. *Identificaciones basadas en perfil étnico en Granada. Estudio realizado mediante observación y entrevistas directas.* Granada: APDHA. https://apdha.org/media/granada-identificaciones-etnicas-2016-web.pdf.

Smith, Tuhiwai Linda. 2012. *Decolonizing Methodologies. Research and Indigenous Peoples.* London: Zed Book.

Vergès, Françoise. 2021. *A Decolonial Feminism.* Trans. Ashley J., Bohrer. London: Pluto Press.

Zakaria, Rafia. 2021. *Against White Feminism: Notes on Disruption.* New York: W.W. Norton & Company.

δ OPEN ACCESS

Affirming Fissures: Conceptualizing Intersectional 'Ethnic' Feminism in Aotearoa New Zealand

Rachel Simon-Kumar ⓘD

ABSTRACT
Intersectionality, as scholarship and praxis, has traversed boundaries far beyond its roots in Black American feminism into population groups whose histories of marginalization are vastly different to those envisioned by Kimberlé Crenshaw. In translation, intersectionality can articulate with new clarity the voices of the invisibilized but also reveal fundamental fissures. This article discusses these contradictions in the context of "ethnic" populations in Aotearoa New Zealand. Comprising 17% of the total population, ethnic groups are peoples who come from Asia, Latin America, Africa and the Middle East. In this article, I set out to interrogate the viability of an Antipodean ethnic feminism given the distinct backdrop of white-settler colonialism, biculturalism, and multiculturalism extant in contemporary New Zealand. I point to five "fault lines" – around positioning, culture, minoritization, place and the subject – where conceptual clarity will deepen ethnic feminism's theoretical roots and relevance for NZ's fastest growing population group.

Introduction

Unlike any other contemporary feminist concept, intersectionality has had a momentous impact on an array of academic disciplines and, cascading out of academe, on art, film, political life, and, indeed, public imagination. Conceptualized in the late 1960s, intersectionality as theory articulated "home-truths" about African-American women's oppressions (Nash 2011), but since then it has traversed boundaries far beyond its roots in Black feminism. En route, it has been translated, actively reconstituting its fundamental meanings and relationships as it moves across space and time into populations whose histories of marginalization are vastly different than those envisioned by Kimberlé Crenshaw (1991), a process that is both empowering and challenging. In this essay, I discuss these contradictions in the context of 'ethnic' populations in Aotearoa New Zealand (henceforth, NZ) – formally referring to peoples who have migrated from Asia, Latin America, Africa, and the Middle East.[1] As NZ's third-largest population group, they are constituted in incongruity: as visible minorities, they often share experiences of racialization, yet there are stark heterogeneities in their socio-economic realities. Politically, as relative newcomers, their claims to equal, as much as minority, status are tentative.

'Ethnic feminism,' as I pose it here, is an emergent assemblage of grassroots practice, policy interventions, and fledging critical thought that has no formal core of ideas other than its responsiveness to the needs of NZ's ethnic and migrant women.[2] Set against the backdrop of NZ's distinctive migration histories, white-settler colonialism, official policies of biculturalism[3] and rapid ethno-

---

This is an Open Access article distributed under the terms of the Creative Commons Attribution-NonCommercial License (http://creativecommons.org/licenses/by-nc/4.0/), which permits unrestricted non-commercial use, distribution, and reproduction in any medium, provided the original work is properly cited. The terms on which this article has been published allow the posting of the Accepted Manuscript in a repository by the author(s) or with their consent.

cultural diversification and multiculturalism,[4] ethnic feminism offers a lens for novel reflections on intersectionality as it moves spatially and temporally. As a theoretical foundation, intersectionality validates minority and migrant women's complex identities and experiences of oppression, but it can also reinforce ideological fissures among them.

This essay seeks to sharpen the conceptual terrain of ethnic feminism while also revealing some inherent contradictions and gaps about intersectionality. It charts some of the conceptual fault lines that need attention if intersectionality is to be meaningfully employed, as Davis (2008) notes, for a "successful" ethnic feminist theory. I structure my argument into three main sections. I begin by briefly sketching NZ's migration histories and a profile of its ethnic groups. Following this, I summarize key arguments for the movement of intersectionality theory into non-Black intellectual spaces leading into the core of the article, which develops five conceptual critiques for an Antipodean ethnic feminism. Drawing on illustrative examples from my own research as well as topical issues in NZ's gender-ethnicity politics, this essay is fundamentally an attempt to encourage introspective reflection and wider discussion of the possibilities for intersectionality to enrich an ethnic and migrant feminist theory and vice versa.

Migration histories of ethnic and migrant communities

Māori are acknowledged as the first people to have arrived in NZ circa 1300 CE on *waka* (canoes) possibly from Polynesia. Māori were agro-pastoral people, famed sea-farers and fighters who constructed social, cultural, and faith systems on worldviews that centered on the natural world and ancestral lineages. It would be 300 years before the first Europeans came to NZ shores; early Māori-European relations were marked by co-existence amidst tensions but through the 19th and 20th century, the land and its peoples were usurped as the island-nation was transformed into a colony of the British Empire. The signing of the Treaty of Waitangi (*Te Tiriti o Waitangi*) in 1840 raised expectations that issues of sovereignty, governance, and race relations between the two peoples would be clarified; yet in the decades that followed, Māori experienced significant dispossession of land, loss of culture and languages, increased exposure to disease and death, and forced economic, social, and political marginalization (O'Malley 2019; Radio n.d.; Salmond 1991).

Asian presence – particularly Indian and Chinese – in NZ has been recorded since the 18th century, although they are largely invisible in histories that predominantly recount Māori-European encounters. Records show Indian sailors among the first European ships that docked in NZ (Nachowitz 2015, 2018), while Chinese arrived in the South Island as gold miners a century later. Alongside hardship, overt racism, and isolation (Ip 2013; Leckie 2021), Asians and other racialized minorities were subject to socio-political exclusion by the colonial state. Stereotypical representations drummed up fears of the 'Hindoo' or 'Asiatic/yellow' peril as NZ embraced "White New Zealand" policy through much of the early 20th century (Elers 2018; Ferguson 2003). Indians were entrapped into visions of British colonization of NZ because they were "just in that state of civilization proper to be made useful" (Salmond 1997, 234–35, cited in Nachowitz 2015).

Immigration Reforms in 1987 radically reset the demographic profile of NZ. Until then, the "mother country," Britain, was its traditional trading partner and together with Ireland, its source of immigrant labor. In the wake of the UK's membership of the European Economic Community in 1973, NZ recognized the need to realign its economic and geo-political relationships more globally. Diversifying from its traditional migration pathway, the Reforms introduced a merit-based immigration that soon attracted skilled labor, especially from Asia. Within the short span of three decades, there was a rapid increase in migrants, first from Asia followed by Latin America, the Middle East, and more recently from the African continent.

In 1991, the proportion of Asians/ethnic people in the country was recorded as 3.1%, and in 2006, it was 11.6%. Currently, nearly 27% of NZ's population is born overseas and the ethnic population, nearly half of who arrived less than 10 years ago, sits at 20% (Stats NZ 2019, 2020a, 2020b). By 2043, ethnic groups are projected to become the second largest, i.e., just over a quarter of the total population. A highly skilled population group, they comprise 200 ethnicities and 170 spoken languages; in fact, Hinduism is the third most widely practiced religion in NZ after 'No Religion' and 'Catholicism' (Ministry of Ethnic Communities n.d.). This group's median age of 31.3 reflects the typical working age of the majority of migrants. A third of the ethnic population (around 30%) is young, aged 15–29; this youth cohort includes those who arrived as children with their parents (the "1.5 generation") or born in NZ ("2+ generation") (Lewycka, Peiris-John and Simon-Kumar 2020). The ethnic population also constitutes a heterogeneous and stratified population group who hold a range of permanent, short-term, and temporary migration residential statuses in the country. This complex demographic diversity is vividly mirrored in the pluralistic configuration of identity politics among this group. Those who arrived prior to this period settled as citizens, whereas for many on temporary visas life have been more precarious (Simon-Kumar 2020). Although there are similarities in their structural experiences as migrants, the aspirations of this stratified group for personal development, collective advancement, and social cohesion could not be more different (Simon-Kumar 2020).

NZ rates highly on the MIPEX (Migrant Integration Policy Index[5]), suggesting relatively good pathways for migrant integration economically, socially, and politically. There is a robust network of community-based associations fostering music, art, theater, religion, food, and culture advancing NZ as an ethno-culturally diverse society. A dedicated minister and Ministry for Ethnic Communities serve the needs of this group while also promoting diversity and social cohesion more generally. In recent years, there has been a prominent shift in the framing of multiculturalism as aligning with responsibilities to indigenous Māori.[6] Official narratives of "diversity as strength" and "the ethnic advantage" are tempered by everyday realities of socio-political exclusion, barriers to advancement, and systemic racism (Malatest International 2021). The killing of 51 Muslims at NZ mosques in 2019 by a white supremacist and anti-Asian violence in the wake of COVID-19 are reminders of their ongoing vulnerabilities.

Intersectionality and emergent ethnic feminism

Since intersectionality was coined in 1989 in response to the erasure of African-American women's subjectivity in single-axis anti-discrimination law, there has been considerable debate about its movement across disciplines, groups, and borders. In a suite of articles written a decade ago, Crenshaw and colleagues point out that intersectionality as a theoretical framework is intended to be generative, transcending the specific context of Black women. In that light, they refer to inter-sectionality as a theory that is "provisional," a "work-in-progress," and "incomplete"; the gender-race multiple-axis discrimination is merely "one way" to understand specific structures of power and there is "possibility for agents to move intersectionality to other social contexts and group formations" (Carbado et al. 2013, 304; also, Carbado 2013; Cho, Williams Crenshaw, and McCall 2013; Collins 2015). To mobilize its spatio-temporal movements to explain new forms of power structures, they argue that intersectionality must be conceived as more than a rigid and "contained entity" (Carbado et al. 2013, 304) – rather, it is an "analytical sensibility," "disposition," and a "way of thinking," thus shifting its emphasis to "what intersectionality *does* rather than what it *is*" (Cho, Williams Crenshaw, and McCall 2013, 795; emphasis added). As they note:

> What makes an analysis intersectional is not its use of the term "intersectionality," nor its being situated in a familiar genealogy, nor its drawing on lists of standard citations ... what makes an analysis intersectional—whatever terms it deploys, whatever its iteration, whatever its field or discipline—is its adoption of an intersec-tional way of thinking about the problem of sameness and difference and its relation to power. (Cho, Crenshaw, and McCall 2013, 795)

With this malleability, however, comes responsibility. While endorsing these efforts of transdisciplin-ary knowledge production – and the attendant displacement of its original subject – Crenshaw and colleagues also appeal against its distortion. This would involve, at the least, keeping intersectionality's aim of uncovering multiple and complex dimensions of power front and center of any social analysis using rigorous methodological tools. Further, they hope that scholars will work toward mainstreaming and integrating intersectionality so as to transform their own disciplines as well as to continue to build bridges and coalitions into the core theory (or what they call "centrifugal forces"), rather than remain as isolated and radicalized positions within their own fields thereby limiting intersectionality's potential and also risking the possibilities of enabling disruptive identity politics (or "centripetal forces") (Cho, Crenshaw, and McCall 2013).

These provisos are pivotal to thinking about NZ ethnic feminism. Historically, ethnic women migrated as partners of male migrants, when permitted entry at all. In the late 20th and early 21st century, occupational shortages in childcare, aged care, nursing and allied health fields meant that ethnic women have migrated in their own right as skilled workers. Like the wider ethnic population, ethnic women are a heterogeneous group stratified across the social, economic, and political spectrum. There are, however, shared exposures to multiple layers of oppression: these include *sexism* from dominant Eurocentric NZ society as well as from their own conservative traditional cultures; *racism* from wider society; systemic *invisibility* in mainstream economic and political systems; *exploitation* from capitalist structures that historically have diminished the labor of women of color; and *selective hypervisibility*, for example, in the context of some religious practices or discussions of sexuality (Simon-Kumar 2009).

The idea of 'ethnic feminism' has been constituted against this backdrop. Within some current public and political discourse, ethnic and migrant women are recognized as a marginalized group. In the strongest showing of race/ethnicity-gender advocacy, a suite of legislation and government prohibitions have been actioned as an outcome of grassroots women's organizing and advocacy. These relate to Female Genital Mutilation/Cutting (1996); Minors (Court Consent to Relationships) Legislation Act (2018) against underage marriage; dowry abuse (noted in the Family Violence Act, 2018); and visas for migrant victims of family violence, among others. Women-specific ethnic organizations have existed since post-World War Two to ensure the continuity of language and culture, but by the 1990s, ethnic organizations "*led by* ethnic women *for* ethnic women" were addressing concerns of settlement and integration, women's rights and autonomy, safety, and freedom from violence (Leckie 1993; Simon-Kumar 2019b). Family violence within ethnic communities, particularly, has become a focal galvanizing issue that has led to the establishment of feminism-led community organizing toward reflection and action; *Te Aworerekura*, NZ's first National Strategy to eliminate Family Violence and Sexual Violence, recognizes the unique contexts of violence in ethnic communities (Ministry of Justice 2021). In 2003, CEDAW's *Fifth Period Concluding Statement on NZ* makes no more than a passing mention of the discrimination and xenophobia faced by migrant and ethnic women. In its subsequent periodic reports (see CEDAW 2012, 2018, 2022) ethnic minority and migrant women garner special attention as disadvantaged groups facing multiple discriminations: "women with disabilities, *women of ethnic and minority communities*, rural women and *migrant women*, who may be more vulnerable to *multiple forms of discrimination* with respect to education, health, social and political participation and employment" (CEDAW 2012, Clause 35, emphasis added). Forums such as Ethnic Minority Women's Rights Alliance Aotearoa (EMWRAA), a community-government alliance since 2012, attract political attendance and response at the highest ministerial levels.

Even as grassroots activism, politics, and policy work with and among ethnic women have thrived and gained visibility, feminist theorizing within the particular context of biculturalism-multiculturalism has lagged. In the early decades of Asian migration post-1987, it was common to see feminist scholars adapt and improvise post-colonial feminism to migrant issues in NZ (e.g., Mohanram 1999; Pio 2007; Simon-Kumar 2009). However, as the ethnic "migrant" assumes the subjectivity of a NZ "citizen," the post-colonial feminist frame has become less tenable. It is not without basis that Gunew (2004, 15) argues the relationship between postcolonialism and multi-culturalism to be an "uneasy one." While the former is a retrospective study of "specific historic legacies," multiculturalism "deals with the often compromised management of *contemporary* geopolitical diversity in former imperial centers as well as in their ex-colonies" (Gunew 2004, 15, emphasis added). Multiculturalism, concerned with migrant and refugee transnational flows, is centered on goals such as social cohesion, inclusion and diversity, distinct from those of postcoloni-alism. such as social cohesion, inclusion, and diversity. Although, arguably, histories of colonization frame the current relationships between migrants and the white settler state, their struggles for identity and belonging go beyond the immediate postcolonial objectives of de-centering Eurocentrism – although both, as Gunew (2004, 29) reminds us, have a "shifting and shifty role to play." In NZ, these transitions in identity are unsurprisingly reflected in feminist intellectual and literary scholar-ship. The longer ethnic minorities spend as citizens, the greater the likelihood of distancing from their identities as migrants – and academics are no different in this regard. Further, there is greater imperative to develop a theory that recognizes migrants' roles as *Tangata Tiriti* or *tauiwi* (translated as "people of the Treaty") to refer to all non-indigenous settlers to the land, distinct from the positionalities of post-colonial Third World subjects (see, for example, Terruhn and Cassim 2023). There is also a new generation of young ethnic feminists who no longer identify as being Third World and for whom postcolonial critical frameworks, while a useful heuristic, hold little immediate relevance (e.g., Ng 2017; Golbakhsh 2020).

It is into this theoretical void that intersectionality has breathed new life. There is a rise in feminist writing in NZ that draws on intersectionality as a frame to express ethnic communities' collective experiences of disadvantage (e.g., Kohli 2015; Nakhid et al. 2015; Soltani 2018; Sumihira 2020). However, the turn to intersectionality has been rapid and there has been insufficient engagement with the deeper conceptual issues that accompany the movement of ideas across contexts. Despite its notable gains in policy, there is, for instance, no overarching narrative of what ethnic and migrant feminism is about or "what it does"; aside from a focus on ethnic women as an identity, it is unclear as to what novel insights and structural analyses ethnic feminism offers. Is ethnic feminism, as Nash (2011) noted, a general theory of identity or specifically of marginalization? What relationship does it hold to "place" – places of origin and place in NZ? In other words, if intersectionality is to be more than another theoretical "buzzword" (Davis 2008) wrapped into an ethnic feminism, its blind spots and creases need scrutiny.

Fault lines for a theory

The growing popularity of intersectionality for explaining the lives of NZ's ethnic women and as the basis for advocacy on their behalf calls for the critical examination of some of its underlying assertions. In this section, I identify five domains for theoretical critique – related to positioning, culture, minoritization, place, and the subject – drawing on illustrative examples to explore unresolved tensions in ethnic feminist thought, politics, and practice.

Positioning and intersectionality theory

Crenshaw's definition of intersectionality is inspired by Black feminist ideas of "multiple jeopardy" (King 1988), or the idea that women of color experience amplified discrimination different from that experienced by their male minority or female majority counterparts. Her assertions center fundamen-tally on the oppression and omissions of multiple identities. She argues that minority women are endowed with multiple, simultaneous – and importantly – historically marginalized identities that compound oppression exponentially, not additively (Crenshaw 1991). To be a black (or ethnic) woman is an entirely new identity independent of being a woman or a black alone, multiplying the impact of simultaneous interlocking systems of discrimination (Collins 1990; King 1988). To invoke multiple jeopardy draws on histories of colonization, patriarchy, and capitalism, and their contem-porary manifestations as structural and institutional racism and sexism. Additionally, Crenshaw highlights the omissions in current anti-discriminatory perspectives and practices in recognizing the significance of multiple axes of difference.

NZ ethnic women's claims to historical marginalization are complicated given the recency of their presence in the country and the broad contradictions of their lived realities. There are three prevailing representations of contemporary ethnic populations: first, as a group whose lives are precarious and vulnerable; second, as peoples who enrich NZ's cultural diversity; and third, as outsiders competing with local NZers for its resources, including welfare (Simon-Kumar 2020). These contradictory representations are mirrored in the lives of women as well. In many facets of life, ethnic women are disproportionately impacted and vulnerable to a range of societal structures. At the same time, given particular immigration incentives on which they entered the country, they also contribute skilled labor and are either employed or employable. Although there are variations among them, ethnic and migrant groups tend to be working or middle-class, have the potential to be generally socially mobile and access reasonable standards of living compared to Māori or Pacific communities where substantive, generational inequity is persistent (Friesen 2020). Take ethnic-gender wage comparisons. Although Asian women earn less than European/Pākehā women and men in all ethnic categories, they are by no means the worst paid among women of color; Pacific women consistently are in the lower rungs of earnings (Public Service Commission 2022; Stats NZ 2022). In health development indicators, ethnic populations, regardless of gender, generally benefit from "the healthy migrant effect" in many measures of wellbeing (Mehta 2012) in comparison with Māori or Pacific health outcomes. Ethnic women also experience a doubled-edge effect of having marginal identities. Representations of migrants as hardworking 'model' minorities are both salutary and a caricature. In NZ's mixed member proportional electoral system, ethnic women are sometimes preferred to ethnic men because they 'tick' multiple-diversity boxes (Barker and Coffé 2018).

The contradictions and instability of 'privilege-marginal' positioning constrain an unqualified adoption of multiple jeopardy perspectives, calling for alternative framings of intersectionality. Among the more prominent is Nira Yuval-Davis, who advances a 'situated analysis' approach highlighting complex and contingent societal grids of power that can impact anyone not only racialized women. A situated analysis framing framing, as she argues, "could ultimately avoid the risk of exceptionalism and of reifying and essentializing social boundaries" but also better encompasses complex real-life distributions of social privilege and disadvantage (Yuval-Davis 2015, 93). Similarly, Hancock (2007) suggests that in lieu of an *a priori* determination of race, class, and gender, intersectionality would be better served by "fuzzy logic," allowing for empirical investigation to reveal interactive, mutually constitutive and unpredictable relationalities. McCall (2005), likewise, proposes *intracategorical* (that assumes a fixed, unified intersectional race, gender, class core), *intercategorical* (that uses these categories in a provisional way to explain inequities), and *anticategorical* intersectionality (that deconstructs and eschews fixed categories altogether as "social fictions" focusing instead on the conditions that produce complex groupings and inequalities). Of these three, the latter two offer more promise to better portray ethnic women's realities.

The first theoretical challenge I would like to signal for the development of robust ethnic feminist analyses is the clarification of the specific intersectionality theory applied to a structural analyses of ethnic women's lives. Typically – and dominantly reflected in advocacy claims – ethnic women are positioned as subjects of multiple jeopardy even though it defies their lived experiences (Nash 2011). Situated analyses, intercategorical, or anticategorical perspectives, could more productively re-focus away from the marginalized subject (the who) to that of which aspects of social identity are pertinent to specific moments of marginalization. Multiple jeopardy risks too singular a perspective, while situated analyses open theoretical possibilities for historical and lived complexities. Context-specific analyses of marginalization in this sense could also better reflect contemporary institutional and policy effects, where they have or have not been effective. Further, contingent intersectionality could both stave off competition among minority groups as well as eschew false alliances based on thinly shared experiences of othering. It also calls for a feminist theory that is not deterred by, but instead is productively grounded in, contradiction and nuanced understandings of marginalization. The risk here is that political gains for minority groups typically demand a framing of need, injury, and injustice.

The conceptual clarity around culture and essentialism

The place of culture and multiculturalism is another unwieldy and contested factor in intersectionality theorizing among NZ's ethnic feminists. Scholarship since the 1990s (e.g., Gutmann 2004; Kymlicka 1995) advocates liberal democracy for multi-ethnic societies as necessarily based on the recognition of ethno-cultural group differences. For ethnic minorities in white-settler societies, cultural distinctiveness is a significant pillar of multicultural claims, where the entitlement to culturally differentiated practices frays is in relation to women's rights. Scholars (Okin 1999; Shachar 2000) point out that cultural rights potentially disenfranchise women from access to liberal rights and legitimize the dictates of patriarchy wrapped up as tradition in exercising control over ethnic minority women's decisions around marriage and family, clothing, sexuality, and career. NZ's ethnic feminists both embrace and shun the idea of 'culture'; it is used to lobby for specialized claims to programs and services, but culture is also posed as a primary source of their oppression. The focus on culture highlights the internal practices of the group specifically its gendered ideologies and relations, often overlooking the materiality of ethnic women's lives in relation to broader systems of white-settler societies. Ethnic feminist theory needs a deeper engagement with culture as a political dynamic.

The developments around ethnic domestic and family violence are a case in point. Violence against women was one of – indeed, the singular – issue that NZ ethnic/migrant women first mobilized around in the 1990s. Grassroots anti-violence activism and scholarly analyses of the drivers of migrant women's vulnerability to violence highlighted a complex plethora of structural, post-migration, and cultural factors (see Simon-Kumar 2019a; Simon-Kumar et al. 2017) although the role of culture is differentially highlighted by key actors in these narratives. In official documents, there is a tendency to underplay the role of culture. A 2011 Ministry for Women report on ethnic violence, for instance, presents culture as benign but open to abuse by "some" men: "[t]he most salient [issue] was the way that *some men* used their culture and religion, and their standing in the community, to rationalize their coercive behavior" (Levine and Benkert 2011, 5, emphasis added). There are also attempts to distance the generalized/macro culture from the particular/micro societal values as seen in the 2019 government report which noted that study-participants "were adamant that *culture in itself was not a cause of family violence*, [but] when victims are recent migrants it is *relevant to consider the 'norms and values'* of their homeland" (Immigration New Zealand 2019, 11, emphasis added). Begum and Rahman (2016), similarly, focusing on Muslim communities, distinguish (patriarchal) local traditions and culture from religion, and point to the active distortions by the former leading to misinterpretations of the latter. Somasekhar (2016) harnesses a version of tradition and culture that is static and restrictive among diasporic populations although becoming progressively liberal in countries of origin. Rather than culture per se, it is the anachronistic version adopted by migrants that is the problem. Feminist grassroots activists are more explicit in positioning culture as patriarchal, instrumental to gender biases, and implicated in the socialization of men (and some women) to commit violence (Nair 2017). They also point to structural organization of cultures, particularly collectivism, that normalizes violence by erasing the interests of individual women in favor of the family or community (Shakti International 2019). On the other hand, some feminists favor a more genial and transformative view of culture, focusing on its potential in addressing violence against women (Simon-Kumar et al. 2017).

While a shared understanding in and of itself is not a feminist expectation, the lack of depth of theorization of a core concept impacting women's lives is. Is culture an ally, or is it ethnic minority women's strongest source of oppression? Is culture to be understood as a group definition, a set of practices, and norms/values? Each has different implications for women's lives and rights. There are also contradictions in the way that culture is reflected in feminist praxis and scholarship; at one level, culture is blameworthy for ethnic women's oppressions, yet community activists also advocate for 'culturally sensitive, competent, and appropriate' services. There is a particular representation of culture that rationalizes gender oppression; in most narratives, its more abhorrent practices (e.g., dowry, honor-based violence or forced marriages) are highlighted as rationale for ethnic women's claims of marginalization. These claims are legitimized through the construction of an "essentialized" ethnic female subject, typically, a recent migrant who is English-language- and social network-deprived as well as financially- and visa-dependent. Also in this frame, culture is constructed as an imported problem in need of re-purposing in NZ. A deep analytical account of culture – as group, boundaries, practices, values – would more clearly address systemic power. It would also recognize that culture is not standalone but profoundly reconstituted in relation to class, religion, and region. A fuller theoretical engagement with culture would feed directly into the relationship of ethnic feminists to the state, on which there is an over-reliance for resources and policy settings. As it stands, there is ambivalence as to the role of the multicultural state, whether it is to arbitrate *against* regressive culture or in stark opposition, if its responsibility is to deliver culture-based services for women. In the context of the UK, multiculturalism in recent decades has seen shifts from secular feminist services to multi-faith feminist provision (Anitha and Dhaliwal 2019; Dhaliwal and Pragna 2012), a move that could be either beneficial or a cause for worry. Given these complexities, an intersectional theory would do well to clarify the connections between culture, feminism and multiculturalism.

Clarifying minority among minorities

A third conceptual clarity for NZ ethnic feminism relates to the understanding and representation as an ethno-cultural minority among other minorities – particularly Māori and Pasifika women – and also prospects for shared struggle against systems of oppression that impact all women of color.

Current scholarship on relationships among minority groups takes one of two routes. The first folds inter-ethnic relations into broader discourses and practices of white/majority racism, in effect, categorizing different minority groups as distinct and unconnected, positioning their political identities solely in relation to their particular experiences of subordination; as Omi and Winant (as quoted in Kim 1999, 105–106) stated, ". . . [n]ative Americans faced genocide, blacks were subjected to racial slavery, Mexicans were invaded and colonized, and Asians faced exclusions." This framing envisions all ethnicities in relation to a "black-white" binary and inadvertently locates racial groups in a hierarchy in a *competitive model* with minority groups jostling with each other to become the preferred "model minority" (Chou and Feagin 2015; Wong and Halgin 2006). Alternatively, there are efforts to explore relationships among minorities using relational perspectives noting that "colonialism and white supremacy have been relational projects" (Molina, HoSang, and Gutiérrez 2019, 3; see also, Nguyen and Velayutham 2018). At one level, relationality, informed by intersectionality, focuses on developing co-operation and a sense of commonality through complex understandings of shared disadvantage; studies show that greater contact between the two communities, perceived similarities in skin tone, and heightened ethno-political consciousness encourage solidarity and coalition-building among minorities (Kaufmann 2003; Wallsten and Nteta 2017). Other, scholars eschew the idea of "independent, already formed groups" (Rodriguez-Muniz, as cited in Molina, HoSang, and Gutiérrez 2019, 7) and instead explore racialization as constituted through the process of relationships. As Molina, HoSang, and Gutiérrez (2019, 7) note, race is not a defining characteristic of a person; instead, "it is better understood as the space and connections between people" so much so that "ethnoracial boundaries, identities, and political affiliations do not precede, but rather are *the effects* of these relations."

Feminist scholarship in NZ is still nascent to the possibilities of developing theory on minority–minority relationships and an air of "suspicion and controversy" (Lowe 2015, 496) still hangs over discussions of multiculturalism and biculturalism. Certainly, in the 1990s wave of Asian migration, feminist solidarity among women of color seemed far from practical or feasible. The late arrival of Asian migrants into the country, the latent privilege ascribed to their skilled economic status, and their political ambivalence as outsiders generally led to wariness. Writing in 1996, Mohanram highlights states of skepticism – not sisterhood – between migrants and other feminists of color:

> If Mohanty's concept of a common context of struggle held sway, then we would see the forging of alliances between the various "blacks"- Māori, Asian, Pacific Islander women in Aotearoa/New Zealand. But no such alliances exist. Rather, Asians in particular are perceived as usurpers of that which rightfully belongs to the Māori rather than as kindred victims of the global economy. (Mohanram 1996, 52)

In the new millennium, a new generation of scholars seek to re-frame the Māori-migrant relationships using indigenous principles and values. *Manaakitanga* or the Māori custom of care and respect (Kukutai and Rata 2017) and *whakawhanaungatanga* or relationship-building (Rata and Al-Asaad 2019) underpin meaningful and decolonized ways in which minorities may forge connections. On the face of it, the divergent histories, political claims, systems and structures of tradition and culture, and gender ideologies among minority groups caution against simplistic gestures of shared struggles. However, relational perspectives might offer ethnic feminism possible analytical tools to reassess the effect of contingent histories in the emergence of identities and oppression, its relation to the Treaty (as *Wāhine Tiriti* or Women of the Treaty, perhaps), the contours of feminist alliance building, and the work of decolonization and nationhood more broadly.

The issue of moral politics and place

A fourth issue for consideration in the development of intersectional perspectives in ethnic feminism relates to the effect of place and the attendant shifting of politics and morality that accompanies geographical transitions. What might be a socially just position, claim, or entitlement in one country becomes morally ambiguous and even untenable simply through the act of migration.

An illustrative example here relates to abortion rights and sex selection. Sex selective abortion, arising from son-preference in Asian, particularly Indian and Chinese societies, has been discussed since the 1980s when population-level sex-ratio discrepancies raised concerns about "missing women" (Bongaarts and Guilmoto 2015; Sen 1990). More recently, sex selection practices have been noted among migrants, including second-generation Asian migrants (e.g., Dubuc and Coleman 2007; Wanigaratne et al. 2018) in Canada, the US, UK, Europe and Australia, among others, pointing to ongoing effects of culturally driven gender bias. In recent research on sex selection in NZ, my colleague and I (Simon-Kumar and Paynter et al., 2021) found no signs of population-based sex ratio discrepancies at birth for babies born among ethnic communities in NZ and concluded that sex-selective abortion practices, even if prevalent, are rare.

In 2020, as the NZ government started to debate a change in abortion legislation, sex selection became the foremost concern that framed the pro v. anti-choice debates. Since 1978, New Zealand has had legislation strictly regulating abortion; it was located in the Crimes Act, and termination was allowed only under the strictest conditions and oversight. The move to decriminalize abortion removed it from the Crimes Act into the domain of health where termination, like any other medical condition, would be part of practitioner-client decision-making (see Abortion Legislation Act, 2020).[7] Given the charged debate centered around sex selection, the Act specifically notes that it "opposes the performance of abortions being sought solely because of a preference for the fetus to be of a particular sex" (Abortion Reform Act 2020, S21). Interestingly, Asian practices of sex selection became the fulcrum of the Parliamentary debates on both sides of the argument, for and against, any law change.

Among ethnic women Parliamentarians, there was a fractured view on the reform. Although all ethnic women politicians supported access to abortion generally, some chose to reject the Bill because the issue of sex selection, in their view, was poorly clarified. Positions fell along party lines with left-of-center Labour and Green Party's ethnic women MPs in Parliament all voting for the Bill and right-of-center National's ethnic woman MPs against. Those who voted for the Bill did so because it removed "the need to lie to get an abortion that many women have felt over the years," the "delays that many women have faced in trying to access an abortion," and because it was "good legislation" (Priyanca Radhakrishanan, Labour Party, voted "for"; Hansards 2020a). Ethnic women politicians who voted against did so because the Bill had not considered that sex selection is a "reality in the world. Yes, sex-selective abortions happen, and in some communities, they happen more than in others" and because the wording of clauses on sex selection in the new Act might create ethnic profiling when ethnic women seek abortion (Parmjeet Parmar, National Party, voted "against"; Hansards 2020b).

The sex selection v. abortion rights debate aptly illustrates the complexity and fissures of intersectional perspectives and the role of geography in constructing a moral feminist politics. In the geographical location of the global south, feminist politics of empowerment coalesces into a singular politics that privileges the rights of the unborn girl child. In the Asian diaspora, it is more complex. For ethnic feminists, to take a pro-abortion stance resting solely on a woman's liberal right to abortion risks being supportive of anti-girl child practices. Ethnic feminists who lobby for a regulated abortion environment in the interest of the girl-child risk becoming aligned with anti-choice conservatives. As a via media, to institute enhanced monitoring of ethnic couples requesting in-vitro diagnostic testing would be acceding to ethnic/racial profiling. The very same issue moved into the geopolitical place of western multi-ethnic nations, reconstitutes meanings and politics in entirely different ways.

The lesson here is that ethnic feminism is not an extension or continuation of global south feminism. To conceptualize the two as similar, albeit enacted in different geographical contexts underestimates the constitutive impact of migration and place. The political allegiances and coalitions in the global south do not readily roll over into a post-migration context; rather, ethnic feminism is new wine and should be encased in new bottles. Yet, the threads of continuity with the "home country" cannot be ignored either. What goes on back home very much impacts gender relations in migrant enclaves. Ethnic feminism must be balanced between these two very different obligations.

The concern with the subject

Nancy Fraser (2005), feminist philosopher, argues the case for different sets of rules in a "post-Westphalian, post-Keynesian" globalizing world. She posits that the principles of justice within the sovereign boundaries of a liberal democratic state cannot be applied directly into a transnational context. As Fraser (2005, 100) notes, "the idea that state-territoriality can serve as a proxy for social effectivity is no longer plausible." Citizens in a liberal state must be cognizant of wider cross-border inequities and the impacts that their claims for justice have on those who are less able to voice them. Fraser (2005, 97) points out that "the Keynesian-Westphalian frame is a powerful instrument of *injustice*, which gerrymanders political space at the expense of the poor and despised." In re-thinking justice in a post-Westphalian/global world, she points out the need to rework the "underlying grammar" of injustice, specifically, the subject or the 'who' of injustice.

In this regard, she points to two justice frames that are typically applied to questions of global injustice. In the first, the affirmative frame, the liberal state is seen as the legitimate boundary for determining claims for equality and justice. The underlying assumption is "that what makes a given collection of individuals into fellow subjects of justice is their shared residence on the territory of a modern state and/or their shared membership in the political community that corresponds to such a state" (Fraser 2005, 98). The second, transformative frame, recognizes the limitations of the stand-alone state and the inadequacy of its principles of justice as the basis of equity ("the state-territorial principle no longer affords an adequate basis for determining the 'who' of justice in every case"). Fraser notes that typically justice frames are grounded in those who are directly subject (the "all subjected") to or impacted by injustice; instead, in a transnational world, she advocates for a principle of "all affected." The all-affected principle holds that individuals and groups have moral standing as subjects of justice when they are impacted by institutional frameworks that shape their respective life possibilities even when they are not bound by geographical proximity.

Fraser's all-affected principle has particular salience for the development of an ethnic feminism. What responsibilities, if any, do ethnic minority migrant women's claims for justice have in relation to disadvantaged women in their countries of origin, in the global south? In demanding equality and equity, do ethnic women place as comparators other citizens within New Zealand (men and women of all ethnicities) or do they balance their claims in response to potential impacts on minority women globally? What should be the "underlying grammar" of ethnic feminism?

An example where questions of this nature come to the fore relates to recent petitions by the New Zealand Prostitutes Collective (NZPC)[8] to remove Section 19 of the Prostitution Decriminalization Act or PDA (2003). New Zealand became the first country in the world to decriminalize prostitution with the passage of the PDA. The Act, the outcome of considerable organized grassroots activism led by the NZPC, specifically states that its purpose is to decriminalize prostitution (while not endorsing or morally sanctioning prostitution or its use) and to create a framework that is human rights and public health focused, rather than punitive and criminal in intent. The PDA has sought to give sex workers the same rights and access to welfare, health, and safety conditions as other workers and to regulate businesses that operate in the sector under the same laws and controls as other businesses (Section 3). Section 19 of the Act focuses on immigration implications of the decriminalization of the sex industry. It specifically forbids the granting of an immigration visa in a case where anyone has: (a) provided, or intends to provide, commercial sexual services; or (b) acted, or intends to act, as an operator of a business of prostitution; or (c) invested, or intends to invest, in a business of prostitution (Section 19, Clause 1).

In recent years, the NZPC has been lobbying to have the legislative restriction of Section 19 lifted on the grounds that it enhances vulnerability and the abuse of migrant sex workers. Their case argues that despite the legal constraints, the reality of migrant women's lives are such that there is the practice of sex work among them. The restrictions of Section 19 prohibit them from accessing much-needed healthcare and welfare and, if anything, make them vulnerable to human trafficking (SEXHUM 2021). Furthermore, if they are apprehended while undertaking sex work, migrant women face criminalization and deportation. As the NZPC (2021, 6) petition notes: "There is no good reason to single out sex workers; it is discriminatory and stigmatizing, particularly for people of color who have English as a second language." The NZPC also seeks amendments to the legislation so that there is freer movement across New Zealand borders for the purpose of providing sex work services and without the need for declaring this intent on their visa. The organization, however, does continue to support the provision of the legislation that forbids anyone interested in operating or investing in sex work business in the country (NZPC 2021). NZPC's recommendations echo the CEDAW, which upholds amending Section 19 "with a view to reducing its negative impact on migrant women" (CEDAW 2018, Section 28 (a)). Several NGOs and grassroots organizations approached by NZPC have signed on to these changes, although there is a lack of clarity as to whether they are supporting the welfare of migrant sex workers currently residing within the country or making a case for de-regulating immigration policy to permit sex work.

This issue is grounded in Fraser's definition of rights and claims within and outside the state-territory and is illustrative of how an ethnic feminist perspective contends with 'who' is the main subject of its theorizing. Are the rights extended to migrant women practicing as sex workers in the country justifiable within an ethnic feminist perspective? Should claims of justice extend to the opening of immigration policy to enable the free entry of migrant workers from the global south given conditions of extant inequalities already present there? While the changes to Section 19 provide an example, it is not an isolated one. Similar questions may also be raised around practices of overseas arranged marriage or state coverage of injury that occurred prior to migrant women's arrival in New Zealand. Should the underlying grammar of justice for ethnic feminism be contained within the borders of New Zealand? Should it cover those who are its citizens or residents only? Should it be restricted to concerns here and now, or should ethnic feminism apply a broader spatio-temporal breadth in determining the scope of their struggles? In other words, ethnic feminism necessarily must clarify the subject of its liberatory doctrine.

Conclusion

Intersectionality has been a *tour de force* since its appearance on the critical theory landscape 30 years ago. It has given voice and visibility to women in the intersections of marginalized multiple social identities, and produced cutting edge analytical and methodological tools to understand deeply masked structures of power. Its rapid translation across disciplines, groups and space has, as yet, been its most triumphant and challenging movement.

This article, conceptualized against the backdrop of Antipodean ethnic minority and migrant women's experiences, is an attempt to challenge the boundaries of ethnic feminism, and in its wake, to formalize the normative foundations of intersectionality theory as it settles on new ground. The five areas of concerns outlined here, by no means exhaustive, challenge NZ's ethnic feminism to reflect on its foundations as it articulates the conditions of a vastly heterogeneous population. The concerns about positioning of identity, culture, minoritization, place, and subjects of identity point to broader engagement with intersectionality as theory itself and its responsibilities to centrifugal movement, building bridges and coalitions as envisioned by Crenshaw. Is ethnic feminism an expression of what intersectionality 'does' or 'can do'? What analytical sensibilities and dispositions is it generating – and what short, medium and long-term emancipatory goals are in its sights? These questions for introspection, I hope, will deepen its theoretical roots.

Theoretically, ethnic feminism is still very much a work-in-progress beset with self-contradiction. Anchored as it is to public funding, the theory has developed from a praxis that posits ethnicity as a fixed marker of identity. It currently presents as a theory of marginalization, while its putative subjects strain to reconstruct themselves as citizens in more complex ways, not merely as migrants (Ahluwalia 2001). There are possibilities ahead for NZ ethnic feminism – to reconstitute as a generalized theory of identity for a rapidly changing population and in relation to evolving histories and peoples (Molina, HoSang, and Gutiérrez 2019). In this form, it has the potential to offer pluralistic perspectives that would neither spiral into essentialized obsolescence nor be held captive by narrowly defined identity politics (Davis 2008; Nash 2011). It is to this task, then, that NZ ethnic minority feminists must now turn.

Notes

1. The definition of 'ethnic' used here broadly reflects that used by New Zealand's Ministry of Ethnic Communities (https://www.ethniccommunities.govt.nz/community-directory/), although there are some important differences. Unless specifically noted, I do not count Continental Europeans as ethnic for the specific purpose of this article. Further, given its particular evolution, there will be overlaps with the term "migrant" (although all ethnic people are not migrants and vice versa) and the term "Asian" (encompassing East, South, and South-East Asians) which for a long time was NZ's main ethnic group.
2. For the purposes of this article, the focus is on cis-women and heteronormativity, as much of mainstream ethnic and migrant women's needs are expressed within this implied context. The contours of queer/rainbow ethnic feminism equally deserve attention.
3. The term "biculturalism" has historically been used variously in NZ (Hayward 2012). In the 18th century, biculturalism was commonly understood as the relations between two cultures, i.e., Māori and Pākehā/European settlers. By the early 20th century – despite the signing of Te Tiriti o Waitangi/The Treaty of Waitangi that protected an equal partnership between Māori and Pākehā/Europeans – bicultural relations were progressively erased under assimilationist policies. In the 1970s and 80s, against a backdrop of Māori language renaissance and protests for sovereignty, an official policy of biculturalism was adopted with the aim of reforming the state sector through the institutionalization of *te reo* and Māori cultural traditions and recognition and practical implementation of the Treaty partnership. Many Māori intellectuals found bicultural policies to be restrictive in scope and called instead for broader constitutional reform in a landmark report *Matike Mai* (Hearn et al. 2016) that centers the Treaty as a framework for NZ's multicultural transitions.
4. Multiculturalism has been used in the scholarship variously: (a) descriptively, as the demographic diversity of a society; (b) as a set of aspirational goals of social cohesion and racial equity for such societies and (c) as a state-sponsored intervention aimed at achieving these goals. In this article, my references to multiculturalism are aimed at the latter two descriptions.
5. See https://www.mipex.eu/new-zealand.
6. See Multicultural NZ, https://multiculturalnz.org.nz/.
7. See https://www.legislation.govt.nz/act/public/2020/0006/latest/LMS237550.html.
8. See https://www.parliament.nz/en/pb/research-papers/document/00PLSocRP12051/prostitution-law-reform-in-new-zealand.

Acknowledgements

This essay was completed during my NZ Fulbright Fellowship (2022-2023) at Georgetown University, Washington DC. I am deeply indebted to Nadia Brown, Priya Kurian, Naomi Simon-Kumar and two anonymous reviewers for constructive feedback on earlier versions of this essay. The views expressed in this article are mine alone.

Disclosure statement

No potential conflict of interest was reported by the author(s).

ORCID

Rachel Simon-Kumar (iD) http://orcid.org/0000-0002-4866-5226

References

Ahluwalia, Pal. 2001. "When Does a Settler Become a Native? Citizenship and Identity in a Settler Society." *Pretexts: Literary & Cultural Studies* 10 (1):63–73. doi:10.1080/713692599.

Anitha, Sundari, and Sukhwant Dhaliwal. 2019. "South Asian Feminisms in Britain: Traversing Gender, Race, Class and Religion." *Economic and Political Weekly* 54 (17): 37–44.

Barker, Fiona, and Hilde Coffé. 2018. "Representing Diversity in Mixed Electoral Systems: The Case of New Zealand." *Parliamentary Affairs* 71 (3):603–32. doi:10.1093/pa/gsx073.

Begum, Fariya, and Anjum Rahman. 2016. Crisis Intervention for Muslim Women Experiencing Sexual Violence or Assault/Good Practice Responding to Sexual Violence - Guidelines for Mainstream Crisis Support Services for Survivors. *TOAH-NNEST*. http://toahnnestgoodpractice.squarespace.com/crisis-support-services

Bongaarts, John, and Christophe Z. Guilmoto. 2015. "How Many More Missing Women? Excess Female Mortality and Prenatal Sex Selection, 1970-2050." *Population and Development Review* 41 (2):241–69. doi:10.1111/j.1728-4457.2015.00046.x.

Carbado, Devon W. 2013. "Colorblind Intersectionality." *Signs: Journal of Women in Culture & Society* 38 (4):811–45. doi:10.1086/669666.

Carbado, Devon W., Kimberlé W. Crenshaw, Vickie M. Mays, and Barbara Tomlinson. 2013. "Intersectionality: Mapping the Movements of a Theory." *Du Bois Review: Social Science Research on Race* 10 (2):303–12. doi:10.1017/S1742058X13000349.

CEDAW. 2003. Draft Report, Consideration of Reports of States Parties, Twenty-Ninth Session 30 June-18 July 2003, CEDAW/C/2003/II/CRP.3/Add.6/Rev.1

CEDAW. 2012. *Concluding Observations on the Seventh Country Report (2012)*, Fifty-Second Session, CEDAW/C/NZL/CO/7.

CEDAW. 2018. *Concluding Observations on the Eighth Periodic Report of New Zealand (2018)*, CEDAW/C/NZL/CO/8.

CEDAW. 2022. *List of Issues and Questions Prior to the Submission of the Ninth Periodic Report of New Zealand.* CEDAW/C/NZL/QPR/9

Chou, Rosalind, and Joe Feagin. 2015. *The Myth of the Model Minority Asian Americans Facing Racism.* London and New York: Routledge.

Cho, Sumi, Kimberlé Williams Crenshaw, and Leslie McCall. 2013. "Toward a Field of Intersectionality Studies: Theory, Applications, and Praxis." *Signs: Journal of Women in Culture & Society* 38 (4):785–810. doi:10.1086/669608.

Collins, Patricia Hill. 1990. *Black Feminist Thought: Knowledge, Consciousness, and the Politics of Empowerment.* New York: Routledge.

Collins, Patricia Hill. 2015. "Intersectionality's Definitional Dilemmas." *Annual Review of Sociology* 41:1–20. doi:10.1146/annurev-soc-073014-112142.

Crenshaw, Kimberlé. 1991. "Mapping the Margins: Intersectionality, Identity Politics, and Violence Against Women of Color." *Stanford Law Review* 43 (6):1241–99. doi:10.2307/1229039.

Davis, Kathy. 2008. "Intersectionality as Buzzword: A Sociology of Science Perspective on What Makes a Feminist Theory Successful." *Feminist Theory* 9 (1):67–85. doi:10.1177/1464700108086364.

Dhaliwal, Sukhwant, and Pragma Patel. 2012. "Feminism in the Shadow of Multi-Faithism: Implications for South Asian Women in the UK." In *New South Asian Feminisms: Paradoxes and Possibilities*, eds. Srila Roy. New York: Zed Books 169–88. 10.5040/9781350221505.ch-008

Dubuc, Sylvie, and David Coleman. 2007. "An Increase in the Sex Ratio of Births to India- Born Mothers in England and Wales: Evidence for Sex-Selective Abortion." *Population and Development Review* 33 (2):383–400. doi:10.1111/j.1728-4457.2007.00173.x.

Elers, Steve. 2018. "A 'White New Zealand': Anti-Chinese Racist Political Discourse from 1880 to 1920." *China Media Research* 14 (3): 88–98.

Ferguson, Philip. 2003. *The making of the White New Zealand policy: Nationalism, citizenship and the exclusion of the Chinese, 1880-1920*. Diss. University of Canterbury.

Fraser, Nancy. 2005. "Re-Framing Justice in a Globalizing World." *Anales de la Cátedra Francisco Suárez* 39: 89–105.

Friesen, Wardlow. 2020. "Quantifying and Qualifying Inequality Among Migrants." In *Intersections of Inequality, Migration and Diversification*, eds. Rachel Simon-Kumar, Francis Collins, and Wardlow Friesen. Cham: Palgrave Macmillan, 17–42. doi:10.1007/978-3-030-19099-6_2.

Golbakhsh, Ghazaleh. 2020. *The Girl from Revolution Road*. New Zealand: Allen & Unwin.

Gunew, Sneja. 2004. *Haunted Nations: The Colonial Dimensions of Multiculturalisms*. London, New York: Routledge.

Gutmann, Amy. 2004. *Identity in Democracy*. Princeton, NJ: Princeton University Press.

Hancock, Ange-Marie. 2007. "When Multiplication Doesn't Equal Quick Addition: Examining Intersectionality as a Research Paradigm." *Perspectives on Politics* 5 (1):63–79. doi:10.1017/S1537592707070065.

Hansards. 2020a. "Abortion Legislation Bill - in Committee - Part 1." NZ Parliament Transcript. https://www.parliament.nz/en/pb/hansard-debates/rhr/combined/HansDeb_20200310_20200310_20

Hansards. 2020b. "Abortion Legislation Bill — Third Reading." NZ Parliament Transcript. https://www.parliament.nz/en/pb/hansard-debates/rhr/combined/HansDeb_20200318_20200318_24

Hayward, Janine. 2012. "Biculturalism." *Te Ara – the Encyclopedia of New Zealand*, June 20. https://teara.govt.nz/en/biculturalism

Hearn, Jeff, Sofia Strid, Liisa Husu, and Mieke Verloo. 2016. "Interrogating Violence Against Women and State Violence Policy: Gendered Intersectionalities and the Quality of Policy in the Netherlands, Sweden and the UK." *Current Sociology* 64 (4):551–67. doi:10.1177/0011392116639220.

Immigration New Zealand. 2019. "Recent Migrant Victims of Family Violence Project 2019: Final Report." Wellington, New Zealand. https://www.mbie.govt.nz/dmsdocument/12138-recent-migrant-victims-of-family-violence-project-2019-final-report

Kaufmann, Karen M. 2003. "Cracks in the Rainbow: Group Commonality as a Basis for Latino and African-American Political Coalitions." *Political Research Quarterly* 56 (2):199–210. doi:10.1177/106591290305600208.

Kim, Claire Jean. 1999. "The Racial Triangulation of Asian-Americans." *Politics and Society* 27 (1):105–38. doi:10.1177/0032329299027001005.

King, Deborah K. 1988. "Multiple Jeopardy, Multiple Consciousness: The Context of a Black Feminist Ideology." *Signs: Journal of Women in Culture & Society* 14 (1):42–72. doi:10.1086/494491.

Kohli, Ambika. 2015. "Forced and Underage Marriages in New Zealand: Some Reflections on Public and Private Patriarchy and Intersectionality." *International Journal for Intersectional Feminist Studies* 1: 58–70.

Kukutai, Tahu, Arama Rata. 2017. From Mainstream to Manaaki: Indigenising Our Approach to Immigration. In *Fair Borders? Migration Policy in the Twenty-First Century*. Wellington: Bridget Williams Books, 26–44. doi:10.7810/9780947518851_2.

Kymlicka, 1995. Multicultural Citizenship: a Liberal Theory of Minority Rights. Oxford:Clarendon Press.

Leckie, Jacqueline. 1993. "Immigration, Ethnicity and Women's Organisations." *Women Together-A History of Women's Organisations in New Zealand. Ngā Rōpū Wāhine O Te Motu*, ed. Anne Else. Wellington: Daphne Brasell Assoc. Press, 499–512.

Leckie, Jacqueline. 2021. *Invisible: New Zealand's History of Excluding Kiwi-Indians*. Massey University Press.

Levine, Marlene, and Nicole Benkert. 2011. "Case Studies of Community Initiatives Addressing Family Violence in Refugee and Migrant Communities: Final Report." In *Ministry of Social Development and Ministry of Women's Affairs*, Wellington, New Zealand. https://women.govt.nz/library/case-studies-community-initiatives-addressing-family-violence-refugee-and-migrant

Lewycka, Sonia, Roshini and Peiris-John, and Rachel and Simon-Kumar. 2020. "Inequality and Adolescent Migrants: Results from Youth 2000 Survey." In *Intersections of Inequality, Migration and Diversification*, eds. Rachel Simon-Kumar, Francis Collins, and Wardlow Friesen. Cham: Palgrave Macmillan, 109–29. doi:10.1007/978-3-030-19099-6_6.

Lowe, John. 2015. "Multiculturalism and Its Exclusions in New Zealand: The Case for Cosmopolitanism and Indigenous Rights." *Inter-Asia Cultural Studies* 16 (4):496–512. doi:10.1080/14649373.2015.1103010.

Malatest International. 2021. *Drivers of Migrant New Zealanders' Experience of Racism. New Zealand Human Rights Commission*. https://apo.org.au/node/311552

Manying, Ip. 2013. "Chinese immigration to Australia and New Zealand: Government policies and race relations." In *Routledge handbook of the Chinese diaspora*, ed. Chee-Beng Tan. Routledge, 156–75.

McCall, Leslie. 2005. "The Complexity of Intersectionality." *Signs: Journal of Women in Culture & Society* 30 (3):1771–800. doi:10.1086/426800.

Mehta, Suneela. 2012. "Health Needs Assessment of Asian People Living in the Auckland Region." *Northern District Health Board Support Agency*. Auckland, New Zealand.

Ministry of Ethnic Communities. n.d. Community Directory. https://www.ethniccommunities.govt.nz/community-directory/

Ministry of Justice. 2021. *Te Aworerekura: Strategy and Action Plan*. https://www.tepunaaonui.govt.nz/national-strategy/#download

Mohanram, Radhika. 1996. "The Construction of Place: Māori Feminism and Nationalism in Aotearoa/New Zealand." *NWSA Journal* 8 (1): 50–69.

Mohanram, Radhika. 1999. *Black Body: Women, Colonialism, and Space*. Minneapolis: University of Minnesota Press.

Molina, Natalia, Daniel Martinez HoSang, and Ramón A. Gutiérrez eds. 2019. *Relational Formations of Race: Theory, Method, and Practice*, Berkeley, CA: University of California Press. doi:10.2307/j.ctvcwp0dz.

Nachowitz, Todd. 2015. "Earliest Indian Presence in Aotearoa (1769–1809) and Settlement according to the New Zealand Census (1861–2013)." In *Workshop on Indian Migration to the Pacific & Indian Ocean States*. Christchurch, New Zealand: University of Canterbury, April 15. https://www.wgtn.ac.nz/nziri/documents/nachowitz.pdf

Nachowitz, Todd. 2018. "Identity and Invisibility: Early Indian Presence in Aotearoa New Zealand, 1769–1850." In *Indians and the Antipodes: Networks, Boundaries, and Circulation*, eds. Sekhar Bandyopadhyay and Jane Buckingham. Delhi: Oxford University Press, 26–61. doi:10.1093/oso/9780199483624.003.0002.

Nair, Shila. 2017. "Elephant in The Therapy Room: Counselling experiences of ethnic immigrant women survivors of family violence in Aotearoa, New Zealand." Master's Thesis. University of Auckland.

Nakhid, Camille, Anna Majavu, Lisa Bowleg, Shelagh Mooney, Irene Ryan, David Mayeda, Menghzu, Fu, Huhana Hickey, Karanina Sumeo, Shakeisha Wilson, et al. 2015. "'Intersectionality Revisited: Moving Beyond the Contours of Race, Class, gender' - Notes on an Intersectionality Symposium." *New Zealand Sociology* 30 (4):190–98.

Nash, Jennifer C. 2011. "'Home truths' on Intersectionality." *Yale Journal of Law and Feminism* 23 (2): 445–70.

Ng, Emma. 2017. *Old Asian, New Asian*. Wellington, New Zealand: Bridget Williams Books. doi:10.7810/9780947518509.

Nguyen, Tran, and Selvaraj Velayutham. 2018. "Everyday Inter-Ethnic Tensions and Discomfort in a Culturally Diverse Australian Workplace." *Social Identities* 24 (6):779–94. doi:10.1080/13504630.2017.1329655.

NZPC. 2021. We are Seeking Your Support to Amend Section 19 of the Prostitution Reform Act 2003. *Petition Document*

Okin, Susan M. 1999. *Is Multiculturalism Bad for Women?*. Princeton, NJ: Princeton University Press. doi:10.1515/9781400840991-002.

O'Malley, Vincent. 2019. *The New Zealand Wars | Ngā Pakanga O Aotearoa*. Wellington, New Zealand: Bridget Williams Books.

Pio, Edwina. 2007. "Ethnic Minority Migrant Women Entrepreneurs and the Imperial Imprimatur." *Women in Management Review* 22 (8):631–49. doi:10.1108/09649420710836317.

Public Service Commission. 2022. Raraunga Ohumahi — Taiutu Workforce Data - Remuneration/Pay. https://www.publicservice.govt.nz/research-and-data/workforce-data-remunerationpay/

Radio NZ. n.d. *The New Zealand Wars Collection*. https://www.rnz.co.nz/nzwars

Rata, Arama, and Faisal Al-Asaad. 2019. "Settlers of Colour: Whakawhanaungatanga as a Māori Approach to Indigenous–Settler of Colour Relationship Building." *New Zealand Population Review* 45: 211–33.

Salmond, Anne. 1991. *Two Worlds: First Meetings Between Maori and Europeans, 1642-1772*. Honolulu: University of Hawaii Press.

Salmond, Anne. 1997. *Between worlds: early exchanges between Māori and Europeans 1773-1815*. Auckland: Viking.

Sen, Amartya. 1990. "More Than 100 Million Women are Missing." *New York Review of Books*, December 20. https://www.nybooks.com/articles/1990/12/20/more-than-100-million-women-are-missing/

SexHum. 2021. "Sexual Humanitarianism: Understanding Agency and Exploitation in the Global Sex Industry." Policy Report, European Research Council ERC-COG-2015-682451.

Shachar, Ayelet. 2000. "On Citizenship and Multicultural Vulnerability." *Political Theory* 28 (1):64–89. doi:10.1177/0090591700028001004.

Shakti International. 2019. "Ethnic Domestic Violence Response Framework and Best Practice Guidelines." Auckland, New Zealand. https://shaktiinternational.org/wp-content/uploads/2019/11/Shakti-Report-2019-part-3.pdf

Simon-Kumar, Rachel. 2009. "The 'Problem' of Asian Women's Sexuality: Public Discourses in Aotearoa/New Zealand." *Culture, Health & Sexuality* 11 (1):1–16. doi:10.1080/13691050802272304.

Simon-Kumar, Rachel, Priya A. Kurian, Faith Young-Silcock, and Nirmala Narasimhan. 2017. "Mobilising Culture Against Domestic Violence in Migrant and Ethnic Communities: Practitioner Perspectives from Aotearoa/New Zealand." *Health & Social Care in the Community* 25 (4):1387–95. doi:10.1111/hsc.12439.

Simon-Kumar, Rachel. 2019a. Ethnic Perspectives in Family Violence in Aotearoa New Zealand, ed. Anne Else. Issues paper 15. New Zealand: Family Violence Clearinghouse. https://nzfvc.org.nz/issues-paper-14-ethnic-perspectives-family-violence-aotearoa-new-zealand.

Simon-Kumar, Rachel. 2019b. "Immigration, Ethnicity and Women's Organisations." In *Women Together: A History of Women's Organisations in New Zealand/Ngā Rōpū Wāhine o te Motu*. Ministry for Culture and Heritage.

Simon-Kumar, Rachel. 2020. "Justifying Inequalities." In *Intersections of Inequality, Migration and Diversification*, eds. Rachel Simon-Kumar, Francis Collins and Wardlow Friesen. Cham: Palgrave Macmillan, 43–64. doi:10.1007/978-3-030-19099-6_3.

Simon-Kumar, Rachel, Francis Collins, and Wardlow Friesen, eds. 2020. *Intersections of Inequality, Migration and Diversification*. Palgrave Macmillan.

Simon-Kumar, Rachel, Janine Paynter, Annie Chiang, and Nimisha Chabba. 2021. "Sex Ratios and 'Missing women' Among Asian Minority and Migrant Populations in Aotearoa/New Zealand: A Retrospective Cohort Analysis." *BMJ Open* 11 (11):e052343. doi:10.1136/bmjopen-2021-052343.

Soltani, Anoosh. 2018. "Muslim women's embodied geographies in Hamilton, Aotearoa New Zealand: An intersectional approach." Diss. University of Waikato.

Somasekhar, Sripriya. 2016. "'What will people think?' Indian Women and Domestic Violence in Aotearoa/New Zealand." Diss. University of Waikato.

Stats NZ. 2019. "New Zealand's Population Reflects Growing Diversity." https://www.stats.govt.nz/news/new-zealands-population-reflects-growing-diversity

Stats NZ. 2020a. "2018 Census Totals by Topic – National Highlights (Updated)." https://www.stats.govt.nz/information-releases/2018-census-totals-by-topic-national-highlights-updated/

Stats NZ. 2020b. "Ethnic Group Summaries Reveal New Zealand's Multicultural Make-Up." https://www.stats.govt.nz/news/ethnic-group-summaries-reveal-new-zealands-multicultural-make-up/

Stats NZ. 2022. "Gender and Ethnic Pay Gaps: Stats NZ's Action Plan 2022/23." Accessed 25 January 2023. https://www.stats.govt.nz/corporate/gender-and-ethnic-pay-gaps-stats-nzs-action-plan-2022/.

Sumihira, Ai. 2020. "Intersectionality and Sisterhood in the Time of Covid-19." *Aotearoa New Zealand Social Work* 32 (2):49–54. doi:10.11157/anzswj-vol32iss2id743.

Terruhn, Jessica, and Shemana Cassim, eds. 2023. *Transforming the Politics of Mobility and Migration in Aotearoa New Zealand*. New York: Anthem Press.

Wallsten, Kevin, and Tatishe M. Nteta. 2017. "Race, Partisanship, and Perceptions of Inter-Minority Commonality." *Politics, Groups & Identities* 5 (2):298–320. doi:10.1080/21565503.2016.1164065.

Wanigaratne, Susitha, Pamela Uppal, Manvir Bhangoo, Alia Januwalla, Deepa Singal, and Marcelo L. Urquia. 2018. "Sex Ratios at Birth Among Second-Generation Mothers of South Asian Ethnicity in Ontario, Canada: A Retrospective Population- Based Cohort Study." *Journal of Epidemiology & Community Health* 72 (11):1044–51. doi:10.1136/jech-2018-210622.

Wong, Frieda, and Richard Halgin. 2006. "The 'Model Minority': Bane or Blessing for Asian Americans?" *Journal of Multicultural Counseling and Development* 34 (1):38–49. doi:10.1002/j.2161-1912.2006.tb00025.x.

Yuval-Davis, Nira. 2015. "Situated Intersectionality and Social Inequality." *Raisons politiques* 58 (2):91–100. doi:10.3917/rai.058.0091.

OPEN ACCESS

Intersectional Politics of the International Women's Strike

Fernando Tormos-Aponte, Shariana Ferrer-Núñez, and Carolina Hernandez

ABSTRACT

Increasingly, progressive organizing faces pressures to adopt intersectional forms of solidarity. Intersectional solidarity consists of an ongoing process of creating ties and coalitions across social group differences by negotiating power asymmetries. This approach to organizing is not a static outcome that movements achieve and preserve. Movements that seek to enact intersectional solidarity must engage in ongoing struggles to sustain it. This article focuses on the case of the International Women's Strike (IWS) of 2017 and 2018 in Spain. We use this case to identify circumstances that can lead to failures to sustain intersectional solidarity and the consequences of the ruptures that follow. In the case of the International Women's Strike, initial calls to organize around the subject of women and women's labor mobilized broad support in 2017. Black women in Spain affiliated with a group known as Afroféminas called on expanding the subject of local IWS mobilization to center the experiences of Black subjects. In a broadly circulated announcement, Afroféminas called out this experience and announced that they would not participate in the International Women's Strike. The case of the International Women's Strike in Spain showcases an instance under which the search for intersectional solidarity can generate broad intersectional consciousness even when it leads to separate organizing tracks. The development of autonomous Black activist spaces informed the continuity and deepening of intersectional consciousness but limited the magnitude of the praxis (e.g. Afroféminas did not participate in the broader praxis that generated disruptive tactics and mobilized larger masses). In choosing to consider racism as a form of violence within one system of capitalist exploitation, limited notions of subjectivity dominated IWS. On the other hand, Afroféminas' withdrawal of participation limited the scope of praxis and raised questions about the representativeness and inclusiveness of the broader movement. Thus, intersectional and oppositional consciousness can emerge from the withdrawal of intersectionally marginalized groups from coalition work while challenging the enactment of mass intersectional praxis.

Introduction

Increasingly, progressive activists are under pressure to adopt intersectional forms of solidarity. Intersectional solidarity consists of an ongoing process of creating ties and coalitions across social group differences by negotiating power asymmetries (Tormos 2017). This approach to organizing is not a static outcome that movements achieve and preserve. Movements that seek to enact intersectional solidarity must engage in ongoing struggles to sustain it. Movements that fail to enact or sustain intersectional solidarity tend to face critiques about their representativeness (authority that a movement has to make claims on

---

This is an Open Access article distributed under the terms of the Creative Commons Attribution-NonCommercial-NoDerivatives License (http://creativecommons.org/licenses/by-nc-nd/4.0/), which permits non-commercial re-use, distribution, and reproduction in any medium, provided the original work is properly cited, and is not altered, transformed, or built upon in any way. The terms on which this article has been published allow the posting of the Accepted Manuscript in a repository by the author(s) or with their consent.

behalf of various groups), thus affecting their standing in the public eye and among policymakers. Further, those excluded from broader movements face challenges mobilizing broader masses and diffusing their ideologies and goals. Failures to enact intersectional solidarity weaken movements all around.

This article examines the intersectional politics of the international women's strike (IWS) in 2017 and 2018. We draw from original interview data, news articles about the strike, and social media observations to theorize how progressive movements, such as the IWS, articulate and seek to sustain popular mobilization. We are particularly interested in a phenomenon we term intersectional synthesis, which refers to the dialectical relationship between an intersectional consciousness and an intersectional praxis (Tormos-Aponte and Ferrer-Núñez 2020). Focusing on how movements develop an awareness of oppression and how these consciousnesses motivate and are motivated by praxis provides critical insight into the ways movements build their agendas, prioritize certain issues and tactics, choose and promote leaders, and make space for different social groups and perspectives.

We seek to build on our initial efforts to identify and theorize the dialectical relationship between intersectional consciousness and praxis. We use the case of the IWS of 2017 and 2018 to identify circumstances that can lead to failures to sustain intersectional solidarity and the consequences of the ruptures that follow. We find that the dialectical processes that we describe as intersectional synthesis can have different outcomes. In instances when movements are able to cope with internal differences through effective negotiations and redistributions of power, intersectional syntheses can sustain solidarity across differences. In instances in which activists do not deem power to be adequately redistributed, the experiences of the multiply marginalized in praxis can further shape their consciousness in ways that signal a need to rupture coalitional approaches to addressing their distinct issues, thus weakening solidarity across differences.

Power negotiations within movements can expand or contract the subject of their struggle. Bridge builders, who tend to be women of color, often seek to expand the subject of a movement and spread awareness of intersectional forms of oppression and approaches to building solidarity. However, this labor can be ineffective when dominant groups reject pressures to redistribute power among social groups in movements. Limited notions of a movement's subject that focus on the issues of dominant subgroups can mobilize broad support across different social groups, but movements struggle to sustain solidarity across differences without expanding the subjective focus of their mobilization and developing new consciousness through awareness of the experiences of multiply marginalized groups in ways that inform future praxis.

IWS efforts to mobilize as women with platforms that recognized shared and distinct experiences were sufficient to ignite broad mobilization in 2017. Once mobilized, new experiences are gained in coalitional politics, and these form new consciousnesses and claims for shifting the way the movement is organized and the issues that are prioritized. Moving forward, these experiences leading into the 2018 strike had shaped consciousness and praxis in ways that signaled to some multiply marginalized groups that pursuing a coalitional approach within IWS was not aligned with their political objectives to subvert intersectional forms of marginalization.

Intersectionality and intersectional consciousness

We build on the tradition of the project of intersectionality. Intersectionality is a political project with activist and intellectual roots that emerged from the critiques Black, queer, and Latina feminists levied against second-wave feminism and civil rights organizing (Combahee River Collective [1977] 1995). This project brought light to the lived experiences of multiply marginalized subgroups (Cohen 1999a, 1999b). Black and Latina queer feminists especially highlighted the need for movements that centered lived experiences shaped by the interactions of multiple systems of oppression, including but not limited to gender, race, class, sexuality, and nationality, among others (Collins 2015).

Analyses of policy silences, how policies neglect and oppress multiply marginalized groups, led Kimberlé Crenshaw (1989) to coin the term intersectionality, thus naming a project whose tradition has been traced back to the centuries-old activism of leaders like Maria Stewart, Savitribai Phule, and Sojourner Truth, and contemporary manifestation of intersectional praxis like the Combahee River

Collective. Intersectionality is a project that focuses on identifying, critiquing, and subverting advocacy and policy silences (Einwohner et al. 2021; Hancock 2011; hooks 1981; Strolovitch 2007). It is a project that resists essentialism, thus rejecting biological, static, and additive notions of identity (Hancock 2007; Weldon 2006b). This project also raises awareness of the subjugation and appropriation of the knowledge that multiply marginalized people produce (Alexander-Floyd 2012; Collins 1990, 2015; hooks 1981).

Emerging from social movements, scholars working at the margins of higher education have pushed to sustain and grow the project of intersectionality (Beaman and Brown 2019). These efforts face numerous challenges, including neglect of intersectionality as a framework for the study of social movements (Irvine, Lang, and Montoya 2019; Liu 2017), the term's capture among non-Black academics, and a dismissal of Black women's activist and intellectual labor that led to the term's growing popularity (Alexander-Floyd 2012).

Intersectionality has now garnered significant attention among social movement scholars. Studies on intersectionality and social movements include those that conceptualize intersectionality as a kind of coalition (Adam 2017; Chun, Lipsitz, and Shin 2013; Cole 2008; Gawerc 2021; Laperrière and Lépinard 2016; Luna 2016; Roberts and Jesudason 2013; Roth 2021; Tungohan 2016; Verloo 2013), an organizing approach (Çağatay 2023; Einwohner et al. 2021; Tormos 2017; Tormos-Aponte 2019), a distinct way of shaping a movement's agenda (Strolovitch 2007; Smooth and Tucker 1999), a series of issues that motivate movement participation (Fisher et al. 2018), a kind of discourse that movements use (Fisher, Dow, and Ray 2017; Heaney 2021), or a framework that scholars can use to study movements (Liu 2017).

In our view, intersectionality proposes a distinct approach to building solidarity among activists. We term this approach the intersectional solidarity organizing approach. We refer to the consciousness that motivates critique and organizing against multiple, compounding sources of oppression as intersectional consciousness and the agency associated with this approach as intersectional praxis. The idea of intersectional solidarity stems from the pioneering work of feminist scholars of color who have theorized about this approach to building solidarity (Cho, Crenshaw, and McCall 2013, Collins and Chepp 2013; Hancock 2011; Townsend-Bell 2011). Intersectional solidarity is a form of solidarity that places the issues of multiply marginalized groups at the center of organizing. Although movements vary in terms of how they enact intersectional forms of solidarity, this organizing approach tends to prioritize the issues of multiply marginalized groups, promotes their leadership, respects their autonomous spaces, and seeks consensus while avoiding the practice of suppressing difference and dissent (Dhamoon 2011; Einwohner et al. 2021; Strolovitch 2007; Tormos 2017; Tormos-Aponte 2019; Weldon 2006a; Smooth and Tucker 1999). Activist labor to enact and sustain intersectional solidarity consists of iterative negotiations of power differences in the quest to cope with and address unequal social formations. Enacting intersectional solidarity is not a linear process that reaches a static and final outcome. Movements that enact this approach to organizing can fail to sustain it, while those who fail to enact it can find ways to adopt it in subsequent struggles.

We argue that the process of enacting and sustaining intersectional solidarity is a dialectical process whereby notions of oppression within movements interact with efforts to enact anti-oppressive praxis in ways that mutually inform and shape each other. This process, which we refer to as an intersectional synthesis, is the dialectical relationship between intersectional consciousness and intersectional praxis. Intersectional consciousness refers to the awareness of multiple marginalizations that exist in societal and movement settings. These are individual and collective understandings of oppression that consider how interacting systems shape lived experiences and conditions of marginalization. These complex understandings of oppression can emerge in movement settings through ongoing deliberation processes and efforts to achieve social justice. These understandings of oppression can deepen activist engagement (Earl, Maher, and Elliot 2017), generate new coalitions (Roberts and Jesudason 2013), and foster solidarity across different social groups. Intersectional consciousness emerges within movements among individuals and collectively (Cho, Crenshaw, and McCall 2013; Cole 2008; Curtin, Stewart, and Cole 2015; Greenwood 2008; Irvine, Lang, and Montoya 2019; Tormos-Aponte 2019).

The labor of raising intersectional consciousness and brokering relationships, also known as bridge-building, tends to rest on the shoulders of women of color (Daniel and de Leon 2020; Montoya and Seminario 2022; Moraga and Anzaldua 1983; Robnett 1996; Terriquez 2015). Movement participants and organizers engage in collective action with a priori understandings of oppression, which can evolve as they engage in internal movement deliberation, contention, and praxis (Tormos-Aponte and Ferrer-Núñez 2020; Townsend-Bell 2011). Townsend-Bell (2011) describes this as a process of identifying what is relevant to activists. Engaging in contention is a process that generates solidarities (Fantasia 1988) and understandings of the marginalized lived experiences that motivate activism (Cho, Crenshaw, and McCall 2013).

Impactful efforts to develop intersectional consciousness can inform praxis within movements and coalitions (Gawerc 2021; Roth 2021). An intersectional praxis refers to the actions that movements and organizers take to confront the systems, institutions, and norms that produce intersectional forms of marginalization. Movements and organizers can strive to enact intersectional praxis through recognitions of intersectional marginalization, representation of multiply marginalized groups in movement leadership, prioritizing the issues of multiply marginalized groups, allocating resources and energies to addressing these issues, compensating the labor of bridge builders, enabling inclusive and deliberative decision-making processes, and making space for the autonomous organizing of multiple marginalized groups (Laperrière and Lépinard 2016; Roberts and Jesudason 2013; Strolovitch 2007; Tormos-Aponte 2019; Weldon 2006a).

Methods: case and sources

This article draws data from public declarations of activist groups, media interviews, news reports covering the strike across Latin America and Spain, blog posts, existing literature on the IWS of 2017 and 2018, and interview data. We use these sources to identify themes that emerge from the data, paying particular attention to issues of representation, agenda setting, and autonomous organizing of multiply marginalized groups in the movement. This analytical approach allows us to build on the notion of intersectional synthesis, identifying dynamics that precede and follow instances in which movements struggle to cope with challenges associated with adopting intersectional approaches to organizing. This article also engages in collaborative ethnography among the authors, allowing reflection on experiences in organizing and embracing the development of movement-generated theory. Further, we build on Shariana Ferrer-Núñez's autoethnography as an organizer and founder of the Puerto Rico-based Colectiva Feminista en Construcción. In doing so, we take activist insights as crucial sources of knowledge production and theory generation and seek to prefigure reciprocal scholar-activist relationships that break with extractive academic traditions that take activist knowledge without attribution.

Autoethnographies have advanced the study of intersectional solidarity (see, for example, Tormos-Aponte and Ferrer-Núñez 2020; Tungohan 2019). This method combines "the personal and the scholarly" in aims of strengthening and promoting movement-emergent theory by taking lived experiences as key sources of knowledge generation (Burnier 2006, 412; Tungohan 2019). Natasha Behl describes it as a "practice of critical reflection on the embodied experience of knowledge making" whose goal is to disrupt the "subject – object separation by placing the researcher's experience at the center of the phenomenon under investigation" (Behl 2017, 584).

International women's strike

The IWS emerged from a global context marked by the relative strength of right-wing and neoliberal forces, which had come to power in Mexico, Spain, Argentina, Brazil, Poland, and the US, among other contexts. This wave of right-wing ascensions to power ignited a sense of urgency and threat against marginalized peoples. In Poland in October of 2016, more than 100,000 rose against the country's ban on abortion. That same month, violence against women, including the violent murder of

Lucía Pérez, ignited mobilization under the slogan #NiUnaMenos in Argentina, Chile, Guatemala, Mexico, and Uruguay, among other countries. This slogan continued reverberating globally, deployed again as feminists called for action. In November 2016, Donald J. Trump's election signaled a turning point in US politics for many, igniting the largest mobilization in US history at the time – the Women's March in January 2017. The Women's March, following the Trump presidential inauguration, mobilized more than four million marchers across the US.[1] and formed part of what became known as The Resistance (Fisher 2019).

Social movement scholarship has debated about what constitutes an opportune international climate for mobilization. Theorized elements of these transnational opportunity structures include the creation or changes of institutions of global governance, whether activists think that they can succeed, the support of powerful states, the adoption of international trade agreements, whether activists are subject to repression, and shifts in international conflicts (Bartley 2007; Carothers 2016; Kay 2005; O'Neill 2004, Simmons 2009; and; Von Bülow 2010). Transnational IWS mobilization emerged in spite of the inopportune national and international political climate. Activists faced the rise of right-wing national governments in Mexico, Spain, Argentina, Brazil, Poland, and the US, among other contexts, and the continuity of right-wing forces in various powerful states, thus, obstructing the ability among activists to rely on the support of a powerful state, a theorized element of transnational political opportunity structures. No major changes had taken place in the intergovernmental landscape. The Trump administration had blocked the proposed Transatlantic Trade and Investment Partnership and announced the intent to withdraw from the Paris Accord on Climate. The emergence of a transnational mobilization of the breadth and magnitude of the IWS was not theoretically expected. While the strength of right-wing forces at this juncture did not signal obvious openings for transnational mobilization, it was precisely the increased strength of right-wing forces internationally that motivated activism to resist these forces. The hostile climate for transnational feminist mobilization did not preclude the struggle to build intersectional solidarity across differences.

As a transnational campaign, IWS sought to move beyond resistance. IWS gave substantive content to the resistance to right-wing forces by articulating grievances and agendas for just futures. Doing so in a hostile political climate required organizing labor. This labor intentionally sought to articulate an intersectional form of solidarity. Leaders of the Una Menos (2018) movement wrote:

> As women of the world, we find ourselves in a process of existential revolution. On March 8, 2017, we united to show our force: we staged the first international women's strike, in a transnational, multilingual, intersectional, and heterogeneous articulation, in which fifty-five countries participated. We began to forge a new internationalism.

Through participant-observation of the IWS, Çağatay (2023) found that an intersectional understanding of solidarity was among the three guiding principles of IWS organizing.[2] This intersectional approach to organizing made space for the co-existence of distinct notions of systems of oppression among organizers. One perspective pushes for a dynamic understanding of oppression resulting from multiple interacting systems of oppression. On the other hand, a Marxist feminist approach promotes the notion that only one system of oppression exists, capitalism, and that racism and imperialism are constitutive of the latter. Proponents argued: "the root of the problem is capitalism, and that racism and imperialism are integral to the latter" (Arruzza, Bhattacharya, and Fraser 2019). This approach has called for a greater recognition of social reproductive labor.[3] Despite these differences of perspectives, power asymmetries across social groups, and the decentralized approach to organizing transnationally, organizers across distinct national and regional settings and social groups coordinated mass mobilization, recalling and building on histories of transnational feminist movements.

The 2017 IWS was born out of a context of heightened mobilization against capitalist exploitation, the right-wing's ascendance, gender-based violence, and authoritarian repression. In the weeks prior to international women's day, activists issued broad calls to strike and mobilize against right-wing and neoliberal forces across the world. In the United States, the Women's Strike Platform centered around five main points – a demand to end gender violence in institutionalized and domestic life, a call for reproductive justice for everyone, to institute labor rights and a robust welfare system, a commitment to anti-racist and anti-imperialist feminism, and a call for environmental justice. The platform connected each issue to the struggles of women of color, immigrant women, and trans women. In the demand to end gendered violence, the IWS noted that this meant an end to police brutality and immigration raids. In the call for reproductive justice, the platform emphasized a definition of women that included women of color and both cis and trans women. The platform highlighted the need for free abortion access and affordable healthcare. Further, the IWS platform emphasized women's autonomy over their bodies. Organizers tied the history of forced sterilization for women of color to the attack on abortion rights as issues rooted in control over women's bodies.

The labor and reproductive labor rights contained in the platform demanded a 15 USD minimum wage, free universal childcare, maternity leave, paid sick leave and family leave, and the right to organize a union in the workplace. It also recognized that formal and informal labor must be paid fairly and equally. Additionally, the extensive 2017 US platform centered an anti-racist and anti-imperialist feminism that distinguished it from neoliberal approaches to feminism, which focus on women's incremental progress within existing systems of oppression. The platform tied White supremacy to a history of colonialism in the country, and argued that this legacy manifested in the present day as police brutality, militarization, and mass incarceration. The platform's call demanded the decolonization of Palestine, support for the Black Lives Matter movement, and support for Immigrants' rights. The list of demands also included a demand for a sustainable future and the protection of natural resources. This was especially critical after the Dakota Access Pipeline protests of 2016 where police brutality and violence against Water Protectors followed the protests.[4]

Throughout the world, other IWS platforms shared a call for a new feminist internationalism, where women's issues were articulated as intersectional and heterogenous. These IWS platforms called for freedom from racism, colonialism, and labor exploitation and argued that these freedoms go hand in hand with liberation from gendered oppression. The strike then, strived to be more than a singular event, but a sustained movement and effort to disrupt other forms of violence.[5]

IWS in Spain and Latin America

This call resonated with Black feminists, who recognized the global nature of the crisis affecting women and rejected being victimized as part of it. Building off of centuries-long organizing traditions against imperialism, colonialism, racism, human rights violations, and sexism in Latin America (Laó-Montes 2016; Marino 2019), Black feminists articulated platforms and mobilized struggles that centered community autonomy and multiple forms of marginalization. The prominent Black feminist collective, Afroféminas, announced that they would join the 2017 strike in Spain, urging world governments to take immediate action to ensure women's well-being. Their demands emphasized immediate access to free healthcare, including reproductive rights, protection of the planet, a stop to domestic violence, and an establishment of serious legal sanctions for criminals in cases of rape, domestic violence, and other kinds of gendered crimes.[6] In Nicaragua, the Afrolatinamerican, Afro-Caribbean, and Diasporic Women's Network joined the call of "Not one less!" The call to end all forms of misogyny, femicide, and violence against women especially resonated amongst Black Nicaraguan women given the then-recent assassination of Vilma Trujillo, a young woman tortured and assassinated at the hands of a religious leader who claimed to be conducting an exorcism.[7] Organizations like La Via Campesina brought together peasant, indigenous women, and afro-descendant women in Honduras to march against gendered violence and corporate exploitation. Their call included a demand for reproductive justice, just agrarian land reform, and environmental protections given the recent death of Indigenous environmental activist Berta Caceres.[8] Across the Caribbean, Black feminist organizations created their own hashtag, #LifeinLeggings, to protest sexual violence, rape culture, and to overcome the myth that sexual harassment only occurs because of women's choice of dress. The hashtag united hundreds of women and emphasized women's autonomy, equal education for women, reproductive justice, LGBT rights, in addition to protesting all forms of violence against women. As in Nicaragua, Jamaican women like those in the radical organization Tambourine Army, also protested gendered violence in religious spaces.[9] Strike organizers managed to mobilize demonstrators in the Global North and the Global South while using discourse that recognized differences among women and called for solidarity across these differences (Çağatay 2023).

Demonstrators in over 50 countries echoed these calls for action, creating a transnational mobilization (Ni Una Menos 2018). In Spain, a general strike backed by unions mobilized more than 5 million to engage in work stoppages, garnering widespread support according to public opinion polls, with one poll estimating strike support at 83%, becoming the movement with the highest mobilization capacity in Spain (Portos 2019).[10] In the US, more than 60 demonstrations mobilized thousands.[11] In Brazil, the 2017 IWS brought hundreds of protestors out. Demonstrators called for the resignation of conservative president Michel Temer, notorious for taking office after the impeachment and removal of President Dilma Rousseff, his misogyny, reflected in his mostly male cabinet, and his initiatives cutting gender equality programs and ministries around racial, women, and human rights. In Nigeria, students and activists joined the international ONE campaign protesting disparities in women's education by staging walk-ins and a 5 km march. In Turkey, a politically diverse set of women's rights groups under the coalition "Women are Stronger Together" (KBG Coalition), mobilized over 10,000 demonstrators in Istanbul to march in protest of violence against women.[12] The march also included men and women from labor unions, student groups, and LGBT groups (Çağatay 2023). IWS showed promise of becoming a popular vehicle for social change that mobilized the type of alliances that many recognized were needed to transform intersecting systems of oppression.

For instance, Arruzza, Bhattacharya, and Fraser (2019) feminist manifesto (Feminism for the 99%), inspired by the IWS for which they organized, calls for broad-based alliances that take differences seriously in efforts to build transformative mass mobilization:

> ...the differences, inequalities, and hierarchies that inhere in capitalist social relations do give rise to conflicts of interest among the oppressed and exploited. And by itself, the proliferation of fragmentary struggles will not give birth to the sort of robust, broad-based alliances needed to transform society. However, such alliances will become utterly impossible if we fail to take our differences seriously.

Similarly, Taylor (2017) recognizes the need for a "much bigger movement to win." Emejulu (2017), however, raised concerns about the use of populist politics in efforts to build broad mobilization under the Feminism for the 99% banner. In Emejulu's view, Feminism for the 99% sought to combine populist and feminist approaches to building transnational solidarity for gender and racial justice. Yet, populism's long standing reliance on homogeneity as a motivation for broad mobilization stands in contrast to the recognition and negotiation of differences that intersectional feminist politics seek to place at the center of efforts to build movements that avoid neglecting the issues of multiply marginalized groups. The promise of Feminism for the 99% as a new form of populist and feminist politics, Emejulu (2017) argues, is its effort to build a majority consisting of the dispossessed and multiply marginalized. Çağatay (2023) observes that IWS enact solidarity amongst multiply marginalized groups in three ways: through coalitions across political identities, linking struggles across scales (from local to global), and by expanding the traditional reach and subject of disruptive tactics and labor solidarity.

Scholars and activists calling for intersectional approaches to building solidarity found promise in broad-based mobilizations like the International Women's Strike, which sought to center intersecting issues of oppressed multitudes and ground itself in grassroots mobilization. Yet, calls for mobilization and platforms paid less attention to the means that would enable such alliances and sustain a movement that draws support from, addresses the issues of, and mobilizes different multiply marginalized social groups. While some deploy notions of shared experiences under authoritarianism and capitalist exploitation to motivate mobilization, emphasizing commonalities while discursively recognizing differences did not sustain mobilization of the magnitude of 2017. In the following

Challenges of enacting intersectional solidarity

The 2017 IWS was notable for its attempts to bridge distinct struggles under the broader umbrella of a feminist labor strike. Drawing support from some labor unions, women's organizations, and collectives, the strike brought hundreds of thousands of women to the streets in protest and millions to strike. In Spain, the 2017 IWS consisted of a coalition of over 400 groups, which made up the 8 M (8th of March) Commission. The 8 M Commission: "As part of a lengthy preparatory process," so the sentence reads "As part of a lengthy preparatory process, the 8M Commission sought to organize women across distinct struggles under the themes of the rejection of gendered violence and discrimination in the workplace, rejection of neoliberal policies and anti-LGBT legislation, a call to legal access to abortion, and a protest of the feminization of poverty, amongst other causes (Campillo 2019).[13] The 8 M Commission released a Manifesto outlining the IWS's demands (Sandu and Fernández 2021). The IWS encompassed diverse sets of issues under the banner of, "We, the women of the world..." It was an opportunity for multiply marginalized women to come together and join against intersecting structures of oppression. The IWS was seen as evolving from a 4th wave tradition of feminist practice based in social group difference and an intersectional analysis of how gendered issues are compounded by other systems of power, such as colonialism, neoliberalism, racism, class, nationalism, among others.

Initially, various Black feminist organizations, joined the strike given the initial intersectional frameworks of the Commission. However, in practice, multiply marginalized participants of the 8 M commission and IWS took issue with what Sandu and Fernandez (2021) describe as a "sisterhood solidarity" approach that subsumed the unique concerns of Black, racialized, and immigrant women under a hegemonic category of "women." In this approach, issues of gender violence, gendered workplace harassment and discrimination, and queer issues were posed mostly in relation to White middle-class women and without referencing how marginalized women experience these issues in compounding fashion. These issues were further compounded by experiences of exclusion of Black women organizers in broader women's movement organizing spaces and exhaustion stemming from their unsuccessful attempts to move dominant subgroups to center the struggles of multiply marginalized groups.[14]

The discontent with the 8 M's insufficient focus on minority women was only exacerbated by the Spanish and international media's refusal to cover non-White middle-class women's issues because they were deemed outside of the feminist movement and too complex for audiences (Sandu and Fernandez 2021; Fernandez 2018). Sandu and Fernández (2021) note that by using a master frame of "women " and "sisterhood" for the Strike, the 8 M Commission took an additive instead of an intersectional approach. The collective identity of "women" was assumed to stem from a central shared experience, primary to all other experiences of oppression even along the lines of race, class, and disability. The experiences of Black, immigrant, trans, disabled, and working-class women within the 8 M strike therefore lacked visibility. Further, the 8 M Strike missed an opportunity to demonstrate how issues of gendered violence and gendered oppression are connected and deeply interrelated with other systems of oppression.

By 2018, AfroFéminas released a statement announcing that they would not join the 2018 IWS. Stating, "We believe that our decision is the only possible decision we could make as Black and racialized women in this country [Spain]," Afrofeminas cited the lack of representation and "complete invisibilization" of Black women in the movement, in addition to the lack of media coverage and prioritization to the issues of racial inequality as a feminist issue (Afrofeminas 2018). Other groups emphasized these claims. Spanish minority feminist groups such as Afroféminas, Spanish Roma Serseni, Black Feminist Association EFAE, and Gitanas Feministas por la Diversidad, were left to do the bulk of the bridge-building work within the 8 M Commission to bring critical awareness to issues of racialized gender discrimination and violence against immigrant agricultural and domestic laborers (Sandu and Fernández 2021).

Interactions with groups who withdrew their participation focused on asking for explanations for their withdrawal, instead of engagement in inclusive deliberative processes aimed at reshaping movement praxis in light of these discussions.[15] These interactions stemmed from the expectation among dominant subgroups that those withdrawing had a duty to explain themselves. Black women who opted to withdraw assumed a burden of explaining their exclusion through constant media inquiries, social media exchanges, and private communications. Black women organizers did not perceive that these requests for explanations for their withdrawal were genuine, particularly after their explanations were met with responses that attempted to dissipate concern by pointing to the existence of a committee that dealt with the issues of immigration and racism. Instead, these responses were deemed to be instances of tokenization.[16]

Discussion

The 2017 IWS and the instances of mobilization that preceded it demonstrated the possibility of mobilizing broad-based demonstrations across social group differences and national contexts. Yet, by 2019, these mobilization efforts had significantly diminished in magnitude and geographical reach. Various multiply marginalized groups had abstained from rejoining the strike while others publicly announced a rupture with IWS groups. Here we seek to make sense of this rupture in light of notions of intersectional solidarity. If intersectional solidarity refers to an ongoing process of creating ties and coalition across social differences by negotiating power asymmetries, we ask: what does this negotiation of power asymmetries look like in this context? What happens when negotiations do not take place or when parties to these negotiations do not agree with the process and how it shapes movement praxis? Intersectionality can be a critical lens that helps us understand the differences between social groups in relation to structures of power and how these differences shape organizing structures, discourses, agendas, and social movement politics more generally. The ways in which organizers approach negotiations of difference can shape the extent to which building and sustaining coalitions is possible. How organizers issue, treat, and reject or embrace criticism can shape the course of negotiations of difference and whether those who hold the power reshape power asymmetries in movements.

Organizers come into mobilization having developed consciousness that may align with distinct intellectual and activist traditions. In the case of Spain's IWS, Afroféminas collective Antoinette Torres emphasizes that Black feminism has its own history, rooted in racial and anti-colonial struggle, a parallel history that is separate from the White feminism portrayed by the strike. In Torres' view, these differences aided the lack of representation and visibility of Black women in the movement and the failure to prioritize the issues of multiply marginalized groups beyond the discourses deployed to mobilize them.[17] Afroféminas's experience in IWS organizing spaces shaped their decision to withdraw from 8 M coalitional work in 2018. These accounts of the experience of Afroféminas in Spain's IWS signal the need for movements to adopt intersectional forms of solidarity in their praxis, and that recognizing intersecting forms of marginalization in platforms might ignite mobilization but is not a sufficient condition to sustain it.

8 M organizer June Montero responded to Afroféminas withdrawal and argued that it did not signal the 2018 strike's failure. Rather, she argued:

> The strike's proposals were clear–that all women would have a voice and that they could participate in one form or another. In respect to whether all women felt included, I think that racialized women did a lot of voice; in fact, inside of the 8 M Commission exists the Comission of Migration and Antiracism, which was also very active during the entire process and participated from the core of the 8 M Commission. Thanks to this we are all part of the process, and there are no borders, like last year. Instead, the perspective of racialized women and the fight against racism is transversal. At the start of the Commision, the first action of the week was a feminist protest against the CIE Aluche. (Madrid's Immigrant Detention center)

Yet, the presence of a committee on migration and against racism was not enough to signal a broader commitment to anti-racism and immigration justice. Sandu and Fernández (2021) point to the work that minority feminist groups such as Afrofeminas, Black Feminist Association EFAE, Roma Serseni, Gitanas Feminstas por la Diversidad did to bring awareness to issues of gender discrimination and violence against immigrant agricultural and domestic laborers within the 8 M Commission, reproducing dynamics whereby bridge-building and intersectional consciousness raising work predominantly falls on women of color who are not made visible and substantively represented in movement leadership.

Media portrayals of the strike also posed challenges for negotiations among different social groups. June Fernández recalls that media reports ignored demands specifically calling to address issues of multiply marginalized groups.[18] Media portrayals of IWS tended to ignore trans issues, issues at the intersection of gender and race, and colonialism, among other issues for which outlets used their discretion and power to determine what would be too "difficult" for popular audiences. In doing so, IWS faced obstructions to its efforts to popularize an intersectional agenda for justice and shift public consciousness about intersecting forms of oppression. In turn, these obstructions shaped the extent to which IWS and its coalition partners were able to represent and advance the demands of multiply marginalized groups publicly.

Ultimately, these challenges led to an "us vs them" dynamic within the organizing 8 M Commission. Autonomous organizing spaces are not antithetical to intersectional solidarity. Rather, many argue that autonomous organizing spaces help engender forms of oppositional "double consciousness" or "mestiza consciousness" for marginalized groups (Mansbridge 2001; Martinez 2002). Oppositional consciousness allows marginalized groups to articulate the dynamics of their oppression and mobilize broader coalitions to stand in solidarity with their struggle (Weldon 2006a). Marginalized groups or "internal minorities" within movements have found effective ways to push for prioritizing their demands within movements through autonomous organizing (Ferree and Ewig 2013 Weldon 2006a, 2011). Autonomous spaces for organizing allow multiply marginalized groups to create counter-publics where they can develop counter-hegemonic ideas and strategize ways to advance their claims within and beyond movement and coalitional spaces.[19] Autonomous organizing allows multiply marginalized groups to speak for and represent themselves, thus enhancing the standing that anti-oppressive movements have as representatives of those they claim to advocate for. Non-additive historical perspectives that decenter white women's organizing reveal autonomous organizing spaces to be critical components of building intersectional feminist movements (Blackwell 2011).

Autonomous organizing need not entail a complete rupture from broader movement bodies. Activists and intellectuals working within Black feminist traditions have simultaneously organized autonomously while calling on broader movements to enact solidarity with multiply marginalized groups (Combahee River Collective [1977] 1995). Transnational feminist organizing had successfully adopted autonomous organizing of multiply marginalized groups as a norm of inclusion, enabling their enhanced political impact on the adoption of the United Nations Convention on the Elimination of All Forms of Discrimination Against Women (Weldon 2006a). Yet, transnational feminist organizing had often struggled with tensions in its efforts to sustain solidarity across groups (Weldon 2006a), including but not limited to in Latin American human rights organizing (Marino 2019). These experiences signal the non-linear dynamics of enacting and sustaining intersectional solidarity.

Afroféminas founder Antoinette Torres recalls how Black feminist traditions informed their decision to withhold their labor from 8 M organizing, recognizing its "history, rooted in racial and colonial struggle, a parallel history that is separate from the White feminism portrayed by the strike. That is why Black women decided to go their own way for 8 M 2018."[20] For Blakey, Machen, Ruez, and Montoya and Seminario (2022), Afrofeminas' decision to break from the strike demonstrates the political enmeshment of subjectivities. Afrofeminas rupture from the 8 m Commission built off of a long history of Black feminist resistance to systems of oppression and white supremacy. Critique and disruption challenge eurocentric hegemonic assumptions of a White middle class feminist norm, and was a way of negotiating differences of power across spheres of political life.

We theorize that rupture, such as the one observed among Afroféminas and 8 M, can be an act of intersectional solidarity insofar as it is an instance of the processes of negotiating power asymmetries intended to insist on the need to recognize the issues of multiply marginalized groups, represent them in movement leadership, prioritize their issues in movement agendas and actions (not just mission statements), and allocate support for the labor of multiply marginalized groups. Çağatay (2023) observes similar dynamics in IWS organizing in Turkey, where "inclusive agendas were easier to maintain than inclusive organizing on the ground."

Afroféminas did not signal a complete rupture and unwillingness to engage in future coalitional work. Rather, as Yania Concepción of Afroféminas argues, the separation from the strike after being invisibilized is not an act of isolation. Concepción affirmed the possibility of forming alliances and joining future struggles.[21] Yet, the conditions for sustaining the bridging, intersectional consciousness-raising, and intersectional praxis labor of Black women had not been generated. This case suggests that the degree of organizing autonomy can shape the progress of negotiations of power differences. Further, the presence of committees and caucuses focused on the issues of multiply marginalized groups may not be enough to build oppositional consciousness if they are not sufficiently autonomous from dominant subgroups.

The imminent and recurrent nature of an annual strike posed yet another challenge for organizing. The recurrent character of an annual strike created pressures and reminders to consider whether the dialectical relationship between intersectional consciousness and praxis had advanced sufficiently to merit renovating activist commitments to the tactic and movement leadership. Upon reconsideration of the political goals that IWS advanced, groups like Afroféminas determined that the coalitional approach to advancing Black women's struggles was not effective. Disruptive tactics can create a kind of binary whereby supporting the strike becomes a choice. The imminence and recurrence of this decision can limit the time and space that movements might need to engage in the complex dynamics of intersectional coalition building and solidarity.

Conclusion

Coalitions and alliances are strategic, and in this case, militant. Their creation need not to emerge from opportune contexts. IWS organizing emerged forcefully in spite of a hostile political climate. Complete agreement on all issues and movement agenda priorities among activists is not a precondition of coalition-building, and yet, experiences of disagreement in praxis can be indicative of the possibility of collaborating to advance shared political objectives.

Those who withdrew publicly from IWS no longer saw in IWS a praxis that informed and was informed by intersectional consciousness. This withdrawal is not a refusal to be in solidarity, but a rejection of being in coalition and participating in a particular action because Afroféminas did not see themselves reflected in the movement's priorities, and instead, saw themselves excluded. Further, activists raised concern about experiencing violence in coalitional work, where their identity as political subjects was being compromised. Black feminist organizers did not conceptualize their withdrawal from IWS as a call to retreat from organizing, but rather, an investment in the Black political consciousness and power.

Withdrawing Black women's labor within movements that fail to enact intersectional praxis while claiming to prioritize their issues has been used as a tactic to pressure more privileged subgroups throughout negotiations of power differences. In doing so, multiply marginalized groups can withdraw consent to be represented by a movement's leadership and erode the public standing that anti-oppressive struggles seek in efforts to bring about social change. This withdrawal and rupture, however, have important implications for the public standing of the movement and its prospects for political influence and social change.

Intersectional solidarity is not a linear process that inevitably leads to progress, whereby there is a problem, theory is applied, intersectional consciousness becomes commonly accepted, praxis is adjusted accordingly, and movements achieve unity in diversity. Because intersectional solidarity is rooted in a commitment to critiquing interlocking systems of power (Collins 2015), intersectional solidarity must act as a kind of synthesis whereby intersectional consciousness continuously informs and is informed by the praxis of a movement. There are instances in which calls to unity, even when issued in good faith, can still result in exclusions. The experiences of multiply marginalized groups with IWS's praxis informed a kind of oppositional consciousness over the limited and essentialist notion of the subject of "woman" in the movement. This oppositional consciousness, in turn, informs a distinct praxis.

Afroféminas's praxis of intersectional solidarity meant negotiating unequal power through generating rupture. The rupture informs the continuity and deepening of intersectional consciousness but limits the magnitude of the IWS's praxis (i.e., Afroféminas no longer informs the broader praxis that generates disruptive tactics and mobilizes larger masses). In doing so, this rupture also has consequences for the praxis that persists among those whose limited notion of subjectivity persists. For instance, the absence of Afroféminas and the public critique raises questions about the representativeness (authority that a movement has to make claims on behalf of various groups) of the broader movement, the IWS. What could have been a broad intersectional struggle turns into an intersectional consciousness without praxis and a praxis without intersectional consciousness.

Notes

1. https://www.washingtonpost.com/news/monkey-cage/wp/2017/02/07/this-is-what-we-learned-by-counting-the-womens-marches/
2. The other two guiding principles that Çağatay (2023) identifies are an acknowledgment of the systemic dynamics of oppression that lead to the deterioration of women's lives globally and a broad definition of labor that highlights the value of women's work in all spheres of life.
3. Arruzza (2016), Arruzza, Bhattacharya, and Fraser (2019), and Bhattacharya (2017) are among the best known articulations of this perspective.
4. https://www.facebook.com/profile/100068253660802/search/?q=platform
5. https://read.dukeupress.edu/critical-times/article/1/1/268/139321/Call-to-the-International-Women-s-Strike-March-8
6. https://afrofeminas.com/2017/03/08/paro-internacional-de-mujeres/
7. https://themis.org.br/red-afro-nicaragua-se-pronuncia-ante-femicidios-y-violencia-de-genero/
8. https://viacampesina.org/es/honduras-las-mujeres-hondurenas-tambien-paramos/
9. https://www.stabroeknews.com/2017/03/13/features/in-the-diaspora/international-womens-day-caribbean-marching-solidarity-lifeinleggings-end-violence-women-girls/;
    https://www.theguardian.com/world/2017/mar/10/jamaica-caribbean-tambourine-army-sexual-violence
    https://lifeinleggings.org/about-us/origin-story/
10. https://english.elpais.com/elpais/2018/03/08/inenglish/1520498047_423763.html
11. https://docs.google.com/spreadsheets/d/1Cq-9bGjHBkoaqkLr9IwxKD8O8gtOcorlTdRkRThRl6o/edit#gid=1527464273
12. https://www.theguardian.com/world/live/2017/mar/08/international-womens-day-2017-protests-activism-strike-live
13. https://www.jacobinmag.com/2018/09/argentinas-anticapitalist-feminism
14. Interview with author 5/6/23.
15. Interview with author 5/6/23.
16. Interview with author 5/6/23.
17. https://www.eldiario.es/desalambre/feminismo-mujer-racializada-afrofeminas_1_2236855.html
18. https://www.pikaramagazine.com/2018/05/del-espejismo-de-la-igualdad-al-desbordamiento-de-la-huelga-feminista/
19. See Fraser (1992) and Young (2000) on the importance of counter publics.
20. https://www.eldiario.es/desalambre/feminismo-mujer-racializada-afrofeminas_1_2236855.html
21. https://www.briega.org/es/entrevistas/entrevista-a-yania-concepcion-feminismo-blanco-lo-ha-centralizado-como-si-todo-hubiera

Acknowledgement

APC charges for this article were fully paid by the University Library System, University of Pittsburgh

Disclosure statement

No potential conflict of interest was reported by the author(s).

References

Adam, Erin. 2017. "Intersectional Coalitions: The Paradoxes of Rights-Based Movement Building in LGBTQ and Immigrant Communities." *Law & Society Review* 51 (1):132–67. doi:10.1111/lasr.12248.

AfroFeminas. 2018. "Por qué Afrofeminas no se une a la huelga feminista." March 5. https://afrofeminas.com/2018/03/05/porque-afrofeminas-no-se-suma-a-la-huelga-feminista/

Alexander-Floyd, Nikol G. 2012. "Disappearing Acts: Reclaiming Intersectionality in the Social Sciences in a Post-Black Feminist Era." *Feminist Formations* 24 (1):1–25. doi:10.1353/ff.2012.0003.

Arruzza, Cinzia. 2016. "Functionalist, Determinist, Reductionist: Social Reproduction Feminism and Its Critics." *Science & Society* 80 (1):9–30. doi:10.1521/siso.2016.80.1.9.

Arruzza, Cinzia, Tithi Bhattacharya, and Nancy Fraser. 2019. *Feminism for the 99 Percent: A Manifesto*. Brooklyn, NY: Verso.

Bartley, Tim. 2007. "Institutional Emergence in an Era of Globalization: The Rise of Transnational Private Regulation of Labor and Environmental Conditions." *American Journal of Sociology* 113 (2):297–351. doi:10.1086/518871.

Beaman, Jean, and Nadia, Brown. 2019. "Sistas Doing It for Themselves: Black Women's Activism and #blacklivesmatter in the United States and France." In *Gendered Mobilizations and Intersectional Challenges: Contemporary Social Movements in Europe and North America*, eds. Jill Irvine, Sabine Lang, and Celeste Montoya. London: Rowman & Littlefield, 226–43.

Behl, Natasha. 2017. "Diasporic Researcher: An Autoethnographic Analysis of Gender and Race in Political Science." *Politics, Groups & Identities* 5 (4):580–98. doi:10.1080/21565503.2016.1141104.

Bhattacharya, Tithi, ed. 2017. *Social Reproduction Theory: Remapping Class, Recentering Oppression*. London: Pluto Press.

Blackwell, Maylei. 2011. *Chicana Power!: Contested Histories of Feminism in the Chicano Movement*. Austin, TX: University of Texas Press. doi:10.7560/725881.

Burnier, DeLysia. 2006. "Encounters with the Self in Social Science Research: A Political Scientist Looks at Autoethnography." *Journal of Contemporary Ethnography* 35 (4):410–18. doi:10.1177/0891241606286982.

Çağatay, Selin. 2023. "If Women Stop, the World Stops": Forging Transnational Solidarities with the International Women's Strike. *International Feminist Journal of Politics*. doi: 10.1080/14616742.2023.2170259.

Carothers, Thomas. 2016. "Closing Space for International Democracy and Human Rights Support." *Journal of Human Rights Practice* 8 (3):358–77. doi:10.1093/jhuman/huw012.

Cho, Sumi, Kimberlé W. Crenshaw, and Lesie McCall. 2013. "Toward a Field of Intersectionality Studies: Theory, Applications, and Praxis." *Signs* 38 (4):785–810. doi:10.1086/669608.

Chun, Jennifer Jihye, George Lipsitz, and Young Shin. 2013. "Intersectionality as a Social Movement Strategy: Asian Immigrant Women Advocates." *Signs: Journal of Women in Culture & Society* 38 (4):917–40. doi:10.1086/669575.

Cohen, Cathy J. 1999a. *The Boundaries of Blackness: AIDS and the Breakdown of Black Politics*. Chicago: University of Chicago Press.

Cohen, Cathy J. 1999b. "What is This Movement Doing to My Politics?" *Social Text* 61: 111–18.

Cole, Elizabeth R. 2008. "Coalitions as a Model for Intersectionality: From Practice to Theory." *Sex Roles* 59 (5–6):443–53. doi:10.1007/s11199-008-9419-1.

Collins, Patricia Hill. 1990. *Black Feminist Thought: Knowledge, Consciousness, and the Politics of Empowerment*. Boston, MA: Unwin Hyman.

Collins, Patricia Hill. 2015. "Intersectionality's Definitional Dilemmas." *Annual Review of Sociology* 41 (1):1–20. doi:10.1146/annurev-soc-073014-112142.

Collins, Patricia H., and Valerie Chepp. 2013. "Intersectionality." In *Oxford Handbook of Gender and Politics*, eds. Georgina Waylen, Karen Celis, Johanna Kantola, and S. Laurel Weldon. New York: Oxford University Press, 57–87.

Combahee River Collective. [1977] 1995. "Combahee River Collective: A Black Feminist Statement." In *Words of Fire: An Anthology of African American Feminist Thought*, ed. Beverly Guy-Sheftall. New York: New Press, 232–40.

Crenshaw, Kimberlé W. 1989. "Demarginalizing the Intersection of Race and Sex: A Black Feminist Critique of Antidiscrimination Doctrine, Feminist Theory and Antiracist Politics." *University of Chicago Legal Forum* 8:139–67.

Curtin, Nicola, Abigail J. Stewart, and Elizabeth R. Cole. 2015. "Challenging the Status Quo: The Role of Intersectional Awareness in Activism for Social Change and Pro-Social Intergroup Attitudes." *Psychology of Women Quarterly* 39 (4):512–29. doi:10.1177/0361684315580439.

Daniel, Meghan, and Cedric de Leon. 2020. "Leadership Succession in Intersectional Mobilization: An Analysis of the Chicago Abortion Fund, 1985–2015." *Mobilization: An International Quarterly* 25 (4):461–74. doi:10.17813/1086-671X-22-4-461.

Dhamoon, Rita Kaur. 2011. "Considerations on Mainstreaming Intersectionality." *Political Research Quarterly* 64 (1): 230–43.

Einwohner, Rachel L., Kaitlin Kelly-Thompson, Valeria Sinclair-Chapman, Fernando Tormos-Aponte, S. Laurel Weldon, Jared M. Wright, and Charles Wu. 2021. "Active Solidarity: Intersectional Solidarity in Action." *Social Politics: International Studies in Gender, State and Society* 28 (3):704–29. doi:10.1093/sp/jxz052.

Elliott, Thomas, Earl Jennifer, and V. Maher Thomas. 2007. "Recruiting Inclusiveness: Intersectionality, Social Movements, and Youth Online." In *Non-State Violent Actors and Social Movement Organizations*, ed. Julie M. Mazzei. Bingley, UK: Emerald Publishing Limited, 279–312. doi:10.1108/S0163-786X20170000041019.

Emejulu, Akwugo. 2017. "Feminism for the 99%: towards a populist feminism?: Can Feminism for the 99% succeed as a new kind of populism?." *Soundings: A Journal of Politics and Culture* 66: 63–67.

Fernandez, June. 2018. "Del espejismo de la igualdad al desbordamiento de la huelga feminista. *Pikara Magazine*." *Pikara Magazine*, May 18. https://www.pikaramagazine.com/2018/05/del-espejismo-de-la-igualdad-al-desbordamiento-de-la-huelga-feminista/

Ferree, Myra Marx, and Christina Ewig. 2013. "Global Feminist Organising: Identifying Patterns of Activism." In *The Women's Movement in Protest, Institutions and the Internet: Australia in Transnational Perspective*, eds. Sarah Maddison and Marian Sawer. New York: Routledge, 148–62.

Fisher, Dana R. 2019. *American Resistance: From the Women's March to the Blue Wave*. New York: Columbia University Press.

Fisher, Dana R., Dawn M. Dow, and Rashawn Ray. 2017. "Intersectionality Takes It to the Streets: Mobilizing Across Diverse Interests for the Women's March." *Science Advances* 3 (9):eaao1390. doi:10.1126/sciadv.aao1390.

Fisher, Dana R., Lorien Jasny, and Dawn M. Dow. 2018. "Why are we here? Patterns of intersectional motivations across the resistance." *Mobilization: An International Quarterly* 23 (4): 451–68.

Fraser, Nancy. 1992. "Rethinking the Public Sphere: A Contribution to the Critique of Actually Existing." *Social Text* 25 (25/26):56–80. doi:10.2307/466240.

Gawerc, Michelle I. 2021. "Coalition-Building and the Forging of Solidarity Across Difference and Inequality." *Sociology Compass* 15 (3):e12858. doi:10.1111/soc4.12858.

Greenwood, Ronni Michelle. 2008. "Intersectional Political Consciousness: Appreciation for Intragroup Differences and Solidarity in Diverse Groups." *Psychology of Women Quarterly* 32 (1):36–47. doi:10.1111/j.1471-6402.2007.00405.x.

Hancock, Ange-Marie. 2007. "When Multiplication Doesn't Equal Quick Addition: Examining Intersectionality as a Research Paradigm." *Perspectives on Politics* 5 (1):63–79. doi:10.1017/S1537592707070065.

Hancock, Ange-Marie. 2011. *Solidarity Politics for Millennials: A Guide to Ending the Oppression Olympics*. New York: Palgrave Macmillan.

Heaney, Michael T. 2021. "Intersectionality at the Grassroots." *Politics, Groups & Identities* 9 (3):608–28. doi:10.1080/21565503.2019.1629318.

hooks, bell. 1981. *Ain't I A Woman: Black Women and Feminism*. Boston: South End Press.

Inés Campillo. 2019. 'If we stop, the world stops': the 2018 feminist strike in Spain. *Social movement studies*. 18 (2): 252–58. doi:10.1080/14742837.2018.1556092.

Irvine, Jill, Sabine Lang, and Celeste Montoya. 2019. *Gendered Mobilizations and Intersectional Challenges : Contemporary Social Movements in Europe and North America*. Lanham, MD: Rowman & Littlefield.

irvine, Jill, Lang Sabine, and Montoya Celeste. 2019. "Introduction: Gendered Mobilizations and Intersectional Challenges." In *Gendered Mobilizations and Intersectional Challenges: Contemporary Social Movements in Europe and North America*, eds. Jill Irvine, Sabine Lang, and Celeste Montoya. Lanham, MD: Rowman & Littlefield, 1–22.

Earl, Jennifer, Thomas V. Maher, and Thomas Elliott. 2017. "Youth, activism, and social movements." *Sociology Compass* 11 (4): e12465.

Kay, Tamara. 2005. "Labor Transnationalism and Global Governance: The Impact of NAFTA on Transnational Labor Relationships in North America." *American Journal of Sociology* 111 (3):715–56. doi:10.1086/497305.

Laó-Montes, Agustín. 2016. "Afro-Latin American Feminisms at the Cutting Edge of Emerging Political-Epistemic Movements." *Meridians* 14 (2):1–24. doi:10.2979/meridians.14.2.02.

Laperrière, Marie, and Eléonore Lépinard. 2016. "Intersectionality as a Tool for Social Movements: Strategies of Inclusion and Representation in the Québécois Women's Movement." *Politics* 36 (4):374–82. doi:10.1177/0263395716649009.

Liu, Callie Watkins. 2017. "The Anti-Oppressive Value of Critical Race Theory and Intersectionality in Social Movement Study." *Sociology of Race & Ethnicity* 4 (3):1–16. doi:10.1177/2332649217743771.

Luna, Zakiya. 2016. "'Truly a Women of Color Organization': Negotiating Sameness and Difference in Pursuit of Intersectionality." *Gender & Society* 30 (5):769–90. doi:10.1177/0891243216649929.

Mansbridge, Jane. 2001. "The Making of Oppositional Consciousness." In *Oppositional Consciousness: The Subjective Roots of Social Protest*, eds. Jane Mansbridge and Aldon Morris. Chicago: University of Chicago Press, 1–19. doi:10.7208/chicago/9780226225784.001.0001.

Marino, Katherine M. 2019. *Feminism for the Americas the Making of an International Human Rights Movement.* Chapel Hill, NC: The University of North Carolina Press. doi:10.5149/northcarolina/9781469649696.001.0001.

Martinez, Theresa A. 2002. "The Double-Consciousness of Du Bois & the Mestiza Consciousness of Anzaldua." *Race, Gender & Class* 9 (4): 158–76.

Montoya, Celeste, and Mariana Galvez Seminario. 2022. "Guerreras Y Puentes: The Theory and Praxis of Latina(x) Activism." *Politics, Groups & Identities* 10 (2):171–88. doi:10.1080/21565503.2020.1821233.

Moraga, Cherrie, and Gloria Anzaldua. 1983. *This Bridge Called My Back : Writings by Radical Women of Color.* 2nd ed. New York: Kitchen Table, Women of Color Press.

O'Neill, Kate. 2004. "Transnational Protest: States, Circuses, and Conflict at the Frontline of Global Politics." *International Studies Review* 6 (2):233–51. doi:10.1111/j.1521-9488.2004.00397.x.

Portos, Martin. 2019. "Divided We Stand, (Oftentimes) United We Fight: Generational Bridging in Spain'S Feminist Movement and the Cycle of Antiausterity Mobilizations." *The American behavioral scientist.* Accessed September 4. doi:10.1177/0002764219831730.

Rick, Fantasia. 1988. *Cultures of Solidarity: Consciousness, Action, and Contemporary American Workers.* Oakland: University of California Press. doi:10.1525/9780520909670.

Roberts, Dorothy, and Sujatha Jesudason. 2013. "Movement Intersectionality: The Case of Race, Gender, Disability, and Genetic Technologies." *Du Bois Review: Social Science Research on Race* 10 (2):313–28. doi:10.1017/S1742058X13000210.

Robnett, Belinda. 1996. "African-American Women in the Civil Rights Movement, 1954-1965: Gender, Leadership, and Micromobilization." *American Journal of Sociology* 101 (6):1661–93. doi:10.1086/230870.

Roth, Silke. 2021. "Intersectionality and Coalitions in Social Movement Research—A Survey and Outlook." *Sociological Compass* 15 (7):e12885. doi:10.1111/soc4.12885.

Sandu, Adriana, and Victoria Pérez Fernández. 2021. "The Fight Goes On! Intersections of Oppression in the Spanish Feminist Movement." *Journal of International Women's Studies* 22 (9): 207–21.

Simmons, Beth A. 2009. *Mobilizing for human rights: international law in domestic politics.* Cambridge University Press.

Smooth, Wendy, and Tamelyn Tucker. 1999. "Behind but Not Forgotten: Women and the Behind-The-Scenes Organizing of the Million Man March." In *Still Lifting, Still Climbing*, ed. Kimberly Springer. New York: New York University Press, 241–58. doi:10.18574/nyu/9780814786802.003.0019.

Strolovitch, Dara. 2007. *Affirmative Advocacy: Race, Class, and Gender in Interest Group Politics.* Chicago: University of Chicago Press.

Taylor, Keeanga-Yamahtta, ed. 2017. *How we get free: Black feminism and the Combahee River Collective.* Haymarket Books.

Terriquez, Veronica. 2015. "Intersectional Mobilization, Social Movement Spillover, and Queer Youth Leadership in the Immigrant Rights Movement." *Social Problems* 62 (3):343–62. doi:10.1093/socpro/spv010.

Tormos, Fernando. 2017. "Intersectional Solidarity." *Politics, Groups & Identities* 5 (4):707–20. doi:10.1080/21565503.2017.1385494.

Tormos-Aponte, Fernando. 2019. "Enacting Intersectional Solidarity in the Puerto Rican Student Movement." In *Gendered Mobilizations and Intersectional Challenges: Contemporary Social Movements in Europe and North America*, eds. Jill Irvine, Sabine Lang, and Celeste Montoya. Lanham, MD: Rowman & Littlefield, 171–88.

Tormos-Aponte, Fernando, and Shariana Ferrer-Núñez. 2020. "Intersectional Synthesis: A Case Study of the Colectiva Feminista En Construcción." In *Latinas and the Politics of Urban Spaces*, eds. Sharon Navarro and Lilliana Saldaña. New York: Routledge, 53–66. doi:10.4324/9781003128649-4.

Townsend-Bell, Erica. 2011. "What is Relevance? Defining Intersectional Praxis in Uruguay." *Political Research Quarterly* 64 (1):187–99. doi:10.1177/1065912910382301.

Tungohan, Ethel. 2016. "Intersectionality and Social Justice: Assessing Activists' Use of Intersectionality Through Grassroots Migrants' Organizations in Canada." *Politics, Groups & Identities* 4 (3):347–62. doi:10.1080/21565503.2015.1064006.

Tungohan, Ethel. 2019. "Equality and Recognition or Transformation and Dissent? Intersectionality and the Filipino Migrants' Movement in Canada." In *Gendered Mobilizations and Intersectional Challenges: Contemporary Social Movements in Europe and North America*, eds. Jill Irvine, Sabine Lang, and Celeste Montoya. Lanham, MD: Rowman & Littlefield, 208–25.

Una Menos, Ni. 2018. "Call to the International Women's Strike – March 8, 2018." *Critical Times* 1 (1):268–69. doi:10.1215/26410478-1.1.268.

Verloo, Mieke. 2013. "Intersectional and Cross-Movement Politics and Policies: Reflections on Current Practices and Debates." *Signs: A Journal of Women in Culture and Society* 38 (4):893–915. doi:10.1086/669572.

Von Bülow, Marisa. 2010. *Building Transnational Networks Civil Society and the Politics of Trade in the Americas*. Series: Cambridge Studies in Contentious Politics. New York: Cambridge University Press. doi:10.1017/CBO9780511761171.

Weldon, S. Laurel. 2006a. "Inclusion, Solidarity, and Social Movements: The Global Movement Against Gender Violence." *Perspective on Politics* 4 (1):55–74. doi:10.1017/S1537592706060063.

Weldon, S. Laurel. 2006b. "The Structure of Intersectionality: A Comparative Politics of Gender." *Politics & Gender* 2 (2):235–48. doi:10.1017/S1743923X06231040.

Weldon, S. Laurel. 2011. *When Protest Makes Policy: How Social Movements Represent Disadvantaged Groups*. Ann Arbor, MI: University of Michigan Press.

Young, Iris Marion. 2000. *Inclusion and Democracy*. New York: Oxford University Press.

🔓 OPEN ACCESS

Confronting Anti-Muslim Racism and Islamism: An Intersectional Perspective on Muslim Women's Activism in Germany

Fatima El Sayed

ABSTRACT
This article explores how Muslim women's activism unfolds in the context of anti-Muslim racism and Islamism in contemporary Germany. In particular, it identifies both gendered forms of anti-Muslim racism and Islamism encountered by Muslim women's organizations and ways they respond to it. Drawing on theories of intersectionality and boundary making, this study identifies the most common strategies used to confront anti-Muslim racism and Islamism and their implications for intersectional boundary making. For this purpose, six expert interviews with representatives of major Muslim women's organizations were conducted and supplemented by data from internet research and participatory observation. Based on a Grounded Theory-inspired approach, the findings show that the responses of Muslim women's organizations to anti-Muslim racism and Islamism reconfigure group boundaries. They create more inclusive spaces in which boundary formations by religion, race, and ethnicity and gender are transcended.

Introduction

Pressures on Muslims in Germany have increased both on an individual level as well as on collective actors, such as mosque communities and Muslim organizations (Amiraux and Jonker 2006; Jonker 2006; Peucker 2019). While Islam and Muslims have been a contentious topic within public discourse in Germany for more than two decades (Cesari 2013), the spread of right-wing populism in recent years has sparked anti-Islamic sentiments all over Europe (Kaya and Tecmen 2019). Terrorist attacks carried out by Muslim radicals in several European countries and the US have sustained anti-Muslim attitudes and nourished the image of Muslims as a security threat (Cesari 2010). Consequently, suspicion toward Muslims and Muslim communities has grown and created a climate of mistrust and hostility (Ajala 2014). Despite repeated assertions by German politicians and state officials that they do not confuse Islamists with "ordinary" Muslims (Shooman and Spielhaus 2010), policy measures adopted within the framework of the war against terror have indiscriminately harmed Muslims as a whole (Monshipouri 2010). Several studies have indicated detrimental effects of counter-terrorism measures that put Muslims under general suspicion (Blakemore and Awan 2013; Kundnani 2014; Spalek 2012). Similarly, scholars have stressed the effects of anti-Muslim discourses on social cohesion within Western societies as they have contributed to an alienation and discrimination of Muslims and inhibited their active and equal participation in public, social, and political life (Peucker and Akbarzadeh 2014).

Simultaneously, Islamist actors have sought to spread their ideologies within Muslim communities and promote a uniform version of Islam. They have accused communities of blasphemy for not complying with

---

This is an Open Access article distributed under the terms of the Creative Commons Attribution-NonCommercial-NoDerivatives License (http://creativecommons.org/licenses/by-nc-nd/4.0/), which permits non-commercial re-use, distribution, and reproduction in any medium, provided the original work is properly cited, and is not altered, transformed, or built upon in any way. The terms on which this article has been published allow the posting of the Accepted Manuscript in a repository by the author(s) or with their consent.

this singular interpretation of Islam (Akbarzadeh 2020; Ceylan and Kiefer 2018). In some instances, Islamist groups have actively recruited individuals for their political purposes and have instigated them to commit violent acts (Abou Taam et al. 2016).

A recurring trope that has been used both within anti-Muslim discourse and Islamist rhetoric is the image of the powerless and submissive Muslim woman. While Islamists abide by strict gender norms that disadvantage women and promote patriarchal interpretations of Islam, public debates about Islam and Muslims in Europe reinforce gendered/intersectional Islamophobia along the axes of gender, race and ethnicity and religion by reproducing stereotypical images of Muslim women (Alimahomed-Wilson 2020; Van and Margaretha 2016; Zahedi 2011). Both discourses depict Muslim women as passive, powerless subjects who either need rescuing from allegedly violent and oppressive Muslim men or protection from a hostile, non-Muslim majority society and Western ideologies. Consequently, Muslim women's agency has been neglected and their activism and social contribution has been invisibilized (Korteweg and Yurdakul 2021). This is despite the fact that voluntary work within religious facilities in Germany is carried out mostly by women (Kausmann et al. 2017). However, women are rarely in positions of power and decision making (Kausmann et al. 2022; Zahedi 2011). This also applies to Muslim women who have been actively involved in community work but have often been marginalized within conventional structures such as mosques and major umbrella organizations (Spielhaus 2012). While some women have created space for themselves within established structures, others have founded their own organizations to represent their specific interests and needs, both within majority society and their own communities (Kuppinger 2012).

In both cases, Muslim women have actively engaged in community building and contributed to a diversification of Muslim civil society in Germany. While they have challenged mainstream discourse about Islam and Muslims within mainstream society, they have also initiated critical debates within Muslim communities (Kuppinger 2012). As such, they have become significant actors of social change in a gendered way. To understand how Muslim women's activism unfolds in contemporary Germany, I focus on their experience of anti-Muslim racism and Islamism and their response strategies to both. More specifically, I look at the extent to which Muslim women's organizations are concerned with Islamism and anti-Muslim racism, what strategies they have developed vis-à-vis these two forces, and what their strategies tell us about identity and belonging in Germany.

In this article, I aim to contribute to the existing literature on Muslim women's activism in two ways. First, I explain how Muslim women are in a double-bind as gender has become a contentious issue that has seen increasing political instrumentalization by proponents of anti-Muslim racism and Islamism alike (Joly and Wadia 2017; Spielhaus 2019). To understand dynamics within Muslim communities that shape the recognition of Islam and Muslim life in Europe, particularly Germany, I provide a closer examination of Muslim women's activism as part of Muslim community building. Since most academic research has predominantly focused on major Turkish umbrella organizations as representatives of Islam and Muslims in Germany, the diversity and heterogeneity of Muslim actors has been overlooked, specifically from a gendered lens. Therefore, I respond to the repeated scholarly critique of the homogenization and essentialization of Islam that conceals the heterogeneity of Muslim lives in Germany focusing on Muslim women's activism (Peucker 2017; Shooman and Spielhaus 2010).

My second contribution is to show how Muslim communities, particularly Muslim women's organizations, experience the social pressures of anti-Muslim racism and Islamism and how these pressures shape their identity formation, positioning, and Muslim community building in general. This is an unexplored field, which justifies the novelty of my work.

This article is structured as follows: I will first give a broad overview of Muslim women's activism in Western societies. Following a brief definition of the terms "anti-Muslim racism" and "Islamism," I will explain how both forces shape Muslim women's activism. I will then introduce my theoretical framework of boundary making and, more specifically, intersectional boundary making. In the data and methods section, I provide detailed information about the sample, the data gathering process, and the evaluation method. Based on the theoretical framework I previously outlined, I will analyze the

88 INTERSECTIONAL (FEMINIST) ACTIVISMS

response strategies of Muslim women's organizations and the implications for their boundary making. In conclusion, I will discuss my main findings and offer suggestions for future research.

Muslim women's activism in western societies

Several studies from the Netherlands (Van Es and Van den Brandt 2020), Britain (Joly and Wadia 2017; Lewicki and O'Toole 2017; Wadia 2015), France (Amir-Moazami, Jacobsen, and Malik 2011; Joly and Wadia 2017; Jouili 2011, 2015; Jouili and Amir-Moazami 2006; Pojmann 2010), the US (Bullock 2005; Wang 2017; Zahedi 2011), and Canada (Bullock 2012; Jafri 2006; Zine 2012) demonstrate the long history of Muslim women's activism and engagement in the social, political, and religious sphere. As these studies show, Muslim women's social activism has mainly evolved out of a desire to represent Muslim women's interests, to promote a better understanding of Islam, or to serve the community and/or general society. A key issue around which Muslim women have (been) mobilized is the headscarf controversy that has unfolded, particularly in France, Germany (Korteweg and Yurdakul 2021), and parts of Canada (Lépinard 2020). However, the issue of the Islamic veil and related stereotypes and stigmatization seem to transgress national borders of Western nations, as examples from the US or Great Britain suggest (Alimahomed-Wilson 2020; Chakraborti and Zempi 2012). In addition, Muslim women have been critically engaged in theological debates, sometimes advocating for feminist or gender-sensitive readings of the Quran (Hammer 2020). The attacks of 9/11 and the subsequent securitizing discourse that raised political awareness among Muslim women across Western countries have been a major catalyst for the growth in Muslim women's community organizing (Wadia 2015; Zahedi 2011). This resonates with other studies on Muslim civic engagement that note a growing number of new organizations following 9/11 (Amath 2015; Cheikh Husain 2020).

In Germany, scholars have only recently paid attention to the diverse landscape of Muslim organizing beyond the major Turkish umbrella organizations and their associated mosque congregations (Ceylan 2006; Halm 2013; Peucker 2017). As recent studies show, Muslim civil engagement in Germany is heterogeneous in terms of both organizational forms and ethnic backgrounds (Mykytjuk-Hitz 2015; Peucker 2017), and it has professionalized (Peucker and Akbarzadeh 2014). Forming a vital part of Muslim community life, Muslim women have been active within mosque congregations and major umbrella organizations but have also founded their own organizations and initiatives (Spielhaus 2012). Although some organizations were already established in the 1990s, little systematic research on Muslim women's activism has been conducted in Germany. This study aims to fill this gap by contributing to the scholarly understanding of Muslim women's activism under the particular conditions of Islamism and anti-Muslim racism.

Muslim women's activism between anti-Muslim racism and Islamism

Research on anti-Muslim racism has expanded in recent years, generating a variety of empirical studies in Muslim-minority countries and provoking academic debates on the adequate terminology and its definitions (Bleich 2011; Bravo López 2011; Çakir 2014; Hafez 2019; Pfahl-Traughber 2012). While Islamophobia has become a common term to describe the exclusion of and discrimination against Muslims on the grounds of their assumed religious affiliation, some scholars have criticized the term as misleading for several reasons. First, the suffix "phobia" is associated with psychological illness and only addresses a general fear of Islam. Second, by focusing on the non-Muslim subject's fear, it gives precedence to this perspective and neglects that of those affected by it. Third, the term implies fear of and hostility toward the religion of Islam and not Muslims themselves (Attia 2015). Finally, the term does not explicitly imply a recognition of the structural and institutional dimensions of Islamophobia (Shooman 2011).

An alternative term that has gained popularity, especially in the German context, is anti-Muslim racism. In comparison to Islamophobia, anti-Muslim racism is more all-encompassing as it refers to the structural and institutional implications of anti-Muslim hatred and discrimination. As such, it directs attention toward different levels of its manifestation and is more adequate for the study of organization's experiences. Building on the definitions of scholars such as Attia (2009, 2013, 2018), Yasemin Shooman (2014, 2010) and Mario Peucker (2019), I define anti-Muslim racism as the stigmatization, discrimination, marginalization, and social exclusion of Muslims or those perceived as such. As a "structural feature of [German] society" (Attia 2013, 4) anti-Muslim racism manifests on four different levels: "the structural level, the level of institutional discrimination, the discursive level, and the subjective level" (Attia 2013, 6). While most incidents of anti-Muslim racism that organizations experience might be mediated through interpersonal interaction, the underlying logic is usually structural, institutional, or discursive in nature.

While discourses on Islamism have been described to have had detrimental effects on Muslim communities as they have fueled anti-Muslim sentiments and led to general suspicion and mistrust toward Muslims (Amiraux and Beauchesne 2020; Fekete 2009), there is evidence that Islamism or Islamic extremism itself has exerted pressure on Muslim communities in Western countries (Pfaff and Gill 2016).

A variety of terms have been used in academic literature to describe the phenomenon of the politicization of Islam and related activities and movements (Akbarzadeh 2020; Esposito and El-Din Shahin 2013; Pfahl-Traughber 2008; Roy 1994; Tietze 2003). The most common ones are Islamism and Political Islam. While both terms are often used as synonyms, some scholars, such as the political scientists Cesari (2021) and Mandaville (2014), argue for a more differentiated approach to these two concepts. According to Cesari (2021, 2), Political Islam might be defined "[...] as a political culture that is the outcome of the dual processes of nationalization and reformation of the Islamic tradition." As such, it represents a "governmentality" of which Islamism, understood "[...] as the religiously based form of political mobilization [...] is one of the many outcomes [...] (Cesari 2021, 2). In line with Cesari, Mandaville (2014, 22) describes Islamism as a subset of Muslim politics, "[...] one that seeks to create a political order defined in terms of Islam (usually a *shar'iah*-based state)." As such, Islamism represents a challenge to democratic and secular orders that reject the primacy of a certain religion in the public and political sphere and guarantee equal treatment to all citizens regardless of their religion or worldview (Cesari 2015).

What continues to be ambiguous with regard to the identification of Islamist actors is whether the assumed intentionality is sufficient to qualify an actor as Islamist and how evidence about this intentionality could be provided (if it is not revealed by the respective actor itself). As some scholars have pointed out, this ambiguity and lack of clear criteria has often resulted in an arbitrary labeling of Muslim groups, activities and religious practices considered to be at odds with "Western values" as Islamist. Furthermore, it has legitimized measures taken within a security policy framework such as surveillance, ideological interventions, and the funding of radicalization prevention (Abbas 2011; De Koning 2020; Fekete 2009; Fox and Akbaba 2015).

Aware of the controversies surrounding the term Islamism, I use it for the purpose of this study as it is the most common term in academic literature and best captures the phenomenon explored. By the term Islamism, I refer to ideologies, movements and groups that reject Germany's democratic system and seek to establish a political and social order based on an exclusivist interpretation of Islam (Akbarzadeh 2020; Esposito and El-Din Shahin 2013; Mandaville 2014; Pfahl-Traughber 2008).

Based on evidence from other Western countries such as the US, Australia, and Great Britain, Muslim women's organizations in Germany are assumed to experience a highly gendered form of anti-Muslim racism and Islamism (Alimahomed-Wilson 2020; Povey 2009; Zahedi 2011). In this context, Islamism manifests in the support for patriarchal order and conservative social mores that neglect Muslim women's agency and depict them as weak, passive, and in need of protection. Anti-Muslim racism is similarly expressed through Orientalist images that paint a homogenous picture of Muslim women along race and ethnicity and gender lines (Zahedi 2011). In both cases, Muslim women are denied agency and represented as victims who need to be rescued from allegedly violent and oppressive Muslim men or protected from a hostile, non-Muslim majority society and Western ideologies

(Zahedi 2011). As I will show later, these discourses have symbolic and material consequences for Muslim women's organizations. While anti-Muslim racism might manifest at the institutional level resulting in the exclusion or discrimination of Muslim women's organizations, Islamism might express itself in verbal assaults of Muslim women's organizations, the instrumentalization of their work, and the recruitment of Muslim women Islamists' political purposes (Termeer and Duyvesteyn 2022).

In this context, Muslim organizations have taken on a variety of new responsibilities and tasks (Cheikh Husain 2020). While they have had to defend themselves against accusations by political and media representatives (Mykytjuk-Hitz 2015), they have also had to assist their members in coping with the challenges of radicalism and anti-Muslim racism (Cheikh Husain 2020). On the other hand, they have been instrumentalized within Islamophobic discourses that label women's organizations as progressive per se and in opposition to conventional, established male-dominated organizations or mosques (Brown 2008). What has been overlooked is the positioning and self-identification of Muslim women's groups and organizations within the community and the social and political field, which is far more complex and transcends the simplified, dichotomous divide.

The following section will introduce the theoretical framework that will be used to analyze the strategies of Muslim women's organizations and related boundary (de-)construction.

Boundary theory

As a highly politicized topic in Europe, Islam and Muslims have become a central issue within the boundary-making literature (Alba 2005; Bowen 2014; Foner 2015; Yurdakul and Korteweg 2021; Zolberg and Woon 1999). Muslim women's organizations are key sites to understand how Muslims in Germany draw and transform social boundaries. Such boundary drawing and transformation emerge as a byproduct of their civic engagement against anti-Muslim racism and Islamism.

The central theoretical vantage point of this work is "boundary theory." According to Lamont and Molnár (2002, 168), boundaries can be conceptualized as essential "symbolic resources [...] in creating, maintaining, contesting, or even dissolving institutionalized social differences." They differentiate between symbolic and social boundaries. *Symbolic boundaries* are considered "tools by which individuals and groups struggle over and come to agree upon definitions of reality" (Lamont and Molnár 2002, 168). As such, they form basic tenets for groupness and social cohesion and structure our affective social landscapes of similarity, closeness, and belonging and make processes of demarcation visible.

Social boundaries represent the manifestation of differentiations into material and non-material conditions. These boundaries are separating lines along which people acquire resources and define individual social status and access to social opportunities, rights, or institutions (Lamont and Molnár 2002). In contrast to symbolic boundaries, social boundaries presuppose a broad consensus and are reflected in stable behavioral patterns (Lamont and Molnár 2002). This speaks to another helpful conceptualization of boundary making by Alba (Alba 2005), who distinguishes between bright and blurred boundaries. While bright boundaries are widely agreed upon and are quite stable and clear, blurry ones are ambiguous and allow for more individualistic behavior, such as self-representation. Whether a boundary is classified as bright or blurry depends on its institutionalization within the social and political field (Alba 2005).

In my study, I make use of that body of literature focusing on symbolic boundary drawing to identify how boundaries are mediated through anti-Muslim racism and Islamism and how these boundaries influence the work of Muslim women's organizations. Adopting an agency-centered perspective, I explore Muslim women's response strategies and their implications for the (re-)construction of boundaries within Muslim communities, civil society, and broader society. To identify Muslim women's organizational response strategies to anti-Muslim racism and Islamism, I draw on the work of Michèle Lamont et al. (2016). Rather than using it as a deductive theoretical framework, I adapt and expand the proposed framework according to the empirical findings. Following a description of Muslim women's response strategies, I inquire what implications these strategies have for the organizations' self-identification and positioning as well as community building and groupness, both in relation to broader society and Muslim communities in Germany.

Intersectional boundary making

Boundary construction is a matter of ethnic, racial, and/or religious identity as much as it is one of gender identity. Against the background of Muslim women's embeddedness in unequal power hierarchies, which are mainly structured along the axis of gender, race, ethnicity, and religion, an analysis of their response strategies vis-à-vis anti-Muslim racism on the one hand, and Islamism on the other, requires the adoption of a multi-layered intersectional approach. Thus, intersectionality represents a further theoretical vantage point, both as an analytical tool as well as a methodological approach.

The term "intersectionality" was first introduced by the Black Feminist scholar and activist Kimberlé Crenshaw (1989, 1991) with the aim of problematizing the construction of marginalization within institutionalized discourses and took into account the unique and invisible specificity of overlapping systems of oppression. Intersectionality was defined as the "complex, irreducible, varied, and variable effects which ensue when multiple axis [sic] of differentiation – economic, political, cultural, psychic, subjective and experiential – intersect in historically specific contexts" (Brah and Phoenix 2004, 76).

To date, the studies on boundary making in the literature have only occasionally applied an intersectional approach. This is noteworthy since much of the scholarly literature has been concerned with the construction of minority groups and questions related to their (non-)belonging on the grounds of different identity markers. One of the few examples is the empirical study by Gökce Yurdakul and Anna C. Korteweg (2013) on "honor" killings and forced marriage debates in the Netherlands, Germany, and Britain. Through their careful analysis of different categories and their entanglement, they show how social divisions such as gender, sexual orientation, citizenship status, and religion play into boundary-making processes and determine actors' preference for a certain strategy.

In this study, I use intersectionality both as methodology and analytical tool. Following Lutz (2015), intersectional methodology can be made productive in various steps in the qualitative research process. While it may serve as a valuable point of reflection of partiality in interview situations and allows the researcher to be attentive to which identity categories are being evoked at which point of the conversation, it further allows for an analysis that considers the contingent, simultaneous activation of multiple symbolic boundaries and identities of Muslim women organizations. Analyzing the strategies of Muslim women organizations against Islamism and anti-Muslim racism in Germany, special attention will be paid to the interplay of the identity categories of gender, ethnicity, race, and religion.[1]

Methods & data

This study draws on six in-depth interviews with representatives of leading Muslim women's organizations during June and December 2022 across Germany. The interview data is supplemented by information from the organizations' websites and ethnographic data collected during a conference in November 2022.

Due to a lack of data on Muslim women's organizations in Germany, a mapping of Muslim women's organizations was devised. For this purpose, internet research was conducted. As many organizations are not easily identifiable as Muslim through their name, the results were rather limited. A further obstacle in identifying Muslim women's organizations via internet search was outdated or lack of information on the organizations' websites. The collected information on Muslim women's organizations in Germany was substantiated and supplemented through personal networks and expert interviews with community leaders.

The sampling follows an explorative research design since Muslim collective organizing, particularly Muslim women's activism in Germany, remains under-researched. The selection of Muslim women's organizations was based on three criteria: (1) The organization self-identifies as Muslim and female; (2) The organization must be led by Muslim women and decision-making must lie in their hands, with the majority of members and/or constituency Muslim and female; (3) The organization is independent of other Muslim (umbrella) associations.

Using these criteria, I identified 21 formalized Muslim women's organizations in 14 different cities. Most of them are located in western Germany, particularly in North-Rhine Westphalia, the most populous federal state, which also ranks among the regions as home to the highest migrant and Muslim populations in Germany (Pfündel, Stichs, and Tanis 2021). Only one organization was identified in eastern Germany, in the federal state of Saxony. This is hardly surprising as the proportion of migrants and racialized people, especially Muslims, is quite small in this region compared to the rest of Germany (Pfündel, Stichs, and Tanis 2021).

As previous studies have emphasized, most Muslim and particularly female Muslim engagement is not formalized and thus invisibilized (Kuppinger 2012; Spielhaus 2012). This could mainly be attributed to the lack of stable funding and reliable resources – a problem that is common to all Muslim organizations in Germany that do not receive funds from abroad. Compared to other Western countries, such as the US or Canada, Muslims in Germany mostly belong to socially disadvantaged segments of the population and lack the funds to finance their organizations (Chbib 2010; Foner and Alba 2008).

Another aspect that has been mentioned by the organizations' representatives and came up during my ethnographic fieldwork are the high administrative barriers to eligibility for state funds. Even for those organizations that are formalized, securing funds represents a major obstacle. As a result, a considerable number of organizations relies upon donations and voluntary work (Muckel et al. 2018; Mykytjuk-Hitz 2015).

Initially, the identified Muslim women's organizations of the sample were contacted via e-mail; however, the response rate was low. Another strategy was therefore chosen that proved more effective. In November 2022, I attended a conference in the city of Duisburg that was hosted by two Muslim women's organizations and dealt with the topic of Muslim women's organizations as civil society actors in Germany. This gave me the opportunity to converse with representatives of Muslim women's organizations and Muslim female activists in person and to invite them for interviews.

In addition, I learned about the organizational landscape, the organizations' histories, motivations, structures, financing, collaborations, and challenges. While the event was generally characterized by a trusting and cooperative atmosphere, discussions about resources and marginalization within Muslim women's organizations revealed different experiences, positionalities, and interests. Issues that seemed to be relevant to all participating organizations were funding, professionalization, and the long-term perspectives for Muslim (women's) organizations in Germany.

The final sample of this study consists of six organizations out of a total number of 21 (Table A1). One of them might be designated as an interest group, while the other five represent welfare organizations that are located in Berlin and in three large cities in the federal state of North-Rhine Westphalia. Two organizations operate on a federal level, while all the others work on a local and occasionally state level. The organizations researched vary considerably in size, degree of professio-nalization, and finances. However, they all report a lack of sustainable financial resources and rely on membership fees and project-based funding. It is worth noting that the majority of organizations have been established as a response to the specific exclusion and discrimination of (visibly) Muslim women. This corresponds with the study of Cheikh Husain (2020) and Peucker (2019) that observed an increase of Muslim activism due to the rise of anti-Muslim sentiments. Initially focusing on Muslim women's empowerment through social services, advanced training programs, the provision of safer spaces and job opportunities, most organizations have extended their offers and target groups to include especially vulnerable minorities, such as (migrant) women of color and refugees. A shared goal of all Muslim women's organizations is to combat gender inequality as well as all forms of discrimina-tion based on religion, race, and ethnicity.

All the interviews were conducted in German and recorded; then I fully transcribed and partially translated them into English. All respondents who were interviewed on behalf of their organizations were chairwomen with decision-making powers and founding members of their respective groups, except for one, a prevention project leader. The interviewed representatives have all been active for over 10 years and have considerable knowledge and experience in community organizing. Half of them are German citizens of Turkish descent; the other half are white German Muslim converts. While nearly all of them wear headscarves and are thus visibly identifiable as Muslims, they differ in relation to their ethnic and racial identity, which shapes their varying positionalities and experiences as representatives of their organizations.

The women's different standpoints are further influenced by their ages, which range between 35 and 67, as well as their educational level. Although all the organizations' representatives have university degrees, they do not all have an academic background. This is particularly relevant with regard to the networks they are able to build, their self-image, and their positioning.

I acknowledge that my approach and method are significantly shaped by the theoretical perspective I adopted, as well as by my own social positioning. As an academic and visibly Muslim woman of color, I could relate to the experiences of discrimination that were reported in the interviews. Furthermore, my being perceived as a member of the Muslim community and my familiarity with internal issues and debates facilitated the conversations and created common ground. However, discussing the organization's experiences of anti-Muslim racism and Islamism seemed to cause occasional discomfort. Due to the sensitive information shared, the disclosure of which might have harmful effects on the organization, most interview partners asked to remain anonymous. To protect their anonymity, direct quotations are not attributed to a particular organization's representative since they might be easily identified. In cases where names are mentioned, pseudonyms are used. Drawing on the basic analytical tenets of the Grounded Theory approach, the original interview material, interpretive prior knowledge, and interpretations from the analysis entered into an iterative process of constituting, examining, and refining interpretive hypotheses. This process is enabled by using computer-assisted qualitative data analysis, namely the software MAXQDA. Coding of the corpus followed instructions formulated by Grounded Theory (Corbin and Strauss 1990). I started with open coding to identify main categories relating to experiences of and strategies against anti-Muslim racism and Islamism. Categories were built through comparisons across the whole corpus and refined through the creation of subtypes. Finally, I used axial coding to explore the relationships between different categories of experiences and response strategies and the implications for intersectional boundary making.

Findings

Response strategies of muslim women's organizations against anti-Muslim racism

Muslim women's organizations have developed a wide range of strategies to respond to the experiences of exclusion and stigmatization based on their gender, religious and racial/ethnic identities. While some of the described strategies relate to specific incidents of anti-Muslim racism, others are broader and more constant. These strategies include concrete actions as well as (counter-)narratives. The most common ones are trust and network building and the activation of existing contacts and networks. Further response strategies entail confrontation, showing attitude/authenticity and acting against stereotypes.

Trust and network building

Most Muslim women's organizations in this study have a diverse network that consists of politicians, state authorities, academics, church representatives, civil society actors, and Muslim communities. While network building and cooperation are common strategies of civil society organizations, these strategies have proven to be of particular importance for Muslim women's organizations in confronting anti-Muslim racism. As the findings show, trust and network building is the most frequent strategy that runs through all cases of the study. It includes personal meetings with stakeholders, participation in working groups, attendance of conferences and public events, (interreligious) dialogue work, (formalized) collaborations, and the staging of public events as well as inviting guests to visit the organization's own facilities. A central goal of all these endeavors is to build trust and overcome suspicion that is often fed by anti-Muslim discourses and media coverage (Shooman 2014; Shooman and Spielhaus 2010). This is illustrated by the following statement:

> I continue to try and clarify my concerns to people who know me – just raising awareness through meeting with people, exchanging views and explaining what's going on, not apologetically, just (showing) that I am "normal" – so that they get to know me.

Another organization's representative highlights the importance of establishing mutual trust and trustworthy networks, particularly with regard to the organization's progress:

> We invite as many people as possible to visit us and see us at work; then they leave with a positive impression. And the next time there's a project, they say, "Oh, we know them; we might as well fund them." This has always been our strategy.

As the quotation indicates, these partnerships are perceived as particularly important as they provide access to material resources such as state funds or facilities as well as non-material resources such as information, credibility, and legitimacy.

It is worth noting that most organizations have established long-standing ties to academics with whom they collaborate and stay in regular contact to exchange information. In one instance, for example, the materials used by the respective organization in its prevention work were developed by researchers from the University of Osnabrück in Lower Saxony.

However, as nearly all of the organization's representatives mention, network building and maintaining is very time and resource consuming, including on an emotional level. This is reflected by the statement of one interviewee:

> We bend over backwards by "inviting everyone," especially the media if possible, and in general. (. . .)

Relating to the networking with policy makers at the federal level, another organization's representative states:

> We can no longer afford to keep traveling at the organization's expense to random meetings where you end up getting barely a word in with someone; it doesn't pay.

Although trust and network building represent a strategy that requires both large material and non-material resources, in most cases it has proven successful in confronting anti-Muslim racism as it blurs existing symbolic boundaries that separate Muslim women's organizations from other social and political actors. As a long-term strategy, building and maintaining relationships might result in reliable allyships that might transform the position of Muslim women's organizations in the future.

Activation of networks and support by allies

While networks have a general merit to Muslim women's organizations due to their position at the lower end of the social and political power hierarchy, they have proven to be especially important in instances of anti-Muslim racism.

Thus, another common response strategy vis-à-vis anti-Muslim racism is the activation of networks and support from allies. As the reports of organizations' representatives indicate, networks are activated either in cases where organizations are denied funding, their credibility is questioned, or they are excluded from committees and memberships in majority institutions.

In some instances of anti-Muslim racism, such as the exclusion from working groups or the denial of membership in an umbrella organization, allies advocate for the respective organization and use their power position to exert pressure on involved institutions or persons. In other situations, allies share important information needed to confront the person or institution in charge. This is illustrated by the following case in which the respective organization was suspected of being Islamist and the organization's representative contacted her allies for support:

(...) of course, those from the associations and within the administration who knew me went and had a word with the others to tell them off. So first I had to say, "Wait a minute! Let me have a look at what kind of network I have and how to get everyone involved so I can get some people behind me."

As this quotation indicates, the interviewee seems to be aware of the organization's rather weak discourse position and its limited power to influence or convince other actors (of its innocence) in the case of such allegation. Instead, the organization opts to activate its allies and to let them advocate for it. While this strategy seems more promising, it nevertheless reproduces existing power hierarchies as Muslim women's organizations are dependent on other actors' support and do not become visible as agents.

In another incident, a Muslim women's organization was denied membership in one of Germany's major social welfare umbrella organizations, which provides access to information, networks, training, and funds. As the chairwoman reports, the organization was only admitted as a member after an ally – a former member of the umbrella organization – complained:

I made quite a fuss about this, and then at some point I approached a former state executive (...) and said, "(...) I'm writing a press release that says we are not being admitted to the Paritätische (German Parity Welfare Association). Would you take a look at it?" Then he said he couldn't imagine that it would be in the (federal) state's interest to exclude us, and that he would speak with Mr. Sauer, the state secretary about it.

What the above examples show is that many Muslim women's organizations have succeeded in building trustworthy relationships with actors from civil society, the administration, politics and academia that have proven essential in confronting anti-Muslim racism and its related impacts. While anti-Muslim racism has reaffirmed and strengthened already existing boundaries through othering that is expressed in suspicion, allegation, and other forms of stigmatization, it has similarly motivated Muslim women's organizations to form new alliances. As Muslim women's organizations have become members in German majority institutions and have collaborated with a variety of other (non-Muslim) actors, they have contested institutionalized social differences (Lamont et al. 2016). This has not only transformed the perception of Muslim women's organizations by parts of majority society; it has also strengthened the organizations' sense of belonging.

Confrontation

Another strategy that Muslim women's organizations have deployed vis-à-vis anti-Muslim racism is confrontation, though to a lesser extent than the aforementioned strategies. As the interviews show, confrontation has only been used in cases of more explicit forms of anti-Muslim racism in which actors are assumed to have acted on bad intentions and/or their guilt could be proven. This has been the case in a false media report that was published about one organization, false allegations made by collaborating partners, and the prohibition of ritual prayer in the facilities used by the respective organization.

Although most organizations' representatives refrain from using confrontation as a strategy – since they do not believe in its added value or positive long-term effect – there are single incidents in which they have felt the urgency to clearly set limits by confronting the actors involved.

This is illustrated by the example in which an organization's representative was confronted with false allegations; she was asked by the partner organization whose facilities the organization was using to prohibit ritual prayer during its activities. Confronting the chair of the respective organization, she responded:

You know what? That's discrimination. And if that's the reason why we're not allowed to be here, then I'll go to the district mayor. Then I'll go to [the] anti-discrimination office. This is discrimination. You can't blame me for doing this.

Although the respective Muslim women's organization eventually left the premises and terminated its partnership with the other organization, this confrontation seemed to be important in order to reaffirm the organization's Muslim identity and claim its right to hold ritual prayer. While Muslim women's organizations rely on the intervention by third parties to confront anti-Muslim racism in some instances, in others they directly interact with the person or institution themselves to regain their agency.

Especially in light of prevalent stereotypical images of Muslim women that portray them as passive and helpless, the need for Muslim women('s organizations) to be more confrontational is stressed in this quotation:

> I think we need to go on the offensive as Muslim women. This "I am friendly and patient and I can handle everything" stuff–nothing comes of it. (...) That's why you need to become more assertive and develop some good arguments.

Showing attitude and "authenticity"

A closely related strategy of Muslim women's organizations that aims at reaffirming intersectional identity and related positions and practices in the face of anti-Muslim racism is showing attitude. This strategy has been deployed both as a general strategy and in particular situations in which Muslim women's organizations have been confronted with subtle allegations by other civil society actors or state authorities.

The following statement of one of the organization's representatives highlights the importance to adhere to the organization's intersectional identity by referring to both the religious and gender identity in its name:

> For me as a convert, it's particularly important that Islam has a place in Germany, that Islam becomes socially acceptable, and that with names such as "Meeting Center for Muslim Women," "Muslim Academy," and "Muslim Family Counseling," we as Muslims show (...) that we are here, we belong here, and we are good people.

Although this chairwoman identifies as a (white) native German and race and ethnicity are expected to be less of an issue for her, it seems that her religious identity assigns her a position outside German society; she needs to reclaim her national affiliation and belonging to German society. This indicates that the boundaries toward adherences of Islam are considerably bright and may even be more salient than German ethnicity. However, the respective chairwoman points out that the discrimination experienced by her employees of color differ from hers because they are additionally targeted on the basis of their race and ethnicity.

While most organizations in the study adhere to the principle of showing attitude and authenticity regardless of the consequences, there have also been concrete instances in which they have applied this principle as a concrete strategy against anti-Muslim racism. This is illustrated in an instance in which a civil society actor repeatedly questioned a Muslim women's organization about the image of women it promotes as a way of insinuating that it is too "emancipated" to be compatible with Islam in his view. The chairwoman responded by reiterating her organization's position. She stated:

> Man, I am sick of hearing this and I'm sick of responding to it. He got the same frigging answer from me every time: "[We stand for women's] self-determination. What more can I tell you, Mr. Demirel? [...] I have explained it to you so many times."

As this example shows, in light of a hegemonic discourse that portrays Muslim women as oppressed, Muslim women's positioning as autonomous and emancipated is frequently contested. By reaffirming their autonomy, Muslim women's organizations reshape the boundaries between Islam and secular liberalism to accommodate their intersectional identities.

Acting against stereotypes

Evidence from other accounts similarly indicates that Muslim women's organizations frequently attempt to overcome the discursively constructed binary between Islam and gender inequality that undermines the perception of Muslim women as autonomous and equal actors. While showing attitude and authenticity is rather a strategy with which Muslim women's organizations try to remain true to themselves, the final strategy of acting against stereotypes that I will analyze is more preoccupied with changing others' perceptions of Muslim women and their organizations. While in some instances, acting against stereotypes manifests in concrete actions, in others it is expressed through counter-narratives that aim to challenge widespread stereotypes of Muslim women.

A widely held stereotype confronted by the organizations interviewed is the image of the uneducated, unskilled, and unemancipated Muslim woman. While the portrayal of Muslim women as unemancipated und submissive women goes back to orientalist imaginings (Zine 2006), the perception of Muslim women as uneducated and unskilled is mainly shaped by the immigration of a considerable number of Turkish guest workers to Germany in the 1960s who were predominantly of Muslim origin (Spielhaus 2013). Due to the intersection of Turkish immigrants' Islamic religion and their working-class background, Muslims and particularly Muslim women in Germany have been generally associated with low social class adherence (Nökel 2002).

To disprove this stereotype, Muslim women's representatives often emphasize their high educational level and their academic background as well as the high level of professionalism in their organization. This is illustrated by the statement in which one chairwoman points to the professionality of existing Muslim women's organizations:

> We are empowering German society so it becomes more diverse. We offer expert intercultural training. We don't need to empower ourselves, we are (already) emancipated women. (...) I find it silly that [Muslim women's empowerment] is being propagated again like it was 20 years ago.

In accordance with this assertion of professionalism, the organization's representative stresses the importance of rejecting any project proposal that reproduces this stereotype of Muslim women. She refers to the experience of her own organization that is recognized as a professionally working organization:

> As Muslim women we really need to reject projects where we always [are requested] to emancipate ourselves further, etc. We should actually refuse to do so. Because [our organization] succeeded in earning a good reputation as [run by] professional Muslim women.

As the example indicates, the organization has invested many resources in becoming a professional organization, but also in being perceived as such. This seems to be a precondition to recognition as a serious actor in civil society, but also in fighting general stereotypes toward Muslims and Muslim women in particular.

Another incident in which one of the organization's representatives felt the pressure to counteract the prevalent stereotype of the subaltern, helpless Muslim woman was at a public event to which she was invited. She expressed this as follows:

> I thought to myself: "You are going to say something now. You're not going to leave without saying a word. Otherwise they will have the wrong image of you."

As the statement indicates, Muslim women's organizations are greatly concerned with their external image since it is shaped by gendered anti-Muslim discourses that determine the organizations' scope of action. With confident, articulate representation, they seek to redraw the boundaries that confine them to a powerless position in the social hierarchy. While such boundaries constructed along gender, race, ethnicity and religious lines are blurred, other boundaries such as social class might become more relevant.

Another common stereotype that Muslim women's organizations try to overcome is the image of the narrow-minded, isolated Muslim woman. This is often accompanied by the perception of visibly Muslim women as being conservative and highly devout. As a consequence, Muslim women('s organizations) tend to be perceived as homogeneous and monolithic entities. This image is particularly harmful in the case of welfare organizations as they aim to reach many diverse target groups. Aware of the predominant perception of the headscarf as a symbol of illiberalism and female submission, some Muslim women's organizations intentionally place the headscarf in the background by portraying women of diverse appearances. This becomes evident through the account of one

Muslim women's organization whose representative describes how her group counteracts the mono-lithic image of visibly Muslim women:

> Sometimes we observe [this prejudice] when we take people through the center here, so we introduce our staff like this: we have a number of female employees without headscarves, so we intentionally [say]: "This is Mrs. Mohammed, without a headscarf. And this is Mrs. So-and-So." So they see [women] with and without headscarves. They actually see a diverse mix.

Although most organizations pay particular attention to Muslim women's needs, they nonetheless stress their openness to all women (and families), regardless of their ethnic and racial or religious background. As a result of their experience of stigmatization and exclusion, Muslim women's organizations seek to reconfigure boundaries that separate Muslim women from other women and broader society within the dimension of religion. By accommodating different intersectional identities and positioning, they aim to create inclusive spaces that take post-migrant reality in Germany into account.

Response strategies vis-à-vis Islamism

The coding of the interview data reveals a disproportionate reference to anti-Muslim racism in comparison to Islamism. Thus, Islamism appears to be of less concern to Muslim women's organizations.

This may be attributed to several factors: first, Islamism is not a structural feature of European society, particularly in Germany. While Muslim women's organizations are confronted with anti-Muslim racism through their interaction with state authorities and other civil society actors in their daily work, their exposure to Islamism is rather limited. Similarly, there is no dependent relationship from Islamist actors as it is the case with respect to actors who are involved in incidents of anti-Muslim racism. This reflects the social power hierarchies in which both phenomena of anti-Muslim racism and Islamism are embedded. The rise of social media has also opened new avenues for Islamists to disseminate their ideologies and intervene in public and theological discussions. Second, Muslim women's organizations represent rather controlled spaces insofar as Muslim women decide on their members and constituencies and are able to exclude those who do not comply with their ethical values. However, while the analog public spaces may not be easily accessible for Islamists and their agitation within these spaces is rather limited, they have increasingly made use of new communication channels such as social media to spread their ideology and mobilize support.

Radicalization prevention

While two of the researched organizations report having been targeted directly by Islamist actors, nearly all organizations acknowledge the harmful effects of Islamist ideologies and rhetoric on their constituencies and/or the whole of Muslim communities. Four organizations, having had previous experience with Islamist recruitment in their social environment or being aware of the potential rise of radical tendencies in general, have been active in the field of prevention work. A particular feature of this work provided by Muslim women's organizations is their extended target group that includes, and in some cases specializes in, women and girls.

As the examples of this study show, the organizations pay particular attention to gender-specific dimensions of Islamism by addressing the singular image of (a modest and respectable) Muslim woman that Islamists promote. This entails specific gender norms that relegate Muslim women to the private sphere and requires them to comply with particular regulations as well as codes of conduct and dress. Parallel to anti-Muslim discourses that make demands on how Muslim women should dress to be accepted as equal members of society, Islamists impose their image of a "proper" Muslim female on Muslim women. Through counter-narratives that emphasize the plurality of opinions and chosen lifestyles, Muslim women's organizations seek to counteract Islamists' claim of absoluteness. Rather than conveying a specific role model of (Muslim) women, they encourage their constituencies to develop their own views and critically engage with their religion. This is described in the following account:

> [It is] a prevention program in the sense that extremely radical groups try to push women into a very specific framework with very clear assignments of gender roles that are also highly restrictive with regard to women, with the dictate that they [women] should not question their religion–or anything as a matter of principle–but just do what they're told (...). And this is exactly what we intend to counteract so they [women] don't fall for this, so that they are enabled to act autonomously and make decisions on their own.

Another cornerstone of Muslim women's prevention work is to foster identification with German society through narratives of belonging, leisure activities and meetings with prominent figures who act as role models. However, as many of the organizations' representatives state, strengthening Muslim women's sense of belonging represents a particular challenge in the face of gendered anti-Muslim racism that reaffirms existing social boundaries along the axis of gender, ethnicity, and race. The interviews indicate that most Muslim women's organizations assign a decisive role to anti-Muslim racism within processes of Islamist radicalization. According to them, experiences of discrimination reinforce alienation from broader society, which are then exploited by Islamist actors for their own purposes. This resonates with literature in that field that refers to anti-Muslim racism as one push factor for Islamist radicalization (Abbas 2019; Esposito and Iner 2018; Mansoob and Pavan 2011). Taking the correlation of Islamism and anti-Muslim racism into account, overcoming anti-Muslim racism becomes an important aim in countering Islamism. As a consequence, addressing experiences of discrimination represents an essential component of the organizations' prevention work. However, what their representatives consider problematic is the general securitization of their prevention work that considers all Muslims potential radicals. This confirms previous findings that critically examine Muslim communities' involvement in deradicalization and prevention work (Abdel-Fattah 2020; Spalek 2012; Welten and Abbas 2021; Yousuf 2020) and is reflected in the following statement:

> What also came to my mind with regard to our project is this securitization of our project work. What we do is actually youth work, but we always need to frame it as prevention, as security measures, and that then of course results in this stigmatization of our target group.

Not responding

Similar to the salience of gender in the context of prevention work, gender has been used as a central point of reference and a source of mobilization in instances of Islamist confrontation.

Two organizations reported to have been targeted directly by Islamist actors. In one case, an organization's representative was denounced by an Islamist actor on a social media platform for her "immoral" dress and behavior as she shook hands with a political representative in public. Further hostile comments have appeared on social media platforms in which the appropriateness of the organization's religious position has been questioned or even declared heresy. Through the promotion of an ideal image of a "proper" Muslim woman and the condemnation of all who deviate from it, Islamists draw symbolic boundaries between those who belong to the Muslim community and those who do not.

However, the organization concerned decided either to not respond or delete the defamatory posts. This might be explained by the limited harm these types of Islamist confrontations cause to Muslim women's organizations. Another reason for the choice of not responding might also be the low prospect of the success of other strategies. Nevertheless, these incidents of verbal abuse might have signal effects that legitimize the interference in the self-determination and representation of Muslim women('s organizations). Furthermore, these confrontations might sustain and fuel sexist attitudes and encourage other groups and individuals to engage in such derogatory discourse.

While some cases of censure toward Muslim women can clearly be categorized as Islamist, others are only considered conservative. Although there is some overlap between conservative views and Islamist ideologies with regard to gender norms that assign a privileged position to males, interviewees clearly differentiate between both phenomena. This thorough distinction seems to be of particular importance in a climate where unfavorable attitudes of Muslims are easily dismissed as Islamist and are consequently deemed illegitimate.

Confronting and developing counter-narratives

In another instance, Islamist actors made use of online information provided by a Muslim women's organization regarding an incident of gendered anti-Muslim racism and published it on their own website. In the same vein, Islamists tried to mobilize around Muslim grievances by calling for donations to file an action for Muslim women who are legally forbidden to teach at public schools because they wear headscarves. As these incidents show, Muslim women's experiences of gendered anti-Muslim racism represent an important source of Islamist mobilization. In this context, the work of Muslim women's organizations is misused for Islamists' own purposes. While no action was taken in the former instance, in the latter the organization's representative raised awareness in her social environment and deconstructed the Islamists' contradictory argumentation and abbreviated representation of the incident.

As the organization's representative highlights the development of counter-narratives to confront Islamists' argumentation, the issue is often complicated by the fact that Islamist claims (in relation to anti-Muslim racism) often hold true. However, the conclusions drawn from it are perceived as contradictory and highly problematic since they do not comply with democratic values and a pluralist model of society.

In another incident, an Islamist group posted a photograph and a quote from the aforementioned chairwoman on its website. When the chairwoman found out, she contacted the people responsible and asked them to remove both her picture and her statement from their website. Although her request was honored, her organization was later contacted by a presumably affiliated individual who tried to inquire the reason for her refusal to be cited by the Islamist group. The following account describes her response:

> And then I said, "We have a particular way of working. And this consists of focusing on coalition and communalities, so to speak, and promoting them – but I have the impression that the [other] organization is acting rather divisively and we do not support this way of working, so we do not want to be associated with it."

As the chairwoman's response indicates, the organization clearly distances itself from the Islamist group. However, it does not do so by arguing on ideological or theological grounds, but on ethical ones. While Muslim women's organizations support a pluralist model of society in which different attitudes, identities and lifestyles are recognized, Islamists convey an exclusivist view that draws sharp boundaries around the dimension of "the true" religion. According to their view, anyone who does not comply with their understanding of Islam does not belong to the "true" Muslim community.

Conclusion

In this study I have explored the strategies of Muslim women's organizations vis-à-vis anti-Muslim racism and Islamism in Germany. The findings reveal that Muslim women's organizations are not only disproportionately affected by anti-Muslim racism; they also face verbal assaults and exploitation by Islamist actors who mobilize around grievances of Muslim women.

An intersectional perspective to boundary making reveals the centrality of the social categories of gender, religion, race, and ethnicity within processes of boundary making. While experiences of anti-Muslim racism reaffirm (pre-)existing symbolic boundaries along the axes of religion, gender, race, and ethnicity and define belonging within German society, Islamists primarily refer to gender and religion in their practices of boundary making and determine who belongs to the Muslim community. In both cases, Muslim women's organizations have experienced exclusion and stigmatization based on their gender identity and their right to self-determination has been neglected. In accordance with Lamont et al. (2016), social boundaries and their maintenance have limited the access of Muslim women's organizations to material as well as symbolic resources (Lamont and Molnár 2002) and have thus limited their scope of action.

To overcome boundaries mediated through anti-Muslim racism and Islamism, Muslim women's organizations have developed a variety of response strategies that include trust building and networking, the activation of existing contacts and networks, confrontation, showing attitude and authenticity, and acting against stereotypes. With regard to Islamism, the most common strategies are not responding or removal of social media posts, awareness raising (within the organization and respective social environment), prevention work, counter-narratives, and confrontation.

While strategies of confrontation, showing attitude, and not responding have tended to maintain or even strengthen (pre-)existing boundaries, most strategies have shifted or resolved established boundary (re-)constructs and transformed symbolic boundaries to accommodate intersectional identities that are marginalized within broader society. Within these processes, Muslim women's organizations have (re-)positioned themselves within broader society, but have also sought to include other minority groups, such as migrant and refugee women, as well as other Muslim communities. This has been reflected in both their self-representation and their counternarratives that have emphasized the plurality of views and lifestyles.

By illuminating Muslim women's strategies against anti-Muslim racism and Islamism and analyzing their related boundary making, this study applies an intersectional approach. Doing so, it contributes to the emerging body of literature on intersectional boundary making. In times of polarization from right-wing populists on the one hand and Islamists on the other, an understanding of boundary-making processes is pivotal to the strengthening of democratic forces that foster social cohesion. In addition, this work provides new insights into the dynamics of Muslim communities in Germany and their active contribution to a vital civil society. As the findings show, Muslim women's organizations have access to diverse groups and communities due to their intersectional positioning and are thus able to mediate among different actors by blurring or overcoming existing boundaries along various identity markers.

In order to understand the decisions of Muslim women's organizations to apply certain response strategies, further research inquiring into the determining conditions for their strategic choices is needed. In line with Lamont et al. (2016), this would require an in-depth analysis of the political and social context in which the organizations are embedded and an expansion of the actual sample to include greater regional diversity.

As the study has further shown, most incidents of Islamist agitations have been mediated through digital channels that provide easy access to other actors and allow for a greater degree of anonymity. In light of a relatively young Muslim population in Germany, it is to be expected that digital platforms will become more relevant. Future studies should therefore explore ways that anti-Muslim racism and Islamism are mediated through digital media and the implications for counterstrategies and related processes of boundary making. In addition, a study of informal groups that have been increasingly active on social media platforms would convey a more complete picture of Muslim women's activism in Germany.

Note

1. The meaning of identity categories within intersectional studies is highly contested. While some scholars criticize the use of identity categories as essentializing and homogenizing (Harris 1990; Lugones 2007), rendering internal group hierarchies and marginalization invisible (Cole 2009; Nash 2008), other scholars contend that unitary categories are at the very heart of intersectionality, but need to be reconceptualized (Carastathis 2016). For analytical purposes and in line with scholars such as Belkhir and McNair Barnett (2001) this study explores those four identity categories that seem discursively most salient with regard to Muslim women in Germany.

Acknowledgments

The author would like to thank Gökçe Yurdakul, Özgür Özvatan, Anna Korteweg, the project team, and the members of the Migration Cluster for their generous comments on the draft version. Together with Bastian Neuhauser I presented. I would particularly like to thank all of the organizations' representatives who agreed to be interviewed. An earlier version of this article at the CES conference and the ECPR conference in Summer 2022 and received helpful feedback from the panel and Jean Beaman. The article has also benefitted from thoughtful remarks by the anonymous reviewers and by the editors of the Special Issue, Serena D'Agostino and Nadia E. Brown. Any mistakes remain, of course, my own. I would particularly like to thank all of the organizations' representatives who agreed to be interviewed.

Disclosure statement

No potential conflict of interest was reported by the author.

Funding

This work was supported by the Bundesministerium für Bildung und Forschung (Project Deutscher Islam) [01UG2035]. I acknowledge support by the Open Access Publication Fund of Humboldt-Universität zu Berlin.

References

Abbas, Tahir. 2011. *Islamic Radicalism and Multicultural Politics: The British Experience*. London: Routledge.
Abbas, Tahir. 2019. *Islamophobia and Radicalisation: A Vicious Cycle*. New York: Oxford University Press.
Abdel-Fattah, Randa. 2020. "Countering Violent Extremism, Governmentality and Australian Muslim Youth as 'Becoming Terrorist.'." *Journal of Sociology* 56 (3):372–87. doi:10.1177/1440783319842666.
Abou Taam, Marwan Claudia Dantschke, Michael Kreutzer, and Aladdin Sarhan. 2016. "Anwerbungspraxis Und Organisationsstruktur." In *Salafismus und Dschihadismus in Deutschland. Ursachen, Dynamiken, Handlungsempfehlungen*, eds. Janusz Biene, Christopher Daase, Julian Junk, and Harald Müller. Frankfurt, New York: Campus Verlag, 79–116.
Ajala, Imène. 2014. "Muslims in France and Great Britain: Issues of Securitization, Identities and Loyalties Post 9/11." *Journal of Muslim Minority Affairs* 34 (2):123–33. doi:10.1080/13602004.2014.911583.
Akbarzadeh, Shahram. 2020. "Political Islam under the Spotlight." In *Routledge Handbook of Political Islam*, ed. Shahram Akbarzadeh. New York: Routledge, 1–10. doi:10.4324/9780429425165-1.
Alba, Richard. 2005. "Bright vs. Blurred Boundaries: Second-Generation Assimilation and Exclusion in France, Germany, and the United States." *Ethnic and Racial Studies* 28 (1):20–49. doi:10.1080/0141987042000280003.
Alimahomed-Wilson, Sabrina. 2020. "The Matrix of Gendered Islamophobia: Muslim Women's Repression and Resistance." *Gender and Society* 34 (4):648–78. doi:10.1177/0891243220932156.
Amath, Nora. 2015. *The Phenomenology of Community Activism: Muslim Civil Society Organisations in Australia*. Carlton, Victoria, Australia: Melbourne University Publishing.
Amiraux, Valérie, and Pierre-Luc Beauchesne. 2020. "Racialization and the Construction of the Problem of the Muslim Presence in Western Societies." In *Routledge Handbook of Political Islam*, ed. Shahram Akbarzadeh. New York: Routledge, 363–82. doi:10.4324/9780429425165-27.
Amiraux, Valérie, and Gerdien Jonker. 2006. "Introduction: Talking About Visibility – Actors, Politics, Forms of Engagement." In *Politics of Visibility - Young Muslims in European Public Spaces*, eds. Valérie Amiraux and Gerdien Jonker. Bielefeld: transcript Verlag, 9–20. doi:10.1515/9783839405062-intro.
Amir-Moazami, Schirin, Christine M. Jacobsen, and Maleiha Malik. 2011. "Islam and Gender in Europe: Subjectivities, Politics and Piety." *Feminist Review* 98 (1):1–8. doi:10.1057/fr.2011.9.
Attia, Iman. 2009. *Die "westliche" Kultur und ihr Anderes: Zur Dekonstruktion von Orientalismus und antimuslimischem Rassismus*. Bielefeld: transcript Verlag. doi:10.1515/9783839410813.
Attia, Iman. 2013. "Privilegien sichern, nationale Identität revitalisieren. Gesellschafts- und handlungstheoretische Dimensionen der Theorie des antimuslimischen Rassismus im Unterschied zu Modellen von Islamophobie und Islamfeindlichkeit". *Journal für Psychologie* 21 (1):1–31.

Attia, Iman. 2015. "Zum Begriff des antimuslimischen Rassismus." In *Gespräche über Rassismus. Perspektiven und Widerstände*, eds. Zülfukar Çetin and Savaş Taş. Berlin: Verlag Yılmaz-Günay, 17–29.

Attia, Iman, and Mariam Popal, eds. 2018. *BeDeutungen dekolonisieren: Spuren von (antimuslimischem) Rassismus*. Münster: Unrast.

Belkhir, Jean Ait, and Bernice McNair Barnett. 2001. "Race, Gender and Class Intersectionality." *Race, Gender & Class* 8 (3): 157–74.

Blakemore, Brian, and Imran Awan, eds. 2013. *Extremism, Counter-Terrorism and Policing*. New York: Routledge.

Bleich, Erik. 2011. "What is Islamophobia and How Much is There? Theorizing and Measuring an Emerging Comparative Concept." *American Behavioral Scientist* 55 (12):1581–600. doi:10.1177/0002764211409387.

Bowen, John R., ed. 2014. *European States and Their Muslim Citizens: The Impact of Institutions on Perceptions and Boundaries*. Cambridge: Cambridge University Press.

Brah, Avtar, and Ann Phoenix. 2004. "Ain't I A Woman? Revisiting Intersectionality." *Journal of International Women's Studies* 5 (3): 75–86.

Bravo López, Fernando. 2011. "Towards a Definition of Islamophobia: Approximations of the Early Twentieth Century." *Ethnic and Racial Studies* 34 (4):556–73. doi:10.1080/01419870.2010.528440.

Brown, Katherine. 2008. "The Promise and Perils of Women's Participation in UK Mosques: The Impact of Securitisation Agendas on Identity, Gender and Community." *The British Journal of Politics & International Relations* 10 (3):472–91. doi:10.1111/j.1467-856x.2008.00324.x.

Bullock, Katherine. 2005. *Muslim Women Activists in North America: Speaking for Ourselves*. Austin, TX: University of Texas Press. doi:10.7560/706316.

Bullock, Katherine. 2012. "Toward a Framework for Investigating Muslim Women and Political Engagement in Canada." In *Islam in the Hinterlands: Exploring Muslim Cultural Politics in Canada*, ed. Jasmin Zine 92–111. University of British Columbia Press. doi:10.59962/9780774822749-006.

Çakir, Naime. 2014. *Islamfeindlichkeit : Anatomie eines Feindbildes in Deutschland*. Bielefeld: transcript Verlag.

Carastathis, Anna. 2016. *Intersectionality: Origins, Contestations, Horizons*. Lincoln, NE: University of Nebraska Press. doi:10.2307/j.ctt1fzhfz8.

Cesari, Jocelyne, ed. 2010. *Muslims in the West After 9/11: Religion, Politics, and Law*. London: Routledge. doi:10.4324/9780203863961.

Cesari, Jocelyne. 2013. *Why the West Fears Islam*. New York: Palgrave Macmillan. doi:10.1057/9781137121202.

Cesari, Jocelyne. 2015. "Religion and Politics: What Does God Have to Do with It?" *Religions* 6 (4):1330–44. doi:10.3390/rel6041330.

Cesari, Jocelyne. 2021. "Political Islam: More Than Islamism." *Religions* 12 (5):299. doi:10.3390/rel12050299.

Ceylan, Rauf. 2006. *Ethnische Kolonien*. Wiesbaden: VS Verlag für Sozialwissenschaften.

Ceylan, Rauf, and Michael Kiefer. 2018. *Radikalisierungsprävention in der Praxis. Antworten der Zivilgesellschaft auf den gewaltbereiten Neosalafismus*. Wiesbaden: Springer Fachmedien. doi:10.1007/978-3-658-15254-3_5.

Chakraborti, N., and I. Zempi. 2012. "Gendered Dimensions of Islamophobic VictimizationThe Veil under Attack: Gendered Dimensions of Islamophobic Victimization." *International Review of Victimology* 18 (3):269–84. doi:10.1177/0269758012446983.

Chbib, Raida. 2010. "Socioeconomic Integration of Muslims in Germany and the United States." In *The Many Sides of Muslim Integration: A German-American Comparison*, American Institute for Contemporary German Studies, 13–26. https://americangerman.institute/publication/the-many-sides-of-muslim-integration-a-german-american-comparison/.

Cheikh Husain, Sara. 2020. "Muslim Community Organizations' Perceptions of Islamophobia: Towards an Informed Countering Response." *Religions* 11 (10):485. doi:10.3390/rel11100485.

Cole, Elizabeth R. 2009. "Intersectionality and Research in Psychology." *American Psychologist* 64 (3):170–80. doi:10.1037/a0014564.

Corbin, Juliet M., and Anselm Strauss. 1990. "Grounded Theory Research: Procedures, Canons, and Evaluative Criteria." *Qualitative Sociology* 13 (1):3–21. doi:10.1007/BF00988593.

Crenshaw, Kimberlé Williams. 1989. "Demarginalizing the Intersection of Race and Sex: A Black Feminist Critique of Antidiscrimination Doctrine, Feminist Theory and Antiracist Politics." *University of Chicago Legal Forum* 1989: 139–67, 8.

Crenshaw, Kimberlé Williams. 1991. "Mapping the Margins: Intersectionality, Identity Politics, and Violence Against Women of Color." *Stanford Law Review* 43 (6):1241–99. doi:10.2307/1229039.

De Koning, Martijn. 2020. "The Racialization of Danger: Patterns and Ambiguities in the Relation between Islam, Security and Secularism in the Netherlands." *Patterns of Prejudice* 54 (1–2):123–35. doi:10.1080/0031322X.2019.1705011.

Esposito, John L., and Emad El-Din Shahin. 2013. "Introduction." In *The Oxford Handbook of Islam and Politics*, eds. John L. Esposito and, and Emad El-Din. New York: Oxford University Press, 1–4. doi:10.1093/oxfordhb/9780195395891.001.0001.

Esposito, John L., and Derya Iner, eds. 2018. *Islamophobia and Radicalization: Breeding Intolerance and Violence*. Cham: Palgrave Macmillan. doi:10.1007/978-3-319-95237-6.

Fekete, Liz. 2009. *A Suitable Enemy: Racism, Migration and Islamophobia in Europe*. London: Pluto.

Foner, Nancy. 2015. "Is Islam in Western Europe Like Race in the United States?" *Sociological Forum* 30 (4):885–99. doi:10.1111/socf.12199.

Foner, Nancy, and Richard Alba. 2008. "Immigrant Religion in the U.S. and Western Europe: Bridge or Barrier to Inclusion?" *International Migration Review* 42 (2):360–92. doi:10.1111/j.1747-7379.2008.00128.x.

Fox, Jonathan, and Yasemin Akbaba. 2015. "Securitization of Islam and Religious Discrimination: Religious Minorities in Western Democracies, 1990–2008." *Comparative European Politics* 13 (2):175–97. doi:10.1057/cep.2013.8.

Hafez, Farid. 2019. "Antimuslimischer Rassismus und Islamophobie: Worüber sprechen wir?" In *Antimuslimischer Rassismus und Islamfeindlichkeit*, eds. Bülent Ucar and Wassilis Kassis. Osnabrück: V&R unipress, 57–76. doi:10.14220/9783737009560.57.

Halm, Dirk. 2013. "Muslim Organisations and Intergenerational Change in Germany." *The International Spectator* 48 (1):48–57. doi:10.1080/03932729.2013.758909.

Hammer, Juliane. 2020. "Muslim Women and Gender Justice: An Introduction." In *Muslim Women and Gender Justice: Concepts, Sources, and Histories*, eds. Dina El Omari, Juliane Hammer, and Mouhanad Khorchide. London and New York: Routledge, 1–14. doi:10.4324/9781351025348-1.

Harris, Angela P. 1990. "Race and Essentialism in Feminist Legal Theory." *Stanford Law Review* 42 (3):581–616. doi:10.2307/1228886.

Jafri, Nuzhat. 2006. "The Canadian Council of Muslim Women: Engaging Muslim Women in Civic and Social Change." *Canadian Woman Studies* 25 (3/4): 97–99.

Joly, Danièle, and Khursheed Wadia. 2017. *Muslim Women and Power. Political and Civic Engagement in West European Societies*. London: Palgrave Macmillan.

Jonker, Gerdien. 2006. "Islamist or Pietist? Muslim Responses to the German Security Framework." In *Politics of Visibility*, eds. Gerdien Jonker and Valérie Amiraux. Bielefeld: transcript Verlag, 123–50. doi:10.1515/9783839405062-005.

Jouili, Jeanette S. 2011. "Beyond Emancipation: Subjectivities and Ethics Among Women in Europe's Islamic Revival Communities." *Feminist Review* 98 (1):47–64. doi:10.1057/fr.2011.4.

Jouili, Jeanette S. 2015. *Pious Practice and Secular Constraints: Women in the Islamic Revival in Europe*. Palo Alto: Stanford University Press.

Jouili, Jeanette S., and Schirin Amir-Moazami. 2006. "Knowledge, Empowerment and Religious Authority Among Pious Muslim Women in France and Germany." *The Muslim World* 96 (4):617–42. doi:10.1111/j.1478-1913.2006.00150.x.

Kausmann, Corinna, Nadiya Kelle, Julia Simonson, and Clemens Tesch-Römer. 2022. "Freiwilliges Engagement – Bedeutung Für Gesellschaft Und Politik." In *Freiwilliges Engagement in Deutschland. Der Deutsche Freiwilligensurvey 2019*, eds. Julia Simonson, Nadiya Kelle, Corinna Kausmann, and Clemens Tesch-Römer. Springer VS, 319–26. doi:10.1007/978-3-658-35317-9_16.

Kausmann, Corinna, Claudia Vogel, Christine Hagen, and Julia Simonson. 2017. "Freiwilliges Engagement von Frauen und Männern. Genderspezifische Befunde zur Vereinbarkeit von Freiwilligem Engagement, Elternschaft und Erwerbstätigkeit." Bundesministerium für Familie, Senioren, Frauen und Jugend. Berlin.

Kaya, Ayhan, and Ayşe Tecmen. 2019. "Europe versus Islam?: Right-Wing Populist Discourse and the Construction of a Civilizational Identity." *The Review of Faith & International Affairs* 17 (1):49–64. doi:10.1080/15570274.2019.1570759.

Korteweg, Anna C, and Gökçe Yurdakul. 2021. "Liberal Feminism and Postcolonial Difference: Debating Headscarves in France, the Netherlands, and Germany." *Social Compass* 68 (3):410–29. doi:10.1177/0037768620974268.

Kundnani, Arun. 2014. *The Muslims are Coming! Islamophobia, Extremism, and the Domestic War on Terror*. London: Verso.

Kuppinger, Petra. 2012. "Women, Leadership, and Participation in Mosques and Beyond: Notes from Stuttgart, Germany." In *Women, Leadership, and Mosques: Changes in Contemporary Islamic Authority*, eds. Masooda Bano and Hilary E. Kalmbach. Leiden, The Netherlands: Brill, 323–44. doi:10.1163/9789004209367_017.

Lamont, Michèle, and Virág Molnár. 2002. "The Study of Boundaries in the Social Sciences." *Annual Review of Sociology* 28 (1):167–95. doi:10.1146/annurev.soc.28.110601.141107.

Lamont, Michèle, Graziella Moraes Silva, Jessica S. Welburn, Joshua Guetzkow, Nissim Mizrachi, Hannah Herzog, and Elisa Ries eds. 2016. *Getting Respect: Responding to Stigma and Discrimination in the United States, Brazil, and Israel*, Princeton, NJ: Princeton University Press. doi:10.2307/j.ctv346qr9.

Lépinard, Éléonore. 2020. *Feminist Trouble*. New York: Oxford University Press.

Lewicki, Aleksandra, and Therese O'Toole. 2017. "Acts and Practices of Citizenship: Muslim Women's Activism in the UK." *Ethnic and Racial Studies* 40 (1):152–71. doi:10.1080/01419870.2016.1216142.

Lugones, María. 2007. "Heterosexualism and the Colonial/Modern Gender System." *Hypatia: A Journal of Feminist Philosophy* 22 (1):186–209. doi:10.2979/HYP.2007.22.1.186.

Lutz, Helma. 2015. "Intersectionality as Method." *DiGest: Journal of Diversity and Gender Studies* 2 (1–2):39–39. doi:10.11116/jdivegendstud.2.1-2.0039.

Mandaville, Peter. 2014. *Islam and Politics*. 2nd ed. London: Routledge. doi:10.4324/9781315814773.

Mansoob, Syed, and Sara Pavan. 2011. "Identity and Islamic Radicalization in Western Europe." *Civil Wars* 13 (3):259–79. doi:10.1080/13698249.2011.600000.

Monshipouri, Mahmood. 2010. "The War on Terror and Muslims in the West." In *Muslims in the West After 9/11: Religion, Politics, and Law*, ed. Jocelyne Cesari. London and New York: Routledge, 45–66.

Muckel, Stefan, Lukas Hentzschel, Aiman Mazyek, Bekir Alboğa, Nushin Atmaca, Lydia Nofal, and Ehrhart Körting. 2018. *Die Finanzierung Muslimischer Organisationen in Deutschland*. Berlin: Friedrich-Ebert-Stiftung Forum.

Mykytjuk-Hitz, Karin. 2015. "Die zivilgesellschaftlichen Potentiale von neo-muslimischen Akteuren." In *Religiöse Netzwerke*, ed. Alexander-Kenneth Nagel. Bielefeld: transcript Verlag, 191–214. doi:10.14361/transcript. 9783839427583.191.

Nash, Jennifer C. 2008. "Re-Thinking Intersectionality." *Feminist Review* 89 (1):1–15. doi:10.1057/fr.2008.4.

Nökel, Sigrid. 2002. *Die Töchter der Gastarbeiter und der Islam: zur Soziologie alltagsweltlicher Anerkennungspolitiken: eine Fallstudie*. Bielefeld: transcript Verlag.

Peucker, Mario. 2017. "Muslim Community Organisations – Crucial but Underexplored Facets of Muslim Lives in the West." In *Muslim Community Organizations in the West*, eds. Mario Peucker and Rauf Ceylan. Wiesbaden: Springer Fachmedien Wiesbaden, 1–10. doi:10.1007/978-3-658-13889-9_1.

Peucker, Mario. 2019. "Islamophobia and Stigmatising Discourses: A Driving Force for Muslim Active Citizenship?." In *Islamophobia and Radicalization: Breeding Intolerance and Violence*, eds. John Esposito and Derya Iner. Cham: Palgrave Macmillan, 245–64. doi:10.1007/978-3-319-95237-6_13.

Peucker, Mario, and Shahram Akbarzadeh. 2014. *Muslim Active Citizenship in the West*. London: Routledge.

Pfaff, Steven, and Anthony J. Gill. 2016. "Will a Million Muslims March?: Muslim Interest Organizations and Political Integration in Europe." *Comparative Political Studies* 39 (7):803–28. doi:10.1177/0010414006287237.

Pfahl-Traughber, Armin. 2008. "Islamismus – Der neue Extremismus, Faschismus, Fundamentalismus und Totalitarismus? Eine Erörterung zu Angemessenheit und Erklärungskraft der Zuordnungen." *Zeitschrift für Politik* 55 (1):33–48. doi:10.5771/0044-3360-2008-1-33.

Pfahl-Traughber, Armin. 2012. "Die fehlende Trennschärfe des "Islamophobie"-Konzepts für die Vorurteilsforschung." In *Islamophobie und Antisemitismus - Ein umstrittener Vergleich*, eds. Olaf Glöckner, Michael Spieker, Gideon Botsch, and Christoph Kopke. Berlin and BostonBerlin and Boston: de Gruyter, 11–28. doi:10.1515/9783110265149.11.

Pfündel, Katrin, Anja Stichs, and Kerstin Tanis. 2021. "Muslimisches Leben in Deutschland 2020." *Forschungszentrum Migration,Integration und Asyl*. Nürnberg. https://www.ssoar.info/ssoar/handle/document/73274.

Pojmann, Wendy. 2010. "Muslim Women's Organizing in France and Italy: Political Culture, Activism, and Performativity in the Public Sphere." *Feminist Formations* 22 (3):229–51. doi:10.1353/ff.2010.0015.

Povey, Tara. 2009. "Islamophobia and Arab and Muslim Women's Activism." *Cosmopolitan Civil Societies: An Interdisciplinary Journal* 1 (2):63–76. doi:10.5130/ccs.v1i2.1040.

Roy, Olivier. 1994. *The Failure of Political Islam*. Cambridge, MA: Harvard University Press.

Shooman, Yasemin. 2011. "Islamophobie, antimuslimischer Rassismus oder Muslimfeindlichkeit? Kommentar zu der Begriffsdebatte der Deutschen Islam Konferenz." *Heinrich-Böll-Stiftung*, July 1. https://heimatkunde.boell.de/de/2011/07/01/islamophobie-antimuslimischer-rassismus-oder-muslimfeindlichkeit-kommentar-zu-der

Shooman, Yasemin. 2014. '. . . Weil Ihre Kultur so Ist': Narrative des Antimuslimischen Rassismus. Bielefeld: Transcript-Verl. doi:10.1515/transcript.9783839428665.

Shooman, Yasemin, and Riem Spielhaus. 2010. "The Concept of the Muslim Enemy in the Public Discourse." In *Muslims in the West After 9/11: Religion, Politics, and Law*, ed. Jocelyne Cesari. London and New York: Routledge, 198–228.

Spalek, Basia. 2012. *Counter-Terrorism. Community-Based Approaches to Preventing Terror Crime*. Cham: Palgrave Macmillan. doi:10.1057/9781137009524_2.

Spielhaus, Riem. 2012. "Making Islam Relevant: Female Authority and Representation of Islam in Germany." In *Women, Leadership, and Mosques: Changes in Contemporary Islamic Authority*, eds. Masooda Bano and Hilary E. Kalmbach. Leiden, The Netherlands: Brill, 437–55. doi:10.1163/9789004209367_023.

Spielhaus, Riem. 2013. "Vom Migranten zum Muslim und wieder zurück – Die Vermengung von Integrations- und Islamthemen in Medien, Politik und Forschung." In Islam und die deutsche Gesellschaft, *Islam und Politik*. eds. Dirk Halm and Hendrik Meyer. Wiesbaden: Springer Fachmedien, 169–94. doi:10.1007/978-3-658-01846-7_7.

Spielhaus, Riem. 2019. "Islam and Feminism: German and European Variations on a Global Theme." In *Muslim Women and Gender Justice: Concepts, Sources, and Histories*, ed. Juliane Hammer. New York: Routledge, 46–61. doi:10.4324/9781351025348-4.

Termeer, Agnes, and Isabelle Duyvesteyn. 2022. "The Inclusion of Women in Jihad: Gendered Practices of Legitimation in Islamic State Recruitment Propaganda." *Critical Studies on Terrorism* 15 (2):463–83. doi:10.1080/17539153.2022.2038825.

Tietze, Nikola. 2003. "Islamismus: Ein Blick in die sozialwissenschaftliche Literatur Frankreichs." *Leviathan* 31 (4):556–70. doi:10.1007/s11578-003-0031-z.

Van Es, Margaretha A. 2016. *Stereotypes and Self-Representations of Women with a Muslim Background*. Cham: Palgrave Macmillan. doi:10.1007/978-3-319-40676-3.

Van Es, Margaretha A., and Nella Van den Brandt. 2020. "Muslim Women's Activism and Organizations in the Netherlands and Belgium." *Trajecta Religion, Culture and Society in the Low Countries* 29 (2):191–220. doi:10.5117/TRA2020.2.004.VANE.

Wadia, Khursheed. 2015. "Women from Muslim Communities in Britain: Political and Civic Activism in the 9/11 Era." In *Muslims and Political Participation in Britain*, ed. Timothy Peace. London: Routledge, 85–102.

Wang, Yuting. 2017. "Muslim Women's Evolving Leadership Roles: A Case Study of Women Leaders in an Immigrant Muslim Community in Post-9/11 America." *Social Compass* 64 (3):424–41. doi:10.1177/0037768617713660.

Welten, Liselotte, and Tahir Abbas. 2021. "'We are Already 1-0 behind': Perceptions of Dutch Muslims on Islamophobia, Securitisation, and de-Radicalisation." *Critical Studies on Terrorism* 14 (1):90–116. doi:10.1080/17539153.2021.1883714.

Yousuf, Shereen. 2020. "Muslim Resiliency in the Face of Counter-Terror and Violent Extremism." *Communication and Critical-Cultural Studies* 17 (4):386–94. doi:10.1080/14791420.2020.1829660.

Yurdakul, Gökçe, and Anna C. Korteweg. 2013. "Gender Equality and Immigrant Integration: Honor Killing and Forced Marriage Debates in the Netherlands, Germany, and Britain." *Women's Studies International Forum* 41:204–14. doi:10.1016/j.wsif.2013.07.011.

Yurdakul, Gökçe, and Anna C. Korteweg. 2021. "Boundary Regimes and the Gendered Racialized Production of Muslim Masculinities: Cases from Canada and Germany." *Journal of Immigrant and Refugee Studies* 19 (1):39–54. doi:10.1080/15562948.2020.1833271.

Zahedi, Ashraf. 2011. "Muslim American Women in the Post-11 September Era: Challenges and Opportunities." *International Feminist Journal of Politics* 13 (2):183–203. doi:10.1080/14616742.2011.560038.

Zine, Jasmin. 2006. "Between Orientalism and Fundamentalism: The Politics of Muslim Women's Feminist Engagement." *Muslim World Journal of Human Rights* 3 (1). doi:10.2202/1554-4419.1080.

Zine, Jasmin, ed. 2012. *Islam in the Hinterlands: Exploring Muslim Cultural Politics in Canada*. Vancouver, BC: UBC Press. doi:10.59962/9780774822749.

Zolberg, Aristide R., and Long Litt Woon. 1999. "Why Islam is Like Spanish: Cultural Incorporation in Europe and the United States." *Politics & Society* 27 (1):5–38. doi:10.1177/0032329299027001002.

Appendix

Table A1. Overview of the Organizations Interviewed.

Organization name	City	Number of Members	Founding year	Main Goals	Main Services	Main target group(s)
Coalition of Muslim Women (Aktionsbündnis muslimischer Frauen, AmF)	Wesseling	500	2009	Improvement of Muslim women's political and social participation	Representation of Muslim women's interests	Muslim women
Meeting and Education Center for Women and Families (Begegnungs- und Bildungszentrum für Frauen und Familien, BBF)	Berlin	30	2019	Empowerment and Support of Muslim/Migrant women	Social Services	(Muslim/Migrant) Women and Families
Muslim Women's Center for Encounter and Further Education (Begegnungs- und Fortbildungszentrum muslimischer Frauen, BFmF)	Cologne	100 (employees)	1996	Social Welfare	Social Services	Minorities and disadvantaged persons
Family Education Center MINA (Familienbildungszentrum MINA)	Duisburg	48	2009	Empowerment of Muslim women and women of Color	Social Services	Muslim and minoritized women and children
Women's Initiative for Education and Childcare (Fraueninitiative für Bildung und Erziehung, FIBEr)	Bonn	40	2009	Women's empowerment, integration of immigrant and refugee women	Social Services	Migrant and refugee women
Welfare Services of Muslim Women (Sozialdienst Muslimischer Frauen, SmF)	Cologne	119	2016	Social Welfare	Social Services	Muslim and minoritized women

Solidarity Through Difference? How Italian and Spanish LGBTQIA* Organizations Frame Solidarity Through an Intersectional Lens

Aurora Perego ⓘ

ABSTRACT
Although Western-based LGBTQIA* mobilizations have often been considered rather internally fragmented and isolated from other movements, recent investigations show that LGBTQIA* organizations have increasingly addressed multiple discriminations and built solidarity ties with communities coping with various inequality structures – such as race, class, and dis/abilities. This article addresses this puzzle by analyzing how political solidarity was framed by Spanish and Italian LGBTQIA* organizations during the 2011–2020 decade, paying particular attention to the nexus between diagnostic framing and solidarity discourses. To do so, this article examines the collective action events published on Facebook by LGBTQIA* organizations based in Milan and Madrid. Results show that, while LGBTQIA* actors dealt with cross-sectional issues in both cities, they differently framed problems and articulated diverse solidarity discourses.

Introduction

[W]e will go to the Pride march all together [. . .]. [We want] A home for everybody, otherwise why should we have equal marriage? [We want] Documents for everybody, otherwise what is the point of civil unions? [We want] Immediate jus soli, otherwise the fair recognition of homosexual couples' children will only trace a new discrimination line. [We want] Healthcare for everybody – secular, not binary, free, and unhampered by any permits to stay in the country. [We want] Universal basic income to guarantee a deserving life. - Corpo ai Diritti, 2019[1]

Social movement scholarship has extensively focused on political solidarity between civil society organizations (CSOs), showing that it plays a pivotal role in civil society. Political solidarity indeed motivates people and so on to build a more just society through the development of feelings of belonging (Banting and Kymlicka 2017; Melucci 1996). By doing so, it increases both individual participation in collective actions (Zurcher and Snow 1981), and cooperation between collective actors (Diani 2015; Melucci 1996). Furthermore, the creation of solidarity bonds strengthens marginalized groups' capacity to advocate for their rights and demand justice (Banting and Kymlicka 2017), thus reducing the risk of exclusion of subaltern sectors of the population (della Porta 2013). Hence, shedding light on how solidarity is formed and facilitated provides a thorough understanding of how civil society is sustained.

Scholarship shows that solidarity bonds encompass both a discourse-related dimension, where organizations express solidarity to other groups' claims and actions, and an action-related dimension, where organizations participate in other group's collective actions or engage in the organization of joint events (Banting and Kymlicka 2017; Hunt and Benford 2004). Several factors may affect the emergence and development of solidarity. Solidarity is created when collective actors share collective

---

ⓑ Supplemental data for this article can be accessed on the publisher's website at https://doi.org/10.1080/1554477X.2023.2250036

identities (Taylor and Whittier 1992) and framing strategies (Benford and Snow 2000; Hunt and Benford 2004). Furthermore, solidarity bonds depend on the opportunities or threats provided by the socio-political context in which organizations are embedded (Bieler and Lindberg 2011). With the diffusion of the Internet, scholars have found that solidarity initiatives (Rahbari 2021) and solidarity ties (Diani 2000) are also enhanced by social media platforms' potential to connect activists across national and transnational borders (Ayoub and Brzezińska 2015).

Within this framework, within-field solidarity – namely solidarity bonds developed between groups that are active in the same collective action field – is often more easily created and sustained over time than cross-field solidarity – solidarity bonds developed between organizations belonging to and identifying with different collective action fields (Van Dyke 2003; Verloo 2013).[2] In particular, different collective identities can lead to conflicts, some of which arise around the sources of inequality (such as gender, class, and ethnicity) that differently affect movement actors (Beamish and Luebbers 2009; Cole 2008). Within this framework, Western-based LGBTQIA* activism has been found to be rather internally fragmented and isolated from other fields (Ghaziani, Taylor, and Stone 2016; Seidman 1997). Nonetheless, recent investigations show evidence of local cooperative efforts occurring between LGBTQIA* organizations and other groups (Chironi and Portos 2021; Terriquez, Brenes, and Lopez 2018).

This article addresses this research puzzle by examining the solidarity discourses developed by LGBTQIA* organizations when interacting with other LGBTQIA* organizations (within-field solidarity) and with organizations from other collective action fields (cross-field solidarity) on social media platforms. In particular, it aims to investigate: (1) to what extent and how LGBTQIA* organizations embedded in different socio-political contexts frame problems (known as "diagnostic framing") over time; and (2) how such framing processes accompany the development of different understandings and discourses around political solidarity in the two contexts. To address these questions, the article discusses the results of a frame analysis of the collective action events published in 2011, 2013, 2015, 2017, and 2019 on the Facebook public pages managed by LGBTQIA* organizations based in Milan and Madrid. This analysis unfolds by proposing an intersectional approach to political solidarity, where intersectionality is articulated both as an analytical lens to study how solidarity discourses deal with intersectional privilege and marginalization, and as an empirical question to investigate its possible usage(s) by LGBTQIA* organizations.

The contribution of this article lies in exploring the evolution of framing processes articulated by LGBTQIA* organizations in Southern Europe, a phenomenon that has not been systematically studied yet. In doing so, this research clarifies both how framing processes may accompany the development of different solidarity discourses in the two cities, as well as how they may be shaped by contextual opportunities and threats. Furthermore, it investigates how social media platforms are used by LGBTQIA* activists to articulate solidarity discourses both within the LGBTQIA* field and with collective actors engaging in other social struggles, thus shedding light on their potential for coalition building between marginalized communities.

Political solidarity from an intersectional lens

Political solidarity is rooted in feelings of belonging to a certain collectivity (Melucci 1996; Taylor and Nancy 1992) and in a sense of emotional investment that connects the members of such a collectivity to one another (Gamson 1992b), making them perceive they share common goals and struggles (Hunt and Benford 2004). Within this framework, solidarity is understood as "the ability of actors to recognize others, and to be recognized, as belonging to the same social unit" (Melucci 1996, 23). Such an ability is highly shaped by collective worldviews (Benford and Snow 2000; Hunt and Benford 2004) and can hence be investigated by examining the collective action frames (Benford and Snow 2000) that sustain how solidarity is interpreted and narrated by collective actors.

Feminist scholars have often conceptualized political solidarity in terms of practices through which organizations acknowledge and negotiate power asymmetries both within themselves and between them (Ciccia and Roggeband 2021; Mohanty 2003; Tormos 2017). Against this backdrop, political solidarity has been addressed through the lens of intersectionality (Crenshaw 1989) to grasp "new linkages and positions that can facilitate alliances between voices that are usually marginalized" (Kaijser and Kronsell 2013, 419). In particular, the framework of "political intersectionality" (Cole 2008) serves as an analytical lens to examine the solidarity discourses and practices articulated within and between organizations affected by different inequality structures (Ciccia and Roggeband 2021; Einwohner et al. 2021; Evans and Lépinard 2019). Political intersectionality indeed sheds light on the inner conflicts and differences within groups, as well as on the relations established between organizations characterized by different social positionings and identities. Building on these insights, intersectional solidarity is defined as:

> An ongoing political process of building cooperation by altering power asymmetries within and between organizations and groups located at different intersections of class, race, gender, sexuality, religion and able-bodiedness, and across geographical boundaries. (Ciccia, della Porta, and Pavan 2021, 176)

Intersectional solidarity hence comprises both a discursive dimension, meaning how differences within and between constituencies are framed by collective actors, and a relational dimension, meaning how differences are not only acknowledged, but challenged through collective practices and actions (Ciccia and Roggeband 2021).

To the purpose of this research, the solidarity discourses articulated by LGBTQIA* actors on their social media platforms are examined through an intersectional approach. Intersectionality constitutes the analytical lens (Hancock 2007) to examine how LGBTQIA* organizations both deal with internal heterogeneous social positionings and frame cross-sectional issues and other minorities' concerns. By doing so, intersectionality serves to problematize social movement theorizations and their explanatory power in relation to LGBTQIA* mobilizations and intersectional claims. However, intersectionality also constitutes an analytical focus of this research, since it pays particular attention to the nexus between how the concept of intersectionality is signified and used, and how solidarity is framed by LGBTQIA* organizations.

LGBTQIA* solidarity framing on social media platforms

Scholars have increasingly analyzed the nexus between social media platforms and the development of solidarity ties, showing how the former often function as "strategic communication venues [...] to broaden and accelerate the formation of new collective meanings, frames, and action strategies to challenge the status quo" (Pavan 2017, 435). Through these venues collective actors establish a wide range of emotionally significant interactions that sustain the creation of collective identities (Kavada 2015), strengthen solidarity ties (Diani 2000), and enhance the creation of solidarity initiatives (Rahbari 2021). Furthermore, digital communication platforms play an important role in the development and circulation of solidarity discourses through flyers, political manifestos, and images (Chidgey 2018; Sumiala and Korpiola 2017).

Social media platforms have been extensively deployed by marginalized communities (Mele 1999). In particular, they are useful to LGBTQIA* organizations in several ways. They provide LGBTQIA* communities with venues to explore non-normative lifestyles and to connect with other marginalized individuals (Mainardi and Pavan 2020; Preves 2005; Shapiro 2004).[3] By doing so, they support community-building processes between people that may thus be encouraged to mobilize for their rights (Ayoub and Brzezińska 2015; Mainardi and Pavan 2020). Furthermore, these platforms are strategically deployed by LGBTQIA* organizations to disseminate information on their claims (Berry, Martin, and Yue 2003) and to connect with other LGBTQIA* collective actors across national and transnational borders (Ayoub and Brzezińska 2015). Recent studies also show that some LGBTQIA* organizations have developed transformative media practices by using social media platforms to mobilize multi-identity groups (such as LGBTQIA* racialized communities) and articulate critical reflections on intersectional matrices of power and possible resistances (Costanza-Chock 2018).

Despite these findings, Western LGBTQIA* collective action fields have often been considered rather internally fragmented (Seidman 1997) and isolated from other communities (Strolovitch 2007). Western-based LGBTQIA* activism has witnessed several conflicts since the 1960s, often due to the predominance of (white) cisgender gay men within LGBTQIA* organizations, and the scarce awareness of intersectional privilege and marginalization (Strolovitch 2007; Ward 2008). Furthermore, in line with studies arguing that collective actors showing strong identity traits are less prone to engage in cooperative endeavors (Lichterman 1995), some scholars find that LGBTQIA* organizations may only partially interact with groups marginalized along other inequality lines (Puar 2007; Strolovitch 2007). Nonetheless, other researchers emphasize that LGBTQIA* groups distinguish themselves from other identity-based organizations due to their promotion of a "unity through diversity" logic aimed at celebrating differences instead of creating exclusionary identities (Armstrong 2002). Against this backdrop, recent investigations show evidence of local cooperative efforts, also referred to as "intersectional coalitions" (Adam 2017), occurring between LGBTQIA* organizations and other collective actors, especially racialized communities (Ayoub 2018; Terriquez, Brenes, and Lopez 2018). These cooperative dynamics are accompanied by collective understandings about difference and solidarity (Cole and Luna 2010; Townsend-Bell 2021), that are sustained by framing processes through which collective actors acknowledge differences and challenge inequalities (Ciccia and Roggeband 2021; Ferree and Roth 1998). Combining studies on intersectional solidarity and framing dynamics, the following section will discuss how the framing of problems (diagnostic framing) may accompany and shape different understandings of political solidarity across different socio-political contexts.

The nexus between solidarity discourses, framing, and socio-political contexts

Framing is a crucial aspect in solidarity building, both in its discourse- and action-oriented dimensions (Ciccia and Roggeband 2021; Gamson 1992a; Hunt and Benford 2004). Drawing from Goffman's (1974) pivotal work,[4] collective action frames are defined as "action-oriented sets of beliefs and meanings that inspire and legitimate the activities and campaigns of a social movement organization" (Benford and Snow 2000, 614). In other words, they are interpretative schemas that bring people together and enhance collective action (Benford and Snow 2000). They are forged and negotiated through so-called "framing processes" (Snow and Benford 1988), and understood as dynamic activities through which collective actors signify and interpret the social realities in which they are embedded (Benford and Snow 2000). This interpretive work is undertaken through three main framing tasks: (1) diagnostic framing, which occurs through the punctuation of specific social conditions or events as unjust, and the attribution of responsibilities for such problems; (2) prognostic framing, which entails the proposition of given solutions to tackle such problems; and (3) motivational framing, which provides a rationale for engaging in collective action beyond the punctuation of problems, the attribution of blame, and the propositions of solutions (Snow and Benford 1988).

LGBTQIA* activism has been highly examined through the framing perspective. Collective action frames mobilized by LGBTQIA* actors have been informed by an interplay between "sameness" and "difference" that has accompanied the development of different movements within the LGBTQIA* collective action field (Ghaziani, Taylor, and Stone 2016; Valocchi 1999). Furthermore, LGBTQIA* collective action frames have emerged and developed through dialectical interactions both within the LGBTQIA* collective action field and through other fields. In particular, they are formed through movement-countermovement dynamics in which collective actors frame common threats and enemies in the effort to strengthen the LGBTQIA* collective action field (Ayoub and Chetaille 2020; Dorf and Tarrow 2014; Fetner 2008).

Framing is also a fundamental dimension in the development of solidarity discourses around LGBTQIA* and intersectional issues. By proposing a theoretical model to conceptualize intersectional solidarity, Ciccia and Roggeband (2021) argue that collective actors may frame solidarity and difference through two main frames: the Common Denominator and the Recognition of Difference frames. The former occurs when organizations articulate a "commonality of experiences" narrative, identifying similar issues and problems and minimizing differences (Ciccia and Roggeband 2021, 7). Within this framework, the proposed solutions are thought to address cross-cutting concerns relevant to different organizations and to benefit all of them in a similar fashion (Ciccia and Roggeband 2021). The latter, instead, occurs when organizations articulate a "dialogue across differences" narrative (Ciccia and Roggeband 2021, 7), not only acknowledging the differential social positionings amongst them (Townsend-Bell 2021), but also framing them as structurally entangled (Ciccia and Roggeband 2021, 7–8). Within this framework, the proposed solutions are rooted in the recognition of such differences and are aimed at addressing diverse, but interrelated, problems in specific ways. This framing occurs through the development of a so-called "intersectional consciousness," defined as:

> [A] set of political beliefs and action orientations rooted in recognition of the need to account for multiple grounds of identity when considering how the social world is constructed, when deciding what corrective goals to pursue, and when selecting the appropriate means for pursuing those goals. (Greenwood 2008, 38)

An intersectional political consciousness is expressed through the framing of the social reality in which collective actors are embedded, as well as through problem attribution and solution proposition. However, given the emphasis posed by previous studies on the importance of common threats and enemies on alliance-building (Van Dyke 2003), this article focuses on diagnostic framing and how LGBTQIA* actors collectively identify problems and attribute responsibilities.

Framing in context: socio-cultural opportunities and threats

Framing processes are elaborated within the socio-political and cultural contexts in which collective actors are embedded (Benford and Snow 2000; Snow, Vliegenthart, and Ketelaars 2019). To analyze the relation between framing and context, researchers have considered the political (Diani 1996) and cultural (Goodwin and Jasper 1999) opportunities and constraints that characterize the context in which challengers act, as well as the discursive opportunity structures (Ferree et al. 2002) in which some actors and frames are perceived as more legitimate than others. Given the dynamic nature of framing, framing processes might differ over time, as well as across contexts and collective action fields (Snow, Vliegenthart, and Ketelaars 2019). Therefore, researchers argue for the importance of situating framing in context (Creed, Langstraat, and Scully 2002), i.e., examining the specific socio-cultural opportunities and constraints that characterize the environment in which activists are embedded, as well as their changes over time (Snow, Vliegenthart, and Ketelaars 2019).

Findings on LGBTQIA* solidarity discourses show divergent results, even if scholars tend to argue that external threats may be more salient than opportunities for LGBTQIA* actors to create both cross-field and within-field ties (Adam, Duyvendak, and Krouwel 1999). Several investigations indeed emphasize that LGBTQIA* actors are more likely to build alliances in more conservative or even repressive societies (Ayoub 2016; O'Dwyer 2018). This phenomenon is explained by the fact that LGBTQIA* activists may both unite amongst themselves and join other movements when they identify common threats and enemies, thus suggesting that diagnostic framing may play a pivotal role in the establishment of solidarity discourses (Adam, Duyvendak, and Krouwel 1999). Building on these insights, the following section will discuss how the nexus between solidarity discourses, diagnostic framing, and the socio-political contexts in which LGBTQIA* actors are embedded is empirically investigated in this research.

Methodology

Case selection and time frame

This investigation articulates a comparative research design (George and Bennett 2005) between two most-similar cases (Seawright and Gerring 2008): Milan and Madrid. The two cities are characterized by rather similar local contexts, but dissimilar national legislations in terms of LGBTQIA* rights. Both cities were pioneer in the emergence of LGBTQIA* mobilizations, in the establishment of the first LGBTQIA* organizations in their countries, and in the formulation of LGBTQIA* political claims (Calvo 2011; Cossolo et al. 2019). However, according to the Rainbow Europe Index, while the Spanish legislative system guarantees LGBTQIA* rights in several institutional areas, the Italian legislation recognizes very few rights to the LGBTQIA* community.[5] The Spanish provision of rights to LGBTQIA* individuals started in the 1990s, when national lesbian and gay organizations adopted a "legalist strategy" (Llamas and Vila 1999) aimed at obtaining recognition from public authorities (Calvo 2011). On the contrary, the Italian context has until recently been characterized by the invisibility of LGBTQIA* issues (Grigolo and Jörgens 2010; Prearo 2015). LGBTQIA* individuals and their rights had been long considered private issues worth neither public discussion, nor legislative attention – partly linked to the traditional role played by family and religion in the Italian society (Nardi 1993), as well as to the influence of the Vatican State (Grigolo and Jörgens 2010).

To map the evolution of framing processes, five points in time (2011, 2013, 2015, 2017, and 2019) were selected within the 2011–2020 decade. This time frame was characterized by several occurrences, illustrated in Figure 1, concerning LGBTQIA* rights in Italy and Spain. Firstly, both countries witnessed the emergence of strong anti-gender campaigns (Cornejo and Pichardo 2018; Lavizzari 2020). This period also saw the creation or renewal of coalitions between LGBTQIA* groups and feminist groups (Chironi 2019; Platero and Ortega-Arjonilla 2016), fostered by the enactment of austerity measures (Chironi and Portos 2021). In both countries, such coalitions supported numerous campaigns for the enactment of new laws, such as an Italian law on same-sex marriage and stepchild adoption (Prearo 2021), which was partially approved in 2016, and a Spanish national law to recognize rights to trans* individuals (Platero 2020), which resulted in regional laws enacted by several Spanish regions (amongst which the Community of Madrid) between 2014 and 2018.

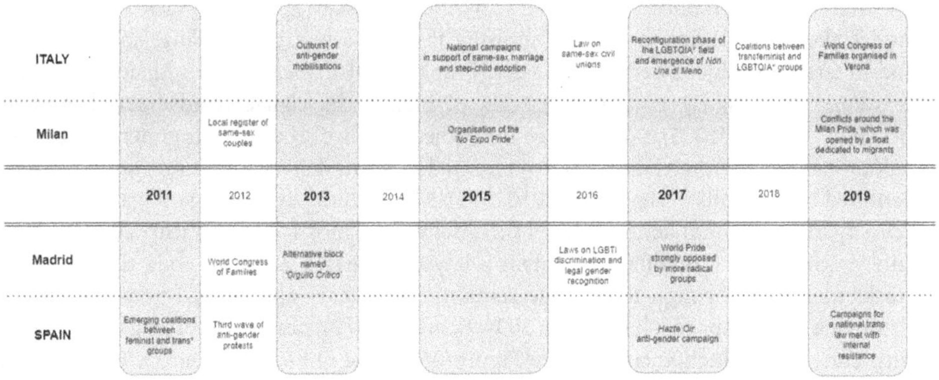

Figure 1. Evolution of Political Opportunities and Threats in Madrid and Milan Between 2011–2020 (Own Elaboration).

Milan and Madrid were protagonists of this decade of changes. In 2012, Milan was the first Italian city to create a municipal register for same-sex couples. However, between the early 2010s and 2015, the city witnessed several mobilizations to oppose Expo 2015 that caused tensions between local LGBTQIA* groups (Bertuzzi 2017). In 2019, the Pride parade was opened by a float dedicated to refugees. During the same period, Madrid was signed by the presence of both strong anti-gender campaigns, such as the 2012 World Congress of Families (Cornejo and Pichardo Galán 2018), and of intense mobilizations for the recognition of trans* rights between 2015 and 2020 (Platero 2020). In 2017, two major but contrasting events took place in Madrid: at the beginning of the year, a new anti-gender campaign started in Madrid before moving to other cities; in June, the World Pride was held in Madrid for the first time. The organization of the World Pride not only heightened within-field conflicts, but also represented an opportunity for less institutionalized groups to increase cooperative efforts (Domínguez and Elpidio 2019).

Units of analysis and data source

This study focuses on LGBTQIA* civil society organizations located in Milan and Madrid that were active on Facebook between 2011 and 2020. To be sampled, the organizations had to identify as part of the LGBTQIA* community and to mobilize to advance the status of LGBTQIA* individuals, no matter whether in the form of service provision, cultural initiatives, or political activities.[6] Regardless of their formalization level, they had to recognize themselves as a constituency and be visible to out-group individuals (Eggert and Pilati 2014) in the digital sphere by managing at least a Facebook public page for at least one year. The sample eventually included 80 and 58 organizations active on Facebook over the decade in Madrid and Milan, respectively (see the online Methodological Appendix for the selection of organizations, and Table A1 for an overview of the sampled organizations and of their characteristics).

To examine the framing strategies developed by LGBTQIA* actors over time, this article focuses on the collective action events promoted on Facebook by the sampled organizations. The posts were retrieved by means of CrowdTangle Team (2020) (please see Table A2 in the Online Appendix for summary statistics of the downloaded posts).[7] Literature on digital activism suggests that Facebook affordances (e.g., no limitations in the number of characters and possibility to reach a broad public) make it an appropriate platform to analyze framing (Guenther et al. 2020). Facebook has also been examined as a tool used to both articulate solidarity discourses (Rahbari 2021) and promote solidarity actions (de Vries, Simry, and Maoz 2015). The frame analysis illustrated below was conducted on the written texts contained in the events.

Coding and analytic strategy

To analyze diagnostic framing tasks, I developed a qualitative coding process in two phases. First, to identify the framing tasks, I followed a "frame semantic grammar" approach (Vicari 2010). According to this model, the main device to identify framing tasks in a text is the clause semantic structure, understood in terms of subject, verb, and object (Franzosi 2010; Vicari 2010). Against this backdrop, when the subject of a clause is a "they" target of blame, the clause is adversarial, and delivers a diagnostic task (Vicari 2010, 510–11). When the subject is a "we" (i.e., the proponent of the collective action itself or a close ally) the clause is self-referential and can deliver different framing tasks, which can be identified based on its verb (Vicari 2010, 511). Modal verbs expressing obligations indicate the moral necessity to perform an action, and as such deliver diagnostic tasks (Vicari 2010, 512).

Secondly, I conducted a qualitative content analysis (Schreier 2012) to code the content of the framing tasks identified through the "frame semantic grammar" approach. I generated the coding scheme through a hybrid approach (Saldaña 2009; Schreier 2012), hence combining a priori deductive coding with emergent inductive coding (see Figure A1 in the Online Appendix). In the first phase, I developed a preliminary codebook based on previous studies on LGBTQIA* collective action frames (Ghaziani, Taylor, and Stone 2016; Valocchi 1999). To assess the validity of this codebook, in the second phase I performed a pilot test on a random sample of 10% of the downloaded events, stratified by year. When finding that previously created codes did not fit the data, I added inductively generated codes to the codebook (Schreier 2012). To conclude, I performed a final round of pilot coding to assess the consistency of my coding by calculating an intra-coder stability measure (Kappa Coefficient = 0.86).[8] Both the pilot test and theoverall coding were conducted in MAXQDA 2020 (Verbi software 2019). The final coding schema is available in Table A3 in the Online Appendix.

To analyze diagnostic framing over time and across cities, this article presents the results of a cross-case analysis (Miles and Huberman 1994). The analysis starts by investigating how diagnosis evolves in Madrid and Milan between 2011 and 2020 respectively (within-case analysis), and then compares the results found in the cases to examined patterns across the cases (cross-case analysis). With regards to the within-case analysis, it examines relations between the codes to identify patterns between the issues framed as problems in the five points in time. It then compares these relations to investigate how they changed over time, with specific attention to their meaning. With regards to the cross-case analysis, a case-oriented replication strategy (Miles and Huberman 1994) is developed to compare diagnostic framing across the two cases.

The evolution of LGBTQIA* solidarity framing in Madrid and Milan

To address the research questions outlined in the introduction, this analysis combines quantitative insights on the absolute and relative frequencies of the different issues coded in the text of the events (illustrated by Figures A2 and A3 in the Online Appendix), with qualitative extracts from the texts. To follow the logic of cross-case analysis (Miles and Huberman 1994), the discussion concerns diagnostic framing over time in Madrid and Milan (within-case analysis) whose evolution is systematically compared through a meta-matrix (cross-case analysis).

Within-case analysis: diagnostic framing in Madrid and Milan over time

During the 2011–2020 decade, the events published online by LGBTQIA* organizations located in both cities increasingly addressed numerous and diverse societal concerns, that can be broadly summarized under three dimensions: (1) issues conventionally related to the LGBTQIA* field of collective actions, such as LGBTQIA*-phobia; (2) issues conventionally considered to affect other communities, such as racism; and (3) issues related to broader processes of social exclusion, such as public cuts and austerity measures. However, while in Milan the focus on these issues raised over time, in Madrid LGBTQIA* collective actors steadily engaged in social concerns and other minorities' issues over the decade. Nonetheless, in Madrid an attention to cross-sectional issues shrank in 2015, perhaps due to organizational campaigns in support of the enactment of two local laws on LGBTQIA*-phobia and trans* rights, and then increases again between 2017 and 2019. By indicating that LGBTQIA* organizations embedded in different contexts similarly engaged with non-LGBTQIA* issues, this evidence is not in line with previous studies according to which collective actors dealing with stronger external threats may be more attentive to cross-sectional concerns (Van Dyke 2003).

However, the ways such concerns were framed changed across contexts. Madrid-based LGBTQIA* concerns were initially discussed by considering the multiple discriminations occurring within the LGBTQIA* field, as exemplified by the following extract:

> Within the lesbian community we are particularly worried for our elderly who suffer from a multiple discrimination: for being women, for being elderly, and for being lesbians. A lot of them experience this [multiple discrimination] and are hence a particularly vulnerable and forgotten community. (Event 2011\2011_492, 13)

In other words, at the beginning of the decade LGBTQIA* issues were framed by emphasizing the heterogeneity of identities and social positionings within the LGBTQIA* field. On the contrary, issues concerning processes of social exclusion were mainly discussed as structural problems equally affecting all members of society, as shown by the following quote:

> We, the common people, are tired of suffering from the consequences of living in a system ruled by the market, which is unbearable and made us victims of a global crisis. (Event 2011\2011_198, 14)

This extract indicates that issues concerning precarity, employment, and exploitation were framed by emphasizing the commonality of experiences lived by individuals besides their personal identities, as exemplified by the expression "We, the common people." In other words, in 2011, LGBTQIA* issues were mainly discussed by acknowledging different social positions and identities within the field, while issues that may affect other communities were mostly addressed by highlighting commonalities beyond collective identities.

Between 2015 and 2019, the framing of LGBTQIA* issues evolved to encompass two main dimensions: on the one hand, LGBTQIA* organizations denounced hate crime against the whole LGBTQIA* community; on the other hand, they discussed the discrimination experienced by some individuals in particular, such as bisexual or trans* people. Furthermore, several events also contained references to LGBTQIA*-phobia together with other processes of marginalization, encompassing not only racism (in 2015) but also ableism, fatphobia, and precarity, stating that "Every form of discrimination (fatphobia, racism, ableism, transphobia, etc.) will be questioned and tackled" (Event 2019\2019_3848, 13). Against this backdrop, the framing of other minorities' issues and social concerns showed two patterns: while most events framed different issues as separated, a minor number discussed them as entangled. Remarkably, when LGBTQIA* organizations framed these concerns as separated, they attributed responsibility to the rise of far-right actors and to their increased visibility in the public arena, as maintained in this extract:

> What is happening goes beyond lesbo-phobic policies that attempt to strip our rights, it [the problem] concerns fascist hate which is directly attacking our lives. Homo- and lesbo-phobic aggressions have risen in the last couple of weeks, as well as racist attacks in the public space. (Event 2019\2019_181, 8)

Interpreting accounts of LGBTQIA*-phobia with concerns over the far-right suggests that problems affecting diverse communities were framed as not interlocking, meaning they are not entangled, as it is instead maintained by scholars and activists developing an intersectional approach to inequalities (Collins 2000). On the contrary, these concerns were framed as emerging from the different sources of inequality, but the responsibility was attributed to the same actor, i.e., the far-right, which was framed as the common enemy (Van Dyke 2003) causing the rise in LGBTQIA*-phobic, racist, and violent attacks to marginalized groups. Against this backdrop, the analysis suggests that different concerns are framed as cross-sectional, but not intersectional. However, especially after the organization of the 2017 World Pride in Madrid, a minor group of events did not discuss only LGBTQIA*-phobia as one of the main problems affecting LGBTQIA* communities, but challenged the structures causing hate crime and LGBTQIA*-phobia, such as hetero-sexism and patriarchy. In this case, different concerns were framed as interlocking, and responsibility was mainly attributed to capitalism. One example of this framing process can be found in the following quotation:

> [They] produce economic growth at the expenses of the most vulnerable people: racialized people, indigenous people, peasants, poor people, migrants, LGBTI and queer people, resisting communities … And it is also produced at the expenses of our surrounding, of other species, and of the ecosystem. (Event 2019\2019_6122, 7)

This extract emphasizes two important dimensions of framing problems as entangled: on the one hand, it suggests that inequalities affecting diverse groups mutually reinforce each other; on the other hand, it indicates that intersectionally marginalized individuals are the ones suffering the most from this entanglement of inequalities. When framing cross-sectional problems in intersectional terms, LGBTQIA* organizations attributed responsibility to capitalism, which was understood as the system through oppressions and inequalities emerge, co-constituting and reenforcing each other to pin marginalized communities against each other.

Differently from Madrid, in Milan there was a slow but progressive increase in the number of issues framed as problems between 2011 and 2020. While the events published in 2011 only focused on discrimination, in 2013 LGBTQIA* organizations started dealing with diverse issues, such as racism and social exclusion, which were not discussed as entangled, but as separated. In 2015, however, LGBTQIA* organizations discussed a wide range of issues, including environmental problems and precarity. LGBTQIA* issues addressed two main concerns: on the one hand, external threats were mainly framed in terms of anti-gender campaigns and LGBTQIA*-phobia; on the other hand, internal conflicts were discussed with reference to homonormativity, pink washing, homonationalism, and invisibility within the community. While external threats were addressed by both more and less institutionalized organizations, internal conflicts were mainly discussed by grassroots groups mobilizing against Expo that, in their words, "becomes a showcase for pinkwashing and homonationalism" (Event 2015\2015_667, 48). These conflicts, however, did not only concern homonormativity and homonationalism, but are also expressed in the following terms:

> Today we must reproach the LGBTQ movement for being so focused on itself, losing the political opportunity to cross its path with that of other social struggles. (Event 2015\2015_1504, 32)

According to more radical LGBTQIA* organizations, not addressing cross-sectional concerns contributed to isolating the Italian LGBTQIA* collective action field, making its struggles less resonant and valid. Against this backdrop, the most discussed cross-sectional struggles concerned social exclusion, capitalism, environmental issues, and racism. While social exclusion, capitalism, and environmental issues were mainly addressed within the framework of No-Expo mobilizations, racism referred to the increased strength gained by far-right activists and parties. Both Expo and far-right actors were hence framed as the common enemy (Van Dyke 2003) targeting differently marginalized communities. As in Madrid, 2017 and 2019 showed the highest heterogeneity of issues framed as problems. However, differently from Madrid, the code-relations matrix (Figure A4 in the Online Appendix) shows that these dimensions are highly discussed within the same events, indicating that different issues were framed as structurally entangled, as exemplified by the following extract:

> [...] Policies against women, lesbians, trans*, [policies] to defend the traditional family and the patriarchal order, attacks to freedom of abortion go hand in hand with the open war against migrants and Roma people. (Event 2019\2019_691, 24)

Within this framework, Milan-based LGBTQIA* organizations did not frame other minorities' concerns as if they were not concerning the LGBTQIA* field, hence in cross-sectional terms, but as an interplay of structural inequalities that reinforce each other, hence in intersectional terms. Furthermore, when these actors also address social exclusion together with cross-sectional concerns, they contribute to re-signifying and redefining it:

> [...] It is more and more evident that it is neither possible, nor legitimate anymore to distinguish between restrictive policies against migrants, security and repression policies, and exclusionary policies: it is not anymore a matter of showing solidarity to migrants [...], but of safeguarding the rights conquered by everybody [*tutti e tutte*] through conflicts and struggles during the last decade. (Event 2019\2019_3304, 19)

Social exclusion is not anymore framed as tackling all aspects of social inequality (Baldassarri and Diani 2007) taken separately, but as acknowledging how all aspects of social inequality are co-constituted and co-articulated. Hence, it is (re-)framed in intersectional terms.

Cross-case analysis: solidarity framing in Madrid and Milan

A combined reading (illustrated by Figure 2) of the evolution of diagnostic framing articulated in the collective action events shared on Facebook by LGBTQIA* organizations indicates that actors based in Madrid and Milan perceived, understood, and framed political solidarity in different ways during the 2011–2020 decade.

	MADRID	MILAN
DIAGNOSTIC FRAMING	From a particular attention to forms of multiple discrimination within the LGBTQIA*, to an increased heterogeneity of issues, including other minorities' concerns, social exclusion processes, and political concerns	From a focus on LGBTQIA* issues, to a redefinition of those issues (including internal conflicts), to a predominance of cross-cutting concerns and other minorities' issues, with social exclusion being redefined as an interplay of inequality structures

Figure 2. Evolution of Diagnostic Framing Tasks in Madrid and Milan Between 2011 and 2020 (Own Elaboration).

In Madrid, LGBTQIA* organizations related to within- and cross-field solidarity through two main patterns. Within-field solidarity was framed by acknowledging the heterogeneity of LGBTQIA* subjectivities and the differential social positionings that LGBTQIA* individuals embody. These stances emphasized that some LGBTQIA* subjectivities, such as trans* people, racialized and/or disabled people, and people from the working class, are more marginalized than others since they defy societal structures that have not been fully challenged yet (such as the gender binary) or they belong to so-called "double minorities" and hence experience multiple discriminations. Within this framework, inequalities were perceived as co-articulating and reenforcing each other, and those considered responsible for such a co-articulation were societal structures, such as capitalism, patriarchy, racism, ableism, and classism. These issues were thus framed as intersectional, meaning that LGBTQIA* actors perceived them as structurally entangled and addressed them at their intersections. This framing process can be interpreted through the Recognition of Differences Frame, meaning that CSOs focus on the specific features of social inequality structures affecting different groups and engage in a "dialogue across differences" (Ciccia and Roggeband 2021, 7). This narrative emphasizes differences with the aim of acknowledging and challenging the interplay of inequalities structures that affect individuals and communities in specific forms.

In the case of cross-field solidarity, instead, inequalities were perceived as stemming from different sources and those considered responsible for heightened inequalities were societal actors, such as far-right parties and activists. Cross-field concerns were hence framed as cross-sectional, meaning that LGBTQIA* actors perceived them as separated from each other and not primarily concerning the LGBTQIA* field. Nonetheless, such actors still considered it crucial to challenge cross-sectional concerns in order to create a more just society. This framing can be interpreted through the Common Denominator Frame, since CSOs focus on cross-cutting concerns that are perceived as equally affecting different groups and are articulated through a "commonality of experiences" narrative (Ciccia and Roggeband 2021). This narrative emphasizes similarities, instead of differences, between differently marginalized groups with the aim of shedding light on shared experiences of inequalities. In the case of Madrid-based LGBTQIA* organizations, the commonality of experiences refers to the increased presence of far-right actors targeting LGBTQIA* communities as much as, and together with, other minorities.

However, a minor number of events published in 2017 and 2019 framed LGBTQIA* issues and other minorities' concerns as structurally entangled. Hence, during the last decade an increasing number of LGBTQIA* organizations based in Madrid framed other minorities' concerns through the Recognition of Differences Frame. This insight points to a gradual and partial evolution from the Common Denominator frame to the Recognition of Differences frame, suggesting that this development could be related to attributing the responsibility of marginalization processes not to societal actors, but to societal structures. Within this framework, depending on who is blamed for the problems framed by CSOs, different "common enemy" narratives (Van Dyke 2003) may accompany the development of an intersectional political consciousness (Greenwood 2008).

In a different fashion, the events promoted by LGBTQIA* organizations based in Milan showed an evolution from the Common Denominator frame to the Recognition of Differences frame. In 2011 the focus was indeed on within-field solidarity, which was discussed by emphasizing common experiences of discrimination, mainly understood as lack of civil rights such as marriage and adoption. Against this backdrop, the emphasis is not on the heterogeneity of identities and experiences within the LGBTQIA* field, but on concerns that are thought to affect LGBTQIA* individuals in the same manner. However, as argued by Ciccia and Roggeband (2021), this framing runs the risk of overlooking specific marginalization processes that only affect some subjectivities, for instance transphobia and double discrimination, thus contributing to the erasure of the experiences of some individuals within the LGBTQIA* spectrum and of people belonging to double minorities (Strid, Walby, and Armstrong 2013). However, in 2015 a cluster of events started addressing internal conflicts in terms of the homonormativity and homonationalism, with more grassroots CSOs criticizing mainstream CSOs for their equality and rights discourses (Prearo 2021), which were perceived as both silencing less normative LGBTQIA* subjectivities, and allying with institutions and industries that were exploiting an equality agenda to legitimize violence against other communities (Puar 2007). Against this backdrop, cross-cutting issues and other minorities' concerns were partially framed in intersectional terms, hence as structurally entangled, with responsibility being attributed to both societal actors and societal structures. In 2019 the majority of events framed LGBTQIA* issues as inextricably intersected with other marginalization processes and cross-cutting concerns, thus mainly through a Recognition of Differences frame. In other words, LGBTQIA* actors framed problems are interrelated, emphasizing that one set of concerns cannot be addressed and challenged without addressing and challenging the others. Yet, they also acknowledged the specificities of different marginalization processes.

These insights suggest that during the 2011–2020 decade LGBTQIA* organizations based in Milan gradually shifted from the Common Denominator frame, mainly focused on within-field solidarity, to the Recognition of Differences frame to discuss both within- and cross-field solidarity. This evolution signals a gradual development of an intersectional political consciousness (Greenwood 2008), which in the case of Milan led to a re-signification of political solidarity. Political solidarity was indeed not anymore narrated as a community (in this case, the LGBTQIA* one) showing solidarity to another community affected by inequalities that were not considered as affecting the former. On the contrary, it was framed as a community understanding these concerns as differently, but intersectionally, affecting all marginalized communities. Solidarity was hence re-signified and re-framed as a horizon through which inequalities are challenged by acknowledging their intersectional nature, while simultaneously recognizing the specific consequences they may have on the lives of differently and intersectionally marginalized communities.

Conclusions: solidarity through difference?

"Solidarity through difference" is not merely the title of this article, but rather the leitmotiv that guided the examination of whether and how LGBTQIA* collective actors articulate solidarity discourses not only through, but also across difference(s). The cross-case analysis outlined above shows that over the last decade LGBTQIA* collective actors increasingly addressed a wide range of issues and concerns. However, the ways such problems were framed changed across context. LGBTQIA* organizations based in Madrid mainly addressed within-field solidarity through the Recognition of Differences frame, hence by acknowledging power asymmetries within the LGBTQIA* field, and cross-field solidarity mainly through the Common Denominator frame, thus by emphasizing the necessity to tackle cross-sectional concerns that were not perceived to be related to LGBTQIA* claims. The presence of both frames in 2011 points to a differentiation between the two frames, which nonetheless decreased over time since cross-cutting issues were to a minor degree discussed through the Recognition of Differences frame in 2019. On the contrary, the events shared by LGBTQIA* organizations based in Milan showed a progressive evolution between the two frames. While events published in 2011 addressed within-field solidarity by articulating an equality discourse through the Common Denominator frame, events published in 2015 and, mostly, 2017 and 2019 discussed both within- and cross-field solidarity in intersectional terms through the Recognition of Differences frame, thus by acknowledging both the structural entanglement between inequality structures and the specific discrimination processes experienced by intersectionally marginalized individuals.

These findings entail two main considerations. On the one hand, social media platforms have been progressively used by LGBTQIA* organizations to address cross-sectional and intersectional concerns, regardless of the context in which they are embedded. This insight suggests that these platforms may play a crucial role in the development of solidarity ties, which sustain marginalized groups' capacity to mobilize, ally, and achieve social change. On the other hand, they indicate that collective actors may be more prone to frame intersectional solidarity discourses when they are embedded in more hostile environments and faced by strong external threats. However, they do not provide evidence of how such discourse may be accompanied by the development of intersectional practices aimed at acknowledging and deconstructing asymmetries within and between organizations. Future research may hence be devoted to filling this gap, shedding further light on the nexus between intersectional solidarity discourses and practices.

This article contributes to the study of intersectional solidarity in several ways. Firstly, it problematizes conventional social movement theories and their explanatory power in relation to LGBTQIA* mobilizations and intersectional activism. Secondly, it explores the development of cross-field solidarity discourses articulated by LGBTQIA* organizations in Southern Europe, a phenomenon that has not yet been systematically studied. Thirdly, it investigates how social media platforms may be used by LGBTQIA* activists to articulate solidarity discourses both within the LGBTQIA* field and with collective actors engaging in other social struggles, thus exploring social media platforms potential for solidarity building. Understanding these issues is of utmost importance to shed light on practices, processes, and tools developed by minoritized groups to overcome differences and build bridges with the aim of creating a more just society.

Notes

1. Extract from the political manifesto of a critical block within the 2019 Milan Pride. Available at: https://www.cantiere.org/28526/pride2019-orgoglio-meticcio-e-lgbtqia/ [Last accessed 25.01.2023]. The original is in Italian. From now onwards, unless differently specified, translations are by me.
2. Expanding on Di Maggio and Powell (1983) and Melucci (1989), collective action fields are understood as localized relational arenas in which various types of organizations act on a recognized area of social life, and in which the mechanisms for the emergence of collective actions are defined (Crossley and Diani 2019).
3. These findings are nonetheless debated. Especially in repressive contexts, social media have been used to both articulate coming-out processes (Birdal 2020) and circulate LGBTQIA*-phobic content (Wijaya 2022), strengthen anti-gender mobilizations (Korolczuk and Graff 2018) and target LGBTQIA* individuals (Steinfeld 2020). Nevertheless, so far LGBTQIA* activists have emphasized the advantages provided by digital media to collective mobilizations over the disadvantages (Ayoub and Brzezińska 2015).
4. The concept of frame was first developed by Goffman (1974), who conceived frames as cognitive schemas that enable individuals to interpret, give meaning to, and label their experiences.
5. Since 2009, ILGA Europe calculates the Rainbow Europe Index, gathering information on national legislations on LGBTQIA* rights. The index currently ranks 49 European countries by measuring six policy areas: equality and nondiscrimination; family; hate crime and hate speech; legal gender recognition and bodily integrity; civil society space; asylum on grounds of gender identity and sexual orientation. More information can be found at: https://www.rainbow-europe.org/.
6. Differently from other studies (e.g., Diani 2015), this research also includes profit organizations, provided that their main activities encompass service provision, cultural awareness, and/or political initiatives. The decision not to exclude these organizations is based on previous empirical evidence, since many LGBTQIA* commercial organizations (such as newspapers, bookstores, and so on) have engaged in identity and solidarity building as much as nonprofit organizations (Armstrong 2002).
7. CrowdTangle Team (2020) is a public insights tool owned and operated by Facebook that allows researchers to retrieve all the Facebook posts published by a list of public pages during a specific timeframe. More information on the tool can be found at: https://www.crowdtangle.com/.
8. When the coding process is conducted by one coder only, intra-coder stability measures help researchers assess the consistency of the codes assigned by one coder to the same coding units in two different points in time (Schreier 2012, 167).

Acknowledgments

I would like to thank Professor Eitan Alimi for sharing with me his thoughts on the topic of collective framing and on my research.

Disclosure statement

No potential conflict of interest was reported by the author.

ORCID

Aurora Perego (iD) http://orcid.org/0000-0003-1576-6757

References

Adam, Erin M. 2017. "Intersectional Coalitions: The Paradoxes of Rights-Based Movement Building in LGBTQ and Immigrant Communities." *Law & Society Review* 51 (1):132–67. doi:10.1111/lasr.12248.

Adam, Barry D., Jan Willem Duyvendak, and André Krouwel, eds. 1999. *The Global Emergence of Gay and Lesbian Politics: National Imprints of a Worldwide Movement*. Philadelphia: Temple University Press.

Armstrong, Elizabeth A. 2002. *Forging Gay Identities: Organizing Sexuality in San Francisco, 1950–1994*. Chicago: University of Chicago Press.

Ayoub, Philip M. 2016. *When States Come Out: Europe's Sexual Minorities and the Politics of Visibility*. Cambridge: Cambridge University Press.

Ayoub, Philip M. 2018. "Intersectional and Transnational Coalitions During Times of Crisis: The European LGBTI Movement." *Social Politics* 26 (1):1–29. doi:10.1093/sp/jxy007.

Ayoub, Philip M, and Olga Brzezińska. 2015. "Caught in the Web? The Internet and Deterritorialization of LGBT Activism." In *The Ashgate Research Companion to Lesbian and Gay Activism*, eds. David Paternotte and Manon Tremblay. New York: Routledge, 225–42.

Ayoub, Philip M., and Agnès Chetaille. 2020. "Movement/Countermovement Interaction and Instrumental Framing in a Multi-Level World: Rooting Polish Lesbian and Gay Activism." *Social Movement Studies* 19 (1):21–37. doi:10.1080/14742837.2017.1338941.

Baldassarri, Delia, and Mario Diani. 2007. "The Integrative Power of Civic Networks." *American Journal of Sociology* 113 (3):735–80. doi:10.1086/521839.

Banting, Keith G., and Will Kymlicka, eds. 2017. *The Strains of Commitment: The Political Sources of Solidarity in Diverse Societies*. 1st ed. Oxford; New York: Oxford University Press. doi:10.1093/acprof:oso/9780198795452.003.0001

Beamish, Thomas D., and Amy J. Luebbers. 2009. "Alliance Building Across Social Movements: Bridging Difference in a Peace and Justice Coalition." *Social Problems* 56 (4):647–76. doi:10.1525/sp.2009.56.4.647.

Benford, Robert D., and David A Snow. 2000. "Framing Process and Social Movements: An Overview and Assessment." *Annual Review of Sociology* 26:611–39. doi:10.1146/annurev.soc.26.1.611.

Berry, Chris, Fran Martin, and Audrey Yue, eds. 2003. *Mobile Cultures: New Media in Queer Asia*. Durham: Duke University Press.

Bertuzzi, Niccolo. 2017. "No Expo Network: A Failed Mobilization in a Post-Political Frame." *Social Movement Studies* 16 (6):752–56. doi:10.1080/14742837.2017.1348943.

Bieler, Andreas, and Ingemar Lindberg, eds. 2011. *Global Restructuring: Labour and the Challenges for Transnational Solidarity*. New York: Routledge. doi:10.4324/9780203842454.

Birdal, Mehmet S. 2020. "The State of Being LGBT in the Age of Reaction: Post-2011 Visibility and Repression in the Middle East and North Africa." In *The Oxford Handbook of Global LGBT and Sexual Diversity Politics*, eds. Michael J. Bosia, Sandra M. McEvoy, and Momin, Rahman. Oxford: Oxford University Press, 267–80. doi:10.1093/oxfordhb/9780190673741.013.16.

Calvo, Kerman. 2011. "Spain: Building Reciprocal Relations Between Lesbian and Gay Organizations and the State." In *The Lesbian and Gay Movement and the State: Comparative Insights into a Transformed Relationship*, eds. Manon Tremblay, David Paternotte, and Carol Johnson. Farnham; Burlington: Ashgate, 167–80. doi:10.4324/9781315556178-12.

Chidgey, Red. 2018. "Feminist protest assemblages and remix culture." In *The Routledge Companion to Media and Activism*, ed. Graham Meikle. London; New York: Routledge, 196–204. doi:10.4324/9781315475059-21.

Chironi, Daniela. 2019. "Generations in the Feminist and LGBT Movements in Italy: The Case of Non Una Di Meno." *American Behavioral Scientist* 63 (10):1469–96. doi:10.1177/0002764219831745.

Chironi, Daniela, and Martín Portos. 2021. "'Together We stand': Coalition-Building in the Italian and Spanish Feminist Movements in Times of Crisis." *European Journal of Politics and Gender* 4 (2):291–309. doi:10.1332/251510821X16135837027525.

Ciccia, Rossella, Donatella della Porta, and Elena Pavan. 2021. "Feminist Alliances: The Ideas, Practices and Politics of Intersectional Solidarity." *European Journal of Politics and Gender* 4 (2):175–79. doi:10.1332/251510821X16177322505899.

Ciccia, Rossella, and Conny Roggeband. 2021. "Unpacking Intersectional Solidarity: Dimensions of Power in Coalitions." *European Journal of Politics and Gender* 4 (2):181–98. doi:10.1332/251510821X16145402377609.

Cole, Elizabeth R. 2008. "Coalitions as a Model for Intersectionality: From Practice to Theory." *Sex Roles* 59 (5–6):443–53. doi:10.1007/s11199-008-9419-1.

Cole, Elizabeth R., and Zakiya T. Luna. 2010. "Making Coalitions Work: Solidarity Across Difference within US Feminism." *Feminist Studies* 36 (1): 71–98.

Collins, Patricia Hill. 2000. *Black Feminist Thought: Knowledge, Consciousness, and the Politics of Empowerment.* 2nd ed. New York: Routledge.

Cornejo, Monica, and J. I. Pichardo. 2018. "From the Pulpit to the Streets: Ultra-Conservative Religious Positions Against Gender in Spain." In *Anti-Gender Campaigns in Europe: Mobilizing Against Equality,* eds. Roman Kuhar and David Paternotte. London; New York: Rowman & Littlefield, 233–52.

Cossolo, Felix, Flavia Franceschini, Cristina Gramolini, Fabio Pellegatta, and Walter Pigino, eds. 2019. *Milano e 50 anni di Movimento LGBT*.* Milan: Il Dito e La Luna Edizioni.

Costanza-Chock, Sasha. 2018. "Transformative Media Organizing: Key Lessons from Participatory Research with Immigrant Rights, Occupy, and LGBTQ and Two-Spirit Movements." In *The Routledge Companion to Media and Activism,* ed. Graham Meikle. London; New York: Routledge, 77–86. doi:10.4324/9781315475059-8.

Creed, Douglas W. E., Jeffrey A. Langstraat, and Maureen A. Scully. 2002. "A Picture of the Frame: Frame Analysis as Technique and as Politics." *Organizational Research Methods* 5 (1):34–55. doi:10.1177/1094428102051004.

Crenshaw, Kimberlé. 1989. "Demarginalizing the Intersection of Race and Sex: A Black Feminist Critique of Antidiscrimination Doctrine, Feminist Theory and Antiracist Politics." *University of Chicago Legal Forum* 1: 139–67.

Crossley, Nick, and Mario Diani. 2019. "Networks and Fields." In *The Wiley Blackwell Companion to Social Movements,* eds. David A. Snow, Sarah A. Soule, Hanspeter Kriesi, and Holly McCammon. 2nd ed. Oxford: Blackwell Publishing, 151–66.

CrowdTangle Team. 2020. *CrowdTangle.* Facebook, Menlo Park, California, United States. [1572083; 1486063].

della Porta, Donatella. 2013. *Can Democracy Be Saved? Participation, Deliberation, and Social Movements.* Malden, MA: Polity Press. doi:10.1002/9780470674871.wbespm065.

de Vries, Maya, Asmahan Simry, and Ifat Maoz. 2015. "Like a Bridge Over Troubled Water: Using Facebook to Mobilize Solidarity Among East Jerusalem Palestinians During the 2014 War in Gaza." *International Journal of Communication* 9: 2622–49.

Diani, Mario. 1996. "Linking Mobilization Frames and Political Opportunities: Insights from Regional Populism in Italy." *American Sociological Review* 61 (6):1053–69. doi:10.2307/2096308.

Diani, Mario. 2000. "Social Movement Networks Virtual and Real." *Information, Communication, and Society* 3 (3):386–401. doi:10.1080/13691180051033333.

Diani, Mario. 2015. *The Cement of Civil Society: Studying Networks in Localities.* New York: Cambridge University Press.

Di Maggio, Paul J., and Walter W. Powell. 1983. "The Iron Cage Revisited: Institutional Isomorphism and Collective Rationality in Organizational Fields." *American Sociological Review* 48 (2):147–60. doi:10.2307/2095101.

Domínguez, Ruiz, and Ignacio Elpidio. 2019. "Neither Resistance nor Commodification: Madrid's LGBT Pride as Paradoxical Mobilization." *Journal of Spanish Cultural Studies* 20 (4):519–34. doi:10.1080/14636204.2019.1689707.

Dorf, Michael C., and Sidney Tarrow. 2014. "Strange Bedfellows: How an Anticipatory Countermovement Brought Same-Sex Marriage into the Public Arena." *Law & Social Inquiry* 39 (2):449–73. doi:10.1111/lsi.12069.

Eggert, Nina, and Katia Pilati. 2014. "Networks and Political Engagement of Migrant Organizations in Five European Cities." *European Journal of Political Research* 53 (4):858–75. doi:10.1111/1475-6765.12057.

Einwohner, Rachel L., Kaitlin Kelly-Thompson, Valeria Sinclair-Chapman, Fernando Tormos, S. Laurel Weldon, Jared M. Wright, and Charles Wu. 2021. "Active Solidarity: Intersectional Solidarity in Action." *Social Politics: International Studies in Gender, State and Society* 28 (3):704–29. doi:10.1093/sp/jxz052.

Evans, E., É. Lépinard, Evans, Elizabeth, and Éléonore Lépinard eds. 2019. *Intersectionality in Feminist and Queer Movements: Confronting Privileges.* London: Routledge. doi:10.4324/9780429289859

Ferree, Myra Marx, William Anthony Gamson, Jurgen Gerhards, and Dieter Rucht. 2002. *Shaping the Abortion Discourse: Democracy and the Public Sphere in Germany and the United States.* Cambridge: Cambridge University Press. doi:10.1017/CBO9780511613685.

Ferree, Myra Marx, and Silke Roth. 1998. "Gender, Class, and the Interaction Between Social Movements: A Strike of West Berlin Day Care Workers." *Gender & Society* 12 (6):626–48. doi:10.1177/089124398012006003.

Fetner, Tina. 2008. *How the Religious Right Shaped Lesbian and Gay Activism.* Minneapolis: University of Minnesota Press.

Franzosi, Roberto. 2010. *Quantitative Narrative Analysis.* Beverly Hills: Sage Publications. doi:10.4135/9781412993883.

Gamson, William A. 1992a. *Talking Politics.* New York: Cambridge University Press.

Gamson, William A. 1992b. "Social Psychology of Collective Action." In *Frontiers in Social Movement Theory,* eds. Aldon D. Morris and Carol McClurg Mueller. New Haven: Yale University Press, 53–76.

George, Alexander L., and Andrew F. Bennett. 2005. *Case Studies and Theory Development in the Social Sciences*. Cambridge; London: MIT Press.

Ghaziani, Amin, Verta Taylor, and Amy Stone. 2016. "Cycles of Sameness and Difference in LGBT Social Movements." *Annual Review of Sociology* 42 (1):165–83. doi:10.1146/annurev-soc-073014-112352.

Goffman, Erving. 1974. *Frame Analysis: An Essay on the Organization of Experience*. Cambridge: Harvard University Press.

Goodwin, Jeff, and James M. Jasper. 1999. "Caught in a Winding, Snarling Vine: The Structural Bias of Political Process Theory." *Sociological Forum* 14 (1):27–92. doi:10.1023/A:1021684610881.

Greenwood, Ronni Michelle. 2008. "Intersectional Political Consciousness: Appreciation for Intragroup Differences and Solidarity in Diverse Groups." *Psychology of Women Quarterly* 32 (1):36–47. doi:10.1111/j.1471-6402.2007.00405.x.

Grigolo, Michele, and Frédéric Jörgens. 2010. "Italy." In *The Greenwood Encyclopedia of LGBT Issues Worldwide*, ed. Chuck Stewart. Vol. 2. Santa Barbara: ABC Clio, 251–68.

Guenther, Lars, Georg Ruhrmann, Jenny Bischoff, Tessa Penzel, and Antonia Weber. 2020. "Strategic Framing and Social Media Engagement: Analyzing Memes Posted by the German Identitarian Movement on Facebook." *Social Media + Society* 6 (1):1–13. doi:10.1177/2056305119898777.

Hancock, Angie-Marie. 2007. "When Multiplication Doesn't Equal Quick Addition: Examining Intersectionality as a Research Paradigm." *Perspectives on Politics* 5 (1):63–79. doi:10.1017/S1537592707070065.

Hunt, Scott A., and Robert D. Benford. 2004. "Collective Identity, Solidarity, and Commitment." In *The Blackwell Companion to Social Movements*, eds. David A. Snow, Sarah A. Soule, and Hanspeter Kriesi. 1st ed. Malden, MA: Blackwell Publishing, 433–58. doi:10.1002/9780470999103.ch19

Kaijser, Anna, and Annica Kronsell. 2013. "Climate Change Through the Lens of Intersectionality." *Environmental Politics* 23 (3):417–33. doi:10.1080/09644016.2013.835203.

Kavada, Anastasia. 2015. "Creating the Collective: Social Media, the Occupy Movement and Its Constitution as a Collective Actor." *Information, Communication & Society* 18 (8):872–86. doi:10.1080/1369118X.2015.1043318.

Korolczuk, Elzbieta, and Agnieszka Graff. 2018. "Gender as 'Ebola from Brussels': The Anticolonial Frame and the Rise of Illiberal Populism." *Signs: Journal of Women in Culture & Society* 43 (4):797–821. doi:10.1086/696691.

Lavizzari, Anna. 2020. *Protesting Gender: The LGBTIQ Movement and Its Opponents in Italy*. New York: Routledge. doi:10.4324/9780429298684.

Lichterman, Paul. 1995. "Piecing Together Multicultural Community: Cultural Differences in Community Building Among Grass-Roots Environmentalists." *Social Problems* 42 (4):513–34. doi:10.2307/3097044.

Llamas, Ricardo, and Fefa Vila. 1999. "Passion for Life: A History of the Lesbian and Gay Movement in Spain." In *The Global Emergence of Gay and Lesbian Politics: National Imprints of a Worldwide Movement*, eds. Barry Adam, Jan Willem Duyvendak, and André Krouwel. Philadelphia: Temple University Press, 214–41.

Mainardi, Arianna, and Elena Pavan. 2020. "LGBTQI Online." In *The International Encyclopedia of Gender, Media, and Communication*, eds. Karen Ross, Ingrid Bachmann, Valentina Cardo, Sujata Moorti, and Cosimo Marco Scarcelli. Hoboken, NJ: Wiley Blackwell, 1–7.

Mele, Christopher. 1999. "Access to Cyberspace and the Empowerment of Disadvantaged Communities." In *Communities in Cyberspace*, eds. Peter Pollock and Marc Smith. New York: Routledge, 290–310.

Melucci, Alberto. 1989. *Nomads of the Present: Social Movements and Individual Needs in Contemporary Society*. Philadelphia: Temple University Press.

Melucci, Alberto. 1996. *Challenging Codes: Collective Action in the Information Age*. Cambridge: Cambridge University Press.

Miles, Matthew B., and A. Michael Huberman. 1994. *Qualitative Data Analysis: An Expanded Sourcebook*. 2nd ed. Thousand Oaks: Sage Publications.

Mohanty, Chandra Talpade. 2003. "'Under Western eyes' Revisited: Feminist Solidarity Through Anticapitalist Struggles." *Signs: Journal of Women in Culture & Society* 28 (2):499–535. doi:10.1086/342914.

Nardi, Peter M. 1993. "The Globalisation of the Gay and Lesbian Socio-Political Movement: Some Observation About Europe with a Focus on Italy." *Sociological Perspectives* 41 (3):567–86. doi:10.2307/1389564.

O'Dwyer, Conor. 2018. *Coming Out of Communism: The Emergence of LGBT Activism in Eastern Europe*. New York: New York University.

Pavan, Elena. 2017. "The Integrative Power of Online Collective Action Networks Beyond Protest: Exploring Social Media Use in the Process of Institutionalization." *Social Movement Studies* 16 (4):433–46. doi:10.1080/14742837.2016.1268956.

Platero, Lucas. 2020. "Redistribution and Recognition in Spanish Transgender Laws." *Politics & Governance* 8 (3):253–65. doi:10.17645/pag.v8i3.2856.

Platero, Lucas, and Esther Ortega-Arjonilla. 2016. "Building Coalitions: The Interconnections Between Feminism and Trans* Activism in Spain." *Journal of Lesbian Studies* 20 (1):46–64. doi:10.1080/10894160.2015.1076235.

Prearo, Massimo. 2015. *La Fabbrica dell'Orgoglio: Una genealogia dei movimenti LGBT*. Pisa: Edizioni ETS.

Prearo, Massimo. 2021. "Italy's LGBT Movement and Interest Groups." In *Oxford Research Encyclopedia of LGBT Politics and Policy*, ed. Donald P. Haider-Markel. Oxford: Oxford University Press, 1058–72. doi:10.1093/acrefore/9780190228637.013.1351.

Preves, Sharon E. 2005. "Out of the O.R. and into the Streets: Exploring the Impact of Intersex Media Activism." *Cardozo Journal of Law & Gender* 12: 247–88.

Puar, Jasbir K. 2007. *Terrorist Assemblages: Homonationalism in Queer Times.* Durham; London: Duke University Press.

Rahbari, Ladan. 2021. "In Her Shoes: Transnational Digital Solidarity with Muslim Women, or the Hijab?" *Tijdschrift Voor Economische En Sociale Geografie* 112 (2):107–20. doi:10.1111/tesg.12376.

Saldaña, Johnny. 2009. *The Coding Manual for Qualitative Researchers.* Los Angeles: Sage.

Schreier, Margrit. 2012. *Qualitative Content Analysis in Practice.* London: Sage.

Seawright, Jason, and John Gerring. 2008. "Case Selection Techniques in Case Study Research: A Menu of Qualitative and Quantitative Options." *Case Studies, Political Research Quarterly* 61 (2):294–308. doi:10.1177/1065912907313077.

Seidman, Steven. 1997. *Difference Troubles.* Cambridge: Cambridge University Press.

Shapiro, Eve. 2004. "Trans'cending Barriers: Transgender Organizing on the Internet." *Journal of Gay and Lesbian Social Services* 16 (3–4):165–79. doi:10.1300/J041v16n03_11.

Snow, David A., and Robert D. Benford. 1988. "Ideology, Frame Resonance and Participant Mobilization." *International Social Movement Research* 1 (1): 197–217.

Snow, David A., Rens Vliegenthart, and Pauline Ketelaars. 2019. "The Framing Perspective on Social Movements: Its Conceptual Roots and Architecture." In *The Blackwell Companion to Social Movements*, eds. David A. Snow, Sarah A. Soule, Hanspeter Kriesi, and Holly McCammon. 2nd ed. Oxford: Blackwell Publishing, 392–410. doi:10.1002/9781119168577.ch22

Steinfeld, Jemimah. 2020. "Forced Out of the Closet: As People Live Out More of Their Lives Online Right Now, Our Report Highlights How LGBTQ Dating Apps Can Put People's Lives at Risk." *Index on Censorship* 49 (2):101–04. doi:10.1177/0306422020935360.

Strid, Sofia, Sylvia Walby, and Jo Armstrong. 2013. "Intersectionality and Multiple Inequalities: Visibility in British Policy on Violence Against Women." *Social Politics: International Studies in Gender, State and Society* 20 (4):558–81. doi:10.1093/sp/jxt019.

Strolovitch, Dara Z. 2007. *Affirmative Advocacy: Race, Class, and Gender in Interest Group Politics.* Chicago; London: The University of Chicago Press. doi:10.7208/chicago/9780226777450.001.0001.

Sumiala, Johanna, and Lilly Korpiola. 2017. "Mediated Muslim Martyrdom: Rethinking Digital Solidarity in the 'Arab Spring'." *New Media & Society* 19 (1):52–66. doi:10.1177/1461444816649918.

Taylor, Verta, and Nancy E. Whittier. 1992. "Collective Identity in Social Movement Communities: Lesbian Feminist Mobilization." In *Frontiers in Social Movement Theory*, eds. Aldon D. Morris and Carol McClurg Mueller. New Haven; London: Yale University Press, 104–29.

Terriquez, Veronica, Tizoc Brenes, and Abdiel Lopez. 2018. "Intersectionality as a Multipurpose Collective Action Frame: The Case of the Undocumented Youth Movement." *Ethnicities* 18 (2):260–76. doi:10.1177/1468796817752558.

Tormos, Fernando. 2017. "Intersectional Solidarity." *Politics, Groups & Identities* 5 (4):707–20. doi:10.1080/21565503.2017.1385494.

Townsend-Bell, Erica. 2021. "Breaking Hegemony: Coalition as Decolonial-Intersectional Praxis." *European Journal of Politics and Gender* 4 (2):235–53. doi:10.1332/251510821X16145402177115.

Valocchi, Steve. 1999. "Riding the Crest of a Protest Wave? Collective Action Frames in the Gay Liberation Movement, 1969–1973." *Mobilization: An International Journal* 4 (1):59–73. doi:10.17813/maiq.4.1.r34444x4376v1x31.

Van Dyke, Nella. 2003. "Crossing Movement Boundaries: Factors That Facilitate Coalition Protest by American College Students, 1930–1990." *Social Problems* 50 (2):226–50. doi:10.1525/sp.2003.50.2.226.

VERBI Software. 2019. *MAXQDA 2020.* Berlin: VERBI Software.

Verloo, Mieke. 2013. "Intersectional and Cross-Movement Politics and Policies: Reflections on Current Practices and Debates." *Signs: Journal of Women in Culture & Society* 38 (4):893–915. doi:10.1086/669572.

Vicari, Stefania. 2010. "Measuring Collective Action Frames: A Linguistic Approach to Frame Analysis." *Poetics* 38 (5):504–25. doi:10.1016/j.poetic.2010.07.002.

Ward, Elizabeth Jane. 2008. *Respectably Queer: Diversity Culture in LGBT Activist Organizations.* Nashville: Vanderbilt University Press.

Wijaya, Hendri Yulius. 2022. "Digital Homophobia: Technological Assemblages of Anti-LGBT Sentiment and Surveillance in Indonesia." *Indonesia and the Malay World* 50 (146):52–72. doi:10.1080/13639811.2022.2010357.

Zurcher, Louis A., and David A. Snow. 1981. "Collective Behavior: Social Movements." In *Social Psychology: Sociological Perspectives*, eds. Morris Rosenberg and Ralph H. Turner. New York: Basic Books, 131–56.

Strategies of Resistance in the Everyday: The Political Approaches of Black Women Living in a Public Housing Development in Chicago

Alex J. Moffett-Bateau 🆔

ABSTRACT

Black women living in poverty in the United States have been shown to develop non-traditional, or what I call extra-systemic, political engagement to combat their vulnerability to government power. With that in mind, I ask the following question: what conceptual framework of "politics" is best suited to fully understanding the politics of poor Black women living in the US? To answer this question, I examined an ethnographic case study of the politics of 31 Black women living in Chicago public housing, over the course of one year (2011 through 2012). The evidence suggests some marginalized Black women incorporate an oft-hidden resistance strategy against forces exerting a disproportionate amount of power over their lives. The political strategies used by the marginalized Black women I observed, were best understood using an expanded extra-systemic conceptualization of politics, informed by Black feminist political theory.

Introduction

Black women living in poverty in the United States have been consistently shown to develop non-traditional, quotidian, or what I call extra-systemic, political engagement to combat their vulnerability to government power and their lack of socio-economic power (Berger 2006; Cohen 2005; Hancock 2004; Williams 2005). With that in mind, I have focused this article on the following question: what conceptual framework of "politics" is best suited to fully interpreting and understanding the politics of Black women living below the poverty line within the United States? Do quotidian political frameworks capture the full socio-political engagement of Black women living below the poverty line in a more robust or complete way?

To answer this question, I examined a single case study of the everyday politics of 31 Black women living in Chicago public housing, over the course of one year (2011 through 2012). I conducted in-depth interviews and gathered ethnographic data while I spent time with Chicago public housing residents across the City of Chicago, attending tenants' meetings, CHA meetings, protests, and other events held during my time there. The case study evidence suggests some marginalized Black women incorporate an oft-hidden resistance strategy against forces exerting a disproportionate amount of power over their lives (Feldman and Stall 2004; Hunt 2010; Scott 1992).

The political strategies used by the marginalized Black women I observed, were best understood using an expanded extra-systemic conceptualization of politics, informed by Black feminist political theory. Building on the work of race, ethnicity, and politics scholars, I argue that by expanding the definitional criteria for what counts as politics and the political, extra-systemic and

---

Author's note: This data is part of a larger data project, featured in the manuscript *Redefining the Political: Black Women Living Below the Poverty Line in Chicago, Black Feminism, and the Politics of Everyday Life*, currently under advanced contract with Temple University Press.

non-traditional conceptions of politics can offer increased accuracy and depth to research on Black women living in poverty within the United States. Ultimately, this article argues all studies of politics benefit by expanding its definitional criteria. The Black feminist extra-systemic conceptual expansion of politics and the political proposed in this article includes traditional forms of political engagement (e.g., voting, writing your senator, etc.) as well what Verba, Schlozman, and Brady (1996) call "the civic," in addition to the extra-systemic elements I suggest in this article (e.g., rioting, storytelling, community cleanup, public school based politics, etc.).

Early findings from US politics scholarship on the political engagement of individual's living below the poverty line indicated marginalized groups did not invest significant time or resources into politics (Campbell et al. 1960; Hancock 2004; Salisbury 1975; Verba, Lehman Schlozman, and Brady 1996). While many US politics scholars limited their conceptions of politics to governance (government power), researchers who studied the socio-political impact of race, gender, and class-based oppression, concluded politics is a form of power that can be cultivated within a variety of institutions, communities, neighborhoods, groups, spaces, places, etc (Cohen 2004; Young 1990). As Iris Marion Young argues,

> Politics touches every aspect of socio-cultural life, there is no escaping the way politics and power are deeply intertwined via marginalization and oppression. Politics in this sense concerns all aspects of institutional organization, public action, social practices and habits, and cultural meanings insofar as they are potentially subject to collective evaluation and decision making. (Young 1990, 23)

At its essence, politics is a manifestation of the hierarchy created by marginalization and oppression (Kim 2003; Young 1990). As a form of power, politics allows one group to exert its power to oppress and marginalize over another group (Young 1990). Politics can also become an attempt to create power which counters government-based power. (Kaba 2021)

However, over time, race, ethnicity, and politics scholars noted existing concepts designed to understand the political engagement of people living in the United States were not completely and/ or accurately capturing the politics of people with marginalized racial identities (Cohen 1999; Isoke 2013; Junn 1999; Simien 2006). Consistently, the political engagement of poor Black women were not fully captured using mainstream large-N surveys or polls, which were organized around traditional conceptualizations of politics and the political (Alexander-Floyd 2017; Harris 2009; Harris-Perry 2011; Jordan-Zachery 2018; Prestage 1991; Simien 2006). Political scientists Zenzele Isoke and Evelyn Simien have both argued that traditional theoretical frameworks for politics and the political frequently miss the politics of poor Black women because those frameworks were originally designed to study the political engagement of middle-class white people living in the United States (Berger 2006; Isoke 2013; Simien 2006). As a result, out of necessity REP, scholars began expanding their conceptual and theoretical frameworks for politics and the political with an eye toward capturing the understudied, and potentially non-traditional, political engagement of Black marginalized communities (Berger 2006; Cohen 2004; Dawson 1994; Isoke 2013; Simien 2006; Spence 2015).

Some of the extra-systemic political strategies described to me during interviews with respondents included but were not limited to: protesting oppressive institutions in their communities, filling in the gaps left behind by public housing authority policies of benign neglect, subverting the formal rules and structures of public meetings, organizing art-shows and community meals, volunteering at local public schools, as well as holding meetings to increase the political confidence of Black residents by educating them on navigating government bureaucracies (Feldman and Stall 2004; Naples 1998; Soss 2002; Williams 2005). While race and gender matter deeply for how politics within Black communities were developed from the 1960's and onward, class sometimes pre-determined who could access particular forms of politics even today (Cohen 1999; Kelley 1996).

Historically the Black working-class engaged in resistance which occasionally took the form of riots, being loud on the bus, or simply refusing to show up to a backbreaking job that underpaid (Carter and Willoughby-Herard 2018; Gore, Theoharis, and Woodward 2009; Kelley 1996). Given the US governments history of intrusion and exploitation of Black women living below the poverty line, a study of the ways poor Black women continue to push back against government power is particularly important (Berger 2006; Harris-Perry 2011; Perry 2013; Richie 2012; Watkins-Hayes 2019). As such, it is critically important to develop concepts and methods capable of accurately capturing and understanding their politics and political worldview (Simien 2006; Weaver, Prowse, and Piston 2019).

Hanchard (2006) contended that the non-traditional aspects of Black political engagement, and the political engagement of many marginalized groups, were in no small part a direct result of oppressive structures and institutions built within the United States to create obstacles for Black communities with a desire to participate in any public, let alone explicitly political, sphere (Hanchard 2006). Simply put, marginalized Black communities created non-traditional political strategies in order to develop the power needed to counter government anti-Blackness (Francis 2014; Williamson, Trump, and Levine Einstein 2018). Ultimately, political scientists continue to find evidence pointing to extra-systemic forms of political engagement (Cohen 2005; Dawson 2003; Hanchard 2010; Perry 2013; Spence 2015).

Scholars have found that adult Black women consistently make-up a large proportion of on the ground grassroots labor throughout Black political work across the United States (Feldman and Stall 2004; Robnett 1997; Williams 2005). Additionally, Black feminist scholars have noted, marginalized Black women found creative and non-traditional means to subvert oppressive power structures generation after generation (Carter and Willoughby-Herard 2018; Cohen 2004; Davis 1983; Jordan-Zachery 2017). They also constituted the majority of the tenants who showed up for tenants' meetings, protests, and CHA Board meetings while I was in the field. Given those realities, I focused on poor adult Black women living in Altgeld Gardens, a Chicago public housing development, for this study.

In this article, I begin with a discussion of the conceptual and theoretical framework developed for this project. In short, the extra-systemic conceptualization of politics and the political is a framework informed by Black feminist political theory and is designed to expand existing conceptualizations of politics. Next, I discuss the methods used to collect the research data. From there, I describe the socio-political context of the case study: The City of Chicago, and the Altgeld Gardens and Phillip Murray Homes Development, a public housing development within the Chicago Housing Authority. Afterwards, I present a discussion of the findings. Finally, I end the article by demonstrating how extra-systemic politics as a concept facilitates a more complete understanding of the politics of Black marginalized communities within the United States.

A conceptual framework

It is important to note I am not making a causal argument; instead, I develop a conceptual framework for expanding existing definitions of politics and the political, hereafter referred to as extra-systemic politics. I use Black feminist political theory, previous race, ethnicity, and politics scholarship, and theories of quotidian politics to build a more robust and comprehensive understanding of *extra-systemic* politics (Berger 2006; Cohen 2004; Cohen and Dawson 1993; Isoke 2013; Kelley 1996; Richie 2012; Scott 1992; Williamson 2016). Quite simply, I developed the extra-systemic conceptual expansion of politics in an effort to further understanding about the socio-political context of an understudied population, whose socio-political knowledge and prowess perpetually go unseen (Michener 2020; Prowse, Weaver, and Meares 2019). Due to the number of respondents who participated in my research, I cannot claim the case examined in this article is applicable to all Black women, or all Black communities within the United States more generally. However, the case does provide important insight into the political lives of marginalized Black communities within the United States (Berger 2006; Cohen 1999, 2010; Watkins-Hayes 2019).

Mainstream feminists and Black feminists have argued for the last few decades there is a critical need to expand definitions, and indeed our wholesale understanding, of what constitutes politics and the political (Cohen 2004; Simien 2006). Nancy Naples (1998) argued contemporary definitions of politics served to obscure and erase the politics of women, and women of color in particular. Whether Black feminist scholars studied the socio-political impact of Black women in Chicago, Newark, or

Brazil, the conclusion remained the same: the politics of Black women were rooted in a socio-political community context which often began in the neighborhood (Berger 2006; Isoke 2013; Perry 2013). It is a politics which understood their socio-political fate is intrinsically linked with Black people throughout their country, and sometimes, Afro-descended people globally (Dawson 1994; Hanchard 2006).

The intervention I am attempting to make is building on Patricia Hill Collins (2019) argument that the Black feminist concept of intersectionality should be used as critical social theory capable of helping us envision future possibilities (Hill-Collins 2019). Keeping Hill-Collins' (2019) intervention in mind, I argue capturing the politics of marginalized Black women requires a more expansive understanding of politics. First and foremost, it requires the researcher and writer to take an intersectional approach to conceptual, theoretical, and methodological design in addition to understanding identity politics. In other words, because the focus of this research centers on a population whose demographics are entirely intersectional (poor Black women living in public housing), the conceptual, theoretical, and methodological organization of this article must be intersectional as well.

As I go on to discuss in the following section, the extra-systemic conceptualization of politics and the political is capable of thinking about and describing the political power at the intersecting point of any number of possibilities. We could think about the intersecting point of neighborhood communities, school-based organizing, union organizing, public housing residents who organize clean-ups of their streets, and highway blockades (as some random examples). This conceptual framework of politics focuses on the process of convincing groups of people to create X thing in order to achieve Y thing, as opposed to being defined by a small group of people (and institutions) with access to government power. The extra-systemic conceptual expansion of politics understands the political as something developed wherever power is created and exchanged.

The concept of extra-systemic political engagement

Political theorists interested in quotidian politics have done important work recognizing the extra-systemic politics of Black folks living in poverty (Hanchard 2006). As political scientist Hanchard (2006) noted, the "explication of quotidian politics serve as a corrective to political and cultural analysis that reduces all politics to the state or macroeconomic factors," in other words, conceptualizations of politics must be expanded to include more than direct engagement with state institutions (Hanchard 2006). Hanchard's quotidian definition of the political is central to the extra-systemic conceptual expansion of politics I propose in this article. In short, Hanchard, argued politics is "the art of the possible, for opportunities and the lack of opportunities in a given situation or dynamic." Simply, politics is about the push to change what is, into something else. Briefly, it is also important to note what Hanchard distinguished as not political. In short, "nonpolitical acts are behaviors that are not generative of political community." This is why drive-by shootings and/or gunplay within neighborhoods are not political. While they may be moments of rebellion or deviance in the strictest sense, in reality, this particular sort of violence causes a "breakdown of political community" (Hanchard 2006).

Scott (1992), Hanchard (2006), and Kelley (1996) all emphasized how struggles over "identity, dignity, and fun" constituted formations of political communities that matter, and have influence and power within broader political conversations (Kelley 1996). As a Black feminist scholar, I am working toward the continuation of the contributions of the aforementioned scholars in the expansion of what we understand as politics. Berger (2006) argued the political work of Black women to "create and re-create a sense of community" often resulted in "labor [that] overlaps and often resists easy public or private distinctions" (Berger 2006). Black feminist scholars asserted time and time again a comprehensive understanding of politics must push back on the desire of socio-political elites to draw firm lines which separated the public and private spheres. Instead, they argued that much of Black women's political work, at the very least, begins in the home or in other spaces often designated as private (e.g., hair salons, church, drug treatment centers, etc.) (Isoke 2013; Mitchell 2020; Williamson 2016).

It is critical that any conception of politics be broad enough to encompass politics which do not fit neatly into categories of "public" vs. "private" space. Young (1990) argued power is, at its root, relational (Young 1990). Specifically, she said "power consists in a relationship between the exerciser and others through which he or she communicates intentions and meets with their acquiescence" (Young 1990). Young was particularly focused on the aspect of politics requiring the power needed for one group to extract their demands from another group. I argue an extra-systemic conceptual expansion of politics, informed by Black feminist political theory, understands politics *as the work of trying to change (for better or worse) the substantive reality of the world (or some part of it).* I use substantive, instead of material, so the conception of extra-systemic politics is flexible enough to encompass the demands for material resources. This allows extra-systemic politics to include "activism at the point of consumption – that is, around housing, food, clothing, and daily life in community spaces," which Rhonda Williams (2005), in addition to other scholars, have pointed to.

But this extra-systemic conception of politics must also be able to capture the type of politics Berger named purposive action:

> One definition of political activity for our purposes is purposive action, which helps to create and define a self or group identity, which then allows for individuals and groups to redress perceived injustices and grievances. (Berger 2006)

In other words, the demand to be recognized as a human within the public and political spheres, who has all the rights every other citizen has (Berger 2006; Harris-Perry 2011). The focus on substantive politics allows extra-systemic politics as a concept to capture the fullness of politics throughout diverse contexts. Like Young (1990), I see extra-systemic politics as ultimately being about striving to successfully achieve a groups' goals, through negotiating, forcing, cajoling, or other behaviors/actions, in order to achieve acquiescence from a specified target (Young 1990). For example, working with NGOs in order to bring global attention to issues of perceived public injustice as a portion of cognitive liberation work, or rioting in order to force a city government into providing additional funding for city public schools.

The extra-systemic conceptual expansion of politics I propose provides a breadth and flexibility that allows students of politics to capture institutional, bureaucratic, cultural, and community-based politics. This framework understands "traditional," "civic," or "quotidian" political work, as all being a part of the spectrum of politics, not separate pieces of a puzzle. As Young (1990) argued, politics does, can, and should, concern all aspects of socio-cultural life, there is no escaping the way politics and power are deeply intertwined under white supremacist heteropatriarchy (Hill-Collins 1998, 2017; Young 1990). Given politics touches every aspect of institutional, bureaucratic, cultural, family, and community life, it becomes quite clear, distinctions of "public" and "private" function as misnomers at best, and distractions at worst.

Theoretical framework: a Black feminist conceptualization of extra-systemic politics

Taken together, my Black feminist informed extra-systemic conceptual expansion of politics argues politics and the political are recognized using the following two requirements. First, the act(s) and/or set of behaviors named as "politics" are rooted in more than one person participating in acts/behaviors aimed at achieving a political goal (in other words, operating within a community toward a common goal). Specifically, this is the set of behaviors/acts people engage in together in order to have their demands met by or on behalf of their target(s). Second, the person(s), groups, people, behaviors, organizations, etc. named as "political" are working to generate substantive change within or for their target(s). In short extra-systemic politics are an effort to achieve some form of change (be it distributive, purposive, material, substantive, socio-cultural, policy, etc.) and engaging in various forms of relational power dynamics.

Within this conceptual expansion, there is no such thing as a "politics" of a singular individual, and there is no such thing as the "political" without power.[1] Note that "politics" always happens with more

130 INTERSECTIONAL (FEMINIST) ACTIVISMS

than one person, given the earlier requirement that politics is "fundamentally relational" and is not something that can be done in isolation (Young 1990). Here I will reiterate for clarities sake, a Black feminist informed conceptualization of extra-systemic politics understands politics as *the work of trying to change (for better or worse) the substantive reality of the world (or some part of it)*. A Black feminist informed conceptualization of the political (in the extra-systemic sense) is as follows: *the groups, people, behaviors, organizations, etc. being named as "political" are engaging in work that seeks substantive changes from the world around them, within or on behalf of their target(s)*.

This extra-systemic conception of politics and the political understands all politics – traditional, quotidian, and/or extra-systemic – to be the work of seeking substantive changes from the world within or on behalf of target(s). I differentiate between "traditional" and "extra-systemic" politics, only to demarcate when I am referencing prior "traditional" conceptions of politics which saw politics as limited to interactions with the government, its representatives, or its institutions. The function of the extra-systemic conception of politics and the political I develop within this article, is to expand how politics and the political are generally understood, not to create additional multiple separate categories. Black marginalized communities require an extra-systemic expansion of politics and the political so their political behavior and political identities can be accounted for and understood in US politics research.

The population: adult Black women living in Chicago public housing

In order to develop an effective extra-systemic understanding of politics informed by Black feminist political theory, the concept(s) must have the capacity to recognize, assess, and legitimize the political work of building intentional community. Black feminist scholars regularly point to the work of story-telling, institutional memory, guardianship of ancestral history, record keeping, community creation, volunteering, and community education as political practices central to Black women and their communities throughout the Afro-diaspora (Berger 2006; Harris-Perry 2011; Isoke 2013; Perry 2013; Williams 2005). While I was in the field, I observed Black women living in poverty who used political tactics like story-telling, informal information dissemination, and a "politics of home-making" (Isoke 2011). The politics of home-making prioritized creating political power via the reclamation of Black women's right to make their homes a site of beauty, comfort, political consciousness raising, community building, and mutual aid (Isoke 2011). Similarly, my experience interviewing respondents in the field reified Williamson's (2016) assertion that story-telling is a primary methodology of Black life. As such, the Black feminist theoretical foundations of this project require I acknowledge the unique intersectional position of poor Black women living in Chicago public housing and the way those identities can, have, and likely will continue to shape their politics and political tactics.

There are a multitude of ethnographic and qualitative projects pointing to the central political and social role Black women occupy within their communities all over the world (Isoke 2013; Perry 2013; Robnett 1997). So much so, Khan-Perry (2013) noted in her study of Brazilian social movements, "Black women shape the everyday and structural conditions of those living 'below the asphalt.'" In other words, Black women across the Afro-diaspora serve as a key and binding tie, holding their communities together via political work that so often eludes the private/public distinction (Hill-Collins 1998). It was no different with the residents I interviewed and observed in Chicago public housing communities.

At the overwhelming majority of tenants organizing meetings, protests, and events, Black women were the only adults present. As has been reported in multiple ethnographies of the political organizing within Black public housing and Black low-income neighborhoods globally, Black women and femmes consistently make up the day-to-day grassroots and administrative labor (Berger 2006; Isoke 2013; Robnett 1997). In short, when it comes to Black politics throughout the global diaspora, Black women are the bodies on the ground doing the day-to-day work (Feldman and Stall 2004; Levenstein 2009; Naples 1998; Robnett 1997).

Given the realities on the ground, in order to fully understand the tenant politics of Chicago public housing my research is focused on adult Black women. In 2011 Black women made up the majority of the residents serviced by the Chicago Housing Authority 84%) they also made up a significant portion of Chicago's urban poor (Housing 2006). In 2004, 39.5% of those serviced by welfare offices in Illinois were Black-Americans (Paral 2004). As such, Black women made up a group that was uniquely and particularly vulnerable to government power (Richie 2012; Ritchie 2017). Their unique vulnerability was a result of living in the United States where anti-Blackness has long been built into social entitlements and public housing policy for the poor (Hancock 2004). That anti-Blackness attached an exceptionally high stigma to any recipients of government support for the poor (Berger 2006; Cohen 1999; Watkins-Hayes 2019).

For example, policy feedback scholar Joe Soss found that SSI recipients were not stigmatized or berated by program officers (Soss 2002). However, AFDC clients viewed the agency as a "pervasive threat in their life, whose limits were unclear" (Soss 2002).[2] Black women living in the poverty in the United States also have increased vulnerability because they have less access to institutional protection (INCITE! Women of Color Against Violence 2016; Richie 2012; Ritchie 2017). They are more likely to die from domestic violence, and more likely to be assaulted by law enforcement, government case workers, or prison corrections officers (Women of Color Against Violence 2016; Richie 2012; Ritchie 2017). Poor Black women are also the fastest growing demographic of incarcerated women in the United States (Ritchie 2017; Western 2007). As a result, focusing on this specific population for the case study enhances understandings of how politics, and political strategies, are shaped and developed by individuals living with multiple sites of marginalization.

The context: public housing within the city of Chicago

The single case used for this study is based in Chicago. The City of Chicago serves as a unique case study for my research, specifically whether an expanded definition of politics and the political is needed in order to fully and accurately understand the political lives of Black women living below the poverty line. Within the city boundaries, Black Americans, Latinos, Asian Americans, and White Americans, live in distinctly different neighborhoods and communities (Hunt 2010; Polikoff 2006; Sampson 2013). As a result of this segregation, racial groups have vastly different lived experiences within the same city. While many Black Americans have little access to healthy food options, many Latinos lack access to basic social services (Sampson 2013). By contrast, white American neighborhoods on the north side have been beneficiaries of heavy economic and social development in hopes of bringing greater tourism to the city (Sampson 2013). Meanwhile, minority residents within the City of Chicago are segregated in terms of housing, and social marginalization. As a result, most job opportunities bring them into contact with more privileged city inhabitants (Feldman and Stall 2004; Polikoff 2006; Ralph 2014).

I interviewed the majority of the respondents in their apartments in the Altgeld Gardens and Phillip Murray Homes development, a public housing development built in the post-World War II period.[3] Altgeld Gardens "sits in one of the city's most isolated areas. The nearest supermarket is miles away, only one bus route serves the development," and it is located next door to a toxic landfill. When visitors drive within a block of the Altgeld Gardens Homes, they are typically inundated with the smell of sewage from the nearby sewage plant. They are overwhelmed with the smell from the street outside of the development, and as the weather gets warmer the smell only gets stronger. Across the street from the Altgeld Gardens Homes are several abandoned steel mills; the area is actually an industrial site. Residents frequently complain about the chemicals emitted from the old mills and the illness that they (allegedly) cause within the community. There have been lawsuits and generations of tenant activism attempting to fight back against the environmental racism foundational to Altgeld Gardens' very existence (Brinson 2004; Cutter, Boruff, and Lynn Shirley 2003; Coffey et al. 2020; Gay 2004; White and Hall 2015).

Down the street from the old mills is a toxic landfill. Originally, the entire area was covered in swamp. In the early 20th century, Poorman Sewage Farm used the swamp as an industrial waste site, and decades later, the City of Chicago filled the swamp and built Altgeld Gardens to house low-income people of color. Years later, the Chicago Housing Authority (CHA) built the Phillip Murray Homes to accommodate the ever-growing number of migrants to the Midwest (Wilkerson 2011).

> Altgeld Gardens was built in 1945 and named in honor of Illinois politicianJohn Peter Altgeld. The Philip Murray Homes were built in 1954 and named in honor of Philip Murray, a visionary leader of the labor movement (Chicago Housing Authority 2023).

All in all, Altgeld Gardens and Phillip Murray Homes public housing development is one large development which accommodates a little more than 1900 row houses (or what respondents called, walk-up apartments vs the high-rise apartments Chicago public housing is well known for) throughout the development (Chicago Housing Authority 2023).

In addition to meeting respondents in their homes and throughout the development, I attended Altgeld Gardens Local Advisory Council Meetings, CHA Central Advisory Council Meetings and CHA Board of Commissioners Meetings. I also traveled to local community organization gatherings, events, and other spontaneous and/or planned political gatherings on the development and across the City of Chicago. Spending time within the housing development itself, as well as observing CHA meetings and gatherings, facilitated a greater understanding of the public and political discourses used to describe public housing spaces and their residents. However, participant observation also allowed me to observe the way spatial environments can shift and change over time to fit the needs and desires of those in power (Hackworth 2014).

Methodological overview

Within this article I examine what conceptualization of politics allows for a complete and accurate understanding of the socio-political lives of marginalized populations. As Prowse, Weaver, and Meares (2019) noted, "subjugated knowledge offers a vital accounting of the American state and the democratic condition in our time" (Prowse, Weaver, and Meares 2019). Said more simply, the words and the wisdom of the women featured in this study can enable a better understanding of the complex interactions between the socio-political as well as spatial conditions of Chicago Public Housing, and the extra-systemic politics these spatial conditions seem to give birth to (Feldman and Stall 2004; Levenstein 2009; Naples 1998; Williams 2005). The methodological design for this research was organized around the intersectional identities of the respondents. As such, the data for this project had three intersecting parts: the ethnographic data, field notes, and in-depth interviews. This facilitated access to multiple points of view, and several social and political networks within the Chicago public housing community.

It is beyond this article to make any broad causal claims about the experiences of *all* Black women living in public housing within the US. Instead, I use ethnography to bring attention to more subtle socio-political experiences that large N survey's sometimes miss (Junn 1999; McKeown 1999; Simien 2006; Small 2009). As Bakshi, Meares, and Weaver (2016) noted, "the traditional survey approaches . . . [come] at a cost. They constrain subversive forms of expression by avoiding the articulation of ideas that the researcher does not ask. Moreover, survey research can sacrifice dynamic interactions for replicability and generalization."

In other words, by focusing on larger data sets, the more subtle nuances found within fine details can be missed (Johnson 2022; Michener 2020; Prowse, Weaver, and Meares 2019). The ethnographic study I analyze in this article brings attention to the unique politics circumscribing a particular group of Black women living below the poverty line in the United States, in service of the theoretical and conceptual development of extra-systemic politics. As a population with a low-number of protections from the state, poor Black women are best suited to fully recount the true nature of the state (Kaba 2021; Richie 2012; Ritchie 2017; INCITE! Women of Color Against Violence 2016. US politics scholars require a full understanding of government domestic power in the United States in order to develop a comprehensive understanding of politics and the political. At its core, politics is the effort to develop power to achieve a particular end goal. Ultimately, all studies of politics in all of its forms, benefit from an extra-systemic expansion of politics: an expanded conceptualization of politics and the political, which includes traditional forms of political engagement (e.g., voting, writing your senator, etc.) as well what Verba, Lehman Schlozman, and Brady (1996) call "the civic," in addition to the extra-systemic elements I suggest in this article (e.g., rioting, storytelling, community cleanup, public school based politics, etc.).

Ethnographic case study

Between April 2011 and April 2012 I conducted a year-long ethnography at the Altgeld Gardens and Murray Homes on the far South Side of Chicago. The data was collected a little over 10 years after the federal government allowed the Chicago Housing Authority to have local control of its public housing once again (Goetz 2013; Hunt 2010; Popkin 2016). As such, it was an appropriate time to assess the political lives of tenants, 10 years into the transition back to local public housing governance. By using the case study method, I was able to interrogate, not only the shifting political identities of CHA tenants, but I was also able to examine the way their lived experiences, and environments contextualize, and in some ways, informed, their understandings of themselves as members of the public sphere (The Black Public Sphere Collective 1995; Squires 2002). In this study, the context cannot be easily separated out from the case itself (Stake 1996). The influence of public housings spatial realities on the political lives of residents cannot be separated from their lived experience within the housing developments.

As is typical in case study methodology, I triangulated the data with three sources of information: I used in-depth interviews, participant observation, and archival analysis to examine my questions. In this study, I conducted in-depth interviews with 31 Black women who were past and present residents of Altgeld Gardens. These interviews allowed me to slowly get to know the women and the nuances of their lives within the housing development and surrounding neighborhoods. I asked questions about how the respondents understand politics as well as questions that examined whether or not they considered themselves to be members of a political community. Most significantly, the in-depth interviews examined how the women felt about Chicago public housing and how they felt about the presence (and/or non-presence) of government actors in their lives. While each in-depth interview was based loosely on the same interview guide, the questions were open-ended in nature so as to allow each individual woman's narrative to develop. It was not my goal to shape how the respondents told their stories. It was my goal to get as close to an authentic self-description of their political lives as possible. All of the interviews were audio recorded and transcribed.

Creating the respondent sample and recruiting participants

All respondents were over 18 years old, and I strove for a diversity of age ranges from young adult to senior women. In order to have diversity in my sample, I recruited potential respondents by posting fliers throughout the housing development. Essentially, there are two units of analysis in my project, the individuals and the development itself. Within the individual unit of analysis, there were actually three different populations: those who were new to public housing, those who were new to Altgeld Gardens, and those who lived in Altgeld Gardens for a significant period of time (10+ years).

I used what some researchers call a snowball or convenience sampling method. I interviewed the women who volunteered for the study who met the specifications of my sample and from there I continued to ask my respondents to recommend other women for the study. This sampling method enabled a better understanding of the community, as well as the political and social networks of the respondents. As has been noted in previous studies of political participation, the political and social network of an individual has one of the largest impacts on their ever-evolving political identity (Verba,

Schlozman, and Brady 1996; Sinclair 2012). As such, understanding the broad networks of the respondents gave me better leverage when constructing a conceptual theory of extra-systemic politics.

Since my data collection included human research subjects, my research project was reviewed by the Institutional Review Board (IRB) at the University of Chicago. The research project was approved by the IRB in 2011, prior to the launch of my fieldwork. All respondents had the opportunity to carefully read a consent form that was approved by the University of Chicago IRB. I also read and reviewed the consent form to each respondent prior to their signing. All consent forms were kept in a separate locked box apart from the data. All of the respondent demographic and identifying information were stripped from the transcripts. Each organization and respondent was given a pseudonym that was used exclusively throughout the project.

Findings

In the following sections, I describe what politics and the political looked like through the lens of an extra-systemic conceptual expansion. Finally, I review the key findings and the central takeaways for students of US politics.

Power within the public housing space

For many respondents, the public housing authority was representative of the government itself (Soss 2002; Soss and Weaver 2017). The bureaucracy of public housing functioned as a stand in for the rest of the city, state, and federal authorities. In the life history of many respondents, it was much later in their adult lives that the voting booth was seen as a form of engagement with the government (Moffett-Bateau 2023). As such, it is critical to consider the spatial context that could allow someone to access the voting booth, the parent-teacher meeting, or the local political organizing meeting. In this way, the spatial realities of public housing itself, as well as the tenants within it, all impact the development of resident political identity, as well as their political behaviors.

When I interviewed Wanda, she would not tell me her precise age, but she was willing to disclose that she was in her forties. She had been living in Altgeld Gardens for most of her life; by 2011, she had lived in Altgeld for almost 40 years. She left the development for a handful of years after taking a job, but ultimately she returned after she gave birth. When I asked her why she chose to return to Altgeld Gardens, she cited her network of support within the public housing development. After spending most of her life in Altgeld, she had access to her mother, her friends, and other family members who were able to help a young mother as she struggled to get on her feet. Wanda's mother was responsible for the founding of a local organization that did work around environmental justice in Chicago public housing (Emily et al. 2020). As a result, Wanda had the opportunity to travel around the country with her mother as well as the opportunity to visit the White House and to meet three sitting presidents. It is no small surprise Wanda was incredibly politically active in the most traditional sense of the word. She conducted voter registration drives every year, she was responsible for organizing multiple protests on the development, and she consistently raised enough grant money to pay everyone who worked in her organization's office, although she was unable to pay herself. As a result, Wanda lived in poverty for most of her life.

Regardless, Wanda continued to be exceptionally active in both the public and the private spheres. In addition to running her organization, she also politicized and, in some ways, radicalized, multiple women throughout the development. Many of her neighbors, who later became respondents, recounted how she dragged them to meetings, to protests, and other activities throughout the development. Not only did her political community remain active both publicly and privately, but Wanda also single-handedly helped many adult Black women become active members within various political communities. Because of her political engagement, Wanda seems like a good place to start when thinking about how Black women living in public housing understand their own power and the power of others.

Because Wanda lived in Altgeld Gardens for most of her life, she had close relationships with most of the maintenance people as well as the managers who oversaw the bureaucracy within the development, the people Michael Lipsky (2010) referred to as "street-level bureaucrats." As a result, whenever Wanda needed something fixed in her home, she was able to get the repair taken care of relatively quickly. In stark contrast, some of the women I interviewed sometimes had to wait weeks, if not months, for things as simple as new light bulbs or as critical as new locks. Interpersonal relationships were everything when it came to overall well-being and personal safety on the development. CHA street-level bureaucrats controlled tenants access to most resources related to their apartments, and sometimes their food stamps, access to educational opportunities, or even childcare. Because of her many personal relationships with management, Wanda was able to keep a cute little dog she took with her everywhere.[4] She also took great pride in her apartment: the walls were painted, and her kitchen was quite clean. It is not an overstatement to say Wanda had a strong sense of self-perceived political power. If she needed something from management, she was able to get it, and even if it required bending the rules, ever so slightly, she knew how to make that happen.

A: [I've] heard different things, that management doesn't let people plant flowers...

W: Yes, they do. They used to give them to you, back in the day. Back in the day they used to give you flowers to plant. But you can do whatever you want to do now. That's not true. If I want to decorate my yard, I can go decorate it. If I need the tools to be able to decorate my yard, they'll give it to you. You just have to leave your state ID or something like that. And then you bring the tools you get your state ID back. So that's not true. Now, what might be true, they might not have the tools, somebody stole them from the inside. It may not be available 'cuz they don't have it no more. But no, you can fix up your own yard. So that's not true. People just don't fix them. Maybe 'cuz I used to do that stuff so much when I was a kid, I would not plant a flower.

A: Yeah, I feel the same way after working in my mom's garden.

W: You see, no, no, no. Vegetable garden, raised bed...I will not garden, period, or take care of a yard. I will pay [somebody] to mow...

A: I feel the same way.

W: ...to mow my yard, or something like that. But I know if I had to put flowers, I mean I got to water and maintain, I'm not doing that. I'm not with that so I just keep my yard. I sweep in front...my neighbor real good, we'll sweep stuff up but I'm not into that because I hated it when I was going it when I was a kid, I guess, unconsciously.

When Wanda was a child growing up in Altgeld Gardens, her mother made her work in the garden every weekend. In her adult life, she had no desire to garden, maintain vegetables, or plant flowers. However, Wanda remained aware of not only the rules around gardening and yard maintenance but also where she could get the tools and other resources should she decide gardening was something that she was interested in doing. Despite her lack of interest in yard upkeep, Wanda made sure her yard was always well cared for. Although CHA maintenance is supposed to do all of the lawn care and maintenance for Altgeld Gardens, many of my respondents complained that it was not adequate. Like Wanda, many respondents took exceptional pride in maintain their front lawn, as well as their home. Being able to access the resources to do so via CHA street-level bureaucrats, was a point of contention throughout the interviews. Respondents asserted their political power in negotiations with CHA in order to get their needs met. I argue being able to access the resources to care for your home is one example of what Williams (2005) "politics at the site of consumption" – in other words, the political work of accessing basic necessities for individual comfort and well-being.

Many senior Black women residents who lived throughout the development took care of cleaning up the streets and performing basic maintenance tasks themselves. Wanda frequently employed young men from around the neighborhood – many of whom she mentored – to do tasks around the house for her like mowing the lawn, fixing a window, and other errands that would keep them out of trouble for the day. Wanda had the ability to not only build relationships within the neighborhood but to create a politics of homemaking where she created safety, comfort, and well-being for herself, her neighbors, and local young people (Isoke 2011). Wanda's politics of homemaking contributed to a personal sense of power which fueled her daily participation within her local socio-political community (Isoke 2011; Williamson 2016). Wanda engaged in political work to not only mentor local young people, but to compensate them while she taught them how to care for a home, *and* how to negotiate CHA bureaucracy in order to do so.

It is in this way the aesthetics of the neighborhood space, in particular the appearance of the individual private sphere, played a role in shaping the individual sense of power, agency, and authority over everyday life. When respondents felt they had no power over their home or themselves, particularly because in the public housing context there was a direct connection between their home and government bureaucracy, it became even more challenging to create an individual sense of power, political identity, and by extension, a sense of political power.

A: Yeah. Are people treated equally in this society?

W: Hell, no, you know that.

A: Who isn't treated equally?

W: The poor. The poor is not treated fairly, because if the poor don't know their power and understand the relationship of the power that they do have, you know. . .power's not defined by wealth. You know what I mean?

A: Absolutely.

W: And power is something. . .power is something that you want to make change or make it better and it gives you that dedication to make that change, you know. So what we don't understand is our power is among the people, but a lot of people think power is associated with how much money you got.

A: Right. Is that a power that you think you have?

W: I don't know. . .no. . .I have an influence power. I can influence people better than trying to acquire people to be on my side. I can influence you. And I can motivate you so my powers is in motivation too because I can motivate you and I can present a picture in a way that you can understand it.

Wanda's point here, about influence being a sort of power was significant. She had the power to influence others, to go wherever she wanted in the development, and to do what she pleased with her apartment. It was a "power-to" which developed her confidence as a member of the political community (Cudd 2006). Significantly, these are not freedoms, let alone power, every respondent had. It was not simply about control; that is, the ability to shape things to your preference. Instead, power, in this framework, was Wanda's sense of her own ability to act, as well as to influence others to act. Wanda could not necessarily control how any woman on the development was going to act on their individual political sensibility. What she did have was a power of influence which facilitated her ability to provide education regarding political skills and community building.

When the government is your landlord, your ability to negotiate the everyday can become a set of experiences which increase your sense of your ability to successfully engage government power or reinforce a generalized sense of political disempowerment. This understanding of government bureaucracies as sources of government power is key when considering why an extra-systemic conceptual expansion of politics and the political is critical (Hackworth 2014; Lipsky 2010; Spence 2015; Watkins-Hayes 2009). As students of US politics, we must have a means to capture the strategies communities use to push back against government power, those we traditionally understand as political, and those we do not. However, resident political power was not simply cultivated in individual homes. Chicago public housing residents also did quite a bit of tenant organizing across the City of Chicago.

The development of subversive resident politics

A central forum for political talk between and amongst CHA residents was the Central Advisory Council Tenant Services Meetings (Eliasoph 1998). Frequently, residents used these meetings as a space to protest potential amendments to housing policy or injustices that touch their lives. For example, one issue which frequently came up during tenant services meetings were observed differences between the treatment of residents who live in high-rise developments (like the former Cabrini Green public housing development) versus those who lived in walk-up developments (like the Altgeld Gardens public housing development). According to tenants at Central Advisory Committee (CAC) meetings, high-rise residents were under a higher degree of surveillance than tenants who lived in other types of developments. High-rise residents had to go through intense security to enter and leave their homes; they were required to show government issued ID to enter the building, and in the absence of identification, tenant guests could not visit resident apartments. High-rise residents consistently complained this constituted unfair and unnecessary surveillance, and they should have greater freedom to come and go as they please.

While on first pass this seems to be a relatively minor issue, it is an example of Eliasoph (1998) public-spirited conversation. The residents were concerned with not only how these surveillance policies affected them individually, but they were also concerned with how it impacted everyone who lived in high-rise public housing buildings. When residents discussed these issues, they almost always framed it as an issue of justice: as fully independent adults living within a democratic society, they should have full access to their places of residence in the way they personally deemed appropriate. What initially began as an issue one person brought up very quickly became an issue multiple residents within the community grabbed hold of and pushed forward.

It is important to note that this form of politics would often be missed by traditional measures of political engagement or behavior. Most of the residents at these meetings were not part of a formal organization, they did not describe their advocacy work as formal protest, and they did not talk about this work as a form of politics. Instead, when I would ask residents what they thought of when I said the word "politics," many mentioned, "white people," "the white house," "Rahm Emmanuel," and occasionally voting. In other words, just like political scientists, they thought of institutions and the people within those institutions who held some measure of political power. On the other hand, the subversive resident politics described above, meets all of the requirements to be considered a form of extra-systemic politics. The fight for residents to be able to independently decide who entered their apartment was: (1) made up of more than two people attempting to use power to create a new possibility which previously did not exist; (2) The community members leading this fight used the power(s) they had access to in order to win a substantive goal from their target (CHA).

Another issue frequently raised at CAC Tenant Services Meetings was the proposed amendment to The Plan for Transformation which would require all residents to be drug-tested in order to live in public housing (Geiger 2013). Over the course of multiple meetings, tenants argued the policy would constitute an invasion of privacy which violated their individual rights. But beyond conceptualizing this as an issue of self-interest, many of the residents I spoke with discussed the negative ramifications drug testing policies would have on the lives of poor people across the City. If residents were required to be drug tested, they worried massive numbers of people would end up homeless and countless families would be destabilized. In many of the mixed-income housing developments drug-testing was already mandatory (mixed-income housing had their own set of rules which were not arbitrated by CHA[5]). Residents at the CAC Tenant Services meetings consistently complained about discriminatory policies they felt were focused on public housing tenants within mixed-income housing.[6]

According to several respondents, some private management companies required public housing residents to be drug-tested, but market-rate renters were excluded from the drug-testing requirement. In this particular policy fight, a group of residents came together to cultivate political power(s) in service of creating a possibility which previously did not exist (a drug-neutral resident policy from

CHA). The community members seeking this possibility sought acquiescence from their target (CHA). Months later, CHA tenants prevailed and CHA street-level bureaucrats rescinded the blanket drug-testing policy (Hampton 2011; Piemonte 2011).

Over time the CAC Tenant Services meetings developed into a space of political learning and political engagement for the Black marginalized communities who lived in Chicago public housing. The meetings served as training grounds for residents: they learned how to speak in front of large groups of people, and they learned which communication strategies worked to effectively shift policy. Residents tried to meet the expectations of both White and Black middle-class CHA board members (Watkins-Hayes 2009). The meetings served as spaces where residents from a wide spectrum of neighborhoods learned about the issues and concerns, they shared in common with one another.

Many residents became regulars at the meetings and showed up early to participate in networking, informal information dissemination, planning, and strategizing. Individuals shared stories with others about what strategies worked when combating the management companies, security guards, or even CHA itself. Residents were able to prioritize and focus on issues like drug testing and Section Three contracts, not only at Tenant Services Meetings but also at CHA Board of Commissioners Meetings and Local Advisory Council meetings. While the neoliberal privatization created via The Plan for Transformation had a number of negative repercussions, a positive result was the training it provided for residents in public-spirited conversation within the unique public spaces it created (Eliasoph 1998; Feldman and Stall 2004; Hunt 2010; Williams 2005).

The creation of resident political imagination

In public meetings, residents were provided a space where they could develop political imagination (Eliasoph 1998). After consistently participating in the meetings, residents were able to make connections between their individual struggles and the political power they held. By bearing witness to residents from other developments as they articulated their visions for a healthy and whole life within their public housing development, new and old residents were able to develop their own political visions for their developments. By observing other residents' participation in the process of political meaning making – the process of articulating their grievances, expectations, and dreams about life in public housing – residents began to cultivate their individual political imaginations. Their political imagination allowed them to see connections between resident quality of life and the political world that could make a better life possible. Significantly, with an expanded extra-systemic conceptualization of politics and the political, students of US politics could have a framework capable of capturing and fully understanding these unique moments of political engagement and political development.

There were a number of public meetings an individual resident could attend on a regular basis. This section focuses on my participant observation at the Altgeld Gardens Local Advisory Council Meetings (LAC), the CHA Board of Commissioners Meetings, and the Central Advisory Committee Tenant Services Meetings. The Altgeld Gardens LAC public meetings occurred monthly in the community center on the development. They were run by the elected LAC resident leadership board and were typically attended by the rest of the council and occasionally an interested resident non-council member. There was always an agenda, and as with all CHA meetings, they were run according to Roberts Rules of Order (but typically the LAC meetings were less formal than other CHA meetings). There was an opening prayer and an approval of the last meeting's minutes, and at that point council business begun. Often, this was a space interested parties, like representatives from CHA family programming or local activist groups, came in and gave presentations about services they provided to the community. The council would also discuss ongoing issues within the development and make decisions about what was needed to address the issues. Sometimes, next steps were as simple as speaking to the management company about broken streetlights (for example). At other times, the proposed solutions were as big as protests against ongoing Section Three CHA construction. Generally, LAC meetings were laid back and informal, as everyone already knew each other. Of the

INTERSECTIONAL (FEMINIST) ACTIVISMS

three meetings of interest here, the LAC meetings ran (on average) for the shortest amount of time, sometimes only lasting 20 minutes.

It is important to note, when asked many LAC members did not consider their activities on the committee to be "political." When I followed up by asking LAC board members whether they participated in a political organization, the majority of them said no. This is despite the fact that most of them ran campaigns in order to get elected to the Council. There were two exceptions to this, the treasurer and the Council president did see themselves as political actors. But the rest of the Council discussed their involvement as simply something they did to help their community (e.g., community work or volunteer work). Understanding the disconnect between traditional definitions of politics and the lived experience of the communities that political practitioners study and engage is critical to gaining better analytic leverage when we analyze the politics of marginalized communities.

Throughout my interviews I asked respondents the survey questions traditionally used by mainstream political science to assess engagement, cynicism, alienation, and efficacy (i.e., I asked respondents questions like, "do you participate in politics?" or "are you involved in any political organizations?"). Routinely, subjects responded "no" to all of the questions regarding their political involvement (with the exception of voting). Yet, when I would follow up with open-ended questions about how they spent their time, I consistently discovered they regularly attended CHA meetings, participated in organizational activities in order to make positive change on the development, or volunteered at the local community center. Ultimately, not only does this suggest more qualitative work is needed within political science to facilitate the development of more useful and accurate conceptual categories capable of capturing the politics of Black marginalized populations (Cohen 1999; Dawson 2003; Harris-Perry 2011; Simien 2006), but it also points to the necessity of an extra-systemic conceptual expansion of politics and the political, informed by Black feminist political theory.

Public meetings as politics in practice

CHA Commissioners Board Meetings were monthly meetings where the broader public could engage with all of the leadership of the Chicago Housing Authority. Typically, this meeting was attended by media, activists, government employees (i.e., local police force, caseworkers, etc.), as well as residents, it was a formal meeting with very little public input. However, residents found creative and imaginative ways to express themselves in this formal space. CAC Tenant Services Meetings were meetings held by the Central Advisory Council every month so where residents could directly communicate with the leadership and staff of CHA. These meetings occupied the middle-space between the Commissioners Board Meetings and the LAC Meetings, in terms of formality. While there was always an agenda and Roberts Rules of Order were supposed to be strictly adhered to, CAC meetings were more likely to be derailed by public outbursts than CHA board meetings, but they were also not run with the ease and familiarity of the LAC meetings.

At every CAC Tenant Services Meeting, a member of the resident council presided over the meeting. This council member would open and close the meeting, kept the meeting on task, and enforced Roberts Rule of Order. Oftentimes, however, this moderator of sorts would use their position of power to bring a particular issue to the forefront of the meeting, forcing the CHA employees to address her concerns in public. For example, a member of the CHA staff (Ms. Frank) was giving a series of routine announcements about various coat drives and, in particular, some graduations CHA was holding in honor of residents who recently graduated from a job readiness preparation program. Suddenly, the council member (Ms. Johnson) who was moderating the meeting became upset.

Ms. Johnson interjected in reaction to the Family Independence Graduation announcement. "I'm taking all of these classes and trainings, and nobody is hiring me and then I get penalized [by CHA, welfare agencies, etc.]. Who is making sure I get hired? You all are having all of these graduations, how many of those people have jobs now? I look outside the window [of her development] all the time and people are working, and they aren't residents."

Ms. Frank responded, trying to move past the issue and appease Ms. Johnson: "It is important to note that there are a number of programs to help tenants get jobs" Ms. Johnson became increasingly aggravated and kept pushing the issue: "but why aren't we working with those contractors that are doing all of the work on the developments?"

Ms. Frank, not having much else to say, replied by saying: "this is why section three is a priority for CHA now."

But Ms. Johnson would not be deterred and instead said "we should be at the table when there are conversations being had [about Section Three]. Stop just saying it and start really working for us."

Here, Ms. Frank couldn't use her typical strategy of telling the residents that she would speak to them at the conclusion of the meeting. Instead, Ms. Johnson was able to expose the ways in which she felt that CHA often tells residents one thing and appears to do another.

This interaction is important for a number of reasons. Ms. Johnson is a veteran CAC member; during the year I was in the field, I saw her at every CAC Tenant Services Meeting and CHA Board Commissioner Meeting I attended. Ms. Johnson was an expert, not only at effective speech strategies (e.g., speaking clearly, loudly, and addressing individual CHA employees by name), but she also learned how to strategically bend meeting rules in order to be heard. In this case, she was able to use her moderator position to bring to the forefront contractors who were doing construction work for The Plan for Transformation on CHA developments but who were not hiring residents to do that work. In "Section Three" of CHA housing policy, CHA committed to making sure contractors working on their housing developments, funded with Housing and Urban Development money, would hire public housing residents (US Department of Housing and Urban Development 2023). In 2011, according to residents, many contractors hired by CHA were not adhering to this policy, and it became a major issue for a number of resident activists – most publicly, Ms. Johnson.

At a CHA Board of Commissioners' meeting, Ms. Johnson was able to strategically use the rules to be heard by the street-level bureaucrats managing CHA (Lipsky 2010). Every Board of Commissioners' meeting had a public comment period, where individuals who signed up before the meeting can speak for a maximum of two minutes. When it was her turn, Ms. Johnson got up and started speaking out about the lack of residents being hired by contractors working on the development. When her time was up, the next individual was called to the front, and the woman promptly deferred her time to Ms. Johnson, who continued speaking for another two minutes. When her time was up, the next person on the list deferred her time to Ms. Johnson. By the time Ms. Johnson was finished, she had been speaking longer than almost everyone else on the agenda, commissioners included. Once again, she was successful; she forced the Chair of the CHA Board of Commissioners to address Section Three and publicly commit to tackling the issue.

While Ms. Johnson may not consider herself an activist or political, her actions as described here say otherwise. Hanchard (2006) argues politics are about the push to change *what is* into *something else*. Ms. Johnson was able to use her position to disrupt the meeting and push the Commissioners to act on an issue that was having a significant impact on the day-to-day life of CHA tenants across the City of Chicago. While traditional frameworks of politics would not capture the political engagement demonstrated above, extra-systemic conceptual expansions of politics and the political allow for a consistent understanding of the politics of extra-systemic political actors like Ms. Johnson.

Interestingly, announcements given by CHA employees at Altgeld Gardens LAC meetings are a site for contentious politics as well.

After the CHA family-programming employee (Ms. Stevens) gave an announcement about services offered for the children who live in Altgeld Gardens, she asked if anyone had any questions. Ms. Smith, a member of the LAC leadership, left her seat at the front of the room, and asked Ms. Stevens if she was aware that the entire sixth grade class at Charger Elementary [one of the public elementary schools on the development] was failing. Ms. Stevens replied that she was not. At this point, Ms. Smith requested that the family programming offices make tutors available to the sixth graders, so that the entire class would not be held back. Ms. Stevens, a bit startled by the request, responded that all of the tutors for Altgeld Gardens were already completely booked. Asked how many tutors there were, Ms. Stevens replied, "two." She then explained that tutors wanted to be paid, and that she would try and find some funding for tutors next year, but she wasn't sure that she would be able to provide any tutors immediately.

After some back and forth between Ms. Smith and Ms. Stevens about whether or not the funding was available for tutors. Ms. Smith, took a step toward Ms.

Stevens and turned toward the rest of the meeting attendees and said "so let me get this straight, you're saying, that you *will not* provide tutors for *our children?*" Ms. Stevens, stammering said, "no, no, no, that is not what I'm saying, I'm saying I will look into it."

Here, Ms. Smith was able to use a relatively routine aspect of LAC meetings, general announcements, to draw attention to an issue that was not present on the formal agenda. When Ms. Stevens asked for questions, as she always does, Ms. Smith was able to force her into a discussion around academic performance at the local elementary school and support services needed for local school children so that they could succeed academically. While Ms. Stevens initially tried to duck and dodge the issue by citing "funding" shortages, when Ms. Smith repeated back to Ms. Stevens what she heard her saying, for the purpose of the formal record, Ms. Stevens quickly agreed to pursue the matter formally by meeting with the principal of Charger Elementary. Ultimately, Ms. Stevens did not want to end up on the LAC meeting minutes (all of which are formally archived at the Chicago Housing Authority Office and are subject to the Freedom of Information Act requests of anyone in the US) as having denied low-income school children adequate tutoring.

This style of contentious (and sometimes disruptive) politics is a skill honed by tenants through attendance at CHA meetings on almost a weekly basis. Attending tenant and CHA meetings helped residents learn the nuances of the rules as well as how to strategically break them. This knowledge provided residents with a platform to give voice to issues, which would otherwise go unheard. It is important to note that this political learning and engagement was also facilitated through the networking and planning that went on before and after every meeting. Generally, after meetings senior residents follow up with tenants who asked questions or made complaints during the public comment period at both the CAC Tenant Services Meetings and the CHA Board of Commissioners Meetings. The senior residents would direct tenants to the CHA employees who committed to speak with them after the meeting, and senior residents also provided tenants with the name and number of their Local Advisory Council (LAC) president if the individual lived in a development with a LAC. For tenants who were concerned about recurring issues, sometimes senior residents met with them before the meeting to organize some type of action in order to get the issue heard in a more effective way.

While some might consider issues like harassment by security guards, lack of access to particular social welfare programs, or lack of access to gainful employment as being "personal" or "nonpolitical," residents saw the connections between their personal lives and the power wielded by government bureaucracies. By being in conversation with one another, residents learned not only Chicago Housing Authority Policy but federal, local, and state policy as well. Residents regularly challenged CHA policy amendments like proposed mandatory drug testing by citing federal housing policy and were able to do so as a result of the political imagination and cognitive liberation developed within these public spaces. Residents learned from each other (through conversation and observation) and from other political actors within these meeting spaces. It was through the intentional cultivation of political imagination that inspired residents to shut down a construction site at Altgeld Gardens because the contractor refused to fulfill Section Three obligations to hire residents onto the work-site. It was also political imagination which inspired residents to have multiple people sign up for speaking time at the CHA Board of Commissioners meeting and "spontaneously" give their speaking time to the resident who was the most skilled and effective public speaker. Ultimately the development of political imagination was a result of the public-spirited conversation created within these public meeting spaces. By leveraging the networks built via extra-systemic political participation in the various councils and CHA meetings, a political power was generated in an attempt to protect residents from the oppressive marginalization which plagued their everyday lives.

Conclusion: key findings within an extra-systemic politics

As a scholar of race and politics, I am invested in understanding the forces shaping the politics of Black marginalized communities in the United States. In this case study, I studied the experiences of Black women living below the poverty line in a public housing development on the south side of Chicago in an effort to flesh out the mechanisms between their lived experiences and their extra-systemic political engagement. Anthropologists, policy feedback scholars, Black feminists, and sociologists have argued people living in poverty have a high level of political knowledge and a unique forms of politics, a politics capable of being understood via an extra-systemic conceptual expansion of politics and the political (Feldman and Stall 2004; Isoke 2013; Kelley 1996; Weaver, Prowse, and Piston 2019). Chicago Public Housing Authority (CHA) sponsored a number of meetings between residents and CHA bureaucrats throughout the month. Those meetings provided residents with the opportunity to express concerns about public housing infrastructure, CHA employees, as well as services provided by local and state government via the Chicago Housing Authority.

CHA sponsored meetings created a public sphere unique to the life experience of public housing residents. Many, if not most residents are limited in their ability to access larger, city-wide public sphere's due to severe constraints on their access to public transportation, as well as the social-political restrictions placed on them due to the intersection of their race, gender, and class identities (Berger 2006; Ralph 2014; Sampson 2013; Watkins-Hayes 2019). On the other hand, CHA meetings provided a space residents could access regularly due to its proximity to their homes, as well as its particular set of rules and logics which they have been taught to engage and strategically use by past and present public housing residents who have acted and continue to act as activist mentors and elders. These public spheres facilitated the development of a political imagination amongst residents that created unique and creative extra-systemic politics.

I began this project centrally concerned with the politics of Black marginalized populations, specifically low-income Black women. In the years following empirical interventions like Cohen's (2010) *Democracy Remixed*, we now know young Black people (and potentially a number of other minority groups) are engaged in politics through means that are not always picked-up using traditional measures. In *Black Visions*, Michael Dawson (2003) made clear Black people in the US have a wide spectrum of political identities demanding a closer look into the political motivations of Black people (beyond an assessment of political alienation from government power generally). In turn, my project contributes to this growing literature around traditional and extra-systemic political participation amongst Black people living in the United States by identifying the conceptual categories and mechanisms which allow extra-systemic politics to take root within Black marginalized communities (Hanchard 2006).

I have created a conceptual category which allows scholars to fully interrogate the political behavior and engagement of Black marginalized groups, and poor Black women in the US specifically. I've provided a framework which will allow students of US politics to measure and understand political behavior and engagement across populations more fully. It is critical for future scholars interested in continuing the theoretical work necessary to fully parse out the politics of marginalized groups, to think through how oppression around a wide range of identities shape the individual relationship to politically important conceptual categories (freedom, joy, political desire, liberation, power, etc.). This project began that work by focusing tightly on how class shapes the political experience of Black women living in public housing. In alignment with the work of past scholars, it is my hope future scholars will continue thinking through the theoretical relationship between liberation and membership in the political community, particularly when it comes to the intersections of race, gender, and class (Alex-Assensoh 1997; Bunyasi and Watts Smith 2019; Cohen and Dawson 1993; Prowse, Weaver, and Meares 2019; Spence 2015). As many a Black feminist has said before, a fully liberated Black citizenship will lead to a society open and free for all people (Blain 2021).

By thinking through how individuals understand their own liberation, their own power, or lack thereof, political scientists can get closer to understanding what Black marginalized people want to accomplish with political power. In a sense, this question is one about desire. What exactly do poor Black women desire from their politics? What does it mean when Black feminists and activists of all sorts make requests for a fully liberated political membership within civil society? Is this desire simply relegated to those Black women who work within political public spheres? Or is a political desire for liberation and/or freedom widely held by all? To use the framework of this project: is there a language of political desire and liberation amongst Black women living below the poverty line? If so, what does that language look like, and what does it mean for the shape and form of their politics? Going forward, if scholars of Black political behavior continue to think broadly about conceptual categories like liberation, joy, and desire, we will have a fuller and more nuanced understanding of who engages in politics and why.

My research attempts to make a theoretical intervention around the way students of US politics understand and measure the political behavior of marginalized Black people. My work builds on research showing neighborhoods shape the type of political community members we become (Cohen and Dawson 1993; Gay 2012; Huckfeldt 1980; Isoke 2011; Perry 2013; Prowse, Weaver, and Meares 2019; Williams 2005; Wong 2012). If one community is fortunate enough to grow up in a neighborhood which facilitates engaged politics, and another community is relegated to neighborhoods which depress political desire, it is a democratic crisis which warrants attention.

Notes

1. To clarify, this does not mean everyone engaging in the "political" has power. But it is to say a definitional requirement for anything considered "political," is the maintenance of power, seeking power, creating power, or even destroying power. Within the relational dynamics of "politics," some form of power is required in order to achieve acquiescence from the target (or on behalf of the target), in order to create the desired change (whatever that may be).
2. AFDC is an entitlements policy for the poor in the United States, the full name is: Aid to Families with Dependent Children (The Assistant Secretary for Planning and Evaluation 2023).
3. Throughout the article I will refer to the Altgeld Gardens and Phillip Murray Homes as "Altgeld," "Altgeld Gardens," or the "Altgeld and Phillip Murray Homes," interchangeably throughout the text. They all refer to the same large walk-up public housing development on the far South Side of Chicago.
4. I should note there was quite a bit of debate around whether or not dogs are actually allowed in CHA apartments. Ultimately, it seemed to be a policy CHA bureaucrats enforce at their discretion since no one ever provided a clear answer.
5. CHA is the Chicago Housing Authority.
6. CAC is the Central Advisory Council.

Disclosure statement

No potential conflict of interest was reported by the author.

Funding

I received support from the University of Chicago Research Initiative Grant, the Carter G. Woodson Pre-Doctoral Fellowship at the University of Virginia, and the Post-Doctoral Fellowship at the University of Connecticut Collaborative for Equity Through Research on Women and Girls of Color.

ORCID

Alex J. Moffett-Bateau (iD) http://orcid.org/0000-0003-3630-4199

Protection of human research participants

University of Chicago, Institutional Review Board (IRB)
Approval Number: AURA IRB: H11204
SBS-IRB
5835 South Kimbark Avenue – Judd Hall 336
Chicago, IL 60,637 SBS IRB website:
http://sbsirb.uchicago.edu/

References

Alexander-Floyd, Nikol. 2017. "Why Political Scientists Don't Study Black Women, but Historians and Sociologists Do: On Intersectionality and the Remapping of the Study of Black Political Women." In *Black Women in Politics: Identity, Power, and Justice in the New Millennium*, eds. Michael Mitchell and David Covin. London, United Kingdom: Routledge, 3–17. doi:10.4324/9781351313681-1.

Alex-Assensoh, Yvette. 1997. "Race, Concentrated Poverty, Social Isolation, and Political Behavior." *Urban Affairs Review* 33 (2):209–27. doi:10.1177/107808749703300205.

The Assistant Secretary for Planning and Evaluation. 2023. "Aid to Families with Dependent Children (AFDC) and Temporary Assistance for Needy Families (TANF) - Overview." United States Government. *Aid to Families with Dependent Children (AFDC) (Blog)*. May 30. https://aspe.hhs.gov/aid-families-dependent-children-afdc-temporary-assistance-needy-families-tanf-overview.

Bakshi, Amar, Tracey Meares, and Vesla Weaver. 2016. "Portals to Politics: Perspectives on Policing from the Grassroots." *Shared Studios*. https://www.sharedstudios.com/research.

Berger, Michele Tracy. 2006. *Workable Sisterhood: The Political Journey of Stigmatized Women with HIV/AIDS*. Princeton, NJ: Princeton University Press. doi:10.1057/palgrave.fr.9400401.

The Black Public Sphere Collective. 1995. *The Black Public Sphere: A Public Culture Book*. Chicago: University of Chicago Press.

Blain, Keisha N. 2021. *Until I Am Free: Fannie Lou Hamer's Enduring Message to America*. Boston: Beacon Press.

Brinson, Clemolyn. 2004. "Altgeld Gardens Lawsuit Settlement." *We the People Media: Residents' Journal* February. https://wethepeoplemedia.org/altgeld-gardens-lawsuit-settlement/.

Bunyasi, Tehama Lopez, and Candis Watts Smith. 2019. "Do All Black Lives Matter Equally to Black People? Respectability Politics and the Limitations of Linked Fate." *Journal of Race, Ethnicity, & Politics* 4 (1):180–215. doi:10.1017/rep.2018.33.

Campbell, Angus, Philip Converse, Warren Miller, and Donald Stokes. 1960. *The American Voter*. Chicago: University of Chicago Press.

Carter, Lashonda, and Tiffany Willoughby-Herard. 2018. "What Kind of Mother is She?: From Margaret Garner to Rosa Lee Ingram to Mamie Till to the Murder of Korryn Gaines." *Theory & Event* 21 (1):88–105. doi:10.1353/tae.2018.0003.

Chicago Housing Authority. 2023. "Altgeld Gardens and Phillip Murray Homes | the Chicago Housing Authority."*Altgeld Gardens and Phillip Murray Homes* (Blog). May 29. https://www.thecha.org/residents/public-housing/find-public-housing/altgeld-gardens-and-phillip-murray-homes.

Coalition to Protect Public Housing. 2006. *Written Submission of the Coalition to Protect Public Housing in Chicago, Illinois USA to the Human Rights Committee at Its 85th Session (2006)*. Chicago, IL: Coalition to Protect Public Housing. https://www.google.com/search?q=http%253A%252F%252Fwww2.ohchr.org%252Fenglish%252Fbodies%252Fhrc%252Fdocs%252Fngos2Fcoalition.doc%26usg%3DAOvVaw26RVNdPGuR6zpbpjUnreOE.&rlz=1C1GCEB_enIN1054IN1054&oq=http%253A%252F%252Fwww2.ohchr.org%252Fenglish%252Fbodies%252Fhrc%252Fdocs%252Fngos2Fcoalition.doc%26usg%3DAOvVaw26RVNdPGuR6zpbpjUnreOE.&gs_lcrp=EgZjaHJvbWUyBggAEEUYOdIBBzY3OWowajeoAgCwAgA&sourceid=chrome&ie=UTF-8&safe=active

Coffey, Emily, Kate Walz, Debbie Chizewer, A. Benfer, N. Emily, Templeton Mark, and Robert Weinstock. 2020. "Poisonous Homes: The Fight for Environmental Justice in Federally Assisted Housing." *Chicago: Shriver Center on Poverty Law*. https://www.povertylaw.org/report/poisonoushomes/.

Cohen, Cathy J. 1999. *The Boundaries of Blackness: AIDS and the Breakdown of Black Politics*. Chicago: University of Chicago Press.

Cohen, Cathy J. 2004. "Deviance as Resistance: A New Research Agenda for the Study of Black Politics." *Du Bois Review* 1 (1):27–45. doi:10.1017/S1742058X04040044.

Cohen, Cathy J. 2005. "Punks, Bulldaggers and Welfare Queens: The Radical Potential of Queer Politics?" In *Black Queer Studies: A Critical Anthology*, eds. E. Patrick Johnson and Mae G. Henderson. Durham: Duke University Press, 21–51. doi:10.2307/j.ctv11cw38r.6.

Cohen, Cathy J. 2010. *Democracy Remixed: Black Youth and the Future of American Politics*. Oxford, England: Oxford University Press.

Cohen, Cathy J., and Michael C. Dawson. 1993. "Neighborhood Poverty and African American Politics." *American Political Science Review* 87 (2):286–302. doi:10.2307/2939041.

Cudd, Ann E. 2006. *Analyzing Oppression*. Oxford: Oxford University Press. doi:10.1093/0195187431.001.0001.

Cutter, Susan L., Bryan J. Boruff, and W. Lynn Shirley. 2003. "Social Vulnerability to Environmental Hazards." *Social Science Quarterly* 84 (2):242–61. doi:10.1111/1540-6237.8402002.

Davis, Angela Y. 1983. *Women, Race and Class*. New York: Vintage Books.

Dawson, Michael C. 1994. *Behind the Mule: Race and Class in African American Politics*. Princeton, NJ: Princeton University Press. doi:10.1515/9780691212982.

Dawson, Michael C. 2003. *Black Visions: The Roots of Contemporary African American Political Ideologies*. Chicago, IL: University of Chicago Press.

Eliasoph, Nina. 1998. *Avoiding Politics: How Americans Produce Apathy in Everyday Life*. Cambridge, United Kingdom: Cambridge University Press.

Feldman, Roberta M., and Susan Stall. 2004. *The Dignity of Resistance: Women Residents' Activism in Chicago Public Housing*. Cambridge, United Kingdom: Cambridge University Press.

Francis, Megan Ming. 2014. *Civil Rights and the Making of the Modern American State*. Cambridge, United Kingdom: Cambridge University Press.

Gay, Claudine. 2004. "Putting Race in Context: Identifying the Environmental Determinants of Black Racial Attitudes." *American Political Science Review* 98 (4):547–62. doi:10.1017/S0003055404041346.

Gay, Claudine. 2012. "Moving to Opportunity: The Political Effects of a Housing Mobility Experiment." *Urban Affairs Review* 48 (2):147–79. doi:10.1177/1078087411426399.

Geiger, Kim. 2013. "Lawsuit Challenges Cha's Drug Testing Policy." *Chicago Tribune*, August 15. https://www.chicago tribune.com/news/breaking/chi-lawsuit-challenges-chas-drug-testing-policy-20130815-story.html

Goetz, Edward, G. 2013. *New Deal Ruins: Race, Economic Justice, and Public Housing Policy*. Ithaca, NY: Cornell University Press. doi:10.7591/9780801467554.

Gore, Dayo F., Jeanne Theoharris, and Komozi Woodward, eds. 2009. *Want to Start a Revolution?: Black Women in the Black Freedom Struggle*. New York: New York University Press.

Hackworth, Jason. 2014. *The Neoliberal City: Governance, Ideology, and Development in American Urbanism*. Ithaca, NY: Cornell University Press.

Hampton, Ivanna. 2011. "CHA Nixes Drug Testing Proposal: Tenants Applaud Decision." *NBC 5 Chicago*, June 22. https://www.nbcchicago.com/news/local/cha-reverses-course-on-drug-testing-proposal/1904131/.

Hanchard, Michael. 2006. *Party/Politics: Horizons in Black Political Thought*. Oxford, England: Oxford University Press.

Hanchard, Michael. 2010. "Contours of Black Political Thought: An Introduction and Perspective." *Political Theory* 38 (4):510–36. doi:10.1177/0090591710366379.

Hancock, Ange Marie. 2004. *The Politics of Disgust: The Public Identity of the Welfare Queen*. New York, NY: New York University Press.

Harris, Duchess. 2009. *Black Feminist Politics from Kennedy to Obama*. London, United Kingdom: Palgrave Macmillan. doi:10.1057/9780230623200.

Harris-Perry, Melissa V. 2011. *Sister Citizen: Shame, Stereotypes, and Black Women in America*. New Haven, CT: Yale University Press.

Hill-Collins, Patricia. 1998. "The Tie That Binds: Race, Gender, and US Violence." *Ethnic and Racial Studies* 21 (5):917–38. doi:10.1080/014198798329720.

Hill-Collins, Patricia. 2017. "On Violence, Intersectionality and Transversal Politics." *Ethnic and Racial Studies* 40 (9):1460–73. doi:10.1080/01419870.2017.1317827.

Hill-Collins, Patricia. 2019. *Intersectionality as Critical Social Theory*. Durham: Duke University Press.

Huckfeldt, R. Robert. 1980. "Variable Responses to Neighborhood Social Contexts: Assimilation, Conflict, and Tipping Points." *Political Behavior* 2 (3):231–57. doi:10.1007/BF00990481.

Hunt, D. Bradford. 2010. *Blueprint for Disaster: The Unraveling of Chicago Public Housing*. Chicago: University of Chicago Press. doi:10.7208/chicago/9780226360874.001.0001.

INCITE! Women of Color Against Violence. 2016. *Color of Violence: The Incite! Anthology*. Durham, NC: Duke University Press. doi:10.1215/9780822373445.

Isoke, Zenzele. 2011. "The Politics of Homemaking: Black Feminist Transformations of a Cityscape." *Transforming Anthropology* 19 (2):117–30. doi:10.1111/j.1548-7466.2011.01136.x.

Isoke, Zenzele. 2013. *Urban Black Women and the Politics of Resistance*. New York: Palgrave Macmillan. doi:10.1057/9781137045386.

Johnson, Richard. 2022. "School Choice as Community Disempowerment: Racial Rhetoric About Voucher Policy in Urban America." *Urban Affairs Review* 2 (58):563–96. doi:10.1177/1078087421992122.

Jordan-Zachery, Julia S. 2017. "Beyond the Side Eye: Black Women's Ancestral Anger as a Liberatory Practice." *Journal of Black Sexuality and Relationships* 4 (1):61–81. doi:10.1353/bsr.2017.0021.

Jordan-Zachery, Julia S. 2018. "Resistance and Redemption Narratives: Black Girl Magic and Other Forms of Black Girls and Women's Political Self-Articulations." *National Political Science Review* 19 (2): 2–10.

Junn, Jane. 1999. "Participation in Liberal Democracy: The Political Assimilation of Immigrants and Ethnic Minorities in the United States." *American Behavioral Scientist* 42 (9):1417–38. doi:10.1177/00027649921954976.

Kaba, Mariame. 2021. *We Do This Til We Free US: Abolitionist Organizing and Transforming Justice.* Chicago: Haymarket Books.

Kelley, Robin D.G. 1996. *Race Rebels: Culture, Politics, and the Black Working Class.* New York: Free Press. doi:10.2307/2211261.

Kim, Claire Jean. 2003. *Bitter Fruit: The Politics of Black-Korean Conflict in New York City.* New Haven, CT: Yale University Press.

Levenstein, Lisa. 2009. *A Movement without Marches: African American Women and the Politics of Poverty in Postwar Philadelphia.* Chapel Hill, NC: University of North Carolina Press.

Lipsky, Michael. 2010. *Street-Level Bureaucracy: Dilemmas of the Individual in Public Services. Street-Level Bureaucracy: Dilemmas of the Individual in Public Services.* New York, NY: Russell Sage Foundation.

McKeown, Timothy J. 1999. "Case Studies and the Statistical Worldview: Review of King, Keohane, and Verba's Designing Social Inquiry: Scientific Inference in Qualitative Research." *International Organization* 53 (1):161–90. doi:10.1162/002081899550841.

Michener, Jamila. 2020. "Power from the Margins: Grassroots Mobilization and Urban Expansions of Civil Legal Rights." *Urban Affairs Review* 56 (5):1390–422. doi:10.1177/1078087419855677.

Mitchell, Koritha. 2020. *From Slave Cabins to the White House: Homemade Citizenship in African American Culture.* Chicago: University of Illinois Press.

Moffett-Bateau, A. J. 2023. "I Can't Vote if I Don't Leave My Apartment": The Problem of Neighborhood Violence and its Impact on the Political Behavior of Black American Women Living Below the Poverty Line." *Urban Affairs Review* 0 (0). doi:10.1177/10780874231162930.

Naples, Nancy A. 1998. *Grassroots Warriors: Activist Mothering, Community Work, and the War on Poverty.* London: Routledge.

Paral, Robert. 2004. *Welfare Use by Racial/Ethnic Groups and Immigrants in Illinois.* Chicago: Bureau of Refugee and Immigrant Services, Division of Human Capital Development, Illinois Department of Human Service.

Perry, Keisha-Khan. 2013. *Black Women Against the Land Grab: The Fight for Racial Justice in Brazil.* Minneapolis: University of Minnesota Press. doi:10.5749/minnesota/9780816683239.001.0001.

Piemonte, Mary C. 2011. "Board Squashes CHA Drug Testing Plan." *We the People Media | Residents' Journal.* June 21. https://wethepeoplemedia.org/board-squashes-cha-drug-testing-plan/

Polikoff, Alexander. 2006. *Waiting for Gautreaux: A Story of Segregation, Housing, and the Black Ghetto.* Evanston, IL: Northwestern University Press.

Popkin, Susan J. 2016. *No Simple Solutions: Transforming Public Housing in Chicago.* Lanham, MD: Rowman & Littlefield Publishers.

Prestage, Jewell. 1991. "In Quest of African American Political Woman." *The Annals of the American Academy of Political and Social Science* 515 (1):88–103. doi:10.1177/0002716291515001008.

Prowse, Gwen, Vesla M. Weaver, and Tracey L. Meares. 2019. "The State from Below: Distorted Responsiveness in Policed Communities." *Urban Affairs Review* 56 (5):1423–71. doi:10.1177/1078087419844831.

Ralph, Laurence. 2014. *Renegade Dreams: Living Through Injury in Gangland Chicago.* Chicago: University of Chicago Press.

Richie, Beth E. 2012. *Arrested Justice: Black Women, Violence, and America's Prison Nation.* New York: New York University Press.

Ritchie, Andrea J. 2017. *Invisible No More: Police Violence Against Black Women and Women of Color.* Boston: Beacon Press.

Robnett, Belinda. 1997. *How Long? How Long? African-American Women in the Struggle for Civil Rights.* New York City: Oxford University Press.

Salisbury, Robert H. 1975. "Research on Political Participation." *American Journal of Political Science* 19 (2):323–41. doi:10.2307/2110440.

Sampson, Robert J. 2013. *Great American City: Chicago and the Enduring Neighborhood Effect.* Chicago: University of Chicago Press. doi:10.7208/chicago/9780226733883.001.0001.

Scott, James C. 1992. *Domination and the Arts of Resistance: Hidden Transcripts.* New Haven, CT: Yale University Press.

Simien, Evelyn M. 2006. *Black Feminist Voices in Politics.* Albany, NY: SUNY Press. doi:10.1353/book5076.

Sinclair, Betsy. 2012. *The Social Citizen: Peer Networks in Political Behavior.* Chicago, Il: University of Chicago Press.

Small, Mario Luis. 2009. "'How Many Cases Do I Need?': On Science and the Logic of Case Selection in Field-Based Research." *Ethnography* 10 (1):5–38. doi:10.1177/1466138108099586.

Soss, Joe. 2002. *Unwanted Claims: The Politics of Participation in the U.S. Welfare System.* Ann Arbor, MI: University of Michigan Press. doi:10.3998/mpub.16475.

Soss, Joe, and Vesla Weaver. 2017. "Police are Our Government: Politics, Political Science, and the Policing of Race-Class Subjugated Communities." *Annual Review of Political Science* 20 (1):565–91. doi:10.1146/annurev-polisci-060415-093825.

Spence, Lester. 2015. *Knocking the Hustle: Against the Neoliberal Turn in Black Politics*. Brooklyn, NY: Punctim Books.

Squires, Catherine R. 2002. "Rethinking the Black Public Sphere: An Alternative Vocabulary for Multiple Public Spheres." *Communication Theory* 12 (4):446–68. doi:10.1111/j.1468-2885.2002.tb00278.x.

Stake, Robert E., 1996. *The Art of Case Study Research*. Thousand Oaks, CA: SAGE Publications. doi:10.2307/329758.

US Department of Housing and Urban Development. 2023. "Section 3 of the Housing and Development Act of 1968." US Federal Government. *Section 3 of the Housing and Development Act of 1968* (blog). https://www.hud.gov/section3.

Verba, Sidney, Kay Lehman Schlozman, and Henry E. Brady. 1996. *Voice and Equality: Civic Voluntarism in American Politics*. Cambridge, MA: Harvard University Press. doi:10.2307/j.ctv1pnc1k7.

Watkins-Hayes, Celeste. 2009. *The New Welfare Bureaucrats*. Chicago: University of Chicago Press.

Watkins-Hayes, Celeste. 2019. *Remaking a Life: How Women Living with HIV/AIDS Confront Inequality*. Berkeley, CA: University of California Press.

Weaver, Vesla, Gwen Prowse, and Spencer Piston. 2019. "Too Much Knowledge, Too Little Power: An Assessment of Political Knowledge in Highly Policed Communities." *The Journal of Politics* 81 (3):1153–66. doi:10.1086/703538.

Western, Bruce. 2007. *Punishment and Inequality in America*. New York, NY: Russell Sage Foundation.

White, Brandi M., and Eric S. Hall. 2015. "Perceptions of Environmental Health Risks Among Residents in the 'Toxic Doughnut': Opportunities for Risk Screening and Community Mobilization." *BMC Public Health* 15 (1):1230. doi:10.1186/s12889-015-2563-y.

Wilkerson, Isabelle. 2011. *The Warmth of Other Suns: The Epic Story of America's Great Migration*. New York: Vintage.

Williams, Rhonda Y. 2005. *The Politics of Public Housing: Black Women's Struggle Against Urban Inequality*. Chicago: University of Chicago Press.

Williamson, Terrion L. 2016. *Scandalize My Name: Black Feminist Practice and the Making of Black Social Life*. New York, NY: Fordham University Press.

Williamson, Vanessa, Kris Stella Trump, and Katherine Levine Einstein. 2018. "Black Lives Matter: Evidence That Police-Caused Deaths Predict Protest Activity." *Perspectives on Politics* 16 (2):400–15. doi:10.1017/S1537592717004273.

Wong, Cara J. 2012. *Boundaries of Obligation in American Politics: Geographic, National, and Racial Communities (Cambridge Studies in Public Opinion and Political Psychology)*. New York, NY: Cambridge University Press.

Young, Iris Marion. 1990. *Justice and the Politics of Difference*. Princeton, NJ: Princeton University Press.

Feminists, Nationalist, Combatants, Activists. A Conversation with Vjosa Musliu on the Multi-Faceted Role of Women in Kosovo

Vjosa Musliu and Enduena Klajiqi

In the second half of the 20th century, women in Kosovo were organized in a multi-layered activism: they fought for national liberation against Serbia's oppressive regime, and at the same time, they were fighting against their own patriarchal system. How did solidarity translate to activism in support of this dual liberation?

Within Yugoslavia, Kosovo was the least developed region in all socio-economic parameters. The literacy rate among Kosovo Albanians was the highest in the federation, and this rate was even higher among women. The symbolic and materiality of the Yugoslav experience had rendered the *Albanian person* in the former Yugoslavia a secondhand citizen. At the bottom of this secondhand layer was *the Albanian woman*. This image of the vile Albanian man and the Albanian woman as a mere biological entity would remain reinstated for decades to come. In Serbia, this image would not only become a tool to justify and legitimize a brutal crackdown against the Albanians in the 1990s; it would also come to define the very Serbian metaphysics.

In 1986, the Serbian Academy of Sciences and Arts published a memorandum reinstating that Albanians in Kosovo were a danger to the Serbian nation because of their innate vile and dangerous ethnic traits. The inherent violence of the Albanian man was, among others, explained as a result of them treating the Albanian women as "machines of reproduction." In the Serbian discourse, the Albanian woman is constructed as a mere biological entity whose main function is to birth more vile Albanian men who would later threaten the very essence of the Serbian nation. I remember once having a conversation with Lepa Mladenović – a Serbian activist with the Women in Black – who told me this story (the paraphrasing is mine):

> As a young woman, I had a genuine interest in the women's traditional attire of nations and cultural groups. I was even acquainted with the different traditional costumes of the many indigenous groups in Peru for instance. And then I realized that I knew nothing about the traditional attire of Albanian women. These women, these people lived only a seven-hour drive from Belgrade. I knew nothing about Albanian women. I knew next to nothing about Albanians. And I came to realize that there was a proper policy and politics that had made it impossible for me and the rest of the people around me from knowing the Albanians. It was easier to know them through slurs and pejorative tropes.

On the one hand, as a country that belonged to the nonaligned movement, Yugoslavia was (self-)adored as the pinnacle of *good socialism*: high standards of living, high socio-economic mobility molded around "brotherhood and unity," and a respectable international standing. With the Constitutional changes in 1974, differently from the rest of the countries in the Eastern Block, Yugoslavia developed its own self-managing socialism whose main feature came to be decentralization. This new system allowed for more freedom of thought, speech, and mobility, among others. Such a political constellation enabled the organization of a major feminist conference in 1978 in Belgrade - "Drugarica Zena. ZenskoPitanje – Novi Pristup" (Comrade Woman. The Women's Question: A New Approach?" - that brought together, for the first time, Eastern and

Western feminists in a socialist country. Through this dialogue with Western feminists, the Yugoslav feminists managed to articulate their version of feminism within socialism, the first in the socialist East (see Lorand 2018). Taking stock of these specific conditions of Yugoslav socialism, Krasniqi and Petrovic (2019) argue how this enabled Yugoslav feminism to emerge as more progressive: neither weary nor adoring Western feminism.

On the other hand, paradoxically, the making of this prosperous Yugoslavia was made possible through its internal coloniality: the Yugoslav project was enabled, if not perpetuated, by the silencing and the structural discrimination of primarily the Albanians (Limani, 2017a; 2017b; Hetemi, 2020) and the Roma (Savić, 2022; 2018; Sardelić, 2021).[1] Owing to what others have called "the colonization" of Kosovo by Serbia after World War I (Rexhepi 2023), the creation of the Albanian other – the *barbarian* within Yugoslavia (Stavrevska et al. 2023) as well as the creation of the Albanian other as "the negro of the Serb" (Arsenijevic 2007) – would continue throughout the Yugoslav Kingdom and the Yugoslav Socialist Federation. For example, many have pointed out the medical apartheid in the Yugoslav public medical sector in Kosovo throughout 1970s and 1980s, and complete segregation of the same in the 1990s (on the 1990s period, see the questions below). In recent testimony, Ivanka Pllana, a Croatian-origin medical doctor working in the health sector in Kosovo during this period, showcases how the othering of the Albanian was also present in the health sector. The Albanian patient, she argues, was sidelined, oftentimes not admitted and routinely seen as a less-than-human subject that cannot be treated in public hospitals by Serbian doctors and staff (Pllana 2021).

The compressed overview above depicts the structural discrimination of the Albanians inside Yugoslavia. At the final layer of this discrimination, we find the Albanian woman.[2] The feminist movements that would emerge in Kosovo throughout these decades (the late 1960s, 1970s, and onwards) are in and of themselves *intersectional*, in that they were born, molded, and conditioned by a set of gender, ethnic, religious, cultural, and socio-economic conditions. Within the Yugoslav experience, feminist movements in Kosovo were, in a way, never confronted with simply *the gender war*. By default, given the structural oppression of the Albanian persona, the othering of the Albanian to the limits of dehumanization, the *gender* aspect of feminist activism ran in parallel with multiple layers of wars.

How can an intersectional approach to feminist activism in Kosovo aid us in conceptualizing the feminist activist landscape in Kosovo during the 1990s? How can intersectionality aid us in highlighting the political act of solidarity?

In 1969, the University of Prishtina – the first university in the Albanian language – was opened in Kosovo. The Constitutional changes of 1974 brought new freedoms and rights for ethnic and cultural minorities in the federation. Kosovo Albanians were swift to take stock of the short-lived favorable policies and translated them primarily into developing education structures. The University of Prishtina would soon become the place and the space of activism, resistance, and political mobilization. This became a new impetus for Albanian subjects (women/men) to pursue higher education and become politically involved.

However, there is a trap in searching for feminist activism primarily in the "educated" layers of society or in the idea that political activism is quintessentially linked with knowledge acquired from traditional schooling. Without necessarily having an established educated mass in the traditional sense of the word, we see encounters of women-led activism in Kosovo. For example, in the face of structural oppression from Belgrade, from 1960s onwards several so-called "illegal groups" - underground movements - came to the fore in Kosovo seeking greater rights and many of them sought unification with Albania. At the core of these activists were women activists such as Sabile Keçmezi Basha. The works of Eli Krasniqi (Krasniqi 2011, 2021) and Itziar Mujika Chao (2020) have shed quite some light on the indispensable role of women in these movements. These groups evolved in their political

150 INTERSECTIONAL (FEMINIST) ACTIVISMS

objectives throughout time – with nationalism always at the core – whereas in the 1980s they directed their efforts in advancing women's rights in the 1980s (Krasniqi 2011), and some of these groups went on to spearhead the founding of the Kosovo Liberation Army (KLA) after 1989 (Krasniqi 2021). Atdhe Hetemi (2019) has documented at length the instrumental role that illegal activist groups and women had in these student protests in the late 1960s and 1980s Kosovo. These illegal groups had clear links with the student protest in 1964 and were organizers of the student protest in 1997 (Hetemi 2019) In these protests, women activists played a key role whereas women such as Trendeline Labinishti carried the Albanian flag at the 1981 student demonstration at great personal risk (Hetemi 2019).

In the 1990s, Yugoslavia gradually fell apart with wars waged by Serbia in Slovenia, Croatia and Bosnia and Herzegovina. Once he came to power, Serbia's former President Slobodan Milosevic revoked the status of autonomy for Kosovo and effectively eroded all political rights for the Kosovo Albanians, expelling them *en masse* from public jobs and public life. Schools in Albanian language were closed; public servants were laid off from work. Hospitals, courts, cultural centers, and sports venues became homogenous Serbian spaces. During this period, Kosovo Albanians organized them-selves in a parallel system – a state within a state. Private houses (of mostly Albanian diaspora members) were turned into make-shift schools with pupils attending lectures sitting crammed in living room sofas using their laps as writing desks. According to the initiative "House Schools,"[3] there are 403 private houses in Kosovo where parallel education has taken place during the 1990s. Kosovo Albanian teachers resumed teaching in-house schools initially for free and then with a gradual pay that was gathered through what today can be called "crowdfunding." Given that they were challenging the very Serbian – the Yugoslav state – these house schools operated in secrecy. As was evidenced during the European nomadic biennale "Manifesta" held in Prishtina in 2022, it was usually women who would do the day-to-day tending of and maintenance of the house schools and would make sure that there was enough wood in the fire log and fresh tea/coffee for the teachers. The Hertica House School, located in Prishtina is a typical example of this. While the head of the family gave up his two-floor house in service of schooling and decided to live with his seven-member family in a two-bedroom house in the same yard, it was his wife and his daughters who would also take care of the house school. "I would wake up at six in the morning, prepare the tea for when the teachers arrive [. . .] During winter my mother would wash the wet socks of pupils who had walked for miles to get to school" (Manifesta Biennal 2022).

During the 1990s, we see women-led activism taking a comprehensive scale: there is a series of women-led and women-organized protests against the violence of the Serbian military against Albanian civilians. An all-women protest on March 8, 1998, with hundreds of women holding loaves of bread in front of the barricades of the Serbian police became the symbol of resistance. In this period, new grassroots organizations and initiatives were formed to foster resistance and solidarity in the face of repression. For example, the initiative "Motrat Qiriazi" (The Qiriazi Sisters) led by two sisters: Igballe and Safete Rogova (from Prishtina) engaged with a minuscule, yet largely impactful campaign against illiteracy among young women and girls in rural Kosovo (Musliu 2021). Named after The Qiriazi Sisters who opened the first school in the Albanian language toward the end of the 19th century, Igballe and Safete Rogova would travel on their own in mountainous and inner villages around Kosovo to convince the elderly men to allow their girls to attend school. Though their primary aim was the emancipation and literacy of young women and girls, to the elderly, they would frame this as an act of resistance against Serbia's repressive regime. Another example is the work of the initiative "Mother Tereza" NGO led by Vjosa Dobruna, among others. Throughout the 1990s, they offered medical and health-related services to the Albanian community in Kosovo. Evidently, while activism was a core component of these initiatives, they functioned as public/state institutions.

What are the legacies of the feminist movements in Kosovo duringthe 1990s and what are the lessons that it can deliver to feminist solidarities worldwide?

For me, the entire decade of the 1990s is a fascinating period of self-organization, radical activism and the notion of solidarity laid bare for the greater good: liberation. We are talking about an entire "state-like" apparatus that was financed, organized, and carried out with what today can be called crowdfunding (the so-called three percent fund), managed by Kosovo's government in exile (Germany and Switzerland), supported by central committees within Kosovo, recorded by a massive administrative mechanism, and carried out in private spaces: formal schooling took place in private homes; 140 medical caretook place in private homes; cultural and political activities took place in coffee bars; nightlife and entertainment took place inprivate basements (see for more Kosovo 2.0, 2016). Oftentimes, the activists would be involved in the parallel state institutions through multiple formats, serving for a variety of institutions in a day entirely as volunteers. Solidarity was the modus operandi of the Kosovo Albanian population at the time and served as the main proponent of resistance. On top of it all, this entire societal and political organization took place in secrecy: it was a state within a state. Women and feminist activists played a prominent role in this elaborate state-like apparatus, from holding ministerial roles inthe self-organised government, diplomatic delegations, engaging in activism in women's reproductive health, founding medical emergency response schools, all the way to initiating campaigns of reconciliation of blood feuds within the Albanian community. The unprecedented circumstances notwithstanding and with the full-blown war afoot, one notices multiple forms of ethnic, civic, sexual, and feminist activism taking place, albeit subordinated to the bigger and totalizing cause: liberation.

Some would suggest that gender amnesia has been in place in Kosovo regarding women's contributions in the passive and active resistance.

From 1999 to date, Kosovo has been the site for the deployment of the full spectrum of structures of Western liberal interventionism and state building, starting with NATO intervention, the UN mission, the EU mission, and the programs of the World Bank and the IMF, among others. One of the defining characteristics of these structures of intervention and statebuilding has been their ability to *restart* time in Kosovo (Musliu 2017). With their intervention and deployment, they introduced "Year Zero" for Kosovo according to which everything that had existed before – governmental, social, and political legacy – had to be sidelined if not erased to make room for a new future. The new future had its own activism, the right way [in italics] of thinking about gender, the right way [in italics] if thinking about gender and emancipation, the right way [in italics] of building a state, and so forth (Musliu, 2021). To this end, the legacy of parallel statebuilding was deemed irrelevant and non-compliant with the Western/European project and at the same time, the socialist legacy of (pre-)parallel statebuilding was deemed outdated and thus undesirable.

The arrival of international peacekeeping also transformed the landscape of feminist activism in Kosovo with new gender, ethnic, and class entities. In the Western liberal state building trajectory, the materiality of Kosovo is very much conceived as male though gender equal in its architecture; women combatants who joined the Kosovo Liberation Army (KLA) in the late 1990s (see for more Ferizaj, 2024). For example, the grassroots (feminist) activism of the 1990s would soon come to be replaced and/or transformed with donor-oriented NGOs and think tanks whose architecture and work would be contingent on donor organizations and not directly to challenges on the ground. To this day, the international actors, spearheaded by the EU, have been actively involved in peace negotiations between Kosovo and Serbia, and unsurprisingly entire series of negotiations have been carried out by male leaders (international and local) without properly streamlining a gender agenda in these negotiations. This erases the whole presence and tradition of women in formal politics in Kosovo (thinking about active politicians in the 1990s such as Luljeta Pula, Kaqusha Jashari, Melihate Tërmkolli, among others); women combatants who joined the Kosovo Liberation Army (KLA) in 1998–1999; in addition to the feminist activism that existed in various organized formats from 1960s onwards.

This amnesia, or better yet, oblivion to the feminist and women-led initiatives in statebuilding has also been abetted in centers of knowledge production in international studies, international relations, and other social sciences across universities of the so-called "Global North." The story of Kosovo – its resistance, resilience, war period, and postwar statebuilding – has been largely told through the barrel of a gun and the heroism of men on the battlefield and at the negotiation table. Sociologists and anthropologists alike have done a better job in shedding light on the multi-layered activism, fight and resistance that has been carried out by women in Kosovo, and have aptly problematized the multi-layered or intersectional fight; fighting patriarchy and fighting for national liberation from an oppressive regime at the same time. The ethnographic, autoethnographic, and critical turns in IR – primarily in continental Europe – have opened up new possibilities for IR to think of states and statebuilding beyond the Westphalian architecture and take a look at non-male structures and institutions that are co-constitutive to making the state. Together with Itziar Mujika Chao, we have an edited volume coming up in 2024 that conceptualizes feminist state building in Kosovo drawing attention to this legacy in Kosovo (Musliu and Mujika Chao, 2024).

How were the newly transformed dynamics resisted by feminist activists in Kosovo? How did women resist against the state and liberal peacekeeping regime in their exclusion? How did particular subjectivities produce different forms of resistance?

Like I mentioned above, the state building endeavors of women in the 1990s were to a large extent sidelined and replaced with the right way [in italics] of conceiving state building and gender emancipation. However, these right ways were often only performed. Even their own envisioned idea of gender emancipation was initially not enforced, as a gender perspective lacked in the recommendations of statebuilding in post-conflict Kosovo. The United Nations Mission in Kosovo (UNMIK) itself lacked an implementing institution for Resolution 1325, although it specifically targeted post-conflict societies.

Nevertheless, there are various recorded encounters of resistance against the liberal peacekeeping regime and its modus operandi in Kosovo. The activist roots of feminist resistance of the 1990s in Kosovo followed a clear continuation through several protests which were organized. The Women's Forum of LDK (Democratic League of Kosovo) – a catalyst in the mass mobilization of women in Kosovo during the 1990s – continued its activism by organizing the "Complete Freedom and Peace in Kosovo" (own translation) protest on the 8th of March 2001. The protest resisted ideas of the cantonization of the territory of Kosovo and demanded that UNMIK and KFOR oppose solving the issue of Mitrovica by dividing the city. Kosovo Women's Network, an NGO spearheaded by the founder of the "Motrat Qiriazi" association in the 1990s, Igballe Rogova, organized protests against the exclusion of women's involvement in the dialogue process with Serbia and demanded the inclusion of women in the process.

Legacies of resistance in Kosovo were oftentimes negated in the name of neutrality, and in service of the fractions of the liberal peacekeeping model. UNMIK's closure of the Rilindja printing house in 2022 is but one example of this. The closing of this publishing house - a central node in the resistance movement of Kosovo in the 1990s - left much of the archive and legacy of this period in dire archival condition. In later stages, the material was collected and activists such as Ervina Halimi devoted themselves to the revival of the archives of Rilindja through the collection of first manuscripts and the creation of a digital library in order to highlight the centrality of the establishment in the cultural life of Kosovo during Yugoslavia.

A notable form of resistance against the erasure and oblivion of the feminist activist legacy in Kosovo is continually done through the practice of remembrance itself – of the encounters, events, and stories of feminist resistance in Kosovo. The practice of remembrance as a political act has allowed for the revitalization of the feminist resistance movement in Kosovo.

Notes

1. For more on the structural oppression against the Roma in former Yugoslavia, see the book by Julija Sardelic, entitled *The Fringes of Citizenship: Romani Minorities in Europe and Civic Marginalization* (2021, Manchester University Press).
2. For a nuanced overview of the othering of Roma women, see the work of Jashari (2019).
3. https://shtepiteshkolla.org/sq/shtepi-shkolla

Disclosure statement

No potential conflict of interest was reported by the author(s).

Funding

This work was supported by the ZAP start credit [na].

References

Arsenijevic, V. 2007. Our Negros Our Enemies. *The Atlantic*, October 18. https://www.theatlantic.com/daily-dish/archive/2007/10/-our-negroes-our-enemies/224452/)

Chao, Itziar Mujika. 2020. "Women's Activism in the Civil Resistance Movement in Kosovo (1989–1997): Characteristics, Development, Encounters." *Nationalities Papers* 48(5): 843–60.

Hetemi, Atdhe. 2019. Seeing each other. Nesting Orientalisms and internal Balkanism among the Albanians and South Slavs in the former Yugoslavia. In: *Rethinking Serbian-Albanian Relations Figuring out the Enemy*, eds, Gazela Draško and Rigels Halili. Routledge.

Hetemi, Atdhe. 2020. "Student movements: 1968, 1981 and 1997: The impact of students in mobilizing society to chant for the Republic of Kosovo." PhD Diss. Ghent University.

Jashari, Sakibe. 2019. "The Subaltern of the Local: The Roma, Ashkali and Egyptian Women and Statebuilding in Kosovo." In *Unravelling Liberal Interventionism: Local Critiques of Statebuilding in Kosovo*, eds. Gëzim Visoka and Vjosa Musliu. New York: Routledge. doi:10.4324/9780429507649-10.

Kosovo 2.0. 2016. Pristina. https://kosovotwopointzero.com/en/rewind-with-kosovo-2-0-the-90s-magazine-issue-launch/

Krasniqi, Elife. 2011. "Ilegalja: Women in the Albanian Underground Resistance Movement in Kosovo." *ProFemina* 2: 99–114.

Krasniqi, Elife. 2021. "Same Goal, Different Paths, Different Class: Women's Feminist Political Engagements in Kosovo from the Mid-1970s Until the Mid-1990s." *Comparative Southeastern Europoean Studies Journal* 69 (2–3):313–34. doi:10.1515/soeu-2021-0014.

Krasniqi, Vjollca, and Jelena Petrovic. 2019. *Notes on Post-Yugoslav Women's Activism and Feminist Politics*. Belgrade: Fondacija Jelena Šantić.

Limani, Mrika. 2017a. *"Kosovo u Jugoslaviji: Protiv kolonijalnog statusa" në Jugoslavija u istorijskoj perspektivi, Helsinški odbor za ljudska prava u Srbiji*, Beograd, 251–79.

Limani, Mrika. 2017b. "The Albanians of Kosovo in Yugoslavia – the Struggle for Autonomy, YuHistorija Initiative."

Lorand, Zsofia. 2018. *The Feminist Challenge to the Socialist State in Yugoslavia*. Cham: Palgrave Macmillan. doi:10.1007/978-3-319-78223-2.

Musliu, Vjosa. 2017. "Multi-Ethnic Democracy as an Autoimmune Practice: The Case of International Missions in Kosovo." *The British Journal of Politics & International Relations* 19 (1):188–201. doi:10.1177/1369148116672211.

Musliu, Vjosa. 2021. *Europeanisation and Statebuilding as Everyday Practices: Performing Europe in the Western Balkans*. London: Routledge. doi:10.4324/9780429343469.

Pllana, Ivanka. 2021. *"Përtej tregimit."* December 11. https://www.youtube.com/watch?v=2egosBiLtoI

Rexhepi, Piro. 2023. *White Enclosures. Racial Capitalism and Coloniality Along the Balkan Route*. Durham, NC: Duke University Press.

Savić, M. Jelena. 2018. Heroines of Ours: Between Magnificence and Maleficence. In The Romani Women's Movement Struggles and Debates in Central and Eastern Europe, eds. Kóczé Angéla, Zentai Violetta, Jovanović Jelena, and Vincze Enikő. Routledge.

Savić, M. Jelena. 2022. *E, Laute Bašalen Taj Roven: Roma Voices of Sorrow*. European Roma Institute for Arts and Culture. The Romani Canon Project.

Stavrevska, Elena B., Sladjana Lazic, Vjosa Musliu, Dženeta Karabegović, Julija Sardelić, and Jelena Obradovic-Wochnik. 2023. "Of Love and Frustration as Post-Yugoslav Women Scholars: Learning and Unlearning the Coloniality of IR in the Context of Global North Academia." *International Political Sociology* 17 (2):1–20. doi:10.1093/ips/olad008.

Index

Note: **Bold** page numbers refer to tables; *italic* page numbers refer to figures and page numbers followed by "n" denote endnotes.

ability 6, 8, 23, 33–37, 51, 74, 109, 135–36, 142
abortion 62, 73, 77, 117; rights 62, 75
act 8, 10, 15, 24–25, 62–64, 79–80, 99, 129, 136, 140, 142
activism 2, 7, 11, 13, 16–18, 22, 28, 32, 109, 111, 148–52; Muslim women 40
activists 2, 7, 9, 11–12, 32, 34, 44–45, 47, 71–74, 76, 79–80, 112, 139–40, 148–49, 151–52
actors 2, 9–10, 87, 89, 91, 95, 97–98, 101, 109–12, 114, 116–19
Adamu, Fatima L. 34
adult Black women 127, 130–31, 134
Africa/African 32–34, 54; American women's oppressions/subjectivity 54, 56; feminisms 33–34, 41
African feminists 33–34; approaches 36; feminist-focused model of intersectionality 41; Muslim 34; research 35; scholars 33
Afro-diaspora 130
Afroféminas 75, 77–81; praxis of intersectional solidarity 81
Afrolatinamerican 75
Ahmed, Sara 49, 50
Aid to Families with Dependent Children (AFDC) 131, 143n2
Albanians 148–49; language 149–50; women 148–49
all-affected principle 63
alliances 22, 61, 76, 80, 110, 112
Altgeld Gardens Homes 127, 131–35, 137, 140–41; LAC meetings 138–39, 141
Alvarez, Rosío 17
analytical lens 33, 109–10
analytical tools 49, 62, 91
anger 27, 50–51
anti-Blackness 127, 131
antigypsyism 47
anti-imperialist feminism 75
anti-Muslim: discourses 86–87, 94, 98; racism 87–91, 93–96, 98–100; racism and Islamism

87–90, 93, 98, 100–101; racism manifests 89; sentiments 92
antiracism/anti-racist 17, 44, 75, 78; Romani women's struggle 51; struggle 51
anti-Roma: beliefs 50; Europe 50; framework 46; racism 45–51; system 50
Anzaldúa, Gloria 12
Aotearoa/New Zealand 54, 61
Argentina 73–74
armed conflict 34
Arruzza, Cinzia 76
Asia 54–55
Asian Americans 15, 131
Asians 55, 61–62; migrants 61–62
attributed responsibility 116
Australia 48, 62, 89
authenticity 96, 101
autonomous: organizations 12; organizing spaces 79
awareness 71–72, 78
axis of gender 91, 99

Bakshi, Amar 132
Banerjee, Supurna 23
Bano, Bilkis 26
Beckwith, Karen 9
behaviors *8*, 50, 128–29
Behl, Natasha 73
Belgrade 148–49
Belkhir, Jean Ait 101n1
Berger, Michele Tracy 128
Bharatiya Muslim Mahila Andolan (BMMA) 26
Bhattacharya, Tithi 76
biculturalism 54, 61
Bilge, Sirma 45
biological: entity 148; family 25
Black: communities 126–27; feminism 2, 54, 78, 125; and Latina queer feminists 71; low-income neighborhoods 130; marginalized communities 126–27, 130, 138, 142; marginalized populations 48, 128, 139, 142, 143; political behavior 143;

political consciousness and power 80; political
engagement 127; political work 127; politics 130;
population 48; and racialized women 77
Black Americans 131
Black Feminist Association (EFAE) 77–78
Black feminists 17, 34, 58, 75, 91, 125–27,
129–30, 139, 142; and activists 143; concept
of intersectionality 128; conceptualization
of extra-systemic politics 129; hometruth 2;
organizations 75, 77; organizers 80; resistance 79;
scholars 127–28, 130; theorists 32; traditions 79
Black Visions (Dawson) 142
Blackwell, Maylei 11, 12, 17
Black women 23, 33, 35, 41, 49, 51, 56, 77–80,
125–28, 130–34, 142–43; activist 72; and femmes
130; living in Altgeld Gardens 127; living in
public housing 128, 132, 134, 142; organizers 78;
residents 135; shape 130; struggles 80; women's
movement 77
Blakey 79
bodies 24, 75, 90, 130
boundaries 9, 28, 61, 64, 87–88, 90–91, 96–97,
100–101
boundary theory 90
Brady, Henry E. 133
Brazil 73–74, 76, 128
Britain 55, 88, 91
broader movements 71, 79, 81
broader society 90–91, 98–99, 101
broad mobilization 71, 76
building solidarity 71–72, 76, 111, 120

CAC Tenant Services meetings 137–39, 141
Çağatay, Selin 74, 76, 80, 81n2
Canada 62, 88, 92
capitalism 7, 49, 58, 74, 116–18
caste 23, 25, 27–29
categories 7, 15, 17, 24–25, 41, 51, 59, 91, 93,
129–30
CEDAW 57, 64
Central Advisory Council 139
century 46, 55, 57, 132, 148, 150
Cesari, Jocelyne 89
Chao, Itziar Mujika 149, 152
Charger Elementary 140–41
Chicago 125, 127, 130–34, 136, 138, 140, 142
Chicago Housing Authority (CHA) 127, 131–33,
135, 137–40, 142; apartments 143n4; board
meetings 127, 139; Board of Commissioners
Meetings 132, 138, 141; Commissioners'
meetings 132, 138, 140, 141; employees 139–42;
meetings 125, 138, 141–42; office 141; policy
141; staff 139; street-level bureaucrats 135, 138;
tenants 133, 138, 140
Chicago Public Housing 132, 142
Chicanas 11–12, 17; feminism/feminists 12, 17;
intersectionality 11; movement 11–12, 17;

women's history 11; and women's liberation
movement 17
children 11, 26–27, 50, 56, 108, 140–41
Ciccia, Rossella 111
citizenship 22, 25–27, 29
Citizenship Amendment Act (2019) 23, 25–26
civil rights 15, 17, 71, 118
civil society 33, 87, 90, 95, 97, 101, 108, 143; actors
92–93, 96, 98; in Germany 92; organizations
36–37, 93, 108, 114, 118
class 6–8, 10, 12–13, 15–17, 23, 25, 28, 59, 61, 77,
109–10, 139–40, 142
clause 57, 62, 64, 114
coalitions 15, 57, 63, 65, 70, 72–73, 76–78, 80, 100,
113; work 12, 78, 80
codes 98, 114
Cohen, Cathy J.: *Democracy Remixed* 142
collected information 91
collective actions 73, 108, 111, 114–15; events 109,
114, 117; fields 109, 111–12, 117, 120n2; frames
109, 111, 114
collective actors 86, 108–12, 115, 119–20
collective identities 77, 109–10, 115
collective understandings 72, 111
Collins, Patricia Hill 6, 128
color 5–7, 13, 15–18, 32–33, 57, 59, 61, 64, 71–73,
75, 92–93, 96, 131–32; activism 7, 12; feminists
6, 61
Combahee River Collective 17, 71, 79
combinations 13, 33, 35–36, 41
commonality of experiences 111, 118
Common Denominator frame 118–19, 120n4
common threats 111–12
communities 15–17, 22–27, 29, 60–62, 86–88, 90,
93, 110–11, 113–16, 118–19, 126, 128–31, 133,
137–39, 143; based organizations 38, 40; building
87, 91, 130, 136; cleanup 126, 133; members
137–38; work 87, 139
Community-Based Groups (CBOs) 37–39
complete rupture 79–80
complexities 15–16, 35, 61–62
conceptual framework 32, 41, 125, 127–28
conceptualizations 11–12, 35–36, 90, 128, 132
conflicts 35–36, 76, 109, 111, 116–17
confrontation 93, 95, 99, 101; anti-Muslim racism
86, 93–95
connections 18, 38, 40, 48, 51, 61–62, 138, 141
Connell, R. W. 7
consciousness 7–8, 8, 10, 71–72
consent forms 134
constellations 34; of inequalities 33–34, 37–38
constituencies 98, 110, 114
constitution 25–27; changes 148–49
construction 15, 18, 46, 60, 90–91
contemporary: discussion of Latina 17; Germany
87; intersectional 2; manifestations 58, 71;
moments 22, 29

INDEX

contention 73, 135
contexts 7, 9–10, 16–17, 26, 28, 49, 51, 54, 56–58, 73–74, 89–91, 99–100, 112, 115, 119
contractors 140–41
contradictions 15, 54–55, 59–60
Cotera, María 11, 12
council 138–39, 141; member 139
counter-narratives 97–98, 100–101
countries 25–27, 33, 35–37, 40, 55–56, 59, 61–62, 64, 74–77, 108, 113, 128, 148
COVID-19 1, 56
creation 10, 29, 74, 80, 93, 108, 110, 113, 138, 149, 152
Crenshaw, Kimberlé 6, 15, 23, 32–34, 51, 56–58, 65, 71, 72–73, 91, 110; definition of intersectionality 58
Crimes Act 62
critical social theory 128
critique 23, 25, 28–29, 47, 49, 70–72, 79
cross-case analysis 114–15, 117, 119
cross-field solidarity 109, 118–19
CrowdTangle Team 114, 120n7
culture 12, 16, 28, 49, 55–58, 60–62, 65

dalit: community 29; families 27; women 22, 23, 27–28
Davis, Kathy 55
Dawson, Michael: *Black Visions* 142
decolonial: feminism 49; perspective 45, 51; Romani women's struggle 51
decriminalize prostitution 63–64
demands 16, 75, 79, 98, 129
Democracy Remixed (Cohen) 142
demonstrators 76
development 7, 10, 16, 28, 33, 59–60, 62–63, 100, 108–12, 118–20, 131–42; of solidarity ties 110, 119
de-whitening, Roma women 44, 51, 52
diagnostic framing 109, 111–12, 114–15, 117
dialectical relationship 71–72, 80
Diasporic Women's Network 75
differences 6–7, 15, 17, 28–29, 34, 36, 56, 58, 71, 74, 76–78, 110–12, 118–20
differential social positionings 112, 118
Di Maggio, Paul J. 120n2
dimensions 6–7, 11–15, 18, 35, 98, 100, 115, 117; of Latina activism 13; of oppression 7, 11
disciplines 45, 56–57, 64
discourses 28, 72, 76, 78, 87, 89–90, 109, 111, 119
discrimination 15–16, 24–25, 33, 35, 37, 47–48, 57–58, 77, 79, 86, 88–90, 92–93, 95–96, 99, 115–16; and social movements 15
disruptive tactics 76, 80–81
diversification 87
diversity 5, 47, 51, 56, 58, 80, 87, 133; and heterogeneity 87; of Latina activism 5
domestic: laborers 77, 79; violence 75, 131

dominant subgroups 71, 77–78, 80
domination 34, 45–46
double minorities 118

economic activities 32, 36, 40
economic experiences of women 37–38, 41
economic institutions 33–34, 38, 40
education/educational 12, 34, 37–38, 47, 50, 57, 72, 136, 149; institutions 25, 38, 40
8M Commission 77–79
Eliasoph, Nina 137
Emejulu, Akwugo 76
environmental issues 117
environmental justice 75, 134
equality 12, 17, 26, 47, 63, 118
Espinosa-Miñoso, Yuderkys 49
Espinoza, Dionne 11, 12
ethnic communities/groups 55–58, 62
ethnic feminism/ethnic feminist 54–55, 57–58, 60–65; perspective 64
ethnicity 47, 49, 52n2, 56, 61, 63, 65, 87, 89, 91–92, 96–97, 99–100, 125–27
ethnic minorities 57, 60, 64
Ethnic Minority Women's Rights Alliance Aotearoa (EMWRAA) 57
ethnic organizations 57
ethnic populations 54–57, 59
ethnic women 57–60, 62; claims 59–60; MPs 62; parliamentarians 62; politicians 62
Europe/European 44–48, 50, 62, 86–87, 90; academic feminist circles 45; countries 86; economic community 55; modernity 46; political framework of depoliticized culture 45; Roma policies 47; Roma Rights Center 46; states 44; union agency 48
evolution 115, 117–18; of framing processes 109, 113
exclusion 10, 13, 17, 23, 47–48, 77–78, 80, 88, 90, 92–94, 98, 100, 152
existing boundaries 95, 101
existing systems 41, 75
expansive intersectional inquiry 6, 18
experiences: of anti-Muslim racism and Islamism 87; of Black women 41; of discrimination 93, 99; of oppression 55, 77; of Romani women 47, 50–51; of women 2, 33, 38
explanatory power 110, 120
external threats 112, 115–16
extra-system: conception of politics 127–30; elements 126, 133; expansion of politics 130, 133; political engagement 128, 142; political participation 141–42; politics 127–30, 132, 134, 137, 142
extra-systemic conceptual expansion 134, 140; of politics 126–29, 136, 139–40, 142

Facebook 109, 114, 117
Faiz, Faiz Ahmed 26, 30n2

158 INDEX

false allegations 95
families 16, 25, 27, 29, 60, 75, 98, 113, 129, 137, 150; violence 57, 60
far-right actors 116–18
feminism/feminist 2–4, 6–19, 23–30, 32–42, 45–52, 55–66, 71–81, 87–101, 109–20, 126–43, 148–53; activism 7, 22, 35, 149, 151; activists 151–52; in Aotearoa New Zealand 54; consciousness 10; intersectionality 29; mobilization 9; movements 9, 15, 28, 77, 149–50; politics 23, 63, 76; practices 77; resistance 152; scholars 32, 35, 57, 72, 109; scholarship in NZ 61; solidarities 61, 150; studies 50; theory 59
feminization 16, 77
Fernández, Cayetano 46
Fernandez, June 77–79
Ferrer-Núñez, Shariana 73
fight 12, 24, 47, 78, 131, 137, 152
500 Years of Chicana Women's History (Martínez) 11
formal education 35, 37, 40
formal institutions 37, 40
formulation 46–47, 52, 113
"frame semantic grammar" approach 114
framework 2, 5–6, 8–9, 32–34, 72, 109–10, 112, 117–18, 126–27, 129, 136, 138, 142–43
Framework for National Roma Integration Strategies 46
framing processes 109, 111–13, 116, 118
Fraser, Nancy 63, 76
Fundamental Rights Agency (FRA) 48, 52n3

gang-rape 22–23, 27–28
gender-based violence (GBV) 34, 50, 74
gender equality 16, 32–39, 41, 48–49; activism **39**; definitions of 34, 38; institutional barriers **40**; priorities 37–38
gender/gendered 6–7, 9–13, 15–17, 23–24, 34–36, 45, 47–48, 51, 59, 78–79, 87, 91, 99–100, 109–10, 142, 151; analysis 6; anti-Muslim discourses 97; anti-Muslim racism 99–100; biases 60, 62; consciousness 9, 16–17; disparities 35, 40; emancipation 152; forms 89; forms of anti-Muslim racism and Islamism 89; hierarchies 10–11; identity 15, 24, 35, 91, 96, 100; ideologies 17, 62; inequalities 17, 32–33, 35–36, 41, 96; intersectional Islamophobia 87; mobilization 5, 12; mobilizations 9; norms 98–99; oppression 75, 77; perspectives 45, 50, 152; roles 50, 99; salience of 6, 99; violence 74, 75, 77; ways 16, 87
Germany 86–92, 95–98, 100–101, 151; society 96–97, 99–100
Ghana 33, 37–39, **39, 40,** 41
Ghosh, Nandini 23
"Global North" 152
Goffman, Erving 111, 120n4
Gomez, Alma 17
Gopal, Meena 23

government 27–28, 130, 133–34, 136–37; bureaucracies 136, 141; power 125–28, 131, 136, 142
Govinda, Radhika 23
Gowus, Amanda 34
grassroots organizations 38, 60, 64
groupness 90–91
groups 10, 12–13, 15–18, 34–35, 38, 56, 59–61, 63–64, 77–81, 93–94, 108–11, 113, 118, 126, 128–31, 149–50; consciousness 15; of women 32, 34, 41
Gunew, Sneja 57–58
Gutiérrez, Ramón A. 61
"Gypsy criminality" 48

Hanchard, Michael 127, 128, 140
Hancock, Ange Marie 59
Hathras 27–28
headscarves 97–98
Hetemi, Atdhe 150
heterogeneity 2, 5, 15, 18, 54, 87, 118; of identities 115, 118
high-rise residents 137
histories 3, 6, 10, 12, 46, 48–50, 54–55, 58, 65, 74–75, 78–79
homes 27, 29, 50, 63, 92, 108, 128, 130, 132, 135–37, 142
homonationalism 116, 118
homonormativity 116, 118
HoSang, Daniel Martinez 61
Husain, Cheikh 92

identities 5–6, 9, 15–16, 23, 25, 58, 61–62, 65, 109–10, 112, 115, 118, 128, 130; categories 15, 33–34, 36, 41, 91; dimensions 15, 47; politics 56
illegal groups 149–50
immigrant 77, 79; women 75, 77
in-depth interviews 91, 125, 132–33
Index of Agency (IOA) 36–38, 40–41
India 22–26, 29, 55; feminism 22, 23, 28; feminists 23
India Democratic Women's Association 28
India Progressive Women's Association 28
inequalities 6–8, 33–38, 41, 47–49, 51, 59, 64, 109, 111, 116, 118–19; structures 110, 119
injustice 59, 63, 137
institutional/institutions 34, 38, 40–41, 44, 46, 73–74, 90, 94, 96, 126–28, 130, 137, 151–52; barriers 35–37, 41; biases 32–35, 40–41
Institutional Review Board (IRB) 134
International Women's Strike (IWS) 70–71, 73–81
intersecting dimensions 15, 17
intersectional: activism 2, 7, 120; analysis 6, 18, 33, 36, 41, 49, 77; approach 17, 33, 73–74, 76–77, 91, 101, 109–10, 116, 128, 149; boundary 87, 91, 93, 101; consciousness 7, 11, 15, 71–73, 80–81, 112; dimensions 7, 47; discrimination on Romani women 47; experiences of Romani women 45,

47, 50; feminism 3, 22; feminist moments 28–29; feminist pedagogy 22, 29; feminist politics 22, 24, 29, 76; forms 73–74; forms of oppression 11, 71; forms of solidarity 70, 72, 74, 78; identities 13, 18, 25, 41, 96, 98, 101, 132; interventions 12; lens 35–36, 108–9; methodology 29, 91; methods 34, 41; mobilization 2, 5, 13, 15; nature 28, 119; perspectives 62, 86, 100; politics 17–18, 26, 70–71; positioning 7, *8,* 101; praxis 11–14, 18, 71–73, 80; privilege 23, 109, 111; solidarity 70–74, 77–81, 110–11, 120; studies, identity categories 101n1; sustaining 70–72, 79; stigma and discrimination 33; synthesis 71–73; terms 116–17, 119; ways 5, 8, 15, 56

Intersectional Feminist Activism 22

intersectionality 2–3, 5–7, 11, 17–18, 22–24, 28–29, 32–36, 41, 45, 50–51, 54–61, 64–65, 71–72, 91, 109–10; applying 34–35; benefits 34, 41; defining 33; and emergent ethnic feminism 56; and intersectional consciousness 71; and state fragility 35; theory 51, 55, 58–59, 65

intersections 2, 5–6, 12–13, 25, 33, 37, 47, 64, 110, 118, 142

Isasi-Diaz, Ada Maria 19n1

Islam 86–90, 96, 100; gender inequality 96; Muslims in Europe 87; feminisms 33

Islamism 86–91, 93, 98, 100–101; and anti-Muslim racism 87–88, 99; and anti-Muslim racism in Germany 91; and Political Islam 89

Islamists 87, 89, 94, 98–101; actors 86, 89, 98–100; confrontations 99; group 87, 100; ideologies 98–99; radicalization 99

Islamophobia 49, 88

Isoke, Zenzele 126

John, Mary 23

Journal of Women, Politics, and Policy (JWPP) 2

justice 22–23, 26–27, 29, 57, 63–64, 79, 108, 137; frames 63

Kelley, Robin D.G. 128

Khatoon, Asma 26

The Kitchen Table: Women of Color Press 17

knowledge 2, 45, 47, 49, 51, 72–73, 93, 141, 149

Kóczé, Angéla 48, 51

Korteweg, Anna C. 91

Kosovo Liberation Army (KLA) 150–51

Krasniqi, Eli 149

labor 9, 25, 36, 40, 57, 71, 73–75, 79–80, 128; movements 13, 15–16, 132; sectors 37

Lamont, Michèle 90, 100, 101

Latina activism 5–7, 9–10, *11,* 12–13, *14,* 15, 18; dimensions of *14;* model 10; studying *6*

Latin America/Latin Americans 48, 54–55, 75, 79

Latinas 5–18; feminists 13, 17, 71; intersectional activism 5–6, 18; intersectionality 6, 10, 13, 18;

intersectional movidas 12; intersectional praxis 12; labor activism 13; and Latina mobilization 15; mobilization 6, 8–15, 18; mobilization intersectionally 5; movements 6, 10, 13–14; queer feminists 71

Latinos 15–16, 131; communities 16; politics 16; struggles for civil rights and racial justice 15

legislation 22–26, 29, 57, 62, 64

lens of intersectionality 23, 110

Lentin, Alana **44**

levels of privilege 35–38

LGBTQIA 109–20; framed 118–19; Madrid-based 115, 118; movement 117; Western-based 109, 111

liberation 17, 49, 51, 75, 142–43, 151; state 63

Lipsky, Michael 135

lived experiences 2, 5, 17–18, 23, 36, 59, 71–72, 131, 133, 139, 142

local: expertise 45; women's groups **39;** young people 136

Lorde, Audre 51

Lugones, María 51

Lutz, Helma 91

Machen 79

Madrid 109, 112–19

mainstream movements 12, 17

Mandaville, Peter 89

Manorama, Ruth 23

Māori 55, 59, 61–62

marginalization 2, 7, 49, 54, 58–60, 71–73, 75, 78, 89, 91–92, 109, 111, 126; processes 118–19

marginalized: Black communities 127; Black people 143; Black women 125, 127–28; communities 27, 109–10, 116–17, 119, 139; groups 41, 57, 71–73, 76–81, 108, 116, 118–19, 127, 142; identities 34, 58

Martínez, Elizabeth 13; *500 Years of Chicana Women's History* 11

mass mobilization 152

Matache, Margareta 46, 47

McCall, Leslie 59

McNair Barnett, Bernice 101n1

Meares, Tracey 132

meetings 12, 38, 94, 99, 125–27, 134, 137–42

Melucci, Alberto 120n2

member states 41, 47

Menon, Nivedita 23

Menos, Una 74

Mexico 73–74

Migrant Integration Policy Index (MIPEX) 56

migrants 28, 55–62, 65, 92, 101, 116–17, 132; sex workers 64; women 54–55, 57, 64

migration 62–63, 78

Milosevic, Slobodan 150

minoritized groups 2, 15–16, 33, 120

minority: groups 59, 61–62, 91, 101, 142; Muslim populations 37; women 58, 63, 77

160 INDEX

mixed-income housing 137
mobilization 6–7, 9–11, 13–18, 23, 27, 71, 74, 76, 78, 110, 113, 120; efforts 36, 78
modernity 45–46, 51
Mohammed, Wunpini 34
Mohanram, Radhika 61
Molina, Natalia 61
Molnár, Virág 90
Montoya, Celeste 13, 79
Montero, June 78
Morraga, Cherríe 17
mothers 9–10, 26–28, 44, 49–50, 134–35, 150
movements 5–7, 9–10, 12–14, 16, 18, 25–26, 50, 55–56, 58, 70–74, 76–81, 89, 111–12; agendas 12, 80; leadership 73, 79–80; and organizers 73; settings 12, 72; struggle 71, 73
mujerismo 17, 19n1
multiculturalism 55–58, 60–61, 65n4
multi-layered activism 148, 152
multiple: dimensions 6–7, 13; discriminations 57, 115, 118; forms of oppression 10–11; groups 34, 36; jeopardy 58–59
multiply 71–73, 76–81
Muslims 25, 29, 34, 56, 86–93, 95–100; activism 92; actors 87; communities 34, 60, 86–87, 89–90, 93, 98–101; communities in Germany 91, 101; community building 87; community life 88; in Germany 90, 92; groups 89; minority countries 88; and Muslim women 97; organizations 86, 90; politics 89; populations in Germany 92; women 22, 25, 40, 87–93, 96–100; women in Germany 97; women organizations 91; women's activism 88; young population 101
Muslim women: agency 87; community 88; embeddedness 91; empowerment 92, 97; experiences of gendered anti-Muslim racism 100; groups and organizations 90; interests 88; organizations 87–88, 90–101; organizations in Germany 89, 91; organizations reshape 96; organizations support 100; positioning 96; prevention work 99; professional 97; representatives 97; response strategies 90; sense 99
Muslim women's activism 87–88; in Germany 86, 91, 101; in western societies 87–88

Nash, Jennifer C. 58
national contexts 41, 78
national identities 34–35
National Women's Association 26
nationwide protests 28
negotiations 76, 78–80, 135, 151
networks 93–95, 101, 134, 141; building 93–94
New Zealand 54–65; "biculturalism" 65n3; ethnic/migrant women 60; gender-ethnicity politics 55
New Zealand Prostitutes Collective (NZPC) 63–64
NGOs 37–38, 129, 152

Nigeria 33, 38–39, **39, 40,** 76; and Ghana 37–38, 41
#NiUnaMenos 74
non-material resources 94
non-Muslim majority society 87, 89
North-Rhine Westphalia 92

Oliveira, Ana 17
Omi, Michael 16, 61
open intersectional analysis 7–8, 13
oppositional consciousness 79–81
oppression 5–8, 10–11, 23, 28, 45–48, 55, 57–58, 60–62, 71–77, 79, 126; institutions 7, 126; Muslim 87, 89; regime 26, 148, 152; systems of 61, 74, 77, 79; understandings of 72–73
Oprea, Alexandra 50
organization/organizational 12–13, 26, 28, 38–39, 64, 75, 87–88, 90–101, 108–20, 129–30, 134; approach 72; experiences 89, 93; experiences of anti-Muslim racism and Islamism 93; in Germany 92; Muslim identity 95; responses 37, 40; response strategies 90; response strategies to anti-Muslim racism and Islamism 90
Organizations Frame SolidarityThrough 108
organizers 16, 73–75, 78, 150
orientations 6, 15–16, 18
overlapping subsets 7, 9
overrepresentation 48

Paik (2009) 28
pan-ethnic identity 15–16
parallel statebuilding 151
Pardo, Mary 16
participants 36–37, 40–41; observation 132–33, 138
patriarchal violence 28
Perry, Keisha-Khan 130
persecuted minorities 25–26
Peucker, Mario 89, 92
Phillip Murray Homes Development 127, 131, 132
phobia 88, 115–16
platforms 71, 75–76, 78, 110, 114, 119, 141
pluralist model 100
Poland 73–74
police brutality 46, 75
policies 2, 26, 35, 47–49, 58, 71, 117, 129, 137, 140, 148–49; silences 71–72
political/politics 2, 6, 13, 22, 45, 49–51, 57–58, 62–63, 95, 125–43, 148; act 149, 152; activism 16, 149; activities 114, 129, 151; actors 94, 139, 141; behavior 18, 130, 134, 142–43; of Black marginalized communities 127, 142; of Black marginalized populations 139, 142; of Black marginalized women 128; of Black women 125, 128; claims 33, 62, 113; community 63, 128, 133–34, 136, 142; comprehensive understanding of 128, 133; consciousness 6–7, 13, 16, 18, 112, 118–19; definition 47; discourses 57, 132; engagement 125–27, 133–34, 137–38, 140;

INDEX

environments 7–8, 12; field 90; frameworks 46, 125; goals 80, 129; of homemaking 130, 136; identities 61, 76, 130, 133–34, 136, 142; imagination 138, 141–42; institutions 38, 40; intersectionality 33, 110; learning 138, 141; life 54, 79, 86; marginalization 35, 55; mobilization 89, 149; officials 37; organizations 139, 151; participation 47, 57, 133; of poor Black women 126; power 128, 130, 135–38, 141, 143; processes 2, 51; project 33, 44, 71; purposes 87, 90; rights 12, 150; scientist 127, 137, 143; scholars 125–26; solidarity 108–11, 119; spheres 89, 129; strategies 52, 125, 131; tactics 130; theory 125, 127, 129–30, 139; work 128–30, 135–36

politicization 33, 89
Popa, Maria 48
poverty line 125–26, 131–32, 142–43
Powell, Walter W. 120n2
power 2, 23–24, 33, 35, 47–48, 50, 56, 71, 73, 77–80, 125–29, 132–34, 136–37, 139, 141–43; asymmetries 2, 74, 78, 109–10; differences 72, 80; relations 45, 51; states 74
practices 2, 7, 11–12, 17–18, 47, 50–51, 58, 60–61, 64, 72–73, 109–10, 120, 152
praxis 11–12, 33, 65, 71, 73, 78, 80–81
prevention work 94, 98–99, 101
principles of justice 63
private homes 150, 151
privilege 23, 35–38, 40–41, 47, 63
processes of boundary 100–101
progressive movements 17, 51, 71
Pro Human Rights Association of Andalusia (APDHA) 48
project of intersectionality 71–72
Prostitution Decriminalization Act (PDA) 63–64
protests 18, 22, 25–28, 75–77, 125, 127, 130, 134, 137–38, 150, 152
Prowse, Gwen 132
public: events 93, 97; health institutions 38, 40; housing 125, 128, 130–34, 137–38, 142; housing communities 130, 132; housing development 127, 131–32, 134, 137–38, 142; housing residents 125, 128, 136, 140, 142; housing spaces 132, 134; meetings 126, 138–39; policies 2, 35; spaces 26, 98, 116, 141; sphere 133, 142; standing 80

Qiriazi Sisters 150
qualitative content analysis 37–38, 114
quotidian politics 127–28

race/racial 6–7, 10–13, 15–17, 44–46, 48–52, 59, 61, 77, 79, 87, 91–92, 96–97, 99–100, 125–27, 142; antagonism 45, 49; class 14; communities 110–11; formation 16, 50; and gender 7, 13, 15–16, 51; gendered identity 10–11; groups 61, 131; identities 16, 93; inequalities 48, 77; justice 9, 13, 15, 17, 76; justice movements 11, 13;

logics 45, 49, 51; minorities 16; people 44–45, 92, 116; women 45, 49–51, 59, 77–78
racism 2, 44–45, 47–52, 57, 74–75, 77–78, 115–18
racist 49, 116
Rege, Sharmila 28
relationships 33–37, 51, 54, 57–58, 61, 93, 95, 129, 136
religion 23, 25–26, 28, 35, 37, 40, 56, 60–61, 87–89, 91–92, 98–100, 110, 113
representatives 79, 87, 91–95, 99, 130, 138
reproductive justice 17, 75
residents 29, 64, 130–34, 136–42
resilience 27, 29, 152
resistance 11, 26, 28–29, 33, 74, 110, 125–26, 149–52
respondents 92, 126–27, 131–37, 139
response strategies 87–88, 91, 93, 98, 101
right-wing forces 74
Roggeband, Conny 111
Rogova, Igballe 150
Rogova, Safete 150
Roma 46–48, 50, 149; bodies 46; communities 48–50; ethnicization 52n2; ghettos 46, 48; girls 50; individuals 48–49; integration 46–47; patriarchy 50; people 46–47, 50, 117; strategic framework for equality 47; women 48, 50; women's racialization 48
Romani 47; activist 50; children 47
Romani women 44–51; activists and feminists 47; empowerment 50; experience 46; experiences 46, 51; intersectional experience 45, 47, 51; in prisons 48; racialization by reproducing 50; salvation 45; self-agency 50; struggle 48–51
Romnja feminists 47
Rousseff, Dilma 76
Ruez 79
rupture 71, 78–81

salient 7, 10–11, 16, 60, 96, 112
Sandoval, Chela 12
Sandu, Adriana 77, 78
Scheduled Caste/Scheduled Tribe (Prevention of Atrocities) Act 27, 30n3
Schlozman, Lehman 133
scholars 2, 6–7, 9, 12, 15–18, 57, 60–62, 72, 86, 88–89, 109–12, 126–29, 142–43; and activists 2, 76, 116
scholarship 2, 33, 41, 60, 108; and activism 41
Scola, Becki 2
Scott, James C. 128
self-identification 24, 90
Seminario, Galvez 13, 79
semi-structured interviews 37
senior residents 141
sex 24, 62; selection 62; workers 64
Shooman, Yasemin 89
showing attitude 96, 101

showing solidarity 117, 119
Simien, Evelyn 126
single-axis movements 5, 12–13, 18
single-axis ways 6–7, 11, 13
small groups 12, 24, 128
social: activism 51, 88; boundaries 59, 90, 100;
    capital 36–37, 40; change 76, 80, 87, 119;
    characteristics 23; cohesion 56, 58, 86, 90,
    101; contexts 56, 101; development 35, 131;
    environment 98, 100; exclusion 89, 115–17;
    group differences 70, 77–78; groups 71–72,
    74, 78–79; hierarchy 29, 97; inequality 117;
    institutions 33–34, 36, 38; justice 2–3, 72;
    locations 2, 15; media 98, 99, 101, 109–10,
    119–20, 120n3; movement intersectionality 5,
    11, 13; movement organizations 111; movement
    politics 6, 78; movements 5–7, 9, 12–13, 15,
    18, 49, 72, 130; movement scholars 18, 72;
    movement scholarship 74, 108; movement
    studies 6, 18, 72; networks 133; positionings 93,
    110, 115; pressures 87; pressures of anti-Muslim
    racism and Islamism 87; relations 7, 76; scholars
    11; services 46, 92; struggles 109, 117, 120
socialism 148–49
societal/society 37–38, 49–50, 56–57, 98, 100, 108,
    115, 118, 120, 136, 142, 149; actors 118–19;
    structures 59, 118–19
socio-cultural life 126, 129
socio-cultural opportunities 112
socioeconomic status 35
socio-political contexts 2, 109, 111–12, 127
socio-political exclusion 55–56
socio-political impact 126–27
solidarity 27–28, 61, 70, 72–74, 76, 78–80, 108–11,
    119, 148–51; bonds 108–9; discourses 109–12,
    114, 119–20; framing 110, 115, 117; initiatives
    109–10; ties 109–10, 119
Somasekhar, Sripriya 60
Soss, Joe 131
South Asia 26
Southern Europe 109, 120
Spain 48, 73–77, 113; minority feminist groups 77;
    prisons 48; society 48
sparked anti-Islamic sentiments 86
state: authorities 27, 93, 96, 98; building 151–52;
    effectiveness 33, 35; fragility 32–36, 41; funds 92,
    94; governments 38, 142; ID 135; institutions 33,
    36, 46, 128; policies 16, 141
statement 77, 94, 96–97, 99–100
stereotypes 51, 88, 93, 96–97, 101; of Muslim
    women 97
strategies 2, 37, 49–50, 87, 90–96, 99, 101, 138, 140;
    of Muslim women's organizations 90, 100
"street-level bureaucrats" 135
strong anti-gender campaigns 113
structural: analyses 6, 58–59; barriers 38, 41;
    changes 33, 36, 38, 41, 51; component 44,

48; conditions 44, 130; discrimination 36,
    149; feature 89, 98; inequalities 7, 15, 33, 117;
    locations 7, 13, 18; oppression 149
student protests 34, 150
subject 56, 58–59, 63–65, 71, 73, 76, 81, 114, 139
subjectivities 57, 79, 81, 118
subversive resident politics 137
sustain solidarity 71, 77, 79
symbolic boundaries 90, 99

target groups 92, 97, 99
Taylor, Keeanga-Yamahtta 76
Temer, Michel 76
tenants 125, 127, 130, 133–34, 136–37, 141; services
    meetings 137–38
theoretical framework 32–33, 35, 56, 87, 90,
    126–27, 129
third gender 24–25
Thomasius, Jacobus 46
Torres, Antoinette 78, 79
Townsend-Bell, Erica 73
tradition/traditional: attire 148; forms of political
    engagement 126, 133; of women in formal
    politics 151
transactivists 24–25
Transatlantic Trade and Investment Partnership 74
transgender 24–25, 29; community 22, 24–25;
    persons 24–25
The Transgender Persons (Protection of Rights) Act
    (2019) 24–25
transnational: feminist 79; mobilization 74, 76
transpersons 25
trans women 75
Treaty of Waitangi *(Te Tiriti o Waitangi)* 55, 65n3
Trump, Donald J. 74
trust 93–94; and network building 93–94
tutors 140–41

umbrella organizations 38, 87–88, 94–95
underlying grammar 63
United Nations Convention on the Elimination of
    All Forms of Discrimination Against Women 79
United Nations Mission in Kosovo (UNMIK) 152
United States 5, 16, 33, 35, 41, 73–74, 76, 86, 88–89,
    92, 125–27, 131–33, 141–42; based scholars and
    scholars of American politics 2; politics 74, 134,
    136, 138, 142–43; politics research 130; politics
    scholars 126, 132; politics scholarship 126
universal feminism 44, 51
University of Prishtina 149
University of Valencia 48
urban development 140
Uttar Pradesh 27

Vasquez, Enriqueta L. 12
Vemula, Rohith 26, 28
Verba, Sidney 133

INDEX

Vergès, Françoise 49
violence 23–25, 28, 49–50, 57, 60, 73, 75–77, 79–80, 128, 131–32, 148, 150
vulnerable: groups 34, 38; women 37, 41

Wallace, Adryan 16
Weaver, Vesla 132
websites 91, 100
welfare 59, 64; organizations 92, 97
Western: countries 88–89, 92; feminism 149; feminists 149; ideologies 87, 89; societies 86–88
white: dominant feminisms 17; feminism 45, 48–50, 78–79; German Muslim 93; middle class feminist norm 79; middle-class women 77; women 49–50, 79
white feminists 49–50; agendas 45–50
whiteness 45, 47, 49, 51
whitening 45–48, 50–51; Romani women's intersectional experience 45, 47, 49, 50
white-settler societies 60
Williamson, Terrion L. 130
Williams, Rhonda 129
Winant, Howard 16, 61
within-case analysis 114–15
within-field solidarity 109, 118–19

women 2, 6–7, 9–12, 16–17, 25–27, 32–41, 48–49, 57–64, 73–79, 87, 92–93, 96, 98–99, 132–33, 148–52; activists 149–50; auxiliaries 11; of color 5, 7, 13, 16–18, 57, 59, 61, 71, 73, 75, 79, 127, 131–32; combatants 151; experiences 2, 36, 41; and feminist activists 151; and girls in rural Kosovo 150; in Kosovo 148, 152; led activism 149–50; mobilization *9*, 10, *10*, 16; in movement 9; movements 9; organizations 17, 28, 34, 37–38, 77, 96, 101; rights 12, 45–46, 57, 60, 150; young 150
Women of Color Press 17
Women's March 74
workers 13, 64
working-class women 17, 77

Young, Iris Marion 7, 129
Yugoslavia 148–50, 152; experience 148–49; feminists 149
Yurdakul, Gökce 91
Yuval-Davis, Nira 59

Zambrano, Mayela 16
Zepeda-Millán, Chris 16